40 QUESTIONS ABOUT

THE HISTORICAL JESUS

40 QUESTIONS SERIES

40 QUESTIONS ABOUT
THE HISTORICAL JESUS

C. Marvin Pate

Benjamin L. Merkle, Series Editor

Kregel
Academic

40 Questions About the Historical Jesus
© 2015 C. Marvin Pate

Published by Kregel Publications, a division of Kregel, Inc., 2450 Oak Industrial Dr. NE, Grand Rapids, MI 49505-6020.

This book is a title in the 40 Questions Series edited by Benjamin L. Merkle.

Library of Congress Cataloging-in-Publication Data

Pate, C. Marvin, 1952-
    40 questions about the historical Jesus / C. Marvin Pate.
      pages cm.—(40 questions series)
    Includes bibliographical references and index.
    1. Jesus Christ—Historicity—Miscellanea. I. Title. II. Title: Forty questions about the historical Jesus.
    BT303.2.P377 2015
    232.9'08—dc23

                                       2014034520
ISBN 978-0-8254-4284-1

Printed in the United States of America

15 16 17 18 19 / 5 4 3 2 1

To David T. McCallum (1985–2002),
whose Christ-like legacy continues to
exceed beyond his brief life on earth

Contents

Part 3: Questions About Jesus' Life and Teaching

Part 4: Questions About Jesus' Crucifixion and Resurrection

Introduction

Why another book about Jesus, one might ask, especially since thousands of books and articles have been written about him in the last two hundred years or so? (When I was in graduate school, one of my professors remarked that he had personally read over a thousand books about the first quest for the historical Jesus. And that did not include the massive literature regarding the second and third quests for the historical Jesus. See the discussion in Part I of this work). Well, to draw on John 21:25, to do proper justice to Jesus would require enough books to fill the whole earth. Even allowing for the irony of John's statement, it suggests that there is plenty to be written about Jesus—Messiah of Israel, Savior of the world, and Lord over the universe. So my answer to the question of why one more book about Jesus is—there is always room for one more.

But reading the plethora of materials about Jesus reveals that not all treatments of him are complimentary. Indeed, perhaps half of that literature denies that we can ever know the historical Jesus because the four gospels are not reliable and what they present to us is rather the Christ of faith, the Christ the church concocted, not the real Jesus. One of the purposes of this book is to categorically deny the validity of the skeptical approach to the Gospels that is represented in the preceding description and has become so fashionable for scholars and laity alike today.

Yet, even the positive readings of the Gospels in works about Jesus (and there are some wonderful works out there to be read—see our Selected Bibliography at the end of this volume) seem forced to make a choice in what the authors present about Jesus. On the one hand, there are many books that focus only on the background issues of the relationship of the historical Jesus to the Christ of faith. This includes discussions of source, form, and redaction criticisms as well as evaluations of the "criteria of authenticity" (the so-called "guidelines" that help readers of the Gospels determine which words and deeds of Jesus actually go back to him). And, personally, I have found the conservative usage of these methodologies to be quite helpful, though not without qualification. Unfortunately, however, this approach rarely seems to get around to actually telling the story of Jesus as found in the canonical gospels. On the other hand, many other fine books about Jesus only summarize his life, ministry, death and resurrection as based on the Gospels. This is of course praiseworthy, but in today's world such an approach has become insufficient due to the rise in doubt among the masses, precisely about the trustworthiness of the Gospels.

Hence, the purpose of this present investigation concerning Jesus is to offer both the necessary background issues of how the historical Jesus relates to the Christ of faith as well as summarizing what Jesus actually said and did according to the Gospels. In other words, the needs and deficiencies of the quest to know Jesus by current society demand such a book as we are offering here.

The aforementioned debate provides the rationale for the unfolding of this work. Thus, Part 1 interacts with questions about the more academic study of Jesus: Are the Gospels reliable, and on what basis? What shall we do with twentieth-century methods like source, form, and redaction criticisms in light of the latest research? Where are we today in terms of the three quests for the historical Jesus? Moving beyond these initial questions, we consider related topics like what role does the Old Testament play in understanding Jesus Messiah? How are we to appraise oral tradition in the Jesus material? What do non-biblical sources say about Jesus? How shall we view the New Testament apocryphal gospels? And what does the rest of the New Testament tell us about Jesus? All of this sets the stage for the following units that cover the more practical aspects of Jesus' life and ministry.

Part 2 asks key questions about Jesus' birth and childhood, examining everything from the miraculous nature of his birth to questions about his family and his socio-economic background.

Part 3 deals with Jesus' life and ministry, treating the most significant aspects recorded in the Gospels. This unit also summarizes Jesus' teaching, his key message—the dawning of the kingdom of God—and how the evangelists present that theme. This section also examines Jesus' predictions about the future, especially the fall of Jerusalem to the Romans in AD 70 and his second coming.

Part 4 answers pertinent questions about Jesus' last week on earth, where he went between his death and resurrection, the reality of his resurrection, and the nature and purpose of his ascension.

John Donne observed that no one is an island; neither is a book an island unto itself. It requires the effort of numerous people to pull it off. Here I wish to express my sincere appreciation to those who helped make this work a reality. First, it continues to be a pleasure to publish with Kregel Academic, this time around under the eagle eye of the editor of the 40 Questions series, Ben Merkle. I am so thankful for Ben's expertise and patience in helping me craft the vision for this book and then providing insightful guidance throughout the process. Along these lines, I also thank my agent Jack Kragt for helping me to contact Kregel with the proposal for this book. Second, I so much appreciate the two fine students here at Ouachita Baptist University who helped me with the myriad of details that accompanied typing the manuscript, locating sources, and compiling a bibliography—Abbey (Jamieson) Ichter and

Trenton Cooper. Both of these individuals are faithfully preparing to serve the Lord and, indeed, are already doing so. Third, OBU continues to be a wonderful university to run ideas like those in this volume by our students and my colleagues. Indeed, much of the material in this work originated in connection with the Life of Christ course I have taught here. Last, but certainly not least, I thank God every day for Sherry, my soul mate of over thirty-eight years now. Next to Jesus, her encouragement, wisdom, and love have been the driving force of my life.

—C. Marvin Pate

Abbreviations

AB	Anchor Bible
ABRL	Anchor Bible Reference Library
ATR	*Australasian Theological Review*
BECNT	Baker Exegetical Commentary on the New Testament
BTB	*Biblical Theology Bulletin*
BZNW	Beihefte zur Zeitschrift für neutestamentliche Wissenschaft
CBQ	*Catholic Biblical Quarterly*
CTR	*Criswell Theological Review*
DJG	*Dictionary of Jesus and the Gospels*
HKAT	Handkommentar zum Alten Testament
ICC	International Critical Commentary
Int	*Interpretation*
JBL	*Journal of Biblical Literature*
JR	*Journal of Religion*
JSNTSup	Journal for the Study of the New Testament: Supplement Series
JTS	*Journal of Theological Studies*
NCB	New Century Bible
NIGTC	New International Greek Testament Commentary
NovT	*Novum Testamentum*
NTL	New Testament Library
NTS	*New Testament Studies*
NTTS	New Testament Tools and Studies
SBLSP	*Society of Biblical Literature Seminar Papers*
SBLSBS	Society of Biblical Literature Sources for Biblical Studies
SBT	Studies in Biblical Theology
TDNT	*Theological Dictionary of the New Testament. Edited by G. Kittel and G. Friedrich. Translated by G. W. Bromiley. 10 vols. Grand Rapids, 1964–1976.*
TNTC	Tyndale New Testament Commentaries
TS	*Theological Studies*
WBC	Word Biblical Commentary
WUNT	Wissenschaftliche Untersuchungen zum Neuen Testament
ZNW	Zeitschrift für die neutestamentliche Wissenschaft und die Kunde der älteren Kirche

BACKGROUND QUESTIONS ABOUT THE "HISTORICAL" JESUS

Questions Related to the
Quest for the Historical Jesus

What Is at Stake Regarding the Four Gospels?

What is at stake concerning the four gospels is nothing less than historic Christianity. No Gospels, no Jesus; no Jesus, no Christianity. This chapter offers a rationale for the first part of this book since it is rather technical in nature, yet of extraordinary importance. Accordingly, two questions undergird Part 1 of this work: Are the four gospels reliable and why are only those gospels included in the New Testament? Because the first question has been bandied about for centuries we will spend the bulk of our time in this chapter introducing the second question, since it was unanticipated by many.

Are the Four Gospels Reliable?

One of my students approached me recently, obviously upset. The student had just finished a class in which the professor cast doubt on the reliability of the Gospels by comparing them to the game of whispering in a person's ear a statement, and then having that person whisper the same statement to the individual next to him or her—continuing around the circle until it came back to the first person who started the statement, with the humorous result that the original statement nowhere matched the statement at the end. The professor said that is how the four gospels came into being. Jesus made his statements and performed his deeds in the AD 30s, but that these were passed along only in oral form and not written down. By the time the four gospels were composed in the 60s and later, based on the traditions of Jesus passed along for decades, they nowhere matched what Jesus actually said and did. Thus, the Gospels dare not be trusted. This story could be repeated hundreds of time, upsetting the faith of the unsuspecting.

But most Christians have not read their gospels in that fashion. Rather, for centuries, the laity in the churches read the Gospels as trustworthy accounts of the life and ministry of Jesus of Galilee. The Gospels were authored by some of those who followed Jesus and therefore provided eyewitness accounts of what Jesus actually said and did. For them, the story line of the canonical gospels goes something like the following: Jesus was miraculously conceived by the Holy Spirit in the womb of Mary (the virgin birth). He was born in Bethlehem and then later moved with his family to Nazareth of Galilee. At the age of about thirty years old, Jesus was baptized by John the Baptist in the Jordan River, a sign of the beginning of Jesus' public ministry. Jesus then went into the Judean desert to be tempted by Satan but prevailed over the tempter by being obedient to his heavenly Father. After that, Jesus called twelve men to be his disciples. These men witnessed firsthand the many miracles that Jesus performed, heard his declaration that the kingdom of God had arrived, marveled at his teaching with authority, joined him in prayer, observed the opposition to him by the religious establishment of the day, followed him as he entered Jerusalem to be received as Israel's Messiah-King, participated with him in a Passover meal/Lord's Supper, stood by as he was arrested by the temple police and Roman escort, watched him die a cruel death on the cross (at least John did), and celebrated his bodily resurrection from the dead.

But such a straightforward reading of the four gospels has been greatly challenged by liberal theologians since the late eighteenth century. It is that skeptical mentality that appeals to the circle game referred above. Two biblical scholars especially expressed their mistrust of the Bible in general—and in the Gospels in particular—over two centuries ago. The first theologian to protest the reliability of the Bible was J. P. Gabler. Gabler championed three points about the Bible: (1) the Bible should only be read for what it reports rather than what it prescribes; (2) the Bible is filled with contradictions; and (3) it is natural in origin, not supernatural. The net result of these three claims was to deny that the Bible is the Word of God, thereby destroying its historical reliability. This new approach to the Bible that Gabler fostered was called the historical-critical method.[1]

If Gabler called into question the dependability of the Bible in general, then H. Samuel Reimarus called into question the reliability of the four gospels. Writing about the same time as Gabler, Reimarus put a wedge between the Jesus of history and the Christ of faith by asserting that the latter was the portrait that emerged from the canonical gospels, but which was a fabrication of the early church. Consequently, the former—the historical Jesus—has been lost to posterity, never to be recovered. In specific, Reimarus scurrilously claimed that the historical Jesus never called himself to be the Messiah. Rather, Jesus was an ordinary Jew who died without seeing the Messiah or the kingdom of God arrive in history. But after Jesus' death, according to Reimarus, the disciples made up the legend of the resurrection thus making Jesus into a supernatural being

---

1. J. P. Gabler, "About the Current Distinction of Biblical and Dogmatic Theology and the Right Definition of Their Goals" (inaugural address, University of Astdorf, March 30, 1787). Published in *Opuscula Academica* 1 (1831): 179–94.

who should be worshipped as on par with God.[2] Since Reimarus's essay, many a scholar came to deny the reliability of the four gospels.

Though both Gabler and Reimarus's arguments have been resoundingly defeated in the years that have passed, the die had been cast regarding the historical reliability of the Bible and the Gospels in particular. Armed with the historical-critical method, liberal biblical scholars now offered a considerably paired down account of the life of Jesus: Jesus was a Jew who was baptized by John the Baptist, lived a controversial life in his relationship with the Jewish and Roman authorities, and was accordingly crucified under the governorship of Pontius Pilate. And that's it! No miracles; no kingdom of God; no atoning death; nor resurrection; no matter. Such a skeptical attitude even affected one of the greatest presidents in American history—Thomas Jefferson. Jefferson famously doubted the supernatural and miracles reported in the Gospels, so he extracted everything miraculous in them thereby producing a miracle-less version of the four gospels. I have read "Jefferson's Bible" and one will find no miraculous Jesus therein, only his moral teachings.

While this skeptical portrait of Jesus of Galilee was the favorite of much of academia, it has only been rather recently, in the last twenty years or so that the laity has latched onto this understanding of Jesus and the Gospels. The first part of this book is devoted to re-establishing the reliability of the four gospels, critiquing the usual tactics of the historical-critical approach as well as high-lighting the newest developments in the discussion. Thus, we will discuss oral tradition and the Gospels, the authorship of the four gospels, and non-biblical testimonies regarding the historical Jesus. Assuming that we can discover the historical Jesus, what portrait of Jesus best characterizes him—apocalyptic, Gnostic, Cynic, or what? When we have dealt with these issues and more related to the four gospels in Part 1, the reader will have reached great confidence about Jesus, in specific, that the historical Jesus (the Jesus who really lived) is none other than the Christ of faith (the Jesus presented to us in the Gospels).

Why Are Only the Four Gospels in the New Testament?

Once some of the contemporary laity rejected the reliability of the four gospels, it was ripe for wrestling with a second question rather recently posed by liberal biblical scholars, namely, why should only the traditional four gospels have a monopoly on the New Testament? Should not other gospels written at the time of the New Testament and beyond—the apocryphal gospels—be included in the New Testament? Such a question goes hand in hand with the pluralistic society America, and indeed most of the western world, has become. Thus, a politically correct culture such as we live in today wants to read today's religious pluralism back into the New Testament. If there are conflicting views

---

2. Reimarus (1716–68) wrote his essay anonymously because it was so radical. It was later published by G. E. Lessing.

toward the Gospels today, some reason, then why could not there have been similar conflicts back then? Could it be that the traditional gospels were embraced by the church (the majority), whereas the apocryphal gospels—those as, if not more, reliable—were discounted because those who affirmed them were in the minority? But why should this be? Today, one of the most widely read novels of our time has argued precisely that—*The Da Vinci Code*, by Dan Brown.[3] This work makes the case for the inclusion of non-traditional gospels in the New Testament, if not to replace them. Its formula for success is the mixture of a conspiracy theory, a potent long-held secret, and a good dose of vilifying historic Christianity, especially the Catholic Church.

The basic plot of *The Da Vinci Code* is as follows: Robert Langdon, the hero of the book, is a professor of religious symbology at Harvard whose skill at cracking codes puts him on the trail of a long-held secret by the Priory of Sion. The latter supposedly is a guild (that included people like Sir Isaac Newton, Victor Hugo, and most importantly, Leonardo Da Vinci) with origins back to the Crusades whose task it is to protect the Holy Grail, the chalice from which Jesus drank at the Last Supper. That, however, is but a diversion from the real truth which is that Jesus of Nazareth and Mary Magdalene were lovers who married and bore children. Thus, the real Holy Grail was Mary Magdalene.

However, the ire of the church need not have been raised over this book but for the way Brown presents his fictitious story; namely, he begins his work with a page labeled, "FACT," which claims that "all descriptions of … documents … in this novel are accurate."[4] This gives the distinct impression that the novel is based on sound historical research. The next pages of this chapter beg to differ with Brown's claim that his novel is rooted in fact. Accordingly, we will expose three key errors upon which the novel is based.[5]

Error 1: The true gospels are the Gospel of Mary (Magdalene) and the Gospel of Philip, not the canonical gospels.
Dan Brown's theological perspective is expressed through the British scholar Teabing. Teabing accused early Christianity of waging a conspiracy against the truth. He declares that "more than *eighty* gospels" were considered for the New Testament, but only four were chosen.[6] The former were the historical losers while the latter were the historical winners. The intent of this assertion is

---

3. Dan Brown, *The Da Vinci Code* (New York: Doubleday, 2003). More than 80 million copies of the book have been sold, it has been translated into 44 languages, and a major motion picture directed by Ron Howard and starring Tom Hanks was released in 2006.

4. Ibid., 1

5. Taken from Marvin and Sheryl Pate, *Crucified in the Media: Finding the Real Jesus Amidst Today's Headlines* (Grand Rapids: Baker, 2005).

6. See the review by Ben Witherington, "Review of the Da Vinci Code," *Biblical Archaeological Review* 30, no. 3 (May/June 2004): 58–61 as well as his full book, *The Gospel Code: Novel Claims about Jesus, Mary Magdalene and Da Vinci* (Downers Grove, IL: InterVarsity Press,

obviously to discredit historical Christianity and replace it with the New Testament Apocrypha. In reality, however, there are only about fifty non-canonical gospels.[7]

Here we discuss two of those New Testament Apocrypha—the *Gospel of Philip* and the *Gospel of Mary* (Mary Magdalene). They are the foundation of Dan Brown's thesis that Jesus and Mary Magdalene were lovers who got married. The *Gospel of Philip* surfaced in the Coptic (Egyptian plus Greek) texts at Nag Hammadi. It is thoroughly Gnostic in orientation.[8]

It is the emphasis that the *Gospel of Philip* places on Mary Magdalene that is of immediate interest to us. In saying 32, Mary Magdalene is called Jesus' "companion," a possible reference to Mary as the wife of Jesus.[9] Saying 55b in the *Gospel of Philip* is thought to confirm this interpretation:

> The S[aviour lov]ed [Ma]ry Mag[da]lene more than [all] the disciples, and kissed her on her [mouth] often. The other [disciples' [...]. They said to him: "Why do you love her more than all of us? The Saviour answered and said to them [...]: "Why do I not love you like her?[10]

While the kiss referred to here could be a kiss of Mary's cheek or forehead, in light of saying 32 it could also refer to a kiss on the mouth: "The perfect conceive through a kiss and give birth. Because of this we also kiss one another. We receive conception from the grace which we have among us."

What is clear from these texts is that Mary is favored by Jesus above the twelve disciples, because she shares with him the knowledge (*gnosis*) of the true nature of reality. Nevertheless, even though these non-biblical passages seem to indicate that Jesus and Mary were married, in typical Gnostic fashion, physical marriage is made secondary in importance to the spiritual intimacy between the two of them—that is, their shared *gnosis* (= knowledge).

2004). See also the penetrating critique by Darrell L. Bock, *Breaking the Da Vinci Code: Answers to the Questions Everyone's Asking* (Nashville: Nelson, 2004).

7. See Witherington, "Review of the *Da Vinci Code*," 58–59; and Bock, *Breaking the Da Vinci Code,* 61–62.

8. We will define and critique Gnosticism (the Greek word for knowledge) in subsequent chapters. Here we note that many of the Gnostic apocryphal gospels were discovered at Nag Hammadi, Egypt in 1948. These documents go back to the second to fourth centuries AD. All quotations of the *Gospel of Philip* and the *Gospel of Mary Magdalene* come from Wilhelm Schneemelcer, ed., *New Testament Apocrypha*, trans. R. McLain Wilson, vol. 1 of *Gospels and Related Writings* (Cambridge, UK: James Clarke and Company; Louisville: John Knox Press, 1991).

9. Witherington, however, does not believe this to be the case, because it is far more likely that the word "companion" used here is not a synonym for a spouse, but rather refers to a spiritual "sister" ("Review of the *Da Vinci* Code," 60).

10. The bracketed portions represent words or portions of words not in the text, but which have been filled in due to context, etc., not necessarily the original words intended by the author.

The *Gospel of Mary* (implied Magdalene) is a second-century fragment written in Greek. Like the *Gospel of Philip*, it also places Mary Magdalene on a pedestal above the disciples. The passage below indicates that Jesus entrusted Mary with secret knowledge because he recognized her superior worth. This aroused jealousy in Andrew and Peter. Hence the ensuing tense conversation:

> When Mary had said this, she was silent, so that the Saviour had spoken with her up to this point. But Andrew answered and said to the brethren: "Tell me, what think ye with regard to what she says? I at least do not believe that the Saviour said this. For certainly these doctrines have other meanings." Peter in answer spoke with reference to things of this kind, and asked them [*the disciples*] about the Saviour: "Did he then speak privily with a woman rather than with us, and not openly? Shall we turn about and all hearken unto her? Has he preferred her over against us?" (Papyrus Berolinensis 8502, 17.7–22)

> Then Mary wept and said to Peter: "My brother Peter, what dost thou then believe? Dost thou believe that I imagined this myself in my heart, or that I would lie about the Saviour?" Levi answered (and) said to Peter: "Peter, thou hast even been of a hasty temper. Now I see how thou dost exercise thyself against the woman like the adversaries. But if the Saviour hath made her worthy, who then are thou, that thou reject her? Certainly the Saviour knows her surely enough. Therefore did he love her more than us. Let us rather be ashamed, put on the perfect Man, [form ourselves] as he charged us, and proclaim the gospel, without requiring any further command and any further law beyond that which the Saviour said." (Papyrus Berolinensis 8502, 1–21)

The Gnostic character of this work is evident. Right before the preceding dialogue, Jesus says, "The Son of Man is within you, follow him" (Papyrus Berolinensis 8502, 8.12–9.5). This alludes to the Gnostic idea that humans are divine and need to become aware of such. Another Gnostic thought occurs in the same context, where Mary says she becomes a man, thereby affirming the androgynous nature of humanity.

Although the Gnostic view that God and humans are androgynous seems to argue for equality between the genders, the *Gospel of Thomas* (one of the most important Gnostic gospels) dispels such an ideal:

> Simon Peter said to them [the disciples], "Let Mary leave us, for women are not worthy of life." Jesus said, "I myself shall lead

her, in order to make her male, so that she too may become a living spirit, resembling you males. For every woman who will make herself male will enter the Kingdom of Heaven." (114)

Thus, in the Gnostic approach, women are subservient to men.

The point to be made from all of this is that the Gnostic thought undergirding the *Gospel of Philip* and the *Gospel of Mary* dates no earlier than the second to third centuries AD, precisely the false teaching opposed by the church father Irenaeus (ca. 130–200), Hippolytus (ca. 170–236), and Tertullian (ca. 160–220). This is in utter contrast to the message of orthodox Christianity evident in the first century AD in the four gospels.

Error 2: Jesus is a mere human in the earliest historical sources who was only later divinized at the Council of Nicea in AD 325.

It is argued that this was due to the oppressive tactics of Emperor Constantine, who suppressed the earlier (Gnostic) gospels and replaced them with the four canonical gospels. That is, for the first four centuries after Jesus' death, numerous documents existed chronicling Jesus' life as a mere mortal, but Constantine rewrote history by replacing these with the four canonical gospels.

Nothing could be further from the truth than this theory. The four gospels, which undeniably date to the first century AD, equate Jesus with God. And so did the apostle Paul (see Phil. 2:9–11) where he calls Jesus "Lord," the Greek equivalent of the Hebrew *Yahweh*).

To the contrary, long before Constantine and even before the Gnostic gospels existed, the four gospels of the New Testament were considered authoritative by the churches. Thus, Irenaeus in AD 125 recognizes the "fourfold gospels" (*Heresies,* 3.11.8). Tatian, a student of the church father Justin Martyr, combined the four gospels into one harmony at around AD 175 (called the *Diatessaron*—Greek for "through the four") because they were so well received in the churches. Earlier, Justin himself attested to the canonicity of the four gospels, calling them the memoirs of the apostles (*Dialogue with Trypho,* 103.19). Coming from the late second century AD, the Muratorian canon (a list of the canon named after the man who discovered it) lists the four gospels as authoritative for the church. Origen (ca. 185–254) concurs that only the four gospels should be accepted by the churches (*Homily on Luke 1:1*). By AD 325, Bishop Athanasius in the Eastern church and the papal see in the West recognized only four gospels. Eusebius, the fourth-century AD church historian who wrote *Ecclesiastical History,* quotes with approval Origen's restriction of inspired gospels to Matthew, Mark, Luke, and John.[11]

---

11. The preceding quotations come from Bock, *Breaking the Da Vinci Code,* 120.

Error 3: Jesus was married to Mary Magdalene.

The most provocative claims in *The Da Vinci Code* are that Mary Magdalene (Mary from Magdala, a town on the sea of Galilee; Luke 8:2) was the wife of Jesus and the mother of his children, and that this was a secret the church wanted to cover up to protect the divinity of Jesus. But even if the *Gospel of Philip* and the *Gospel of Mary* (Magdalene) wish to say that Jesus and Mary were married, there is no New Testament evidence for such a notion. We offer here two rebuttals to the preceding hypothesis: first, Jesus was not married to Mary; second, Jesus was never married. First, the Gospels' references to Mary Magdalene show no indication whatsoever that she and Jesus were married. Here are the references:

- Jesus cast seven demons out of Mary (Luke 8:2).
- Mary witnessed Jesus's crucifixion (Mark 15:40–41; Matt. 27:55–56; John 19:25).
- She was present at the burial of Jesus (Mark 15:47; Matt. 27:57–61; cf. Mark 16:1).
- She was the first to see Jesus in his resurrection body (John 20:10–18).
- She along with other women announced Jesus's resurrection to the apostles (Luke 24:10; John 20:18).

The fact that emerges from these references is that, except in John 20:10–18, Mary and Jesus were consistently in the presence of other people when together. In John's account, Mary touched Jesus out of surprise and joy on the first Easter morning. There are no sexual innuendoes in the narrative at all. Mary's embrace of Jesus is born out of spontaneity and reverence. Furthermore, while Mary supported Jesus' ministry, there is not so much as a hint in the Gospels that Mary was an apostle, or enjoyed a privileged place among followers of the historical Jesus; nor was she placed on a pedestal by Jesus, contra the *Gospel of Philip* and the *Gospel of Mary*. Moreover, in the gospel references to Mary and other women followers of Jesus, all the other ladies are connected to males as relatives except Mary, strongly suggesting she had no man in her life, and certainly not Jesus.[12]

Second, there is no good indication that Jesus was ever married. Bock nicely summarizes the evidence that Jesus was single:

> It has long been believed by Christians and scholars that Jesus was single, and there are good reasons for this belief. When He was in ministry, there was no mention of a wife. When He was tried and crucified there was no mention of a wife. Jesus' family members—His mother, brothers, and

---

12. See Bock, *Breaking the Da Vinci Code*, 34–35.

sisters—were mentioned more than once, but never a wife. Nor was there any indication that He was widowed.[13]

It is true that the normal expectation was that Jewish males in Bible times were supposed to be married and have children (Gen. 1:26–28), but there were notable exceptions to that norm. It may well be that the Old Testament prophet Samuel was single, as well as Hosea (until God commanded him to marry Gomer). Certainly the Essenes (the probable authors of the Dead Sea Scrolls) were celibate.[14] And, no doubt, John the Baptist was also single. These individuals apparently felt a calling to forego marriage in order to be able to devote themselves fully to the kingdom of God, as did the apostle Paul himself (1 Cor. 7). This seems to be what Matthew 19:10–12 is saying in describing certain disciples who had chosen to be celibate for the sake of the kingdom. Most scholars believe this reference alludes to Jesus' own justification for remaining single.

Conclusion

This opening chapter has raised two pressing questions about the four gospels. Are they reliable? And are they rightly the only gospels to be included in the New Testament? Our answer to the first question is, "yes," while our answer to the second question is also "yes." But these two questions only represent the tip of the iceberg relative to the historical Jesus. To that discussion we now turn in the rest of Part 1.

REFLECTION QUESTIONS

1. What is at stake regarding the four gospels?

2. How did Gabler and Reimarus attack the Bible and the four gospels, respectively?

3. What is the first error of Dan Brown's *The Da Vinci Code*? What is the response to this error?

4. What is its second error? What is the response to this error?

5. What is its third error? What is the response to this error?

---

13. Ibid., 19, 41–42.
14. See Josephus, *Antiquities of the Jews,* 18.1.5.20–21 and *Jewish Wars,* 2.8.2

Do the Gospels Present an Accurate Description of the Life of Jesus?

Talk about the quest for the historical Jesus might imply that the church has lost the Jesus behind the Gospels. Indeed, that is the conclusion that numerous New Testament scholars have reached over the last two hundred years. This issue boils down to whether or not the four gospels are historically reliable. Those who do not think the Gospels are historically reliable are skeptical that Christianity can ever recover who the real Jesus was and what he did, if anything! However, conservative scholars disagree, arguing instead that the portraits of Jesus in the New Testament gospels are accurate because they are the inspired word of God and also are supported by the historical facts.

So the fundamental query which concerns this opening unit of our book is this: Is the Jesus of history the same as the Christ of faith? In other words, has the later church made Jesus of Nazareth into something other than he actually was on earth? Or was he the Messiah, the Son of God who inaugurated the kingdom of God by performing miracles, revealing God, dying for our sin, and then was raised from the dead? We will attempt to answer these all-important questions by documenting and then responding to the three major criticisms that have been brought against the historical reliability of the four gospels. Those criticisms are, in their basic historical order of appearance, as follows: (1) The four gospels present Jesus as performing supernatural feats, which no scientifically-informed person thinks is possible. (2) The four gospels repeatedly contradict themselves as well as commit historical errors thus undermining their trustworthiness. (3) The three key New Testament disciplines of source, form, and redaction criticisms have combined to refute the claim of the Gospels that they are based on eyewitness accounts.

Rejection Due to Miracles

First, perhaps the oldest criticism raised against the historical reliability of the canonical gospels was, and continues to be, that of skepticism toward the miracles they record. With the entrenchment of the Enlightenment from the sixteenth to eighteenth centuries came a rejection of the supernatural. Such an anti-supernatural bias found its way especially in the polemical writings of David Hume, the Scottish philosopher who rejected the reliability of the Gospels because they purported that Jesus performed miracles. Hume claimed that the probability would be greater for a natural rather than supernatural explanation of any apparently miraculous event. To substantiate this claim, Hume offered four lines of support. (1) No alleged miracle has been ever supported with the testimony of a sufficiently large number of witnesses. (2) People in general crave the miraculous and believe fables more readily than they ought. (3) Miracles occur only among barbarous people. (4) Miracle stories occur in all religions and thereby cancel each other out since they support irreconcilable doctrines.[1]

Such skepticism toward the miracles of Jesus as recorded in the Gospels influenced President Thomas Jefferson to compose his version of the four gospels, which cut out anything that contained the supernatural! Prejudice against the supernatural aspect of the Gospels was championed by eighteenth- to nineteenth-century biblical scholars from Friedrich Schleiermacher to David F. Strauss to J. Ernest Renan. In the twentieth and twenty-first centuries, notable New Testament scholars like Rudolph Bultmann, the Fellows of the Jesus Seminar, and Bart Ehrman have continued the attacks on the supernatural claims made by the four gospels.

The underlying premise of these anti-supernatural scholars is that the universe is a closed system based on natural causes proceeding from inviolable laws of science. This presupposition is fundamentally opposed to the suspension of such laws due to divine intervention. Added to this is Ernst Troeltsch's principle of historical analogy, which essentially declares that we cannot accept reports of miracles in the past because we know that miracles do not happen in the present. The combination of the aforementioned anti-supernatural bias with the principle of historical analogy produced what is commonly called today, the "historical-critical method."

What are we to say to this closed view of the universe that regards the miraculous in the Gospels with deep suspicion? Two responses rightly counter this mindset. First, the commonality of the previous skeptical scholars is that they are restricted to a provincial Western mentality. As Paul Rhodes Eddy and Gregory A. Boyd note, such a viewpoint does not objectively take into account the miraculous phenomena occurring in non-Western cultures

---

1. See David Hume, *Enquiry Concerning Human Understanding*, ed. L. A. Selby-Bigge (1748 repr. Oxford: Clarendon, 1902), section 10.

reported by even Western ethnographers. These include encounters with angels and demons, experiences of instantaneous healings, deceased people coming back to life, and more. The authors write, "Clearly, outside the narrow experience of secularized Western scholars, present human experience is not by any means devoid of the supernatural."[2] Second, it is an undeniable fact that the majority of Western people have never stopped believing in, and occasionally experiencing, what they perceive to be supernatural occurrences.[3] Eddy and Boyd observe that the Gallup polls and others reveal that eighty percent of Americans believe that God performs miracles today.[4] And we might add to this that the scientific community itself has long-since replaced the antiquated view of the inviolability of the laws of Newtonian mechanics with quantum theory in which natural "laws" are recognized as only provisional descriptions of observed regularities in nature.[5] Not long ago I heard a distinguished Harvard physics professor announce that his experimentations worked nine out of ten times, which in his estimation still left room for divine intervention in at least one out of ten times!

Supposed Internal Contradictions and Historical Errors

Second, for years now skeptics of the Gospels have asserted that they are filled with internal contradictions and historical errors. Thus, Craig Blomberg writes, "Because the New Testament has been scrutinized with more intensity than any other work of literature in the history of the world, it is not surprising to discover that virtually every passage in the Gospels has been seen as conflicting with some other passage by someone or other at some time in history."[6] We will now engage these two arguments in order.

Supposed Internal Contradictions

Regarding the supposed internal contradictions, the reality is that when four points are kept in mind the apparent contradictions in the Gospels evaporate.

Literary Arrangement. Literary arrangement explains many notable "discrepancies" in the Gospels such as the different orders of the wilderness temptations of Christ in Matthew and Luke, the timing of the cleansing of the Jerusalem

---

2. Paul Rhodes Eddy and Gregory A. Boyd, *The Jesus Legend: A Case for the Historical Reliability of the Synoptic Jesus Tradition* (Grand Rapids: Baker, 2007), 69.
3. See R. Mullin, *Miracles and the Modern Religious Imagination* (New Haven, CT: Yale University Press, 1996). Craig S. Keener has performed a valuable service in this regard by recording modern-day miracles in his *Miracles: The Credibility of the New Testament Accounts*, 2 vols. (Grand Rapids: Baker, 2011).
4. Eddy and Boyd, *Jesus Legend*, 74.
5. See Craig L. Blomberg, *The Historical Reliability of the Gospels*, 2nd ed. (Downers Grove, IL: InterVarsity Press, 2007), 106.
6. Ibid., 152.

temple by Christ, or the question of whether Jesus celebrated the Passover on the night before he was arrested and crucified. Ancient authors, like modern writers, exercised poetic liberty in rearranging the chronological order of the events of a person's life for the purpose of dramatic presentation. The Statement on Inerrancy of the Evangelical Theological Society agrees, arguing that the gospel authors' literary rearrangement of the chronology of the life of Jesus for their purposes of presentation in no way detracts from the inspired nature of the message of the Gospels.[7] This is just good writing at work. As an example, we may apply this technique to the first of the preceding examples. It is true that Matthew and Luke present the temptations of Jesus in somewhat different order. Thus:

MATTHEW 4:1–11	LUKE 4:1–13
1) Stones to Bread	1) Stones to Bread
2) Temple	2) Kingdoms of the World
3) Kingdoms of the World	3) Temple

Most likely, Luke has the more original order than Matthew as is evidenced, for example, by the first evangelist's propensity to organize his material around the theme of Jesus as the new Moses (note how Matthew clusters the Sermon on the Mount material together to attain that purpose rather than Luke's Sermon on the Plain in Luke 6:17–49). Matthew attaches high value to mountains as the place of divine revelation,[8] which is why he lists as last Satan's temptation of Jesus on a mountain. It was on that mountain that Jesus rejected Satan's offer of the kingdoms of the world if, that is, Jesus would worship him.

Theological Considerations. Second, related to the previous point, theological considerations contributed to the varying literary arrangements found among the four gospels. For example, Matthew portrays Jesus as the new Moses. Mark reveals that Jesus is the suffering Messiah through four passion predictions (Mark 8–10). Luke's extended treatment of Jesus' journey to Jerusalem to be crucified is similar to one of Israel's rejected prophets (Luke 9–19). John presents Jesus as the true Israel who replaced or fulfilled the Old Testament feasts, sacrifices, and temple. The canonical gospel writers organized their respective material to convey the spiritual message the Holy Spirit impressed upon them. Thus, literary arrangement and theological considerations go hand in hand with dismissing apparent contradictions among the Gospels.

---

7. "The Chicago Statement on Inerrancy," in *Inerrancy*, ed. Norman L. Geisler (Grand Rapids: Zondervan, 1979).

8. See, for example, the Sermon on the Mount (Matt. 5–7); the Olivet Discourse (Matt. 24); the Great Commission (Matt. 28).

Cultural Adaptation. Cultural adaptation also explains different descriptions in the Gospels of the same words and deeds of Jesus. For example, Luke famously changes the imagery of his narrative from something distinctively Palestinian to its Greco-Roman counterpart. Three examples will suffice to demonstrate this interpretation of the other synoptic gospels. Blomberg records these instances of cultural adaptation:

> In at least three clear cases, as he writes for the least Jewish audience of all the gospels and with the most fluent Greek style of the four, Luke changes the imagery of his narrative from something distinctively Palestinian to its Graeco-Roman counterpart. The parable of the two builders is the most developed example of this process of "representational change" (Matt. 7:24–27; Luke 6:47–49). Luke adds that the wise man who built his house on the rock "dug down deep and laid the foundation", a practice much more common outside Palestine than within, and turns the description of the storm with its violent wind appropriate for the small, dry Israeli desert river beds suddenly swollen with rain, into a calmer flood, more characteristic of a larger river such as the Syrian Orontes slowly overflowing its banks. So, too, only Luke's version of the parable of the mustard seed has the plant growing in a garden rather than a field (Luke 13:19; cf. Mark 4:31; Matt. 13:31). Jewish purity laws forbade the planting of a mustard seed in a garden, but in the Graeco-Roman world this was a common place practice. And Luke's account of the lowering of the paralytic through the roof of the house where Jesus was teaching removes Mark's reference to "digging", which would have been necessary with the typical thatched roofs of Palestine, and replaces it with a description of the removal of "tiles", more common atop buildings elsewhere in the Roman Empire (Mark 2:4; Luke 5:19). All these changes simply help a non-Jewish audience to picture the scenes more vividly and comprehensibly in their minds, even if the actual details of the imagery have changed.[9]

Corroborating Reports. More than agreement in every little detail, corroborating reports also dismiss apparent contradictions among the Gospels. Thus, on the one hand, the birth narratives of Jesus Christ as recorded in Matthew 1–2 and Luke 1–2 contain differing material:

---

9. Blomberg, *The Historical Reliability of the Gospels,* 162–63.

MATTHEW 1–2	LUKE 1–3
Jesus' genealogy goes back to Abraham	Jesus' genealogy goes back to Adam
Joseph is the focus	Mary is the focus
Herod the Great is introduced	Herod the Great is not mentioned
The Wise Men worship the Christ child	Shepherds worship baby Jesus

Yet, on the other hand, note the twelve major agreements between the birth stories of Matthew and Luke:

1. Jesus' birth is related to the reign of Herod (Matt. 2:1; Luke 1:5).

2. Mary, his mother to be, is a virgin engaged to Joseph, but they have not yet come to live together (Matt. 1:18; Luke 1:27, 34; 2:5).

3. Joseph is of the house of David (Matt. 1:16, 20; Luke 1:27; 2:4).

4. An angel from heaven announces the coming birth of Jesus (Matt. 1:20–21; Luke 1:28–30).

5. Jesus is recognized to be a Son of David (Matt. 1:1; Luke 1:32).

6. His conception is to take place through the Holy Spirit (Matt. 1:18, 20; Luke 1:35).

7. Joseph is not involved in the conception (Matt. 1:18–35; Luke 1:34).

8. The name "Jesus" is imposed by heaven prior to his birth (Matt. 1:21; Luke 1:31).

9. The angel identifies Jesus as "Savior" (Matt. 1:21; Luke 2:11).

10. Jesus is born after Mary and Joseph come to live together (Matt. 1:24–25; Luke 2:4–7).

11. Jesus is born in Bethlehem (Matt. 2:1; Luke 2:4–7).

12. Jesus settles with Mary and Joseph in Nazareth in Galilee (Matt. 2:22–23; Luke 2:39, 51).[10]

---

10. This material is adapted from Joseph A. Fitzmyer, *The Gospel According to Luke I–IX*, AB 28 (New York: Doubleday, 1979), 307.

Actually, the differences in Matthew and Luke concerning the birth of Jesus Christ are easily accounted for once we allow for poetic license and their respective theological messages. Neither author purports to provide the complete account of the birth of their Lord but rather chooses which material to present according to the leading of the Holy Spirit and the spiritual needs of their audiences. Moreover, their agreement in the key areas we noted above corroborates their testimonies and would be accepted in a court of law today. Indeed, modern eyewitness accounts are deemed as legally reliable precisely because they agree in the basic descriptions rather than in the minutiae. In the case of the latter, such testimonies would be thrown out of court for collusion.

Supposed Historical Errors

But what about the accusation that the Gospels contain historical errors which thereby diminish their trustworthiness? Here we treat three famous texts supposedly guilty of blatant historical error. Mark 2:26 refers to King David eating showbread when (*epi*) Abiathar was the high priest (see 1 Sam. 21:1–6). Yet, 1 Samuel 21 clearly states that Ahimelech, Abiathar's father, held that office. It was this "mistake" that caused Bart Ehrman to jettison his conservative faith for liberalism.[11] But John Wenham has made a convincing case for translating the unusual prepositional phrase as, not "when Abiathar was high priest" but "concerning [the passage of Scripture in 1 Samuel 21 that speaks of] Abiathar the High Priest." Indeed, Mark uses *epi* eighteen out of its twenty-one occurrences to refer to location not time. Wenham very plausibly suggests that Mark does this because the passage referred to comes immediately before Abiathar's exploits as High Priest. In the context of the two priests—Ahimelech and Abiathar—the latter is the more noteworthy as the priest who first brought the priesthood to King David's side in his struggle against Saul.[12]

In Matthew 23:35 Jesus accuses the Jewish leaders of having a history of killing Old Testament righteous men, from Abel to Zechariah the son of Berachiah. Yet, the Old Testament says nothing of the prophet Zechariah being murdered. Skeptics of the Gospels seize on this point arguing that Jesus mistakenly confused the prophet Zechariah with another Zechariah, the son of Jehoiada, who was a priest. According to 2 Chronicles 24:20–22, the latter was killed in the temple court. However, rabbinic traditions (e.g., the *Targum* on Lam. 2:20 and the *Midrash Rabbah* on Eccl. 3:16) also refer to Zechariah the prophet as being killed in the temple. On this understanding, Jesus and extra-biblical tradition converge in reporting an actual incident not mentioned in the Old Testament. Other New Testament notables also refer to

---

11. See Bart D. Ehrman, *Misquoting Jesus: The Story Behind Who Changed the Bible and Why?* (San Francisco: Harper-San Francisco, 2005), 9.
12. See J. W. Wenham, "Mark 2:26," *JTS* (1950): 156.

individuals not recorded in the Hebrew Bible but mentioned in non-canonical Jewish literature.[13]

Luke 2:2 refers to a census taken during the time Quirinius was governor of Syria. Historians date that census to AD 6 but Jesus was born in 6 BC. Did Luke make a mistake here? Not if Quirinius was joint-ruler of Syria before he assumed sole governorship in AD 6, as some ancient Roman historians infer (Tacitus, *Annals* 3.48; Florus, *Roman History* 2.31).[14]

Supposed "Assured" Results of Higher-Critical Approaches

A third reason for the modern skeptical appraisal of the historical reliability of the canonical gospels stems from three scholarly disciplines that dominated gospel studies in the twentieth century—source, form, and redaction criticisms. Each of these approaches in their own way have undermined the eyewitness claims of the Gospels. More than the previous suspicions raised against the Gospels (antipathy toward miracles and apparent contradictions and historical errors) these three disciplines have severed the Jesus of history from the Christ of faith. We first describe the three scholarly pursuits with a view to exposing how they eliminated the long-standing tradition by the church that the Gospels were based on eyewitness testimony and then in the chapters that follow we offer a rebuttal to each, arguing instead for the traditional view.

Source Criticism

Source criticism has dominated gospel studies for the last two hundred years. Alternately labeled the "the Synoptic Problem," B. H. Streeter is usually credited with popularizing this approach to the first three gospels.[15] The central concern of the Synoptic Problem is how one is to account for both the similarities and the differences among Matthew, Mark, and Luke. Streeter's work was the culmination of almost two thousand years of attempts to explain that question. His answer was that Mark was the first gospel written and that Matthew and Luke wrote independently of each other but had access to Mark's gospel along with a hypothetical sayings source of Jesus' teaching called "Q," for *Quelle* (German for "source"), containing 235 sayings shared by Matthew and Luke. This "two document theory" was enlarged to include special Matthean material ("M") and special Lukan material ("L"). Although rival configurations appeared along the way, Streeter's theory has won the day.

---

13. See, for example, Hebrews 11:35 with reference to 2 Maccabees and the Jewish mother's hope for the resurrection of her martyred sons, Jude 9 concerning *The Apocalypse of Moses* and its mention of the dead body of Moses, or Jude 14–15 where Jude quotes *1 Enoch* with reference to the coming of the Lord.

14. For further discussion, see C. Marvin Pate, *Luke* (Moody: Chicago, 1995), 24–25.

15. B. H. Streeter, *The Four Gospels: A Study of Origins* (London: Macmillan, 1924; New York: Macmillan, 1925).

Now, the two source theory could be a useful tool to investigate the literary relationships among the Synoptics, but what threatened conservative scholars about this hypothesis was its oft-accompanying denial of the eyewitness nature of the three Gospels; a concern that was also applied to John. Simply put, the concern was this: why would Matthew, a disciple of Jesus, bother to use Mark, a non-disciple of Jesus, as well as the anonymous source "Q"? Luke might be expected to do as much since he was not an apostle. Yet, things got even more complicated because advocates of Streeter's proposal went on to deny that even Matthew and John,[16] two of the twelve apostles of Jesus, were actually the authors of those works ascribed to them. With those denials, the foundation of the eyewitness testimony of the four Gospels collapsed in the minds of many New Testament scholars.

Form Criticism

Before the dust had settled on the debate concerning source criticism, in the 1920s form criticism assumed center stage as the newest approach to the Synoptic Gospels. Rudolf Bultmann was probably the most influential theologian in twentieth-century New Testament scholarship. Based on the works of his colleagues K. L. Schmidt and Martin Dibelius, Bultmann helped to pioneer the application of form criticism to the Gospels with the publication of his monumental work, *The History of the Synoptic Tradition*.[17] Three key components undergird the task of form criticism. (1) The gospel materials should be classified according to their "form"—parables, pronouncement stories, wisdom sayings, apocalyptic statements, miracles or legends, etc. (2) These forms circulated independently of each other in various church communities. For example, pronouncement stories were used in early Christian Jewish debates within the synagogues. Miracles/legends were appealed to by Gentile churches in an effort to win over Greek speaking audiences accustomed to hearing about divine-man miracle workers in their culture. And apocalyptic statements were developed by the early church in the aftermath of the delay of the parousia (the second coming of Jesus). (3) These forms first circulated among the believing communities in oral form and separate from each other for a generation before they were written down as the Gospels we now know. The fundamental assumption driving form criticism was that these materials were not produced by eyewitnesses but rather were the product of communities which had no real contact with the historical Jesus tradition. Indeed, after Bultmann applied the criteria of authenticity to the Gospels (most notably

---

16. John came under scathing attack regarding its claim to be an eyewitness account due to being written in the 90s and containing much material that was different from the Synoptic Gospels.
17. R. Bultmann, *The History of the Synoptic Tradition* (Oxford: Blackwell; New York: Harper & Row, 1968 [German orig. 1921]).

the criteria of multiple attestation and dissimilarity—more on these later in this unit) there was precious little of the sayings and deeds attributed to Jesus that were deemed to be from the historical Jesus. Today, the Jesus Seminar continues Bultmann's radical approach thus severing the Jesus of history from the Christ of faith.

Redaction Criticism
    Coming on the heels of source and form criticisms, redaction criticism in the 1960s to the 1980s focused on the individual evangelists as shapers and editors of the material they inherited from their communities. While this discipline accorded more of a place to the theological efforts of the composers of the Gospels than did form criticism, it still questioned the Gospels as the products of eyewitness accounts. Instead of reporting the history of the real Jesus, the founders of redaction criticism (Günther Bornkamm, Willi Marxsen, and Hans Conzelmann) argued instead that the gospel authors were more interested in crafting their own theologies for their respective communities.
    Space does not permit us in this opening chapter to respond to the above three disciplines and their combined attack on the historical reliability of the Gospels. Rather, in the chapters that follow in Part I we will offer our rebuttal to these criticisms.

Summary
    We began our study with the fundamental question of whether the Jesus of history and the Christ of faith are the same. The decision one arrives at regarding this issue determines whether or not one views the canonical gospels as reliable, no small matter concerning the Christian faith. We began therefore to answer the three major criticisms raised against the four gospels. The evidence as we have studied it through the years has convinced us that the Gospels accurately record the supernatural acts of Jesus. They are historically reliable because the Gospels are indeed based on eyewitness accounts. Having done this, we now need to focus on more background information regarding the Gospels, specifically the three quests for the historical Jesus (see the next two Questions). To put our thesis another way, when we take the Gospels' records seriously what picture of Jesus emerges?

REFLECTION QUESTIONS

1. What is the fundamental question of this chapter?

2. How would you answer the first objection to the reliability of the Gospels regarding miracles?

3. How would you answer the second objection of the reliability of the Gospels regarding their supposed contradictions and historical inaccuracies?

4. How have the three New Testament disciplines of source, form, and redaction criticisms served to undermine the reliability of the Gospels?

5. How would you respond to these three disciplines?

What Were the First Two Quests for the Historical Jesus?

At three different periods during the last few hundred years in New Testament studies, scholars have launched attempts to discover the historical Jesus. These are naturally labeled the "three quests for the historical Jesus." This chapter discusses the first two of those quests while the next chapter focuses on the third quest.

The First Quest for the Historical Jesus (1778–1906)

The assumption that the historical Jesus[1] is not one and the same with the portrait found in the four Gospels was first championed by H. Samuel Reimarus in his article, written anonymously, "On the Aim of Jesus and His

---

1. Besides the works soon to be mentioned in the text, the brief survey we offer regarding the quests for the historical Jesus is indebted to the following studies: Colin Brown, "Historical Jesus, Quest of," in *DJG*, ed. Joel B. Green, Scot McKnight and I. Howard Marshall (Downers Grove, IL: InterVarsity Press, 1992), 326–41; James Charlesworth, "Jesus Research Expands with Chaotic Creativity," in *Images of Jesus Today*, ed. James H. Charlesworth and Walter P. Weaver (Valley Forge, PA: Trinity, 1994), 1–41; John P. Meier, "Reflections on Jesus-of-History Research Today," in *Jesus' Jewishness: Exploring the Place of Jesus in Early Judaism*, ed. James H. Charlesworth (New York: Crossroad, 1991), 84–107; Marcus Borg, *Jesus in Contemporary Scholarship* (Valley Forge, PA: Trinity, 1994); Ben Witherington III, *The Jesus Quest: The Third Search for the Jew of Nazareth* (Downers Grove, IL: InterVarsity Press, 1995); *Jesus Under Fire*, ed. Michael F. Wilkinson and J. P. Moreland (Grand Rapids: Zondervan, 1995), especially Scot McKnight's article, "Who Is Jesus? An Introduction to Jesus Studies," 51–72; Luke Timothy Johnson, *The Real Jesus: The Misguided Quest for the Historical Jesus and the Traditional Gospels* (San Francisco: Harper Collins, 1996); N. T. Wright, *Jesus and the Victory of God* (Minneapolis: Fortress, 1996), 1–224; and especially Craig A. Evans, *Life of Jesus Research: An Annotated Bibliography*, New Testament Tools and Studies 13 (Leiden: Brill, 1989).

Disciples."[2] For Reimarus, the real Jesus was an apocalyptic preacher whose expectation of the soon arrival of the kingdom of God met with stunning disappointment. Christianity would have died were it not for Jesus' disciples, who falsely claimed that Jesus arose and preached his future return and establishment of the kingdom of God. Reimarus' study initiated the first quest for the historical Jesus, a search that spawned the writings of hundreds of books in an attempt to recover the sayings and miracles of the authentic Jesus.[3] Four general approaches can be catalogued in that literature. First, the traditional response consisted of conservative accounts of the life of Jesus such as J. J. Hess' three volumes on *The History of the Three Last Years of the Life of Jesus* (1768–72).[4] Second, the life of Jesus from a liberal, or anti-supernatural, perspective, was put forth by Friedrich Schleiermacher,[5] David Friedrich Strauss,[6] and J. E. Renan,[7] to name a few.[8] Third, from A. B. Ritschl and Adolf Harnack came an emphasis on the ethical life of Jesus, especially the guidelines

---

2. Hermann Samuel Reimarus (died 1768) anonymously wrote and G. E. Lessing published, "Von dem Zwecke Jesu und seiner Junger: Nock ein Fragment des Wolfenbuttelschen ungenannten fragment?" These extracts became known as the Wolfenbuttel fragments (see Brown, "The Quest for the Historical Jesus," 327). For the text, see *Reimarus Fragments*, ed. C. H. Talbert, trans. F. S. Fraser, Lives of Jesus Series (Philadelphia: Fortress, 1970).

3. Albert Schweitzer, *The Quest of the Historical Jesus: A Critical Study of Its Progress from Reimarus to Wrede*, summed up the entire history from the late eighteenth century (Reimarus) to the beginning of the twentieth (William Wrede); see the handy summary (from a conservative point of view) in Charles C. Anderson, *Critical Quests of Jesus* (Grand Rapids: Eerdmans, 1969); or still more schematically, John S. Kselman, "Modern New Testament Criticism," in *Jerome Biblical Commentary*, ed. Raymond Brown, Joseph A. Fitzmyer, and Roland Murphy (Englewood Cliffs, NJ: Prentice Hall, 1968), 2:7–20. A 116-page bibliography, introduced by a 111-page sketch of the chief questers, can be found in Warren S. Kissinger, *The Lives of* Jesus (New York/London: Garland, 1985). A more general bibliography on Christology, including sections on the historical Jesus, is available in Leland Jennings White, J*esus the Christ, A Bibliography* (Wilmington: Glazier, 1988). A useful annotated bibliography is supplied by Craig A. Evans, *Life of Jesus Research* (Leiden, Netherlands: E. J. Bril, 1989). Further methodological considerations and caveats can be found in Ben Witherington III, *The Christology of Jesus*, 1–31; this bibliography comes from Joseph P. Meier, *A Marginal Jew: The Roots of the Problem and the Person* (New York: Doubleday, 1991), 1:34–35, though that author chose not to include a survey of the quests; cf. also E. P. Sanders, *Jesus and Judaism* (Philadelphia: Fortress, 1985); see Evans' list, *Jesus*, 14–17.

4. Cf., for example, A. Edersheim, *The Life and Times of Jesus the Messiah*, 2 vols. (New York: Randolph/London: Longmans, 1883); F. W. Farrar, *Life of Christ* (New York: Dutton, 1874); see also M. J. Lagrange, *The Gospel of Jesus Christ*, 2 vols. (London: Burns, Oates & Washbourne, 1938).

5. F. E. D. Schleiermacher, *The Life of Jesus*, trans. S. M. Gilmour, ed. J. C. Verhegden, Lives of Jesus Series (Philadelphia: Fortress, 1975).

6. D. F. Strauss, *The Life of Jesus Critically Examined*, 3 vols., trans. G. Eliot (London: Chapman, 1846).

7. J. E. Renan. *The Life of Jesus*, trans. C. E. Wilbour (London: Trubner, 1864).

8. The reader is referred to Evans, *Jesus*, 21–22.

for living delineated in the Sermon on the Mount.[9] Fourth, with Albert Schweitzer's work, *The Quest for the Historical Jesus*,[10] which proceeded from Johannes Weiss' groundbreaking study, *Jesus' Proclamation of the Kingdom of God*,[11] the apocalyptic Jesus emerged victorious over its conceptual rivals. In that monumental study, Schweitzer identified three major crises in the quest for the original Jesus: The first was the crisis provoked by Strauss: to investigate the historical Jesus either as a purely historical approach or as a purely supernatural one. The second was posed by the Tübingen school and Schweitzer's teacher, Holtzmann: to investigate the historical Jesus by either following the Synoptic Gospels or John. The third was the choice between Wrede and himself (Schweitzer): to investigate the historical Jesus by characterizing him as either an eschatological or a non-eschatological Jesus. In each case Schweitzer left no doubt as to the path which the reader should follow.[12]

Why Did the First Quest Fail?

As far as Schweitzer was concerned, like Weiss before him, Jesus was an apocalyptic preacher of the coming kingdom of God. Colin Brown summarizes six eschatological aspects of Jesus' teaching, according to Weiss:

> The kingdom was transcendent and supramundane; it belonged to the future; Jesus was not the founder or inaugurator but waited for God to bring it; the kingdom was not identified with the circle of Jesus' disciples: it did not come gradually by growth or development: its ethics were negative and world-denying. Jesus was a rabbi or prophet who believed that in God's good time he would become the Son of Man.[13]

Schweitzer agreed with Weiss' presentation of the historical Jesus, except that whereas Weiss had made eschatology the key to Jesus' teaching, Schweitzer said that it was also the key to the course of Jesus' life. The title *Son of Man* was a designation of the Messiah coming on the clouds as judge. Jesus believed that it was his vocation to become the coming Son of Man. Initially he

---

9. A. B. Ritschl (1822–89) provides the classic liberal view of Jesus; see his *The Christian Doctrine of Justification and Reconciliation*, 3 vols. (1870–74), along with Adolf Harnack (1851–1930), *The Mission and Expansion of Christianity in the First Three Centuries*, trans. and ed. James Moffatt (Gloucester: Peter Smith, 1972). The latter prompted the famous quip by Alfred Loisy, "The Christ that Harnack sees, looking back through nineteen centuries of Catholic darkness, is only the reflection of a liberal Protestant face, seen at the bottom of a deep well" (quoted in Brown, "The Quest for the Historical Jesus," 331).
10. See footnote 3 above.
11. Johannes Weiss, *Jesus' Proclamation of the Kingdom of God*, trans. T. H. Hiers and D. L. Holland, Lives of Jesus Series (Philadelphia: Fortress, 1971).
12. Schweitzer, *The Quest for the Historical Jesus*, 238.
13. Brown, "The Quest for the Historical Jesus," 331.

revealed this messianic secret only to Peter, James and John. Later, Peter told it to the rest of the Twelve. Judas told the secret to the high priest who used it as the ground for Jesus' execution (Mark 14:61–64; cf. Dan. 7:13).

Jesus had sent out the Twelve on a mission to proclaim the coming kingdom of God. He did not expect them to return. The Twelve were the "men of violence" (Matt. 11:12) who would provoke the messianic tribulation that would herald the kingdom. Whereas Weiss believed that one could only wait passively for the kingdom, Schweitzer believed that the mission was designed to provoke that coming. When this did not happen, Jesus was determined to give his own life as a ransom for many (Mark 10:45) and so cause the kingdom to come.[14]

Schweitzer's epoch-making work on the historical Jesus brought an end to the first quest, showing, on the one hand, that the lives of Jesus constructed on the Gospels were but mere reflections of their authors while, on the other hand, arguing that the authentic Jesus was a disillusioned announcer of the coming rule of God, a portrait not too appealing to conservative Christianity.

During the 1920s, Rudolf Bultmann's form critical program attempted to fill the void created by the demise of the first quest for the historical Jesus. Form criticism was pioneered by F. L. Schmidt, Martin Dibelius and Rudolph Bultmann. Schmidt's *The Framework of the Historical Jesus* (1919) claimed that the framework of the gospel stories was created by the evangelists for their own purposes and was historically invalid. Martin Dibelius' *From Tradition to Gospel* (1934) was more positive in relating the gospel traditions to the historical Jesus. With Rudolf Bultmann's *The History of the Synoptic Tradition* (1921), however, form criticism reached the peak of skepticism. There Bultmann eloquently argued that the Synoptics shed light, not on Jesus, but on the *Sitz im Leben* (situation in life) of the early church. The Christ that they preached was not that of the authentic Jesus but that of the Hellenistic church. For Bultmann and his followers, the key criterion for ascertaining genuine sayings and acts of Jesus was the criterion of dissimilarity (only that which is neither Jewish nor is in common with the Hellenistic church is authentic), along with other considerations such as multiple attestation (an authentic saying or act of Jesus must be attested in two or more sources: e.g., Q and Mark), and coherence (the picture that emerges from the criterion of dissimilarity becomes the grid for interpreting the multiple sources). The aforementioned criteria, wedded with Bultmann's de-mythological hermeneutic (an approach that tried to arrive at the core truth behind all the "myths" in the Bible), left little modern relevance for the likes of Schweitzer's apocalyptic Jesus. Instead, born out of the philosophy of existentialism, Bultmann's hermeneutic presented the New Testament as calling people to "authentic existence" by embracing a faith in Jesus without any historical underpinning.[15]

---

14. Ibid., 331–32.
15. More in the next chapter on the criteria of authenticity.

What Was the New (Second) Quest For the Historical Jesus? (1953–Late 1960s)

It is generally agreed that Ernst Käsemann's celebrated paper delivered at a Marburg reunion of Bultmann's former students in 1953, "The Problem of the Historical Jesus,"[16] initiated the second, or new, quest for the historical Jesus. In that paper, Käsemann challenged Bultmann's radical divide between the Jesus of history and the Christ of faith, arguing that the early church held the two together—the exalted and humiliated Lord. To do otherwise was to invite the label of Docetism (the heresy that said that Jesus was divine but not human). The way forward through the impasse was to analyze Jesus' preaching, which signaled the inauguration of the kingdom of God. Käsemann was followed by scholars like Ernst Fuchs,[17] who maintained that Jesus' fellowship with sinners was that of one who acted on behalf of God, and Gunther Bornkamm, who called attention to the presence of the kingdom in Jesus' authoritative words and actions.[18] The latter claimed: "Quite clearly what the Gospels report concerning the message, the deeds, and the history of Jesus is still distinguished by an authenticity, a freshness, and a distinctiveness not in any way effaced by the Church's Easter faith. These features point us directly to the early figure of Jesus."[19]

In America, James M. Robinson and Norman Perrin propagated the new quest. For the former, the question of how the proclaimer of the Kingdom became the proclaimed Christ is answered not by the historical inquiry that characterized the first quest, but rather by existentialism's challenge to follow Jesus by being authentic.[20] The latter, though aligning himself with the new quest, disagreed with that movement's identity of the historical Jesus with the kerygmatic Christ. Not surprisingly, Perrin made much of the Bultmannian criteria for authenticity.[21] Though it should be noted that Perrin did allow for more of the historical Jesus than Bultmann. Thus, Perrin identified the following facts about Jesus: his baptism by John, the proclamation especially in parables of the present and future kingdom of God, a ministry of exorcism, his gathering of disciples across socio-economic boundaries, his sharing a common meal that celebrated their new relationship to God, his challenge to the Jewish teachers of his day, the arousal of opposition that led to his

---

16. E. Käsemann, "The Problem of the Historical Jesus," trans. W. J. Montague, SBT 41 (Naperville, IL: Allenson/London: SCM, 1964).

17. E. Fuchs, *Studies of the Historical Jesus*, trans. A. Scobie, SBT 42 (Naperville, IL: Allenson and London, SCM, 1964).

18. Gunther Bornkamm, *Jesus of Nazareth*, trans. I. McLuskey, F. McLuskey, and J. M. Robinson (New York: Harper & Row; London: Hodder & Stoughton, 1960).

19. Bornkamm, *Jesus of Nazareth*, 24.

20. James M. Robinson, *A New Quest of the Historical Jesus*, SBT 25 (Naperville, IL: Allison; London: SCM, 1959).

21. Norman Perrin, *Rediscovering the Teaching of Jesus* (New York: Harper & Row, 1967), 233.

arrest, his trials by the Jewish authorities on a charge of blasphemy and by the Romans for sedition, and his crucifixion.[22]

Colin Brown summarizes the rather meager impact of the second questers:

> New Quest ended scarcely two decades after it started. Its demise coincided with the end of the Bultmann era and the passing of existentialist philosophy. Despite its emphasis on scholarly rigor, its methods and assumptions were limited to those of the Bultmann school. For all its stress on history, it remained curiously indifferent to the world of first-century Judaism as known from Josephus, the Dead Sea Scrolls, and rabbinic literature. To those engaged in the New Quest the proclamation of the cross was the pivotal event which linked existence with the historical Jesus. By positing the crucifixion of Jesus as a fact, docetism was averted. But little attention was paid to the question, Why exactly was Jesus crucified? Insofar as it was answered at all, it was answered in existential terms. To exclude the close connection between religion, theology, politics, sociology and economics as interrelated factors in answering this question now looks curiously unhistorical and short-sighted.[23]

However, a positive contribution of the new quest was its spawning of the school of redaction criticism, with its recognition that the gospel writers were theologians in their own right, not just compilers of sacred tradition.[24]

REFLECTION QUESTIONS

1. Who began the first quest for the historical Jesus and how did that unfold?

2. Why did the first quest fail?

---

22. Norman Perrin, *The New Testament: An Introduction* (New York: Harcourt, Brace, Jovanovich, 1974), 287–88.
23. Brown, "Quest for the Historical Jesus," 337.
24. For the Synoptic Gospels, see the following redactional studies: Bornkamm, "The Stilling of the Storm in Matthew" in *Tradition and Interpretation in Matthew*, ed. G. Bornkamm, G. Barth and H. J. Held (London: NTL, 1963), 52–57; H. Conzelmann, *The Theology of Luke*; W. Marxsen, *Mark the Evangelist*, which first coined the term, "*Redaktionsgeschichte*." For a thorough attempt to debunk the movement, see Clifton C. Black, *The Disciples According to Mark: Markan Redaction in Current Debate* (Sheffield: JSOT, 1989).

3. After the failure of the first quest for the historical Jesus and before the rise of the second quest, whose theological program ruled the day in New Testament studies?

4. What was the second quest for the historical Jesus?

5. Why did that movement fail?

What Is the Third Quest for the Historical Jesus?

Though some doubt that we should call more recent scholars' preoccupation with the historical Jesus a "third quest,"[1] many believe the label is apropos. Three responses to the previous quests for the historical Jesus can be detected in this current literature: conservative, radical, and cultural. These three responses amount to what today is labeled the "third quest for the historical Jesus." We now describe each. Then we briefly evaluate the criteria for finding the historical Jesus.

The Conservative Response

More conservatively inclined scholars responded to radical form criticism with vigor. C. F. D. Moule (*The Origin of Christology*) rejected the History of Religion School's premise that the historical Jesus was transformed into the Christ of faith under the influence of Savior cults. Rather, argued Moule, titles like "Son of man," "Son of God," "Christ," and "Lord" go back to Jesus himself.[2] Already, Martin Hengel's erudite study had dispelled the Bultmannian myth of any water-tight compartmentalization of Judaism and Hellenism, thus calling for drastic revision of the criterion of dissimilarity (*Judaism and Hellenism*, 1974).[3] Building on the insights of Hengel, I. Howard Marshall, in a series of books, helped to dismantle the radical form critical

---

1. See Stanley Porter's reservations about the nomenclature, *The Criteria for Authenticity in Historical-Jesus Research: Previous Discussion and New Proposals*, JSNTSupp 191 (Sheffield: Sheffield Academic Press, 2000), chapter 1.
2. C. F. D. Moule, *The Origin of Christology* (Cambridge: Cambridge University Press, 1977).
3. M. Hengel, *Judaism and Hellenism*, trans. John Bowden, 2 vols. (Philadelphia: Fortress, 1974 and London: SCM Press; Philadelphia: Trinity Press International, 1989); cf. *The Hellenization of Judea in the First Century after Christ* (London: SCM Press; Philadelphia: Trinity Press International, 1989).

agenda, demonstrating that the Gospels, especially Luke, were reliable historical documents.[4]

The Liberal Response

In light of such a devastating critique of the Bultmannian program, it is surprising that such an approach continued to attract adherents, at least in America. Most notably, it was the Jesus Seminar that systematically applied form-critical criteria to the sayings and acts of Jesus, color-coding them according to their probability of authenticity. It is not surprising, however, given the Bultmannian assumptions of the Fellows of the seminar, that only some eighteen percent of Jesus' sayings and acts are colored red (genuine sayings or acts). The rest fall into the rather nebulous categories of pink, gray and black.[5] Chief among the members of the Jesus Seminar are Burton L. Mack[6] and John D. Crossan,[7] whose separate works envision Jesus to have been a Cynic sage thoroughly immersed in Hellenistic philosophy, not a Jewish apocalyptic seer.

The evaluation of the Jesus Seminar by David Wenham and Steve Walton, however, does not bode well for the future of that approach:

> The Seminar's work has been criticized from all sorts of angles: for the populist voting system (though this is arguably just a reliable way of assessing a scholarly consensus); for the doubtful estimate of the gospel sources; and for its

---

4. I. Howard Marshall, *Luke: Historian and Theologian* (Grand Rapids: Zondervan, 1970); *The Gospel of Luke* (Exeter: Paternoster; Grand Rapids: Eerdmans, 1978); *I Believe in the Historical Jesus* (Grand Rapids: Eerdmans, 1978); "The Synoptic Son of Man Sayings in Recent Discussion," *NTS* 12 (1965–66): 327–51; "The Divine Sonship of Jesus," *Int* 21 (1967): 87–103.

5. See R. W. Funk and R. W. Hoover, eds., *The Five Gospels: The Search for the Authentic Words of Jesus* (Sonoma: Polebridge Press; New York: Macmillian, 1993), 36–37. The Jesus Seminar also published its assessment of the activities of Jesus, following a similar format; cf. R. W. Funk, ed., *The Acts of Jesus: What did Jesus Really Do? The Search for the Authentic Deeds of Jesus* (San Francisco: Harper Collins, 1998). In the Introduction to the first volume, the Fellows offer a survey of the quests for the historical Jesus under the rubric, "The Seven Pillars of Scholarly Wisdom" (2–5): (1) the distinction of the Jesus of history from the Christ of faith; (2) the synoptics are closer to the original Jesus than the gospel of John; (3) the priority of Mark and the Existence of "Q"; (4) Schweitzer's eschatological Jesus; (5) Bultmann's "rescue" of Schweitzer's eschatological Jesus with the existential Jesus; (6) Form Criticism's distinction of oral and written literature; (7) the shift of the burden of proof of historicity of the Gospels from radicals to conservatives.

6. Burton L. Mack, *A Myth of Innocence: Mark and Christian Origins* (Philadelphia: Fortress, 1988).

7. John Dominic Crossan, *The Historical Jesus: The Life of a Mediterranean Jewish Peasant* (San Francisco: Harper-San Francisco, 1991); *Jesus: A Revolutionary Biography* (San Francisco: Harper-San Francisco, 1994).

improbable conclusion. It has been argued that, no less than their predecessors, the Americans have ended up portraying Jesus in their own image—as a reasonable, non-violent anti-establishment figure.[8]

The Cultural Response

Since Ben F. Meyer's insightful study, *The Aims of Jesus* (1979), a third type of study of the historical Jesus has emerged, that of rooting Jesus in the Jewish culture of his day. Meyer has been followed by both Christian scholars, e.g., E. P. Sanders (*Jesus and Judaism*, 1985),[9] G. Theissen (*The Shadow of the Galilean*, 1983),[10] James Charlesworth (*Jesus Within Judaism*, 1988),[11] and especially N. T. Wright (*Jesus and the People of God*, 1992 and *Jesus and the Victory of God*, 1996),[12] and John P. Meier (*A Marginal Jew: Rethinking the Historical Jesus; Mentor, Message and Miracles; Companions and Competitor*),[13] as well as Jewish scholars like Geza Vermes, whose *Jesus the Jew* (1973) and *Jesus and the World of Judaism* (1984) portrayed Jesus against the backdrop of Honi the Circle Drawer and Hanina ben Dosa the Miracle Worker.[14] If these scholars are correct, as they seem to be, an

---

8. David Wenham and Steve Walton, *Exploring the New Testament: A Guide to the Gospels and Acts*, vol. 1 (Downers Grove, IL: InterVarsity Press, 2001), 132. For other critiques of the Jesus Seminar, see Wright, *Jesus and the Victory of God*, vol. 2 of Christian Origins and the Question of God (Minneapolis: Fortress, 1996); Ben Witherington III, *The Jesus Quest: The Third Search for the Jew of Nazareth* (Downers Grove, IL: InterVarsity Press, 1995), 42–57; Richard B. Hays, "The Corrected Jesus," *First Things* 43 (May 1994): 43–48; Evans and Bruce Chilton, eds., *Authenticating the Words of Jesus*, NTTS 28 (Leiden: E. J. Brill, 1998).

9. E. P. Sanders, *Jesus and Judaism* (Philadelphia: Fortress, 1985); *The Historical Figure of Jesus* (London: Penguin, 1993).

10. Gerd Theissen, *The Shadow of the Galilean: The Quest for the Historical Jesus in Narrative Form* (Philadelphia: Fortress, 1987); *Sociology of Early Palestinian Christianity* (Philadelphia: Fortress, 1978); *The Gospels in Context: Social and Political History in the Synoptic Tradition* (Minneapolis: Augsburg Fortress, 1991).

11. James H. Charlesworth, *Jesus Within Judaism*, Anchor Bible Reference (Garden City, NY: Doubleday, 1988).

12. *The New Testament and the People of God*, vol. 1 of Christian Origins and the Question of God (Minneapolis: Fortress, 1992); *Jesus and the Victory of God*, vol. 2 of Christian Origins and the Question of God (Minneapolis: Fortress, 1996).

13. John P. Meier, *A Marginal Jew: The Roots of the Problem and the Person*, vol. 1 (New York: Doubleday, 1991); *A Marginal Jew: Mentor, Message and Miracles*, vol. 2 (New York: Doubleday, 1994); *A Marginal Jew: Companions and Competitors*, vol. 3 (New York: Doubleday, 2001).

14. Geza Vermes, *Jesus the Jew: A Historian's Reading of the Gospels* (New York: Macmillan; London: Collins, 1973) second edition: 1983; *Jesus and the World of Judaism* (Philadelphia: Fortress; London: SCM, 1984). For earlier Jewish attempts to root Jesus in Judaism, see C. G. Montefiore (*Rabbinic Literature and Gospels Teachings* [London: Macmillan, 1930]) and David Flusser (*Jesus* [New York: Herder and Herder, 1969]; *Judaism and the Origins of Christianity* [Jerusalem: Magnes, 1988]; see further Donald A. Hagner, *The Jewish*

overhaul of the criterion of dissimilarity is called for, especially the first aspect—authentic Jesus tradition differs from Judaism. And, one might add, if first-century Palestine was mutually influenced by Judaism and Hellenism, then so should the second aspect of the criterion of dissimilarity be considerably qualified—authentic Jesus tradition must differ from the later Hellenistic church.

The Criteria of Authenticity: An Evaluation

Perhaps the best way to sort through the myriad of articles and books on the criteria of authenticity[15] would be to reduce them to the top three: (1) multiple attestation, (2) dissimilarity, and (3) environment or culture.

First, multiple attestation is the criterion that says that identification of material that appears in more than one independent source (such as material found in both Mark and Q), is therefore attributable to Jesus. One of the earliest scholars to advocate this criterion was F. C. Burkitt:

> It appeared to me that the starting-point we require may be found in those Sayings which have a real double attestation. The main documents out of which the Synoptic Gospels are compiled are (1) the gospel of Mark, and (2) the lost common origin of the non-Marcan portions of Matthew and Luke, i.e., the source called Q. Where Q and Mark appear to report the same saying, we have the nearest approach that we can hope to get to the common tradition of the earliest Christian society about our Lord's words.[16]

Reclamation of Jesus: An Analysis and Critique of Modern Study of Jesus [Grand Rapids: Zondervan, 1984]).

15. For general treatments of these criteria, see, for example, F. C. Grant, "The Authenticity of Jesus' Sayings," in W. Eltester, ed., *Neutestamentliche Studien fur Rudolf Bultmann*, BZNW 21 (Berlin: Topelmann, 1954), 137–43; W. O. Walker, "The Quest for the Historical Jesus: A Discussion of Methodology," *ATR* 51 (1969): 38–56; R. T. France, "The Authenticity of the Sayings of Jesus," in *History, Criticism & Faith: Four Exploratory Studies*, ed. C. Brown (Leicester: InterVarsity Press, 1976), 101–43; R. H. Stein, "The 'Criteria' for Authenticity," in *Studies of History and Tradition in the Four Gospels*, ed. T. T. France and D. Wenham, Gospel Perspectives 1 (Sheffield: JSOT Press, 1983), 225–63; D. Polkow, "Method and Criteria for Historical Jesus Research," in ed. K. H. Richards, Society of Biblical Literature 1987 Seminar Papers, SBLSP 26 (Atlanta: Scholars Press,1987), 336–56; C. A. Evans, "Authenticity Criteria in Life of Jesus Research," *Christian Scholar's Review* 19 (1989): 6–31; Meier, *A Marginal Jew*, 1:167–95; and especially Porter, *The Criteria of Authenticity*.

16. F. C. Burkitt, *The Gospel History and Its Transmission*, 3rd ed. (Edinburgh: T&T Clark, 1911), 147. Some others who make reference to this criterion are: C. H. Dodd, *The Parables of the Kingdom* (Charles Scribner's Sons, 1962), 26–27 and T. W. Manson, *The Teaching of Jesus* (Cambridge: Cambridge University Press, 1935), 10–11.

Burkitt then went on to list thirty-one of these doubly attested sayings.[17] Problems, however, accompany this perspective: (1) it presumes the priority of Mark, something which the revived Griesbach hypothesis resists with its emphasis on Matthew;[18] (2) multiple attestation can prove a tradition to be early, but not necessarily authentic;[19] (3) the negative use of this indication is not valid; thus there is no reason to deny the authenticity of a tradition simply because it is found in only one source.[20] Nevertheless, multiple attestation can provide the probability of the authenticity of sayings. Thus, H. K. McArthur writes:

> My own proposal would be that the order of priority should be reversed so that the criterion of multiple attestation is given first place, at least in order or procedure [instead of the criterion of dissimilarity]. Furthermore I would propose that when three or four of the synoptic sources concur in providing evidence for a given motif in the ministry of Jesus then the burden of proof should be regarded as having shifted to those who deny the historicity of that motif.[21]

Second, dissimilarity is the identification of material that is dissimilar to characteristic emphases of ancient Judaism and/or early Christianity, and is therefore attributable to Jesus. This is the number one criterion enlisted by New Testament scholars to discover what the historical Jesus said and did. Rudolf Bultmann first pioneered this criterion: "We can only count on possessing a genuine similitude of Jesus where, on the one hand, expression is given to the contrast between Jewish morality and piety and the distinctive eschatological temper which characterized the preaching of Jesus: and where on the other hand we find no specifically Christian features."[22] It was with Bultmann's students, however, that the criterion became explicitly reformulated and put into its now common usage. E. Käsemann writes, "In only one case do we have more or less safe ground under our feet; when there are no grounds either for deriving a tradition from Judaism or for ascribing it to

---

17. Burkitt, *The Gospel History*, 147.
18. See especially William R. Farmer, *The Synoptic Problem: A Critical Analysis* (New York: Macmillan, 1964). For the application of the Griesbach theory to Mark, see C. S. Mann, *Mark*, AB 27 (Garden City: Doubleday, 1986). For criticisms of the Griesbach view, see the thorough treatments of Robert Stein, *The Synoptic Problem: An Introduction* (Grand Rapids: Baker, 1987), 29–157; and W. D. Davies and Dale C. Allison, *Matthew* [I–VII], ICC (Edinburgh: T&T Clark, 1988), 1:97–127.
19. For both objections, see Stein, "The 'Criteria' of Authenticity," 230–31.
20. So C. F. D. Moule, *The Phenomenon of the New Testament* (London: SCM, 1967), 71; cf. Burkitt, *The Gospel History*, 167–68.
21. H. K. McArthur, "The Burden of Proof in Historical Jesus Research," *Expository Times* 82 (1971): 118.
22. R. Bultmann, *History of the Synoptic Tradition*, rev. ed. (New York: Harper & Row, 1963), 205.

primitive Christianity, and especially when Jewish Christianity has mitigated or modified the received tradition, as having found it too bold for its taste."[23] Similarly, H. Conzelmann adds, "Whatever fits neither into Jewish thought nor the views of the later church can be regarded as authentic."[24]

Early on, however, Morna Hooker criticized this principle on two grounds: the first problem is that it singled out what is "unique" to Jesus, but not necessarily what is characteristic.[25] In other words, some of Jesus' characteristic teaching might be disregarded because it happens to overlap with Jewish and early Christian analogues. If this criterion is followed too strictly, then the "authentic Jesus" that will emerge will be isolated from his own environment and context.[26] An obvious problem here is that as a Palestinian Jew, Jesus' teaching would regularly reflect Jewish ideas and concepts. Moreover, since the early church found him and his teachings relevant (if it had not, Christianity as we know it would not have emerged), we should expect significant overlap between material attributed to Jesus and material that played an important role in the early community. The basic problem seems to be that the criterion of dissimilarity retains the assumption of form criticism, namely, that what was relevant to the early church must have originated with it and not with Jesus.[27] The second problem is that the criterion presupposes that we possess adequate knowledge of first-century Judaism and Christianity necessary for such comparative analysis.[28] What we think may be distinctive to Jesus may not be after all. For these reasons this criterion has been frequently criticized.[29] Nevertheless, the criterion is helpful, if it is applied properly. But it must be remembered that material that does not meet its requirements has not been proven inauthentic, it simply does not enjoy the relative confirmation that this criterion offers.[30]

In light of the above criticisms, Norman Perrin reformulated the criterion of dissimilarity to say, "Sayings and parables may be accepted as both ancient Judaism and early Christianity."[31] But, as Polkow observes, "characteristic emphases are obviously not the same as anything distinctive or unusual that could be considered under the general labels of ancient Judaism and early

---

23. Ernst Käsemann, "The Problem of the Historical Jesus," in *Essays on New Testament Themes,* trans. W. J. Montague, SBT 41 (Naperville, IL: Allenson and London: SCM, 1964), 15–47 (esp. 36–37).

24. Hans Conzelmann, *Jesus* (Philadelphia: Fortress, 1973), 16.

25. Morna Hooker, "On Using the Wrong Tool," *in Theology* 75 (1972): 570–81 (esp. 574–75).

26. Ibid., 574.

27. Evans, "Authenticity Criteria," 15.

28. Hooker, "On Using the Wrong Tool," 575.

29. Besides those already mentioned, see Stein, "The 'Criteria' for Authenticity," 242–44 and Bruce Chilton, *A Galilean Rabbi* (Wilmington, DE: Michael Glazer, 1984), 86–87.

30. Evans, "Authenticity Criteria," 15.

31. N. Perrin, *The New Testament: An Introduction* (New York: Harcourt Brace Jovanovich, 1974), 281.

Christianity; we are looking for anything unusual that contradicts the norm."[32] Polkow rebuts Perrin on this point, "One major challenge to dissimilarity which necessitates its reformulation is the discovery of the Nag Hammadi material. Thomas, for example, features many parables and aphorisms attributed to Jesus which are clearly dissimilar to characteristic emphases in either Judaism or Christianity, yet are hardly from Jesus."[33]

The third and final criteria we will discuss is that of environment or culture, especially a Palestinian context. Polkow summarizes this criterion:

> According to this criterion if a tradition betrays Palestinian social, domestic, agricultural, religious, etc. customs, this argues that the tradition originated in a Palestinian environment and cannot be a later creation of the Greek, i.e., non-Palestinian church. Again the argument here is that the closer we can trace a tradition to the time and environment of Jesus, the more likely it is that that tradition is authentic.[34]

Joachim Jeremias, the foremost advocate of this approach, observes:

> The pictorial element of the parables is drawn from the daily life of Palestine. It is noteworthy, for instance, that the sower in Mark 4.3–8 sows so clumsily that much of the seed is wasted; one might have expected a description of the regular method of sowing, and that, in fact is what we have here. This is easily understood when we remember that in Palestine sowing precedes ploughing. . . . What appears in the western mind as bad farming is simply customary procedure under Palestinian conditions.[35]

But two objections can be raised against this principle unqualified: (1) since the works of Martin Hengel, the old dichotomy of Judaism and Hellenism

---

32. Polkow, "Method and Criteria," 348.
33. Ibid. This is especially so if Gnosticism (which impacts the *Gospel of Thomas*) post-dated Christianity rather than the reverse, the latter of which Bultmann claimed. Bultmann's writings on the subject include: *Primitive Christianity in Contemporary Setting*; "The New Testament and Mythology" in *Kerygma and Myth: A Theological Debate*, ed. H. E. Bartsch, trans. R. H. Fuller (New York: Harper & Row, 1961), 1–44; *Theology of the New Testament*, vol. 1, part II. But see the penetrating critiques of the theory of pre-Christian Gnosticism by E. M. Yamauchi, *Pre-Christian Gnosticism: A Survey of the Proposed Evidences*, rev. ed. (Grand Rapids: Baker, 1983).
34. Polkow, "Method and Criteria," 236.
35. Joachim Jeremias, *The Parables of Jesus*, rev. ed. (London: SCM; Philadelphia: Westminster, 1972), 11–12.

has fallen;[36] thus both Palestinian, Jewish, and Gentile traits may characterize the historical Jesus; (2) this criterion can only root a saying/act in Palestinian culture, not necessarily in authentic material.[37] But these two objections are offset by those scholars since the 1980s we noted above who plausibly argue that Jesus' Judaism must be considered in discovering the historical Jesus.

Conclusion

This chapter has summarized three positions that comprise the third quest for the historical Jesus, the: conservative, cultural, and liberal schools of thought. Moreover, we evaluated the top three criteria that are followed in order to discover the Jesus of history. While these discussions are quite important to academia and also have profound effect upon the religious scene at large, the humble follower of Jesus who believes in the inspired nature of the canonical Gospels is not too concerned about distinguishing the historical Jesus and the Christ of faith for, to that person, they are the same!

REFLECTION QUESTIONS

1. When did the Third Quest for the historical Jesus begin?

2. What was the conservative expression of that movement?

3. What was the liberal expression of that movement?

4. What was the cultural expression of that movement?

5. What is your assessment regarding the criteria of authenticity?

---

36. Martin Hengel, *Judaism and Hellenism*, trans. John Bowden, 2 vols. (Philadelphia: Fortress, 1974).
37. So Stein, "The 'Criteria' for Authenticity," 238.

What Are the Various Views of the Historical Jesus?

Three major views of Jesus dominated the theological landscape during the twentieth and now twenty-first centuries: (1) the apocalyptic Jesus, (2) the Gnostic Jesus, and (3) the Cynic Jesus.

The Apocalyptic Jesus

The first quest for the historical Jesus came to a crashing halt with the publication of Albert Schweitzer's classic work in 1906, *The Quest of the Historical Jesus*. In his book Schweitzer masterfully demonstrated that the quest for the historical Jesus amounted to nothing more than each interpreter imposing his own opinion of who Jesus really was onto the four gospels. The result was a welter of conflicting offerings of the historical Jesus. As they looked into the waters of the Gospels, what interpreters saw was merely their own reflection: the devotional Jesus, the liberal Jesus, the ethical Jesus, and so on.

For Schweitzer's part, he sided with the position of Reimarus, the view that got the whole quest started in the first place. "Consistent eschatology" is a label that New Testament scholars apply to the works of Albert Schweitzer. "Consistent" means consistent with the futurist view of most Jews at the time of Jesus who thought that the kingdom of God was still in the future, with reference to how Schweitzer interpreted the message of Jesus. Judaism at the time of Christ divided history into two periods: this age of sin, when sin rules, and the age to come, when the Messiah will come to establish the kingdom of God. Schweitzer maintained that Jesus believed it was his vocation to become the coming Son of Man and thereby initiate the kingdom of God.

So, Schweitzer said, Jesus took matters into his own hand by precipitating his death, hoping this would be the catalyst for causing God to make the wheel of history turn to its climax—the arrival of the kingdom of God. But, claimed Schweitzer, Jesus was wrong and he died in despair. So, for Schweitzer, Jesus never witnessed the dawning of the age to come, it lay in the distant future separated from this present age.

Most scholars today give due credit to Schweitzer for demonstrating conclusively that Jesus was indeed an apocalyptic preacher. Conservative gospel scholars, however, disagree with Schweitzer's "consistent" view of Jesus and the kingdom. Rather, they side with Oscar Cullmann that "inaugurated eschatology" is the more accurate (and reverent) view of Jesus and the kingdom. Thus, the kingdom of God did indeed arrive in Jesus' life, death, and resurrection. But it is not yet complete, awaiting the return of Christ. Christians therefore live in the overlapping of the two ages.

The Gnostic Jesus

The Jesus Seminar is a group of radical gospel scholars who began meeting in 1985 for the purpose of color coding the four gospels, which is actually a parody of the red-letter editions of the Gospels (red being the color of Jesus' words in the four Gospels to help distinguish them from the narrator's words in black.)[1] The Fellows (the name of the members of the Jesus Seminar) put a whole new radical twist on color-coding the Gospels. The Fellows arrived at their color-coded translation via the American way. They voted on whether or not the five hundred references comprising Jesus' words and works in the four canonical Gospels were authentic, meaning actually spoken or performed by Jesus. The vote on each saying and act went basically like this:

- a red bead to indicate "Jesus surely said or did this"
- a pink bead for "Jesus probably said or did this"
- a gray bead for "he probably didn't say or do that"
- a black bead for "it's very unlikely that Jesus said or did that"

What were the Fellows' final results? Only eighteen percent of Jesus' sayings and acts in the Gospels were deemed authentic and colored red in their publications *The Five Gospels* and *The Acts of Jesus!*[2] What criteria did the Fellows use to determine what Jesus genuinely said and did? Essentially two assumptions guided them in their decision making. They used the criterion of dissimilarity and the criterion of multiple attestation.

We recall that the *criterion of dissimilarity* states that a saying or deed of Jesus that stands out both from his Jewish heritage and from his later followers (the

---

1. The following section on the Jesus Seminar is adapted from C. Marvin and Sheryl Pate, *Crucified in the Media: Finding the Real Jesus amidst Today's Headlines* (Grand Rapids: Baker, 2005).
2. The two volumes produced by the Jesus Seminar are Robert W. Funk, ed., *The Five Gospels: What Did Jesus Really Say? The Search for the Authentic Words of Jesus* (San Francisco: HarperSanFrancisco, 1997); idem, *The Acts of Jesus: What Did Jesus Really Do? The Search for the Authentic Deeds of Jesus* (San Francisco: Harper-SanFrancisco, 1998).

church) truly goes back to Jesus. In other words, the saying or deed has to be unique, thus dissimilar, from Jesus' Jewish culture or what his followers would say or do. The saying or deed only "counts" if it is in opposition to both groups.

The *criterion of multiple attestation* assumes there are four separate sources that make up the Gospels: Mark, Q (sayings of Jesus not in Mark but in Matthew and Luke), M (material only in Matthew), and L (material only in Luke). They omit John from the discussion because his gospel is different from the Synoptic Gospels. If a saying or deed attributed to Jesus occurs in two or more of these sources, it is thought to be authentic. If it occurs in only one source, it is not thought to be attested to and therefore is not considered authentic. When all is said and done, what is left of the Gospels as a result of the approach? Craig L. Blomberg leaves us in no doubt:

> In the entire Gospel of Mark, there is only one red-letter verse: "Give to Caesar what is Caesar's and to God what is God's" (Mark 12:17). Only fifteen sayings (not counting parallels) are colored red in all of the Gospels put together, and they are all short, pithy "aphorisms" (unconventional proverb-like sayings or parables) particularly the more "subversive" ones. Examples of the former include Jesus' commands to turn the other cheek (Matt. 5:39; Luke 6:29) and love your enemies (Matt. 5:44; Luke 6:27), and his blessing on the poor (Luke 6:20). Examples of the latter include the parables of the Good Samaritan (Luke 10:30–35), the shrewd manager (Luke 16:1–8a), and the vineyard laborers (Matt. 20:1–15). Seventy-five different sayings are colored pink, while at the other end of the color spectrum, several hundred appear in black, including virtually the entire Gospel of John and all of Jesus' claims about himself (e.g., "I am the way and the truth and the life"—John 14:6; "I and the Father are one"—John 10:30; and so on).[3]

So what portrait of Jesus emerges from the above "findings" of the Jesus Seminar? When the preceding two criteria, especially the principle of dissimilarity, are applied to Jesus, he ends up with no connection to his Jewish heritage and no ties to the church he founded. In other words, the Jesus Seminar portrays Jesus as a "talking head" with no body.

So this "talking head" Jesus appears to be is nothing more than a Greek-style philosopher who utters mere moral maxims about how to treat each other, but who makes no claim to be the Messiah, announces no kingdom

---

3. Craig L. Blomberg. "Where Do We Start Studying Jesus," in *Jesus under Fire*, ed. Michael J. Wilkins and J. P. Moreland (Grand Rapids: Zondervan, 1995), 18.

of God, makes no proclamation against sin, and subverts no religious establishment. One wonders why this Jesus was ever crucified. The Jesus of the Seminar might have ruffled some feathers among his fellow Jews, but he would not have undermined their core beliefs.

What the Jesus Seminar foists on to the public is a Gnostic Jesus, one that is more hospitable to radical scholars today. Such a Gnostic portrait of Jesus comes primarily from the apocryphal *Gospel of Thomas*. The *Gospel of Thomas* is a second-century Gnostic reinterpretation of Jesus. The Gnostics were a group of Christians who were considered heretical by the mainstream church. Similar to the Greek philosopher Plato, they taught that the human body is evil and only the soul is good. According to them, in the beginning there was one cosmic spirit-being and no matter. But an evil creator god turned from the one true God and created the world. Gnostics believed that they were not of this world but descendants of the one true God. They thought of themselves as sparks of divine light entrapped by the evil creator god in the material world of his creation. Their goal—their salvation—was to escape this world and re-ascend to the heavenly realm of their origin.

In Christian Gnosticism, the redeemer figure was identified with Christ. He comes, as in other Gnostic systems, to remind Gnostics of their true nature, to awaken them from forgetfulness, and to tell them of their heavenly home. This Christ shares with them secret knowledge (*gnōsis*) which is the means by which they can escape the world of evil and return to God. The *Gospel of Thomas* (second century AD) reflects the outlook of the Gnostic movement in significant aspects. Jesus, for example, speaks as the redeemer who comes from God. He reminds his followers of humanity's forgetfulness and tells how it is in need of enlightenment (*Thomas* 28). He deprecates the world (21:6; 27:1; 56:1–2; 80:1–2; 111:3). He reminds people of their origin (49) and tells them of their needed return to the heavenly home (50). He also speaks of his own return to the place from which he has come (38).

In addition, the *Gospel of Thomas* is individualistic—each person follows his or her own intuition, because that intuition is divine. That is how they follow Jesus. Thus, saying 49 reads, "Blessed are the solitary and the elect, for you will find the Kingdom. For you came forth from it, and you will return to it."[4] In other words, according to the *Gospel of Thomas*, "Christians" possess individually the true knowledge of their origin. Related to this, saying 70 reads, "Jesus said: If you gained this [truth]

---

4. Unless otherwise specified, the quoted translations of the *Gospel of Thomas* in this chapter come from Wilhelm Schneemelcher, ed., *New Testament Apocrypha*, trans. R. McLain Wilson, vol. 1 of *Gospels and Related Writings* (Cambridge, England: James Clarke; Louisville: John Knox, 1991).

within you, what you have will save you. If you do have this in you, what you do not have in you will kill you." So these "Christians" understand that the truth is within them, namely, their origin is heaven, not earth, and it is this knowledge that will save them.

Thomas is also pantheistic—God is in the material universe, the spark of divine in humans. Saying 77 makes this clear: "Jesus said: I am the light that is above them all. I am the all; the all came from me, and the all attained to me. Cleave a [piece of] wood, I am there. Raise up a stone, and you will find me there."

Furthermore, the *Gospel of Thomas* consists of 114 purported sayings of Jesus—with no passion narrative: Jesus does not die for sin and his body is not resurrected. In other words, this apocryphal work is moralistic in orientation. One is saved by following the light within, not by revelation from God from without.

The Jesus Seminar appeals to the *Gospel of Thomas* to prove that early Christianity was pluralistic. That is, they say that some Christians followed the Gnostic *Gospel of Thomas*. The Fellows boast that early Christianity was tolerant of alternative types of Christian faith. They see the Council of Nicea in Asia Minor (Turkey) in AD 325 as the turning point, when the orthodox view won out over the Gnostic approach and wrongly branded the latter heretical.

The Jesus Seminar makes quite an opening statement in its two books: "Beware of finding a Jesus entirely congenial to you."[5] The ironic thing about this comment is that the Jesus Seminar has found in the five "gospels" precisely the picture of Jesus they wanted to find—an individualistic, pantheistic, moralistic, pluralistic, North American Jesus.

The Cynic Sage

The third most influential portrait of Jesus in the last century and today is that of Jesus the Cynic sage, a theory especially advanced by John Crossan and Burton Mack.[6] Craig A. Evans observes this theory:

> Various scholars in the twentieth century have portrayed Jesus as a Pharisee, an Essene, a prophet, a great moral teacher, a philosopher, a charismatic holy man or a magician. These portraits, like Renaissance religious art in which Jesus and his disciples are depicted in sixteenth-century Venetian or Parisian dress, often tell us more about the scholars' biases

---

5. Funk, ed., *The Five Gospels*, 5.
6. John Dominic Crossan, *The Historical Jesus: The Life of a Mediterranean Jewish Peasant* (San Francisco: HarperSan Francisco, 1991); Burton L. Mack, *A Myth of Innocence: Mark and Christian Origins* (Philadelphia: Fortress, 1988); idem, *The Lost Gospel: The Book of Q and Christian Origins* (San Francisco: Harper-San Francisco, 1993).

than they do about Jesus in Nazareth or Jerusalem of the first century. Few are as misleading and distorted as the idea that Jesus was a Mediterranean Cynic.[7]

Cynicism was founded by Diogenes (ca. 412–321 BC). The nickname "Cynic" comes from the Greek word meaning "doggish" or "doglike." Cynics earned this dubious title because of their ragged, unkempt appearance. Attractive apparel and grooming meant nothing to them. And, like dogs, Cynics would urinate and defecate in public. So why in the world would anyone compare Jesus to a Cynic sage? Four points are made by Crossan and Mack in supporting their hypothesis that Jesus was just that, to which we offer our responses.

Similar Dress?

These authors argue that Jesus and the Cynic sages or philosophers dressed in the same manner. The Cynic typically carried a cloak, a beggar's purse and a staff, and usually went barefoot. In a letter to his father, Diogenes says, "Do not be upset, Father, that I am called a dog [=Cynic] and put on a double, coarse cloak, carry a purse over my shoulders, and have a staff in my hand" (*Cynic Epistles* 7).[8] Jesus gave his disciples similar instructions:

- Take nothing for the journey except a staff—no bread, no bag, no money in your belt. Wear sandals but not an extra tunic. (Mark 6:8–9)
- Take no gold, nor silver, not copper in your belts, no bag for your journey, nor two tunics, nor sandals, nor staff; for the laborer deserves his food. (Matt. 10:9–10)
- Take nothing for your journey, no staff, nor bag, nor bread, nor money; and do not have two tunics. (Luke 9:3)
- Carry no purse, no bag, no sandals; and salute no one on the road. (Luke 10:4)

But Evans easily dismisses such proposed similarities between Jesus' afore-mentioned commands regarding dress and Cynic apparel:

> Are Jesus' instructions in step with the Cynic dress code? Clearly not. Jesus' instructions in fact do not agree with Cynic dress and conduct; they contradict them. The very things Jesus tells his disciples not to take with them (no bag, no

---

7. Craig A. Evans, *Fabricating Jesus: How Modern Scholars Distort the Gospels* (Downers Grove, IL: InterVarsity Press, 2006), 100.

8. See ibid., 107, 110. Taken from Abraham J. Malherbe, *The Cynic Epistles*, SBLSBS 12 (Missoula, MT: Scholars Press, 1977).

tunic and no staff either, if we follow the version in Matthew and Luke) are the characteristic markers of the true Cynic, as one observer from late antiquity put it: "What makes a Cynic is his purse and his staff and his big mouth." There is nothing Cynic-like in Jesus' instructions to his disciples.

The only parallel with Jesus is simply in giving instruction with regard to what to wear and what to take on one's journey. The only specific agreement is taking a staff (if we follow Mark; if we do not, then there is no agreement at all). The staff, however, is hardly distinctive to Cynics. On the contrary, in the Jewish context the staff has a long and distinguished association with the patriarchs, such as Jacob and Judah (Gen. 32:10; 38:18), and the great lawgiver Moses and his brother Aaron (Ex. 4:4; 7:9). Moreover, the staff is also a symbol of royal authority, figuring in texts that in later interpretation take on messianic and eschatological significance (for example, Gen. 49:10; Is. 11:4; Ezek. 19:14).[9]

Similar Worldview?

According to Crossan and Mack, Jesus' worldview and the Cynic's worldview were the same. But again Evans rightly discounts a comparison here:

> Besides the question of dress, some scholars suggest that Jesus' worldview is Cynic. Instead of being caught up with materialism and vanity, the Cynic lives a life of simplicity and integrity before God. According to one ancient writer, the "end and aim of the Cynic philosophy . . . is happiness, but happiness that consists in living according to nature." Living according to nature also means treating fellow human beings as equals. A few scholars apparently think that this is more or less what Jesus taught. . . .

Admittedly, all of this criticism could have been uttered by a Cynic. But this represents only one aspect of Jesus' teaching. Jesus criticized some of his critics, but he was not crude, nor did he suggest that religious faith was pointless. Herein lies a telling difference between the world view of Jesus and that of Cynics. Whereas the latter railed against religion because the gods, they thought, were indifferent, Jesus urged his followers to believe in God, because he does take notice and cares deeply. Indeed, some of Jesus' statements we have looked at go on to assure that "your Father who sees in secret will reward

---

9. Ibid., 107–8.

you" (Matt. 6:6, 18). Accordingly, Jesus urges his disciples to pray, "for your father knows what you need before you ask him" (Matt. 6:8). This is not the teaching of the Cynics.

Furthermore, Jesus proclaimed God's rule and urged his disciples to look to God for deliverance. Jesus longed for the redemption of his people and believed deeply that the God of Israel would fulfill the prophecies and promises of old. These hopes and beliefs are not consistent with Cynic ideology.[10]

Similar Ethical Teaching?

Mack makes much of what he perceives to be the resemblances between Q, the sayings of Jesus, and Cynic moral maxims. He claims two things in particular here. First, Q consists of short sayings like the aphoristic style of Cynic philosophers. Second, in keeping with Cynic teaching, Q contains only wisdom statements; statements that are devoid of any apocalyptic orientation.[11] But these two assertions have been roundly criticized by gospel scholars, and for good reason. Regarding the first claim, the sayings of Jesus far and away parallel Jewish wisdom statements that comprise writings like Proverbs, Sirach, and Wisdom of Solomon. Concerning the second claim, it is simply not true that Q contains no eschatological remarks. Note, for example, the mention that the Twelve will reign and judge Israel in the end-time (Matt. 19:28; Luke 22:30); the incomparably powerful end-time judge burning the wicked (Matt. 3:7–12; Luke 3:7–9, 16–17); or Jesus rejecting the wicked at the judgment (Matt. 7:21–23; Luke 13:26–27).[12] Moreover, Second Temple Jewish wisdom literature was filled with apocalyptic statements (see, e.g., the Dead Sea Scrolls [4QMMT, etc.], *4 Ezra,* and *2 Baruch*).

Similar Influence?

Proponents of the Cynic model of Jesus appeal to what they say was the thoroughly Hellenized city of Sepphoris, which lay only four miles north of Nazareth where Jesus was raised. The assumption here is that Hellenistic philosophy like Cynicism must have been present in the culture for Jesus to adopt as his worldview and style of ministry. Indeed advocates of the Cynic model argue that archaeological digs in that city discovered the presence of pig bones, coins with the image of Caesar, pagan idols, and images and mosaics with pagan themes on them. All of these were once offensive to Jews but the gradual Hellenization of Israel in general, and Sepphoris in particular, witnessed the abandoning of their belief in Yahweh. But as a number of recent analyses of Sepphoris have pointed out, the previous claim is most misleading.

---

10. Ibid., 108–12.
11. Mack, *The Lost Gospel,* 1–3.
12. This response comes from Craig S. Keener, *The Historical Jesus of the Gospels* (Grand Rapids: Eerdmans, 2009), 62–63.

Rather, the aforementioned Hellenistic components found at Sepphoris were discovered to have dated from *post*-AD 70, the period after the Jewish revolt against Rome. At that time defeated Israel was converted into a place of pagan practices. But before AD 70, the Jews in Sepphoris and indeed in Israel as a whole staunchly resisted any significant Hellenization of its Jewish faith, even as it had continuously done since the Maccabean revolt in the 160s BC. Thus, it is most significant what was found in excavations of Sepphoris before AD 70 and what was found after that date:[13]

WHAT WAS FOUND BEFORE AD 70	WHAT WAS NOT FOUND BEFORE AD 70
Mikvoth (immersion pools for ritual cleansing)	Pig bones
Menorah	Coins with the image of Caesar
Fragments of stone vessels (faithful Jews preferred stone vessels for ritual cleansing over plastic vessels because the latter were more easily defiled)	Pagan idols and images
	Pagan buildings (odeum, nymphaeum, gymnasium, shrines, for example)

In light of the archaeological evidence as well as the other data offered in response to the Cynic model of Jesus above, Evans' conclusion seems inevitable: "All this evidence leads to the firm conclusion that Sepphoris in Jesus' day was a thoroughly Jewish city. There is absolutely no reason whatsoever to think there may have been Cynics loitering in the streets of Sepphoris, on the lookout for Jewish youths from nearby Nazareth village."[14] We concur and therefore discard the portrait of the Cynic Jesus.

Conclusion

This chapter has grappled with who the real Jesus was: apocalyptic preacher, Gnostic teacher, or Cynic sage? The evidence amassed in this chapter leaves one with a clear response, namely, Jesus was an apocalyptic preacher. But not the kind Schweitzer made him out to be. Rather, Jesus was the Messiah who announced the dawning of the kingdom of God in his life and ministry—a kingdom that will be fully unveiled at his parousia.

---

13. See Evans, *Fabricating Jesus,* 117.
14. Ibid., 117.

REFLECTION QUESTIONS

1. What is the apocalyptic view of Jesus?

2. What is the Gnostic view of Jesus?

3. What is the Cynic view of Jesus?

4. What were the differences in the city of Sepphoris before and after AD 70?

5. What is your view of the historical Jesus?

Questions Related to the
Sources of the Historical Jesus

What Does the Old Testament Teach About the Coming Messiah?

I will answer this question in three steps: (1) the identification of the Messiah in the Old Testament; (2) the fulfillment of Old Testament messianic prophecies related to the life of Christ as presented in the four gospels; and (3) a four-fold response to those who claim that later messianic readings of Old Testament passages are anachronistic and therefore unwarranted.

The Identification of the Messiah in the Old Testament

The Hebrew term behind the English word Messiah means "to anoint" (usually with oil). Throughout the Ancient Near East, the custom of anointing people with oil for special occasions was common. Anointing with oil symbolized purification, but it also symbolized the conferring of power, authority, and honor. Thus, the term Messiah refers to "the Anointed One" or the "One conferred with power, authority, and honor." The New Testament Greek word is *Christos*, from which we get the English word Christ. The Greek word carries the same connotation as the Hebrew word, that of "the Anointed One."

Throughout the prophetic texts of the Old Testament, the promise of future blessings and restoration usually centers around a special person, one who is coming to make all things right. Often this Coming One is described in royal terms. He is the coming righteous and just king, the branch of David, and the Shepherd (royal imagery) who regathers the flock. He is often equated with Yahweh (i.e., the LORD), the God of Abraham, Isaac, and Jacob. He is called Immanuel (God with us), but he is also identified as the Suffering Servant. There are also allusions to the Coming One as prophet and priest.

Thus, in the Old Testament the picture of the Coming One is rather complex, and there is no one central term used to define him. Surprisingly, the specific term Messiah (Anointed One) is used only a handful of times in regard to the future Coming Deliverer (Pss. 2; 110; Dan. 9:25–26; Isa. 61:1), even though the concept is much more common. So in the Old Testament, while it was clear that someone quite special, even divine, was coming to carry out the spectacular works of God, there was no central defining term for what to call him.

It is during Second Temple Judaism (roughly the time between the close of the Old Testament and the coming of Jesus), that the term Messiah became popular among the Jews as the main word for referring to the Coming One predicted by the Old Testament prophets. Unfortunately, however, during this time many of the Jews distorted this term in some regards. Often the term Messiah became tightly associated with Jewish political aspirations of independence from Rome. The term Messiah became disassociated with the concept of the Suffering Servant and with the central concepts of justice and righteousness that had been emphasized in the Old Testament. The Jews wanted a powerful king to lead them to military victory over Rome. Messiah was the word they used for the one that they hoped would deliver them from Roman rule.

As mentioned above, the Greek equivalent term for Messiah is *Christos* (the Christ). When Jesus enters the scene in Palestine, the Greek term Christ was being used like the Hebrew term Messiah and was likewise associated with numerous misconceptions about a Coming One who was strictly a political, military leader who would defeat the Romans. Thus, when Jesus appears in the New Testament gospels, he is cautious about using the term Christ. Jesus is clear about identifying himself with the Coming One that the Old Testament predicted, and the Gospels have numerous passages where Jesus or the gospel writers point out how Jesus fulfills the Old Testament prophecies about the Coming Deliverer (e.g., Matt. 1:22; 2:5–6, 17–18, 23; 4:14–16; 12:17–21; 13:13–15, 35; 21:4–5; 26:3; see also our references below). Yet, Jesus uses the actual term "Christ" sparingly to avoid furthering the misconceptions associated with the term. The gospel writers—as well as Jesus—do clearly affirm that Jesus is "the Christ," and they do use the term occasionally, but in general Jesus himself prefers the term "Son of Man."

However, after the death and resurrection of Jesus, when his ministry could no longer be misunderstood or misconstrued into a political, military rebellion against Rome, the apostles freely use the term Christ, proclaiming clearly that Jesus of Nazareth is "the Christ" of the Old Testament. For example, in Acts 2:36 Peter proclaims, "Therefore let all Israel be assured of this: God has made this Jesus, whom you crucified, both Lord and Christ." In Acts, the apostles proclaim that not only was Jesus the Messiah (Christ) while on earth, but that he is now exalted to the right hand of God and is the reigning messianic king even now, as prophesied by Psalm 110:1, one of the most quoted Old Testament texts in the New Testament.

The identification of Jesus as the Christ became so foundational to the early church, that soon the term Christ became attached to the name Jesus, so that the savior was frequently simply called Jesus Christ. Likewise the early followers of Jesus soon took on the name "Christians." Paul uses the term Christ over four hundred times in his letters, but most of the time he uses the term as the name of Jesus. As did Jesus and the gospel writers, Paul continues to affirm that Jesus Christ was the Coming One the Old Testament predicted and that he did fulfill all that the Old Testament prophesied.[1]

Old Testament Prophecies and the Life of Christ

There are numerous Old Testament prophecies that pointed to and predicted the coming of the Messiah. Many of these are identified in the New Testament as fulfilled in Jesus Christ. These prophecies can be grouped into ten general categories:

1. **Christ's Birth.** Several aspects relating to Christ's birth were foretold in the Old Testament. The Old Testament prophesied that Christ would be a descendant of David (cf. Ps. 110:1 with Matt. 22:43–44; Mark 12:36; Luke 20:42–43), but also of divine origin (cf. Ps. 40:6–8 with Heb. 10:5–9; Ps. 2:7 with Acts 13:33; Heb. 1:5; 5:5; Isa. 7:14 with Matt. 1:21–23). Micah foretold the place of birth, Bethlehem (cf. Mic. 5:2 with Matt. 2:6; John 7:42). Several Old Testament prophets alluded to the opposition that the Messiah would face at birth, seen in the attempt by Herod to kill all the babies in Bethlehem (cf. Hos. 11:1 with Matt. 2:15; Jer. 31:15 with Matt. 2:16–18). The virginal conception of Christ is referred to in Matthew 1:21–23 as the fulfillment of Isaiah 7:14.

2. **Christ's Forerunner.** The Old Testament prophesied that the Messiah would be preceded by a forerunner, fulfilled by John the Baptist (cf. Isa. 40:3–5 with Matt. 3:3; Mark 1:3; Luke 3:4–6; John 1:23; Mal. 3:1 with Mark 1:2; Luke 7:27; Mal. 4:5–6 with Matt. 11:14; 17:12; Mark 9:12–13; Luke 1:17).

3. **Christ's Ministry.** Various aspects of Christ's ministry were foretold in the Old Testament. The Messiah was to be a prophet (cf. Deut. 18:15–16, 19 with Acts 3:22–23; 7:37; Ps. 69:9 with John 2:17; see also Matt. 21:12–16; Mark 11:15–17; Luke 19:45–47). Likewise he was identified as the Suffering Servant of the Lord (cf. Isa. 53:4 with Matt. 8:17; Isa. 61:1–2 with Luke 4:18–21; Isa. 53:12 with Luke 22:37; Isa. 53:3–9 with Mark

---

1. For this discussion see, "Messiah," in Danny Hays, Scott Duvall, and C. Marvin Pate, *Dictionary of Biblical Prophecy and End Times* (Grand Rapids: Zondervan, 2007), 280–82; now updated as *An A to Z Guide to Biblical Prophecy and End Times* (Grand Rapids: Zondervan, 2012), 280–82.

9:12; Luke 18:32; 24:24–25, 46). The Old Testament also pointed to Jesus' eternal priesthood (cf. Ps. 110:4 with Heb. 5:6; 7:17, 21). Numerous texts prophesied that the Messiah would be a king (cf. Zech. 9:9 with Matt. 21:5; John 12:14–15; see also 2 Sam. 7:12). Jesus also taught in parables, a messianic fulfillment of Psalm 78:2.

4. **Christ's Opposition by the Jews.** The Old Testament indicated that the Messiah would be opposed and oppressed by his own people (cf. Isa. 6:9–10 with Matt. 13:14–15; Mark 4:12; Luke 8:10; Isa. 53:1; 6:9–10 with John 12:37–41; Ps. 118:22–23 with Matt. 21:42; Mark 12:10–11; Luke 20:17; Acts 4:11; 1 Peter 2:7–18). Jesus' cleansing of the temple was a part of the motivation for opposition to him by the Jewish leaders, seen in John 2:17 as the fulfillment of Psalm 69:9.

5. **Christ's Betrayal by Judas.** Several Old Testament texts described the betrayal of the Messiah by a close friend (cf. Ps. 41:9 with John 13:18; 17:12; Zech. 11:12–13 with Matt. 27:9–10; see also Ps. 109:8; 69:25 and Acts 1:20).

6. **Christ's Arrest and Abandonment.** The Old Testament prophets declared that the Messiah would be arrested and then abandoned by his friends and supporters (cf. Zech. 13:7 with Matt. 26:30–31; Mark 14:27).

7. **Christ's Death.** The violent death of the Messiah is mentioned in several places in the Old Testament (cf. Ps. 22:18 with John 19:24; Ps. 22:15 with John 19:28; Ps. 34:20; Ex. 12:46; Num. 9:12 with John 19:36; Zech. 12:10 with John 19:32; Isa. 53:7–9 with Luke 18:32; Acts 8:32–35; 1 Cor. 15:3; Deut. 21:23 with Gal. 3:13).

8. **Christ's Resurrection.** The New Testament also identifies several Old Testament texts as pointing to the resurrection of the Messiah (cf. Ps. 16:8–11 with Acts 2:25–28; 2 Sam. 7:12–13 with Luke 18:33; 24:46; Hos. 6:2 with John 2:19–22; 1 Cor. 15:4).

9. **Christ's Ascension.** The Old Testament predicted, not only the suffering of Christ, but also his glorification, seen in his ascension to sit at the right hand of God (cf. Ps. 110:1 with Acts 2:34–35; Ps. 2:7 with Acts 13:33–35; Ps. 68:18 with Eph. 4:8).

10. **Christ's Return.** Jesus' return in glory to earth is predicted in the Old Testament (cf. Dan. 7:13–14 with Matt. 24:30; Mark 13:26: Luke 21:27; cf. Pss. 2:8; 110:1–3, 5–7).[2]

---

2. See ibid., 16–17.

How Much Messianism Is There in the Old Testament?

With this question one reaches a major hermeneutical debate. Despite the numerous messianic prophecies just mentioned as fulfilled in the life of Jesus the Christ, the modern period has witnessed wide scale rejection of messianic prophecy in the Old Testament. Beginning with Anthony Collins' two broadsides against messianic prophecy in the Old Testament (*Discourse of the Grounds and Reasons for the Christian Religion* [1724] and *The Scheme of Literal Prophecy Considered* [1727])[3] and continuing with the works of Sigmund Mowinckel,[4] the Collins,[5] Joseph Fitzmyer,[6] and others, these authors have argued that the Old Testament verses that are supposedly messianic in scope prove not to be when the original context of the passage is taken into account. Most notoriously, Isaiah 7:14 refers only to God's deliverance of Israel from the Syro-Ephraimaite collation in 732 BC, not to Jesus as Immanuel.

But a better way of identifying Old Testament messianic prophecies is being suggested today by other biblical scholars and that is to see what Old Testament texts are considered messianic by later interpreters in Second Temple Judaism. This includes the New Testament itself. Regarding the latter, we noted above the numerous Old Testament texts the New Testament, especially the Gospels, considered to be predictive of Jesus Christ. Here we correlate with Michael F. Bird those Old Testament texts perceived to be messianic by Jewish writers in the Second Temple period. Note the following chart:

Table 1. Old Testament Texts and Messianic Interpretations[7]

OT/HEBREW BIBLE	MESSIANIC INTERPRETATION
Genesis 49:10	4QpIsa frgs. 7–10.iii.25; 4Q252 5.1–7; T. Jud. 22:1–3; 24.1; LXX; Sib. Or. 5.415; Tg. Onq.; tg. Neof.; Justin Martyr, *1 Apol.* 32, 54; *Dial.* 52, 120; Clement of Alexandria, *Paed.* 1.5–6; Irenaeus, *Haer.* 4.10.2

3. These articles are found in J. O'Higgins', *Anthony Collins: The Man and His Works,* International Archives of History of Ideas 35 (The Hague: Nijhoff, 1970), 155.
4. Sigmund Mowinckel, *He That Cometh* (Nashville: Abingdon, 1954).
5. John J. Collins, *The Scepter and the Star: The Messiahs of the Dead Sea Scrolls and Other Ancient Literature,* ABRL (New York: Doubleday, 1995) and Adela Yarbro Collins and John J. Collins, *King and Messiah as Son of God: Divine, Human, and Angelic Messianic Figures in Biblical and Related Literature* (Grand Rapids: Eerdmans, 2008).
6. J. A. Fitzmyer, *The One Who Is to Come* (Grand Rapids: Eerdmans, 2007).
7. Michael F. Bird, *Are You the One Who Is to Come? The Historical Jesus and the Messianic Question* (Grand Rapids: Baker, 2009), 47.

OT/HEBREW BIBLE	MESSIANIC INTERPRETATION
Numbers 24:17	1QSb 5.20–29; CD 7.18–20; 1QM 11.6–7; 4Q175 1.9–13; 1QPsj 9–13; Philo, *Moses* 1.290; *Rewards* 95; T. Jud 24:5; T. Levi 18.3; *y. Ta'an.* 4.5; Tg. Onq.; Justin Martyr, *Dial.* 106; Irenaeus, *Haer.* 3.9.2
2 Samuel 7:12–16	Pss. 89; 132; Sir. 47:11; 4Q174 2.19–3.11; 4Q246 1.8–9; 2.1; 4Q254 4.2–3; 4Q369 frg. 1 2.6; Pss. Sol. 17.4; 4 Ezra 13:32, 37
Psalm 2	4Q174 3.10–13; 3.18–19; Pss. Sol. 17.23; 1 En. 48:10; 4 Ezra 13:32, 37, 52
Isaiah 11:1–6	1QSb 5.22, 25, 26; 4Q161 8, 9, 10, 15–29; 4Q285 5.1–6; 1 En. 62:2; Pss. Sol. 17.24, 29, 36–37; T. Jud. 24:6; T. Levi 18.7; Tg. Isa.; Matt. 2:23; Acts 13:23; Heb. 7:14; Rev. 5:5; 22:16; Justin Martyr, 1 *Apol.* 32; *Dial.* 87; Clement of Alexandria, *Paed.* 1.7
Isaiah 53	1 En. 37–70; Tg. Isa.
Jeremiah 23:5; 33:15; Zechariah 6:12	4Q161 8–10, 15–16, 22; T. Jud. 24:4–6
Daniel 7:9, 13–14	Mark 14:61–62; 1 En. 37–70; 4 Ezra 13; *b. Hag.* 14a; *b. Sanh.* 38b; Justin Martyr, *Dial.* 31–32
Amos 9:11	4Q174 3.10–13

Note also that the above passages and other Second Temple Jewish texts attest to a number of messianic figures, including: Messiah, Son of David, Son of God, Son of Man, the Prophet, Elect One, Prince, Branch, Root, Scepter, Star, Chosen One, Coming One (recall our similar comments above).

Four Responses to the Claim That Old Testament Messianism Is Anachronistic

First, it should be remembered that the Old Testament itself reinterprets earlier texts that place them on a messianic trajectory. For example, 2 Samuel 7:12–16 becomes more messianic in Psalm 89:3–4, 19, while the combination of the "scion" or "branch" of Jeremiah 23:5; 33:15 (cf. Isa. 11:1) with the "servant" of Isaiah 41–53 in Zechariah 3:8 intensifies the messianic hope.[8]

---

8. The later Old Testament's usage of earlier material is a point powerfully made by Michael A. Fishbane's magisterial work, *Biblical Interpretation in Ancient Israel* (Oxford: Clarendon, 1985).

Second, Bird adds to this discussion the following idea:

> What is more, the editing, collecting, and translation of the Hebrew texts also led to the formation of messianism within the interpretive development of the Old Testament itself. When the Prophets or Psalms are read after the Pentateuch, the pentateuchal prophecies are taken up and continued by another series that expresses the particularity of the Davidic covenant and hope. When heard in the context of the Pentateuch and Prophets, the royal Psalms can readily be understood as oracles of the future related to Davidic kingship and national restoration (esp. Pss. 89 and 132).[9]

Third, the later messianic reading of the Old Testament can also be seen in the Greek translation of the Hebrew Bible. Bird writes of this:

> In Num. 24:7 LXX the translators combine the prophetic oracle "There shall come forth a man" with the reference to "Gog" from Ezek. 38–39, with the result that "there shall come a man out of his seed, and he shall rule over many nations; and his kingdom shall be made higher than *Gog*, and his kingdom shall be increased." This is a clear instance of combining the original oracle with exilic hopes for national deliverance from Israel's archenemy of the last days. And also in Hab. 2:3 LXX we find: "For *he* will surely come, and will not tarry," which changes the "it" (i.e., the vision) to a person "he will come" (i.e., a divine agent) in the future. Thus, the messianic interpretation of certain texts in the Second Temple era is merely an extension of what was already happening within the Old Testament itself. The process of the reinterpretation and reapplication of certain texts along royal, messianic, and eschatological lines had long since begun.[10]

Finally, there is something to be said for the fact that the same Old Testament texts are considered messianic by later interpreters. Thus, J. J. M. Roberts argues that if every messianic document had a completely different selection of proof texts, one could grant the capricious nature of their messianic

---

9. Bird, *Are You the One Who Is to Come?*, 45.
10. Ibid., 45.

exegesis, but the fact that certain texts kept being recalled for their messianic content is a highly significant feature of Jewish and Christian interpretation.[11]

These four counter-points to the claim that later messianic interpretation of an Old Testament text is anachronistic have much to commend themselves.

Conclusion

This altogether-too-brief treatment of such an immense topic—Old Testament messianism—has at least broached the subject by covering three points. First, we offered an overview of the traditional view of the role of messianism in the Old Testament. Second, then we noted how the New Testament relates Jesus to Old Testament messianic prophecies. Third, we provided a four-fold defense of the traditional reading of messianism in the Old Testament and in Second Temple Judaism. This much debated topic shows no signs of abating in the future, nor should it given its enormous significance.

REFLECTION QUESTIONS

1. What are the various terms used of the coming Messiah in the Old Testament?

2. What are some of the Old Testament prophecies concerning the Messiah?

3. How does the later Old Testament reinterpret earlier Old Testament texts in a messianic way?

4. Which Hebrew texts does the Septuagint interpret as messianic?

5. What are some Old Testament texts that Second Temple Judaism and the New Testament interpreted as messianic?

---

11. J. J. M. Roberts, "The Old Testament's Contribution to Messianic Expectations," in *The Messiah: Developments in Earliest Judaism and Christianity*, ed. J. H. Charlesworth (Minneapolis: Fortress, 1992), 39–51.

Is Jesus' Life Confirmed by Non-Jewish and Jewish Sources?

Scholars such as Bruno Bauer, Arthur Drews, G. A. Wells, and Robert Price have gone so far as to deny that there was ever a historical Jesus, as outlandish as that may sound.[1] Among other things, they argue that pagan and Jewish remarks concerning Jesus of Nazareth are too skimpy in detail and are mere hearsay without historical validation. And even scholars less skeptical than those who deny Jesus' existence find grounds to question the reliability of those sources outside of the New Testament referring to Jesus. But is this radical assessment accurate? Not at all, for, as the following investigation will demonstrate, extra-biblical records about the historical Jesus are quite reliable. We proceed with this discussion by first examining non-Jewish comments about Jesus after which we look at non-Christian Jewish remarks on the topic.

Early Non-Jewish Sources on Jesus

Here we examine three Roman writers' comments about the historical Jesus—the Roman historians Suetonius, Tacitus, and the Roman governor Pliny the Younger—along with the polemical remarks about Jesus by Celsus the Neoplatonist philosopher.

---

1. B. Bauer, *Kritik der evangelischen Geschichte der Synoptiker*, 2 vols. (Leipzig: Wigand, 1841); Arthur Drews, *The Christ Myth*, 3rd ed., trans. C. D. Burns (1810; reprint., Amherst, NY: Prometheus, 1998); G. A. Wells, *The Historical Evidence for Jesus* (Buffalo, NY: Prometheus, 1982); idem, *The Jesus Legend* (LaSalle, IL: Open Court, 1996); idem, *The Jesus Myth* (Chicago: Open Court, 1999). Even self-professed liberal New Testament scholar Bart D. Ehrman begs to differ with the Jesus legend/myth in his *Did Jesus Exist? The Historical Argument for Jesus of Nazareth* (New York: Harper Collins, 2012).

Suetonius (ca. AD 70–160)

In his life of the Roman emperor Claudius (AD 54–68), Suetonius has an intriguing passage about disturbances in the Jewish community in Rome: "Since the Jews constantly made disturbances at the instigation of Chrestus, he expelled them from Rome" (*Lives of the Caesars* 5.25.4). Most likely, *Chrestus* is a variant spelling of *Christus* (Christ). Many interpreters of this statement, rightly we believe, reconstruct the episode thusly: Jewish Christians in Rome presented Jesus as the Messiah to non-Christian Jews, which resulted in a flurry of debate between the two groups. Claudius, who would not have known the difference between Christian Jews and non-Christian Jews, solved the problem by issuing an edict expelling the whole lot of Jews from Rome, in AD 49. As it stands, Suetonius's statement documents two facts about Jesus—he was a historical person and he was thought by his followers to be the Messiah.

The supporters of the Jesus legend or myth disagree with these conclusions. They offer two demurrals. First, they argue that the attempt to link *Chrestus* with *Christ* is pure speculation. Rather than *Christus* being Christ, he was simply a Jewish agitator with a common name and that he had no association with Christianity. Second, even if the reference is to Christ, it is no doubt dependent upon Christian hearsay, not reality.[2] But these arguments are not convincing. Regarding the first, it is significant that *Chrestus* was a common name among Gentiles but never used by Jews, so far as we know.[3] At the same time, one can easily understand Suetonius mistaking a Jewish title (Christ) he was unfamiliar with for a common Greek name and thus emending it to *Chrestus*.[4] Second, a Roman historian of the stature of Suetonius, who we know had access to Roman libraries and archives, would not pass on hearsay from a discredited minor religious sect.[5] Moreover, since Suetonius is recounting an edict from a Roman emperor it no doubt was contained in official court documents.[6] Third, as a matter of confirmation, it is

---

2. E. Doherty, *The Jesus Puzzle: Did Christianity Begin with a Mythical Christ?* (Ottawa: Canadian Humanist Pub., 1999), 27; see also Wells, *Jesus Myth*, 197–98.

3. As documented by D. Noy, *Jewish Inscriptions of Western Europe*, vol. 2: *The City of Rome* (New York: Cambridge University Press, 1995). This point is made by R. E. Van Voorst, *Jesus Outside the New Testament: An Introduction to the Ancient Evidence* (Grand Rapids: Eerdmans, 2000), 33.

4. So argues Joseph P. Meier, *A Marginal Jew: Rethinking the Historical Jesus*, vol. 1: *The Roots of the Problem and the Person* (New York: Doubleday, 1991), 92.

5. On Suetonius' access to sources, see G. Kennedy, "Classical and Christian Source Criticism", in *The Relationship among the Gospels: An Interdisciplinarian Dialogue* (San Antonio, TX: Trinity University Press, 1978), 141. In *Life of Nero* 16.11–13, Suetonius reveals his antipathy to the Christian movement. He relates Nero's persecution of Christians thusly, "Punishment was inflicted on the Christians, a class of men given to a new and mischievous superstition."

6. See Paul Rhodes Eddy and Gregory A. Boyd, *The Jesus Legend: A Case for the Historical Reliability of the Synoptic Jesus Tradition* (Grand Rapids: Baker, 2007), 177.

telling that Luke reports this same edict as having an impact upon Aquila and Priscilla, two Jewish Christians who left Rome at that very time and resettled in Corinth (Acts 18:2). All of this to say, those who interpret Suetonius' statement above as indicating that Jesus was a real person whom his followers considered to be the Christ seems to be the best reading.

Tacitus (ca. AD 55–117)

Tacitus was proconsul of Asia for two years (AD 112–113) and the author of the *Annals* and the *Histories*. The former covers the period from Caesar Augustus through Caesar Nero (AD 14–68). One portion of the *Annals* is pertinent to our discussion in this chapter, 15.44, which was written around AD 115. Tacitus reports here of Nero's persecution of the Christians in Rome:

> Therefore, to stop the rumor [that the burning of Rome had taken place by order], Nero substituted as culprits, and punished in the utmost refinements of cruelty, a class of men, loathed for their vices, whom the crowd styled Christians. Christus, the founder of the name, had undergone the death penalty in the reign of Tiberius, by sentence of the procurator Pontius Pilatus, and the pernicious superstition was checked for a moment, but in the capital itself, where all things horrible or shameful from every part of the world find their center and become popular.[7]

Taken at face value, Tacitus' statement says four things about the historical Jesus. First, it confirms that the time of Jesus' execution was during the reign of Caesar Tiberius (AD 14–37) and during Pilate's governorship over Judea (AD 26–36). Second, the statement confirms that Jesus' death was by execution order of the Roman governor. Third, it claims that the Christian movement was temporarily suppressed but broke out again even in Rome. Fourth, related to the last comment, Tacitus' report demonstrates that in the span of a mere three decades (since the time of Tiberius and Pilate to Nero), the Christian movement had grown to the point that it could be made a plausible scapegoat for a Roman emperor.[8]

But those who are skeptical of the attestation to the historical Jesus in Tacitus' comment counter with four arguments. First, they claim that Tacitus' statement is a later Christian interpolation. Second, because Tacitus calls Pilate a "procurator" rather than a "prefect," the latter of which is now attested

---

7. Tacitus, *Annals*, trans. C. H. Moore and J. Jackson, LCL, reprint ed. (Cambridge, MA: Harvard University Press, 1962), 283.
8. For these four points see Boyd and Eddy, *The Jesus Legend*, 179.

in an ancient inscription,[9] skeptics decry Tacitus's report as unreliable. Third, Tacitus referred to Jesus as "Christus" instead of his legal name, "Jesus," which reveals that the Roman governor/historian was relying upon popular Christian mythology. Fourth, the trial of a minor insurrectionist would not have been included in Roman records.

We now respond to these arguments in order. First, it is highly unlikely that a later Christian would add to Tacitus's statement such a negative appraisal of early Christianity—"superstition," "disease," and "horrible or shameful."

Second, the evidence for the terms "procurator" and "prefect" suggests that the two were fluid. Thus, while the Pilate stone discovered at Caesarea Maritima gives Pilate the title "prefect," both Philo (*Legacy to Gaius,* 38) and Josephus (*Jewish Wars* 2.9.2.169) refer to Pilate as "procurator," as does Tacitus.

Third, regarding the objection that Tacitus was relying on Christian mythology we may say three things. (1) Tacitus is generally considered to have been too reliable a historian to base his official report on a superstitious religious fringe group. (2) By the second century, the time of Tacitus' writing, "Christ" and "Jesus" were used interchangeably. (3) Tacitus uses the name "Christ" not "Jesus" because he is explaining the origin of the name "Christians."[10]

Fourth, it is almost certain that Tacitus (who was proconsul of Asia and held Roman consulship) found his information about Jesus from official Roman sources.

Thus, we believe the evidence is compelling that Tacitus' report is a trustworthy account of Jesus' crucifixion under Roman order and that Christianity, the movement that proceeded from belief in Jesus, grew to the point some thirty years later that it could be singled out for persecution.

Pliny the Younger (AD 61 or 62–113)

Pliny the Younger was the nephew of the famous encyclopedist, Pliny the Elder, who died during the eruption of Vesuvius in AD 79. The former became the governor of Bithynia in northwestern Turkey early in the second century. In a letter written about AD 111 to the emperor Trajan (AD 98–117), he refers to the burgeoning Christian movement:

> They [the former Christians] assured me that the sum total of their error consisted in the fact that they regularly assembled on a certain day before daybreak. They recited a hymn antiphonally to Christus as if to a god, and bound themselves with an oath not to commit any crime, but to abstain from

---

9. The correct title was identified from the "Pilate stone" found in Caesarea Maritima in 1962. See J. J. Rousseau and R. Arav, "Pontius Pilate's Stone," in *Jesus and His World: An Archaeological and Cultural Dictionary* (Minneapolis: Fortress, 1995), 225–27.
10. See Boyd and Eddy, *The Jesus Legend,* 182–83.

theft, robbery, adultery, breach of faith, and embezzlement of property entrusted to them. After this it was their custom to separate, and then to come together again to partake of a meal, but of an ordinary and innocent one.[11]

In this letter, Pliny the Younger is asking Emperor Trajan for advice on dealing with Christians in his territory. In the course of the letter, Pliny recounts information about Christians he had gathered from people who had defected from the faith under threat of death. Wells doubts the historical significance of the statement: "His letter demonstrates no more than that Christians existed in the early second century and worshipped Christ . . . it represented what, by then, Christians believed, not what was necessarily historically the case."[12] But this no doubt is an overstatement because the governor notes that Christ was worshipped by Christians "as if" he were a god, suggesting that both Pliny and the former Christians he interrogated assumed that Jesus was a historical person. Thus, Pliny was simply reporting that Christians worship this man as a god.[13]

Celsus (second century)

In the late second century, Celsus, the Neoplatonist philosopher, wrote the first known full-scale attack on Christianity, titled *True Doctrine.*[14] Celsus ridicules the idea of the virgin birth of Jesus and claims that he was illegitimately born when Mary committed adultery. He argues that Jesus grew up to be a small and ugly man, that he gathered a small following of sailors and tax collectors, and that he amazed them with displays of sorcery and magic. Celsus further claims that Jesus taught his disciples to beg and steal for a living and that when he died, hysterical women reported a resurrection (see Origen's *Against Celsus* 1.28, 32, 62; 2.6, 32, 44–55; 6.75; 8.41).

Celsus most likely based his pejorative evaluation of Jesus on the New Testament itself, not independent sources. There are two important historical considerations regarding Jesus that can be gleaned from Celsus' derogatory remarks. First, he did not deny that Jesus existed. In fact, no ancient source doubted that Jesus existed. That criticism would have to wait for modern skeptics hundreds of years removed from the first century. Second, Celsus did not deny that Jesus performed miracles, except that Celsus attributed those works to magic and sorcery. Indeed, as we will see below, rabbinic literature did not discount Jesus' miracles but also attributed them to impure sources.

---

11. Pliny the Younger, *Letters* 10.96.
12. Wells, *Jesus Myth*, 197.
13. So Eddy and Boyd, *The Jesus Legend*, 175.
14. While the work is lost, Origen preserved vast portions of it in his rebuttal, *Against Celsus*.

Ancient Jewish Sources on Jesus

Here we examine three famous Jewish sources on the historical Jesus: Josephus' "James Passage," The *Testimonium Flavianum*, and rabbinic traditions.

Josephus' "James Passage"

Flavius Josephus is the most important Jewish historian of the ancient world. His two most significant works are *The Antiquities of the Jews*, which traces Jewish history from creation to his own day, and *The Wars of the Jews* (*Jewish Wars*), which chronicles Jewish history from the Maccabean revolt to the fall of Masada to the Romans in AD 73. Though Josephus is biased in his reporting, most scholars also believe he is a generally reliable historian. The "James Passage" occurs in *The Antiquities of the Jews*. It reads:

> When, therefore, Ananus [the high priest] was of this [angry] disposition, he thought he had now a proper opportunity [to exercise his authority]. Festus was now dead, and Albinus was but upon the road. So he assembled the Sanhedrin of judges, and brought before them the brother of Jesus, who was called Christ, whose name was James. (*Antiquities of the Jews* 20.9.1)

Two main objections have been put forth by skeptics of this report, arguing that it is a later Christian interpolation. First, the mention of "Christ" is not characteristic of Josephus, for the some ten messianic figures that he mentions that lived from AD 6–66 he never calls "Messiah." Second, the negative picture given here of Ananus the high priest does not square with the positive view of the same person Josephus provides in his earlier work, *Jewish Wars* (4.5.2).

Yet, these demurrals are rather easily dispensed with. Concerning the first, Josephus mentions some twenty-one other people with the name "Jesus." As a matter of fact, in the same section of the James text, Josephus refers to a "Jesus, the son of Damneus." As Eddy and Boyd observe, "It seems Josephus simply knew that the brother of James was 'called Christ' by his followers and so distinguished him from the other persons named 'Jesus' he had already mentioned."[15] Moreover, the very fact that Josephus says "who was called Christ" rather than "Jesus the Christ" suggests we are dealing with a historian who merely wanted to identify James by specifying his well-known brother— a brother who had followers who believed he was the Christ.[16] Regarding the second criticism of the authenticity of the "James Passage," Josephus scholars have noticed an unmistakable negative shift in Josephus' general attitude toward Jewish religious and political leadership between *Jewish Wars* and

---

15. Eddy and Boyd, *The Jesus* Legend, 189.
16. Ibid.

Antiquities of the Jews. And the negative view toward Ananus in *Antiquities of the Jews* is consistent with that general shift.[17]

Thus, the authenticity of the "James Passage" should stand and with it the historical reality of Jesus and his brother James, a pillar of the Jerusalem church (see Acts 15; cf. Gal. 1:19; and of course the book of James itself).

The Testimonium Flavianum

Without question the most controversial ancient testimony and the most important witness to the historical Jesus comes from Flavius Josephus—the *Testimonium Flavianum*. It reads:

> About this time there lived Jesus, a wise man, if indeed one ought to call him a man. For he was one who wrought sur-prising feats and was a teacher of such people as accept the truth gladly. He won over many Jews and many of the Greeks. He was the Messiah. When Pilate, upon hearing him accused by men of the highest standing among us, had condemned him to be crucified, those who had in the first place come to love him did not give up their affection for him. On the third day he appeared to them restored to life, for the prophets of God had prophesied these and countless other marvelous things about him. And the tribe of the Christians, so called after him, has still to this day not disappeared. (*Antiquities of the Jews* 18.3.3)

Here we have the most significant Jewish historian in ancient times osten-sibly acknowledging that Jesus existed, was wise, performed miracles, was the Messiah, and was crucified and resurrected according to Old Testament prophecy! Yet, this extant copy has been widely recognized to be inauthentic, for two key reasons. First, the description contains obvious Christian senti-ment from a non-Christian writer the likes of Josephus:

- "*. . . if indeed one ought to call him a man*" is a clear allusion to Christ's deity.
- "*He was the Messiah*" contradicts Josephus' own claim that the Roman general Vespasian (the general who led the Roman assault against Judea in the revolt of AD 66) was the true Messiah (*Jewish Wars* 6.5.4).
- "*On the third day he appeared to them restored to life, for the prophets of God had prophesied these and countless other marvelous things about him*" is patently Christian thought.
- "*And the tribe of the Christians, so called after him, has still to this day not disappeared*" is not the way Josephus describes other religious

---

17. On this point see Meier, *Marginal Jew*, 1:58.

movements, especially as a *"tribe" (phylon),* but it is the way the fourth century Christian historian Eusebius does refer to Christians thus suggesting the term is a later Christian interpolation.

Second, the first Christian to mention the *Testimonium* is the aforementioned Eusebius (*Ecclesiastical History* 1.11). Moreover, earlier church fathers like Irenaeus, Tertullian, and Origen are clearly familiar with *Antiquities of the Jews* but never refer to this passage. This strongly suggests that the *Testimonium* had not yet been written. Confirming this observation is the fact that Origen twice noted that Josephus did not believe Jesus was the Messiah (*Against Celsus* 1.45; *Commentary on Matthew* 10.17).

We now respond to these two objections. Regarding the first criticism, all agree that three of the preceding components are later Christian interpolations which, when removed, nevertheless most likely result in Josephus' authentic text. That should read as follows:

> About this time there lived Jesus, a wise man. For he was one who wrought surprising feats and was a teacher of such people as accept the truth gladly. He won over many Jews and many of the Greeks. When Pilate, upon hearing him accused by men of the highest standing among us, had condemned him to be crucified, those who had in the first place come to love him did not give up their affection for him. And the tribe of the Christians, so called after him, has still to this day not disappeared.[18]

What is left in this passage, as Boyd and Eddy note, is nothing that a Jewish historian could not have said about Jesus. Acknowledging that Jesus was a "wise man" and a doer of "surprising feats" is commensurate with our other sources when they speak of Jesus as a teacher and miracle-worker. Furthermore, the word "tribe" need not have come from a Christian interpolator since Eusebius is the only one we know from antiquity who used that term for Christians.[19]

Concerning the objection that early church fathers except Eusebius did not know of the *Testimonium*, a couple of responses may be offered. (1) The reconstructed original text of the *Testimonium* actually turns out to be a rather negative portrait of Jesus in that it fails to mention that Jesus is the Messiah and it implies Jesus won over people by trickery. Such a negative comment on Jesus would explain why early church fathers did not mention the *Testimonium*—it cast a bad light on the historical Jesus. (2) This also explains why Jerome only mentions in passing this text (*De Viris Illustribus* 13.14) even though he cites

---

18. As found in Eddy and Boyd, *The Jesus Legend*, 193.
19. Ibid.

Josephus over ninety times—the negative tone in the *Testimonium* regarding Jesus served no apologetic function for Jerome.

We conclude this discussion by agreeing with those who think the original version of the *Testimonium* did indeed refer to the historical Jesus and not in the most flattering way.

The Talmud (ca. AD 400–500)

There are a number of polemical passages against Jesus in the *Talmud*, an important collection of writings by the Jewish rabbis. Although the written form of the *Talmud* does not occur before about AD 400, some of the material no doubt circulated earlier in oral form. Regarding Jesus, the *Babylonian Talmud* Sanhedrin 107b reads:

> One day he (Rabbi Joshua) was reciting the Shema (Deut. 6:4) when Jesus came before him. He intended to receive him and made a sign to him. He (Jesus) thinking that it was to repel him, went, put up a brick and worshipped it. . . . And a Master has said, "Jesus the Nazarene practiced magic and led Israel astray."

And the *Babylonian Talmud* Sanhedrin 43a says of Jesus:

> It was taught: On the eve of the Passover Yeshu (the Nazarene) was hanged. For forty days before the execution took place, a herald went forth and cried, "He is going forth to be stoned because he has practiced sorcery and enticed Israel to apostasy. Anyone who can say anything in his favor, let him come forward and plead on his behalf."

As indicated in these passages the *Talmud* does not deny the miracles of Jesus but attributes them to magic. The *Talmud* also contains a number of Ben Pandera stories, according to which Jesus was the son of the Roman mercenary Pandera, "who begot a child with Joseph's adulterous wife, Mary, during her menstrual period."[20] These calumnies were expanded in the Middle Ages into the notorious anti-Christian traditions of a work called *Toledoth Jeshu*.[21]

---

20. The name Pandera is probably a play on the Greek word *parthenos* (virgin). Origen also reports a similar charge made by Celsus, "Let us return, however, to the words put into the mouth of the Jew, where the mother of Jesus is described as having been turned out by the carpenter who was betrothed to her, as she had been convicted of adultery and had a child by a certain soldier named Panthera" (*Contra Celsum* 1.32). It seems that Matthew and Luke's birth accounts of Jesus were written precisely to ward off any such ill speculation about Mary's virgin birth of Jesus.

21. The *Toledoth* may well have been composed as early as the fifth or sixth century. See Edwin M. Yamauchi, "Jesus Outside the New Testament: What is the Evidence?" in *Jesus*

We should mention that there are other ancient non-biblical references to the historical Jesus, namely, the apocryphal gospels, and we will deal with these in a later question. But the sensationalist claims that the Dead Sea Scrolls (ca. 160 BC–AD 70) mention or at least allude to Jesus have been refuted.[22]

Conclusion

We may now conclude this investigation into non-Jewish and Jewish references to Jesus by observing that all of the aforementioned key passages are rather negative in their assessment of Jesus; the only exception is the "James Passage" by Josephus which at best is neutral to Jesus. And, yet, even though these texts are negative toward Jesus they almost begrudgingly admit three data: (1) Jesus lived; (2) he performed miracles (which were attributed to magic or sorcery) and (3) he had followers. This alone refutes the Jesus legend proponents and indeed goes further in acknowledging that there was something supernatural about Jesus of Nazareth.

REFLECTION QUESTIONS

1. What do we learn from Suetonius about Jesus?

2. What do we learn from Tacitus about Jesus?

3. What do we learn from Pliny the Younger about Jesus?

4. What do we learn about James, Jesus' brother, from Josephus?

5. What do we learn from the *Testimonium Flavianum* regarding Jesus?

Under Fire, ed. Michael J. Wilkins and J. P. Moreland (Grand Rapids: Zondervan, 1995), 207–29.

22. See C. Marvin Pate, *Communities of the Last Days: The Dead Sea Scrolls, the New Testament, and the Story of Israel* (Downers Grove: InterVarsity Press, 2000), 78–83.

Are the Apocryphal Gospels a Reliable Source of the Historical Jesus?

The New Testament Apocrypha are various writings imitating the New Testament, produced from the second century up to the middle ages. These works are often written under the assumed names of the twelve apostles and the associates of Christ. Thus, some are gospels, recounting events from the life of Christ before he began his public ministry. Others are similar to Acts, claiming to record episodes from the lives of the apostles after Jesus' ministry. Still others are apocalypses, modeling the format of Revelation, while a few are letters patterned after the New Testament epistles.

Why were the New Testament Apocrypha written? Everett Harrison points out the twofold motivation behind the writing of these works:

> Two factors are largely responsible for the creation of these writings. One was the desire for further information about the life of Jesus and the careers of the apostles. Scripture has little to say about our Lord prior to the opening of his ministry. This gap was an invitation and even a challenge to supply the deficiency by calling upon the resources of the imagination. . . . A second factor was the desire of those with heretical tendencies to foist their ideas on the church with the alleged endorsement of Christ or the apostles. By far the most common of these tendencies was the Gnostic [reinterpretation of Jesus] . . . It was rather easy to claim the authority of Jesus for teaching that went beyond that of the New Testament, since he himself had hinted that he had much to say that he was unable to impart to his disciples at the time (John 16:12). This was an open door for Gnostic

propaganda, especially as it was put into the lips of the resurrected Savior.[1]

The table below classifies the majority of the New Testament Apocrypha, including the Nag Hammadi documents:

	GOSPELS AND RELATED FORMS	
NARRATIVE GOSPELS	REVELATION DIALOGUES AND DISCOURSES	SAYINGS, GOSPELS AND COLLECTIONS
Gospel of the Ebionites	*(First) Apocalypse of James* (NHC V)	*Gospel of Thomas* (NHC II)
Gospel of the Hebrews	*(Second) Apocalypse of James* (NHC V)	*Teachings of Silvanus* (NHC VII)
Gospel of the Nazoreans	*Apocryphon of James* (NHC 1)	
Gospel of Nicodemus (*Acts of Pilate*)	*Apocryphon of John* (NHC II, III, IV, and BG 8502)	
Gospel of Peter	*Book of Thomas the Contender* (NHC II)	
Infancy Gospel of Thomas	*Dialogue of the Savior* (NHC III)	
Papyrus Egerton 2 (a fragment of an unknown narrative gospel)	*Epistula Apostolorum*	
Papyrus Oxyrhyncus 840 (a fragment of an unknown narrative gospel)	*Gospel of the Egyptians*	
Proto-Evangelium of James	*Gospel of Mary* (BG 8502)	
Arabic Infancy Gospel	*Gospel of Philip* (NHC II)	
Gospel of Pseudo-Matthew	*Pistis Sophia*	
	Questions of Mary	
	Questions of Bartholomew	
	Second Treatise of the Great Seth (NHC VII)	

---

1. Everett F. Harrison, *Introduction to the New Testament* (Grand Rapids: Eerdmans Publishing, 1971), 121–122.

	GOSPELS AND RELATED FORMS	
	Sophia of Jesus Christ (NHC III and BG 8502)	
	Two Books of Jeu	
	Bodlian Coptic MC d54 (a fragmentary dialogue between Jesus and John)	
	TREATISES	
On the Origin of the World (NHC II)	Gospel of Truth (NHC 1 and XII)	Treatise on Resurrection (NHC I)
(Coptic) Gospel of the Egyptians (NHC III and IV)	Hypostasis of the Archons (NHC II)	Tripartite Tractate (NHC I)
	APOCALYPSES	
(Coptic) Apocalypse of Elijah	(Latin) Apocalypse of Paul	Concept of Our Great Power (NHC VI)
(Arabic) Apocalypse of Peter	Apocalypse of Sophonias	Book of Elchasai
(Coptic) Apocalypse of Peter (NHC VII)	Apocalypse of Thomas	V and VI Ezra
(Greek/Ethiopic) Apocalypse of Peter	Ascension of Isaiah (chaps. 6–11)	Melchizedek
(Coptic) Apocalypse of Paul (NHC V)	Christian Sibyllines	Mysteries of Saint John the Apostle and the Holy Virgin
	ACTS	
Acts of Andrew	(Coptic) Acts of Peter (BG8502)	Acts of Philip
Acts of Andrew and Matthias	(Greek) Acts of Peter	Acts of Thomas
Acts of John	Acts of Peter and the Twelve (NHC VI)	Kerygmata Petrou
Acts of Paul (and Thecla)		

GOSPELS AND RELATED FORMS		
LETTERS		
Abgar Legend	*Epistle of Pseudo-Titus*	*Paul's Letter to the Laodiceans*
Correspondence between Paul and Seneca		
LITURGICAL MATERIALS		
HOMILIES	PSALMS	PRAYERS
Interpretation of Knowledge (NHC XI)	*Odes of Solomon*	*On the Anointing* (NHC XI)
Kerygma of Peter		*On Baptism A* (NHC XI)
Testimony of Truth (NHC IX)		*On Baptism B* (NHC XI)
A Valentian Exposition (NHC XI)		*On the Eucharist A* (NHC XI)
		On the Eucharist B (NHC XI)
		A Prayer of the Apostle Paul (NHC 1)
KEY TO ABBREVIATIONS: NHC = Nag Hammadi Codex BG = Berlin Gnostic Papyrus[2]		

In a later chapter we will focus on the first motivation above pointed out by Harrison—the appeal to New Testament apocryphal gospels to fill in the details of Jesus' boyhood, especially his purported miracles. This chapter centers on the

---

2. Paul D. Wegner provides this list, *The Journey from Texts to Translations: The Origin and Development of the Bible* (Grand Rapids: Baker, 2000), 159. To this list should be added the *Gospel of Judas,* a New Testament apocryphal gospel that makes Judas a hero by reinterpreting the death of Christ in Gnostic terms. Thus, Judas and Jesus made an agreement secretly that Judas would hand over Jesus to the authorities for the purpose of killing Jesus in order to set his soul free from his mortal body.

second motivation above—the attempt of Gnosticism to support its teachings about Jesus in the New Testament apocryphal gospels. The battle that ensued was nothing less than historic Christianity versus Gnosticism. Had Gnosticism won, with its Platonic disparagement of the body and exaltation of the soul, the message of the Incarnation of Jesus, the God-Man, would have been defeated.

In our own day, no one has made a more concerted effort to legitimize Gnosticism as on par with the canonical gospels than Elaine Pagels, Harrington Spear Professor of Religion at Princeton University.[3] She has long championed the Gnostic cause in American religion. Her best-sellers on the subject include *The Gnostic Gospels; The Gnostic Paul*; and *Adam and Eve*, and *the Serpent*. In a more recent best-seller, *Beyond Belief: The Secret Gospel of Thomas*,[4] Pagels argues that the *Gospel of Thomas* has received a bad rap thanks to the canonical gospel of John. Her title reflects the thesis of her book: the gospel of John presents only one part of the story of early Christianity, and not a very legitimate one at that. She asserts that the gospel of John promotes a religion in which individuals should cognitively believe a set of dogmas about Jesus (that he is the only Son of God, uniquely existing in eternity past, born of the virgin Mary, died for sinful humanity, and arose in bodily form). Anything other than these formulations are to be categorically rejected as heresy. The *Gospel of Thomas*, argues Pagels, presents a more promising path—a religion in which truth is not revelation from God outside the individual but rather truth about God within the individual waiting to be discovered and experienced. The content of that truth is that Christians are actually none other than Christ, newly created in the image of God. Pagels claims vociferously that the gospel of John was written precisely to squash the growing popularity of *Thomas* in the first-century church.

Authority: Where Does It Come From?

The real question here is where does authority come from? What should be the canon? Should it be the New Testament or the apocryphal (non-canonical) gospels of the second to fourth centuries AD? With this question, Pagels goes for the jugular of historic Christianity, arguing that Gnosticism was (and is) just as legitimate, if not more so, an expression of Christianity as orthodoxy. Her question basically is, who made historic Christianity the final say in matters of faith and practice? The key issue behind this question has to do with the New Testament canon—the books that are traditionally included in the New Testament.

"Canon" means rule or measuring stick. Discussions of the final formation of the Bible center on at least two important questions: When were the

---

3. Elaine Pagels' works on Gnosticism are: *The Gnostic Gospels* (New York: Random House, 1979); *Adam, Eve, and the Serpent* (New York: Random House, 1989); *The Gnostic Paul: Gnostic Exegesis of the Pauline Letters* (Harrisburg, PA: Trinity Press International, 1992).

4. Elaine Pagels, *Beyond Belief: The Secret Gospel of Thomas* (New York: Random House, 2003).

books of the Bible determined to be inspired? And what were the criteria for including the present books in the Bible? For our purpose, we will focus only on the New Testament canon. Pagels' thesis is twofold: Before Irenaeus, there was diversity of opinion about the nature of Christ, even in the New Testament itself. In other words, the New Testament canon was open. But from Irenaeus on, an artificial uniformity was imposed on Christianity regarding who Jesus was. Consequently, the historical winners (the four gospels) were officially admitted into the canon, while the historical losers (e.g., the *Gospel of Thomas*) were shunned. After summarizing Pagels' arguments below, we will offer a rebuttal of them, point by point.

Pagels wastes no time in her book *Beyond Belief* debunking the idea that there was a uniform witness to the nature of Christ early on in the history of Christianity. In reality, claims Pagels, there were at least three major competing interpretations of who Jesus was at the time, reflected in the Synoptic gospels, the gospel of John, and the *Gospel of Thomas*.

The Synoptics

Pagels wants to pit the gospel of John against the Synoptic gospels (Matthew, Mark, and Luke) to support her theory that there were diverse, contradictory views about Christ in the New Testament. Thus, she mentions the well-known differences between the Synoptics and John: the Synoptics place Jesus' cleansing of the temple during the passion week, while John situates it at the beginning of Jesus' ministry (John 2:12–22); and the Synoptics equate the Last Supper with the Passover meal, while John does not, for he wishes to equate Jesus' death on the cross with the time of the slaying of the Passover lamb. Most evangelicals are not threatened by these dissimilarities, attributing them to John's poetic license. But Pagels goes on to insist that the Synoptics' view of the nature of Christ is that, though labeled the "Messiah," the "Son of Man," and "Son of God" therein, Jesus was no more than God's *human* agent. These titles were but metaphors not to be pressed literally. According to Pagels, only Luke's gospel says that Jesus was made Lord, but only at his resurrection, not before.

The Gospel of John

According to Pagels, the portrait of Jesus dramatically changes with John, which elevates him to equal status with God. It is only in the gospel of John that Jesus is the unique Son of God, the light of the world, and without parallel among humans. Pagels labels this "higher Christology" (Jesus is God) as opposed to the Synoptics' "lower Christology" (Jesus is mere man).

The Gospel of Thomas

The *Gospel of Thomas*, unlike the gospel of John, teaches that God's light shines not only in Jesus but, potentially at least, in everyone. Thomas's gospel encourages the hearer not so much to believe in Jesus (as John 20:3–31 does), but rather to seek to know God through one's own divinely given capacity, since all are created in the image of God (*Gospel of Thomas*, 3). When the would-be followers of Jesus look within themselves, they discover that not only does Jesus come from the light, so do they (*Gospel of Thomas*, 50). The *Gospel of Thomas* equates humans with Christ (108). Then Pagels asserts: "This, I believe, is the symbolic meaning of attributing this gospel to Thomas, whose name means 'twin.' By encountering the 'living Jesus,' as Thomas suggests, one may come to recognize oneself and Jesus as, so to speak, identical twins."[5] Then approvingly she quotes Thomas in that regard:

> Since you are my twin and my true companion, examine yourself, and learn who you are. . . . . Since you will be called my [twin] . . . although you do not understand it yet . . . you will be called "the one who knows himself." For whoever has not known himself knows nothing. But whoever has known himself has simultaneously come to know the depth of all things.[6]

While Pagels believes that early Christianity offered various contradictory perspectives on Jesus (the Synoptics, John, and *Thomas),* she resonates only with the *Gospel of Thomas'* perspective. She bemoans that the complexity and richness of early Christianity was lost with Irenaeus, second-century bishop of Lyons, France, who imposed, she believes, an artificial uniformity onto the church. Irenaeus was an ardent combatant against Gnosticism, prompting his five-volume polemical work *Refutation and Overthrow of Falsely So-Called Knowledge*, commonly referred to as *Against Heresies*. In those five volumes, the bishop affirmed the notion of "apostolic tradition," that is, the orthodox view of Jesus Christ that had been handed down by the apostles to each succeeding generation, namely, his birth from a virgin, his passion and resurrection in the flesh, and all unique revelatory events that provided atonement for sin. As such, Irenaeus asserts that this apostolic tradition represents the canon of truth, the grid through which to filter out false teaching about Jesus.

According to Pagels, Irenaeus was among the first to champion the gospel of John as the true interpretation of Jesus, linking it to the Synoptics, even interpreting the Synoptics through John's perspective. Consequently, Irenaeus declared that these four gospels exclusively conveyed the true message about Jesus—that he is the unique Son of God whose sacrificial death alone provides forgiveness for sin. Irenaeus secured such a privileged position for the four gospels (read through John's perspective) by mounting a campaign against all apocryphal gospels, demanding they be destroyed.[7]

---

5. Ibid., 57.
6. *Gospel of Thomas*, 138, quoted in ibid, 57.
7. Ibid., 80–81, 86, 89–99, 111–13, 147, 166, 167.

Irenaeus set the church on a path that led to the victory of orthodoxy over alternate expressions of Jesus, culminating in the official approval of the four gospels and the apostolic tradition by Athanasius, the fourth-century champion of orthodoxy. Such a development was aided by the Roman emperor Constantine, whose conversion to Christianity in AD 313 paved the way for the legalizing of Christianity. Using Christianity as the unifying principle for his empire, Constantine convened the bishops of the churches in Nicea, on the Turkish coast, in AD 325 for the purpose of composing a common set of beliefs among Christians—the Nicene Creed. Later, in the spring of AD 367, Bishop Athanasius of Alexandria, Egypt, wrote his most famous letter. In his Easter letter to the churches, Athanasius clarified the picture of Christ that had been sketched out two hundred years before, starting with Irenaeus. First, the bishop censured the heretics:

> [They] have tried to reduce into order for themselves the books termed apocryphal and to mix them up with the divinely inspired Scripture . . . which those who were eyewitnesses and helpers of the Word delivered to the fathers, it seemed good to me . . . to set forth in order the books included in the canon and handed down and accredited as divine.[8]

Pagels remarks:

> After listing the twenty-two books that he says are "believed to be the Old Testament" [based on the Hebrew reckoning], Athanasius proceeds to offer the earliest known list of the twenty-seven books he called the "books of the New Testament," beginning with "the four gospels, Matthew, Mark, Luke, and John," and proceeding to the same list of writings attributed to apostles that constitutes the New Testament today. Praising these as the "springs of salvation," he calls upon Christians during this Lenten season to "cleanse the church from every defilement" and to reject "the apocryphal books," which are "filled with myths, empty, and polluted"—books that, he warns, "entice conflict and lead people astray."[9]

The Argument against Pagels

Pagels makes essentially two arguments. First, she maintains that, before Irenaeus, diversity characterized not only early Christianity but even

---

8. Athanasius, *Festal Letter* 39.3 (AD 367), emphasis added.
9. Pagels, *Beyond Belief*, 176–77.

the New Testament. Second, she argues that a forced uniformity became the mark of the church's teaching from Irenaeus on. We take issue with those two claims.

The Question of Diversity

First, it simply is not true that diversity to the point of contradiction characterizes the Synoptics' relationship to John. Not only does the gospel of John teach that Jesus is God, but so do the Synoptics. This is clear from the Synoptics' titles for Jesus, *contra* Pagels: Messiah, Son of Man, and Son of God. *Messiah* is the Hebrew term for "anointed one" (*Christus*, the Greek term for the same). It is clear from Psalm 2:2, 7 that the term does not refer to a mere man, for there the Lord's Anointed One (Messiah in v. 2) is proclaimed the Son of God (v. 7). Even in a Jewish work written close in time to the New Testament, *4 Ezra*, we see God call that Messiah "my son."

A similar dynamic exists for the title "Son of Man," Jesus' favorite self-reference. This title originated in Daniel 7, where it is the *heavenly* Son of man who receives the kingdom of God (Dan. 7:13–14). "Son of God," as we saw in Psalm 2, elevates the Messiah far above humans. Furthermore, in ancient Egyptian and Mesopotamian thought as well as in the Roman Empire, the pharaoh or king was declared to be the Son of God—one divinely begotten of God. The use of these three titles for Jesus in the Synoptics, then—Messiah, Son of Man, and Son of God—surely demonstrates that they view Jesus as more than a mere man.

Moreover, Pagels asserts that the gospel of John consciously opposed the *Gospel of Thomas*. She says this because she believes that *Thomas* dates back to around AD 50, although most scholars date *Thomas* in the second century. The proof of this, according to Pagels, is that the *Gospel of Thomas* must have been extant in the first century because John criticizes it and paints such a negative picture of the apostle Thomas. Thus, Thomas does not understand that Lazarus will rise from the dead (John 11:14–16); he does not comprehend that Jesus is the way to heaven (14:5–6); and most important, he has to see the risen Jesus before he will believe Jesus is no longer dead (20:24–28). But there is no need to draw the conclusion from these failings of Thomas that John was criticizing a *written* document about Thomas. After all, the first two responses were typical of the misunderstandings of the disciples toward Jesus in general during the life of Christ. Moreover, Nicholas Perrin has conclusively demonstrated that the *Gospel of Thomas* is based on Tatian's *Diatesseron*, *a* harmony of the four gospels, which dates no earlier that AD 170![10]

Furthermore, John 20:24–28 serves the purpose of confirming that Jesus arose bodily from the dead, so Thomas was able to see and touch Christ. But the "target" for this passage need not have been the *Gospel of Thomas*, for

---

10. Nicholas Perrin, *Thomas and Tatian*, Academia Biblica 5 (Atlanta: Society of Biblical Literature, 2002).

the beginning forms of Gnosticism in the first century AD denied the bodily resurrection of Jesus, and John 20:24–28 is better suited as a barb against it. Scholars date the beginnings of Gnosticism—but not the full-blown system presumed in *Thomas*—to the late first century AD, with the *Gospel of Thomas* following decades later. If this is so, then Pagels' entire thesis collapses to the ground, for it cannot uphold a first-century dating of the *Gospel of Thomas*. All of this to say, the four canonical gospels espouse a consistent message about Jesus Christ—though he was fully human, he was fully God.

To summarize, Pagels states that the Synoptics do not agree with John, nor do they agree with the *Gospel of Thomas*. However, the real picture that emerges is that the Synoptics are very similar to John in their portraits of Jesus and together they disagree with the non-canonical *Thomas'* presentation of Jesus as Gnostic. The bottom line is that it is the non-canonical *Thomas* versus the Synoptics and John.

The Question of the Origin of Orthodoxy
Neither will Pagels' second thesis do—that only from Irenaeus on was there a forced uniformity on the church's teaching about Jesus. In other words, she believes Gnostic writings like *Thomas* were held in high regard among Christians, along with the Synoptics and John, until Irenaeus messed things up. But this assumption overlooks a crucial fact: orthodoxy runs throughout the New Testament and is witnessed to consistently up to Irenaeus and far beyond. In the Pastoral epistles (1 and 2 Timothy and Titus) written circa AD 64, the author (Paul) admonishes pastors Timothy and Titus to preserve and protect the "sound doctrine" (1 Tim. 1:10; 6:3; 2 Tim. 1:13; 4:3; Titus 1:9). This sound teaching is no doubt the teaching of the apostles (Acts 2:42) concerning Jesus' birth, death, and resurrection.

Second Peter (ca. AD 64) vows to protect that same truth (1:1; 2), as does Jude (ca. AD 80), urging the believers to defend "the faith which was once for all delivered to the saints" (v. 3 RSV). Most likely, these biblical authors were combating the beginning expressions of Gnosticism. First John (ca. AD 95) rounds out the discussion by providing a more sustained criticism of incipient Gnostic teaching (1:1; 2:22; 3:4, 8–10; 4:2–3).

This is all in keeping with the message of the gospel of John that Jesus is the God-man (see especially the opening statement 1:1–14). Irenaeus and Athanasius were not the first to "impose" the canonical rule of faith. In reality, the Church Fathers all the way from Justin Martyr (early second century AD) to Augustine (early fifth century AD) attest to the orthodox belief in Jesus. We see this from the fact that, while the Fathers quote the twenty-seven New Testament books some 36,000 times (some estimates go much higher), in comparison, their references to the New Testament Apocrypha are negligible. They also chose to read and preach on the twenty-seven New Testament books in their worship services.

Conclusion

When it comes to the proper view of Jesus, the New Testament is our sole authority—not Gnostic books like the *Gospel of Thomas* that tried unsuccessfully to force themselves on the people of God. So out with the Gnostic Jesus and in with the Orthodox Jesus! In other words, the New Testament apocryphal gospels are not reliable sources for the historical Jesus.[11]

REFLECTION QUESTIONS

1. What are the New Testament Apocrypha?

2. What does Elaine Pagels claim regarding the relationship between the *Gospel of Thomas* and the gospel of John?

3. How would you respond to Pagels' claim that diversity to the point of contradiction characterizes the canonical gospels' portrait of Jesus?

4. What evidence invalidates Pagels' contention that Irenaeus forced uniformity onto Christianity?

5. How many times do the church fathers quote the New Testament Apocrypha in their writings and sermons?

---

11. Bart D. Ehrman's newest book puts forth the older view that Jesus' deity is presented in sequential stages, not from the beginning, *How Jesus Became God: The Exaltation of a Jewish Preacher from Galilee* (San Francisco: HarperOne, 2014). But the volume edited by Michael F. Bird offers the far more plausible view that Jesus was God from the get-go. This thesis argues for a high Christology view early on in the New Testament, *How God Became Jesus: The Real Origins of Belief in Jesus' Divine Nature—A Response to Bart D. Ehrman*, Michael F. Bird, Craig A. Evans, Simon Gathercole, Charles E. Hill, and Chris Tilling (Grand Rapids: Zondervan, 2014).

Was the Oral Tradition Regarding the Historical Jesus Reliable?

The Jesus Seminar was a group of some eighty New Testament scholars who convened twice a year from 1985 to 1996 for the purpose of ascertaining which sayings and deeds attributed to Jesus in the four gospels are authentic. The result of their investigation determined that only eighteen percent of the five hundred sayings and deeds attributed to the historical Jesus were viewed by the Jesus Seminar as authentic, that is, uttered and performed by the Jesus of the Gospels!

Now how did the Jesus Seminar reach such an astounding conclusion? Two specific criteria of form criticism and one basic premise of form criticism informed their decision. We dealt with the criteria of dissimilarity and multiple attestation in an earlier question, which are the two main standards used by form critics. Here we focus on the fundamental assumption of the Jesus Seminar that there was a period when the message of the historical Jesus circulated among the churches before it was written down. And during such a period of oral tradition, the church created sayings and deeds that Jesus in fact never said or did. This, then, produced the gap between the historical Jesus (the real Jesus) and the Christ of faith (the production of the church).

In this chapter we will counter the six planks of the form critics' argument that the oral tradition did not accurately pass on the information about the historical Jesus.

The Six Planks of Oral Tradition as Promoted by Form Criticism

The six planks of the form critical assumption that oral tradition adversely effected the message of Jesus are: (1) the assumption of a purely oral period; (2) the assumed lack of a coherent narrative; (3) the assumed lack of a biographical interest; (4) a limited role of eyewitnesses; (5) assumed laws of oral and written traditions; and (6) statements by the risen Jesus that passed as being from his ministry on earth.[1]

1. The Assumption of a Purely Oral Period

Several pieces of evidence indicate that, at the very least, literacy in first-century Judaism was not low, thus dispelling the common claim of form criticism that the transmission period between Jesus and the writing of the Gospels was exclusively oral in nature. First, the treasure trove of writings produced by the authors of the Dead Sea Scrolls (most likely the Essenes at Qumran) strongly suggests that reading and writing in the first century in Israel were widespread. This is especially the case since we know that the Essenes did not live only along the Dead Sea but throughout Palestine from ca. 150 BC to AD 70.[2] Second, related to the previous point, the faith of Jews in the ancient world was rooted in a collection of writings—what we now call the Hebrew Bible together with its translations into Greek and Aramaic. Third, it seems that synagogues were prevalent in first-century Palestine, including Galilee. And the evidence suggests that these synagogues could function as schools for Jewish boys.[3] Fourth, the Gospels consistently portray Jesus as engaging in debates with scribes and Pharisees on scriptural interpretation. From this one can reasonably conclude that Jesus had the educational training needed to debate rather technical points regarding the Torah.[4] Indeed, John 7:15 states that Jesus amazed the crowds by his "learning" (*grammata oiden*), a term that usually included reading skills.[5] Compare this with Luke 4:16–30 which mentions that Jesus read from Isaiah and commented upon it with regard to his own ministry. All of this is consistent with the point made by the Gospels that Jesus was recognized to be a teacher/rabbi.[6]

---

1. This description of the six planks and responses to them are based on Paul Rhodes Eddy and Gregory A. Boyd, *The Jesus Legend: A Case for the Historical Reliability of the Synoptic Jesus Tradition* (Grand Rapids: Baker, 2007), 237–308.
2. See Josephus, *Jewish Wars* 2.8, 2–13. For more discussion of the literature comprising the Dead Sea Scrolls, see my *Communities of the Last Days: The Dead Sea Scrolls, the New Testament and the Story of Israel* (Downers Grove, IL: InterVarsity Press, 2000), chapters 1–2.
3. On the educational role, etc. of the synagogue, see R. Riesner, *Jesus als Lehrer: Eine Untersuchung zum Ursprung der Evenglien-Ueberlieferung* (Tübingen: Mohr Siebeck, 1981), 123–206.
4. Thomas Boomershine argues that this tradition is the most compelling evidence of Jesus' literacy, "Jesus of Nazareth and the Watershed of Ancient Orality and Literacy," *Semeia* 65 (1995): 21.
5. See ibid, 22.
6. Meier rightly remarks of this: "If we take into account that Jesus' adult life became fiercely focused on the Jewish religion, that he is presented by almost all the gospel traditions as engaging in learned disputes over Scripture and *halakah* with students of the Law, that he was accorded the respectful—but at that time vague—title of rabbi or teacher, that more than one gospel tradition presents him as preaching or teaching in synagogues (presumably after and on the Scripture readings), and that, even apart from formal disputes, his

We conclude this first counterpoint to form criticism by stating the obvious: the fact that the Jesus tradition was written down from the beginning disputes the form critic claim that only oral development governed the period from the earthly Jesus to the canonical gospels. No less important is the corollary to this finding—it makes difficult the claim that the pre-gospel tradition was susceptible to any rampant and unrestrained changing of the genuine material associated with the historical Jesus.

2. The Assumed Lack of a Coherent Narrative

Even if (we would say "since") there was writing in the period between the historical Jesus and the recording of the canonical gospels, we still have to reckon with the reality that there was also oral transmission of the Jesus tradition during that time. Was that accurate? More specifically, was the written narrative informing the written gospels simply the early church's superimposing of a fictitious framework on isolated, small units or forms? We answer this question by quoting Eddy and Boyd:

> Early form critics such as Bultmann took it for granted that folk traditions consisted almost exclusively of short vignettes. How could longer narratives, to say nothing of epics, be remembered and transmitted intact orally? While this view is still prevalent today among many in New Testament circles, a significant number of folklorists, anthropologists, and ethnographers over the last several decades have justifiably abandoned it. The reason for this reversal is that empirical evidence has shown it to be demonstrably wrong. A large number of field work studies have "brought to light numerous long oral epics in the living traditions of Central Asia, India, Africa, and Oceania, for example." Hence, as the famed Finnish folklorist Lauri Honko recently noted: "The existence of genuine long oral epics can no longer be denied." In fact, amazingly, scholars have documented oral narratives whose performance lasted up to twenty-five hours carried out over several days.[7]

---

teaching was strongly imbued with the outlook and language of the sacred texts of Israel, it is reasonable to suppose that Jesus' religious formation in his family was intense and profound, and included instruction in reading biblical Hebrew. . . . [Jesus] was literate, and his literacy probably extended beyond the mere ability to sign one's name or conduct basic business transactions ('tradesman's literacy') to the ability to read sophisticated theological and literary works and comment on them ('scribal literacy'). Jesus comes out of a peasant background, but he is not an ordinary peasant" (*A Marginal Jew*, 276, 278).

7. Eddy and Boyd, *The Jesus Legend*, 252–53.

Eddy and Boyd do not miss the enormous significance this model of oral performance has for understanding the Gospels:

> These observations decisively refute the classic form-critical assumption that oral traditions, by nature, do not involve long narratives. Applying this conclusion to the Jesus tradition, there is no longer any justification for supposing the overall narrative framework of the Gospels to be a literary "fiction" imposed on previously autonomous, disconnected units of the oral Jesus tradition.[8]

What this means for the Gospels is that the small independent units of the oral tradition behind the Gospels are not at odds with the historical metanarrative that frames them.[9]

3. The Assumed Lack of Biographical Interest

The assumption of radical form critics throughout the twentieth century was that orally oriented cultures were indifferent to the distinction between historical/biographical and fictional narratives. But this presumption against the historical or biographical nature of the Gospels is now being significantly questioned by those better trained in oral genre. Thus, one of the folklorists who has been at the forefront of this discussion says, "While folklore is present [in orally oriented cultures] so is historical content. Even more importantly, so are historical attitudes of the tradition bearers."[10] The anthropologist Patrick Pender-Cudlip agrees strongly. He argues that "oral tradents" (those entrusted with transmitting oral traditions) demonstrate as much concern to receive and render a precise, accurate and authentic account of the past as do modern literate historians.[11]

It is no surprise, therefore, that scholars are now revisiting the New Testament emphasis on "tradition" and "teachers" in support of the view

---

8. Ibid., 254.
9. Eddy and Boyd comment: "The individually identifiable units of tradition are, in fact, small, discrete units, and they can function relatively independently with respect to order (with limits) and even presence (i.e., within any given performance, oral or written). However, at the same time, they were always-already envisioned within the schematic backdrop (the "mental text") of a lengthy narrative tradition about Jesus" (ibid, 254–55).
10. R. Dorson, "Introduction: Folklore and Traditional History," in *Folklore and Traditional History*, ed. R. Dorson (The Hague: Mouton, 1973), 9.
11. Pender-Cudlip comments, "Both consist of supposedly authentic narratives of past events, both explain and express truths about the present through stories about the past, and both use the present as a model for reconstructing the past. Regarded in this light, the differences between them are mainly technical" (P. Pender-Cudlip, "Oral Traditions and Anthropological Analysis: Some Contemporary Myths," *Azania* 7 [1972]:12).

that the early church accurately passed on the history of the Jesus tradition.[12] Added to the importance of tradition and teachers in the New Testament are the twin themes of "bearing witness" to Jesus and of "remembering" the ministry, death, and resurrection of Jesus within the early church.[13] Thus, as James Dunn has argued, in a predominantly oral community such as the early church, the primary function of these teachers would have been to transmit faithfully the oral traditions regarding the historical Jesus.[14]

These recent findings concerning the accurately passing on of oral traditions do not bode well for the antiquated claim of form criticism that the early church had no historical or biographical interest in the historical Jesus.

4. Limited Role of Eyewitnesses

Three recent authors have provided new research that has devastating results for form criticism's much alleged claim that eyewitnesses played little to no role in the transmission of the Jesus tradition: James Dunn, Samuel Byrskog, and Richard Bauckham. We briefly summarize here their contributions to the debate at hand.

One of the leading proponents of applying interdisciplinary studies of oral traditions to the question of the historical Jesus is James Dunn, eminent New Testament scholar. Dunn argues that gospel scholars need to move beyond the Bultmannian propensity to emphasize early Christian communities as the transmitters of the Jesus tradition. Rather, they should acknowledge the central role Jesus' immediate disciples would have played as eyewitnesses to his life and teaching. Dunn contends that we must not forget the continuing role of eyewitness tradents (i.e., those who passed along the traditions about Jesus), of those recognized from the first as apostles or otherwise authoritative bearers of the message of the historical Jesus. Dunn writes, "In focusing particular attention on the communal character of the early traditioning process we should not discount the more traditional emphasis on the individual figure of authority respected for his or her own association with Jesus during the days of his mission."[15]

---

12. For the importance of the "traditions," see, e.g., 1 Corinthians 11:2, 23; 15:1–3; Galatians 1:9; Philippians 4:9; Colossians 2:6–7; 1 Thessalonians 4:1; 2 Thessalonians 2:15; 3:6. For the importance of "teachers" passing on the Jesus tradition, see, e.g., Acts 13:1; Romans 12:7; 1 Corinthians 12:28–29; Galatians 6:6; Ephesians 4:11; Hebrews 5:12; James 3:1; cf. especially *Didache* 13:2.
13. Eddy and Boyd, *The Jesus Legend*, 266–67. See John 1:7–8, 15, 19, 32; 3:26, 28; 5:32; Acts 1:8, 22; 2:32; 3:15; 5:32; 10:37–41; 13:31; 22:15, 18; 23:11; 26:16; Luke 22:19; 1 Corinthians 11:2, 24–25; 2 Thessalonians 2:5; 2 Timothy 2:8, 14.
14. James D. G. Dunn, *Christianity in the Making*, vol. 1: *Jesus Remembered* (Grand Rapids: Eerdmans, 2003), 176.
15. See Dunn's newest book on the subject, *Jesus Remembered*, 242–43.

Samuel Byrskog has recently provided us with one of the most exhaustive studies on the role of eyewitnesses in the early church.[16] Byrskog approaches the debate well-informed by recent interdisciplinary studies on ancient oral traditions and oral history (the difference between these two is that the former covers a shorter period of transmission than the latter). Byrskog's first contribution in his work is to demonstrate that Greco-Roman social groups generally conform to the pattern of orally dominant cultures regarding their interest in accurately preserving the essence of past events relevant to their self-identity. Next, the author convincingly locates the early Christian movement within this same pattern as is evidenced by their frequent appeals to eyewitness testimony. More specifically, Byrskog makes a powerful case that the early Jesus tradition emphasized the role played by the twelve disciples (with Peter as the main spokesman), several women (with Mary Magdalene at the forefront), and certain family members of Jesus, particularly Mary and his brother James. These, he contends, were the primary oral tradents of the Jesus tradition.[17]

Richard Bauckham has further confirmed the importance of eyewitnesses in reporting the sayings and deeds of the historical Jesus in his monumental work, *Jesus and the Eyewitnesses: The Gospels as Eyewitness Testimony.*[18] Building on the insights of Byrskog, Bauckham offers several additional lines of evidence for the presence and importance of eyewitness testimony in the early church. First, Bauckham plumbs the depths of Papias' famous statements regarding Papias' connection to testimony rooted in eyewitness recollection, concluding that they are indeed reliable.[19]

Second, Bauckham explores the fact that, while the tendency in the gospel tradition is to leave characters unnamed, some nevertheless are named. Bultmann explained this phenomenon by the "law of increasing detail," wherein he assumed that the more the Jesus tradition was passed on the more detailed it became and, in doing so, suggests the Jesus tradition was tampered with all along the way.[20] But Bauckham's research demon-

---

16. Samuel Byrskog, *Story as History—History as Story: The Gospel Tradition in the Context of Ancient Oral History* (Tübingen: Mohr Siebeck, 2000).
17. Ibid., 91.
18. R. Bauckham, *Jesus and the Eyewitnesses: The Gospels as Eyewitness Testimony* (Grand Rapids: Eerdmans, 2006).
19. The earliest form of this tradition is that of Papias, preserved by Eusebius, *HE*, iii. 39.15: "Mark indeed, since he was the interpreter (ἑρμηνευτής) of Peter, wrote accurately, but not in order (οὐ μέντοι τάξει), the things either said or done by the Lord as much as he remembered. For he neither heard the Lord nor followed Him, but afterwards, as I have said, [heard and followed] Peter, who fitted his discourses to the needs [of his hearers] but not as if making a narrative of the Lord's sayings (χυριαχῶν λογίων); consequently, Mark, writing some things just as he remembered, erred in nothing; for he was careful of one thing—not to omit anything of the things he had heard or to falsify anything in them."
20. Ibid., 68, 215, 241, 283, 310, 345, 393.

strates just the opposite—in no case does a character in Mark gain a name in Matthew or Luke, while Matthew and Luke several times drop the name of a character mentioned in Mark. Thus, Bultmann claimed that the flow of the Jesus tradition in terms of detail proceeded from general to specific while Bauckham shows quite the reverse—from specific to general.[21] Bauckham specifies that names such as Cleopas (Mark 15:40), Simon of Cyrene and his sons (Mark 15:21) and four recipients of Jesus' healings were eyewitnesses who not only originated the traditions to which their names are attached but also continued to tell these stories as authoritative guarantors of the traditions.[22]

Third, in a fascinating chapter, Bauckham demonstrates cogently that the various personal names in the Gospels (e.g., Simon, Joseph, Lazarus, Judas, John, Jesus, Matthew, and James) occurred with a high frequency in first-century Palestine. Yet this was not the case for those names in non-Palestine areas. Moreover, the usages of names in the Gospels also correspond closely to the variety of ways in which persons bearing the same very popular names could be distinguished in Palestinian Jewish usage. Bauckham also notes that the lists of the twelve apostles in the Gospels constitute an official order of the early church precisely because those individuals were recognized to be the official tradents of the Jesus tradition;[23] Peter is the authoritative voice behind not only Mark but also Matthew and Luke;[24] the Jesus tradition was passed along by eyewitness testimony not anonymous communities;[25] eyewitness memory is affirmed by recent psychological studies;[26] and the gospel of John is the result of eyewitness testimony.[27]

Thus, the works of Dunn, Byrskog, and Bauckham have demolished perhaps the most important plank of form criticism by showing that the Gospels are indeed rooted in eyewitness testimony and therefore are historically reliable.

5. Assumed Laws of Oral and Written Traditions

Bultmann and his followers assumed that they could confidently make conclusions about the original creation and early transmission of Jesus tradition on the basis of laws about how folk traditions are created, orally transmitted, and creatively expanded.[28] Bultmann claimed that three tools enabled

---

21. Ibid., 291–81.
22. Ibid., 417–19.
23. Ibid., 93–113.
24. Ibid., 155–239.
25. Ibid., 290–318.
26. Ibid., 319–357.
27. Ibid., 358–508. Though Bauckham does not think that the author is John the apostle but another eyewitness by the name of John; here we disagree, since we think John the apostle was the author of the fourth gospel.
28. Bultmann, *The History of the Synoptic Tradition*, 6–7.

one to accomplish the preceding task. We now evaluate those "laws" in light of later evidence.

(1) From the study of how Matthew and Luke used Mark and Q, Bultmann tried to extrapolate these findings to the earlier oral stage. But research in orality studies since the 1960s have shown that oral traditions do not follow linear, unidirectional "laws" (as the literary paradigm thought), but rather follow far more complex, multidirectional paths. Oral variations depend on the performance situation itself—and every performance is, to one degree or another, different from the next.[29]

(2) The second tool Bultmann used in tracking the oral stage of the Gospels was to identify the original, pure type of form of literature, whether pronouncement story, apocalyptic saying, parable, etc. Proceeding back in time before the writing of the Gospels and identifying the original, pure oral form created by the community allowed Bultmann then to sort out the later secondary accretions. But what may be true of written texts is not true of oral traditions. Within two decades of the publication of Bultmann's *History of the Synoptic Tradition*, Milman Parry and A. B. Lord were already providing evidence from field studies demonstrating that no inherent connection can be made in oral traditions between the length and complexity of a form, on the one hand, and how early or late it was, on the other.[30] A corollary of this finding is that no longer can scholars be confident that in identifying the "original, pure" form of the Synoptic material they have discovered the situation in life of the community supposedly producing that form.

(3) We must now also seriously question Bultmann's third tool, that there were universal laws of oral transmission. Bultmann's approach to the development of oral tradition was based on Herman Gunkel's application of form criticism to the Old Testament, especially in his 1901 commentary on Genesis.[31] That, in turn, was rooted in Axel Olrik's understanding of oral tradition, particularly as he analyzed Danish ballads and Danish and

---

29. See L. Marander-Eklund, "Variation in Repeated Interviews: Stories of Childbirth," in *Thick Corpus*, 432; quoted in Eddy and Boyd, *The Jesus Legend*, 297. This observation applies to a wider oral context.

30. Milman Parry, *The Making of Homeric Verse: The Collected Papers of Milman Parry*, ed. M. Parry (Oxford: Clarendon, 1971); A. B. Lord, "The Gospels as Oral Traditional Literature," in *The Relationships among the Gospels: An Interdisciplinary Dialogue*, ed. W. O. Walker (San Antonio,TX: Trinity University Press, 1978). Lord wrote, "Given the nature of oral traditional composition and transmission . . . [it] does not in any way necessarily follow that the shortest is the oldest and the longest the latest or that the crudest is the oldest and the most polished the latest" (53). E. P. Sanders' dissertation confirmed that the Synoptic material did not necessarily grow in length (*Tendencies of the Synoptic Tradition* [New York: Cambridge University Press, 1969], 273–74).

31. H. Gunkel, *Genesis*, HKAT 1/1, 6th ed. (Göttingen: Vandenhoeck & Ruprecht, 1963); idem, *The Legends of Genesis*, trans. W. H. Carruth (New York: Schocken, 1964).

Icelandic sagas.[32] But Olrik's findings have been submitted to criticism because he generalized "laws" of oral tradition for all cultures even though his research was restricted to only one local field.[33] And such a stricture applies as well to Bultmann's universal "laws" of the development of oral tradition. Because the sample field today is much more extensive than it was in the past, and because folklorists utilize recording devices that allow much more detailed analysis of oral performances than was previously possible, experts in the subject now know that variations in oral performances do not conform to "laws of development" but are usually the result of contextual adaptation and/or spontaneous creativity.

We conclude this overall point by noting that rather recent findings have seriously called into question the three tools of Bultmann's agenda of postulating "universal laws" of the development of oral tradition in the Gospels. The tie that binds such criticisms of Bultmann is that oral performances vary according to audience and purpose and therefore may not be generalized into one category.

6. Prophetic Inspiration and Jesus' Sayings

Bultmann proposed the thesis that the early church drew no distinction between prophetic utterances by Christian prophets and the sayings of Jesus in the gospel traditions. That is to say, the early church prophets—inspired by the Spirit of the risen Christ—freely created material that was eventually retrojected onto the Jesus of history.[34] Eugene Boring later provided the definitive defense of the "creative-prophets thesis."[35] Of the many criticisms that have been leveled against this thesis here, we observe that if it is true that early church prophets regularly spoke with the voice of the risen Jesus to address issues the church was facing, and if these sayings were eventually retroactively placed into the mouth of earthly Jesus, then we should expect to find many of those questions the early church faced being addressed by Jesus in the Gospels. But this is precisely what one does not find. Thus, the issue of whether Gentiles who accepted Christ needed to also be circumcised (Acts 15; Galatians; Romans; Philippians 3) is not mentioned in Jesus' teachings in the Gospels. Nor is the issue of *glossolalia* (speaking in tongues) in the Gospels. Neither are the issues of church polity or the role of women in

---

32. A. Olrik's "Epic Laws" was translated into German in 1909 and was utilized by Gunkel in his Genesis commentary. For Olrik's larger work, see his, *Principles for Oral Narrative Research*, trans. K. Wolf and J. Jensen (Bloomington: Indiana University Press, 1992).
33. See B. Holbeck's comments in his "Introduction" to Olrik's, *Principles for Oral Narrative Research*, xxii–iii.
34. Bultmann, *The History of the Synoptic Tradition*, 127.
35. Eugene Boring, *Sayings of the Risen Jesus: Christian Prophecy in the Synoptic Tradition* (New York: Cambridge University Press, 1982); revised as *The Continuing Voice of Jesus* (Louisville: Westminster/Knox, 1991).

worship or eating food dedicated to idols included in the Gospels. If prophets were speaking on behalf of the risen Jesus to the early church on particular matters plaguing the local congregations, then their absence in the Gospels is most puzzling.[36]

Conclusion

This question has been devoted to critiquing the six major planks of the assumption of Bultmann and his followers—that oral tradition significantly changed the Jesus of history into the Christ of faith that we find in the Gospels. But the most recent research available as applied to the aforementioned six planks of argumentation has begged to disagree, rightly claiming that the two—Jesus of history and Christ of faith—are one and the same; this owing to the reliability of the oral tradition that informs our canonical text.

REFLECTION QUESTIONS

1. What was the relationship between written material and oral tradition between the life of Jesus and the writing down of the four gospels?

2. How would you respond to those who maintain that the Gospels do not form a coherent narrative?

3. Who were some of the reliable witnesses to the historical Jesus?

4. How would you correct the radical critics of the Gospels who say there were hard and fast laws of the oral and written traditions about the historical Jesus?

5. What issues in the life of the church would be expected to have surfaced in the supposed statements by the risen Jesus, which were confused with his statements on earth?

---

36. For the other criticisms see Eddy and Boyd, *The Jesus Legend*, 298–305.

What Does the NT (Outside the Gospels) Teach About Jesus' Life and Teaching?

When it comes to the New Testament's usage of the Gospels concerning the historical Jesus, a certain phenomenon meets the reader, namely, while the Pauline and non-Pauline literature make numerous allusions to the Jesus tradition, they actually quote or cite that material only occasionally. Why is this? We will answer that question at the end of our investigation in this chapter. First, this chapter will summarize the New Testament reliance upon the Gospels. We examine the Pauline letters in this regard, after which we look at the non-Pauline letters' usage of the Jesus tradition.

Pauline Literature and the Gospels

Here we summarize Paul's reliance on the Jesus tradition under two categories: the life of Jesus and the teaching of Jesus. The apostle Paul wrote his letters before the canonical gospels were written down (i.e., during the "oral" period). Consequently, we should not expect to necessarily find agreement in exact wording between the two bodies of materials—Paul's letters and the canonical gospels. Nevertheless, we remember from our previous question that both corpuses can be fully trusted for their historical reliability.

Paul on the Life of Jesus

In this section we conveniently categorize Paul's usage of the life of Jesus material as presupposed in the canonical gospels under four topics: (1) Jesus' life, (2) Jesus' miracles, (3) Jesus' death and resurrection, and (4) Jesus' return.

Jesus' Life. Paul gives evidence in his writings that he knew a significant amount of detail concerning the life of Jesus.[1] Consider the following allusions to the Jesus of history:

> He knew Jesus was born and raised as a Jew (Gal. 4:4) and that he was a descendant of Abraham and David (Gal. 3:16; Rom. 1:3). Paul knew Jesus had a brother named James (Gal. 1:19) and perhaps other brothers as well (1 Cor. 9:5). He knew by name a number of disciples who ministered with Jesus, and he knew that Jesus' disciple Peter was married (1 Cor. 9:5). Paul also knew that Jesus was betrayed (1 Cor. 11:23) and that he was executed by crucifixion (1 Cor. 1:17–18; Gal. 5:11; 6:12; Phil. 2:8; 3:18) with the help of certain Judean Jews (1 Thess. 2:14–15). Paul was aware that Jesus instituted a memorial meal the night before his death (1 Cor. 11:23–25), and that Jesus was buried after his death and was resurrected three days later, a fact he refers to frequently and places a great deal of weight on (Rom. 4:24–25; 1 Cor. 15:4–8; cf. Rom. 6:4–9; 8:11, 34; 1 Cor. 6:14; 2 Cor. 4:14; Gal. 1:1; 1 Thess. 4:14). . . in a first-century Jewish context this affirmation inherently implies the resurrection of a physical body in a historical sense. Moreover, Paul knew that Jesus's earthly life was characterized by meekness, gentleness, self-sacrificial love, and humble service (2 Cor. 10:1; Phil. 2:5–7). Paul's central passion was to know and be conformed to Jesus Christ (Phil. 3:8–10), and he consistently held up Jesus's life—and his own life as modeled on Jesus' life—as examples to be emulated (1 Cor. 11:1). In this light, it cannot be regarded as a coincidence that Paul's own thought, attitude, and conduct paralleled closely what we find in the Jesus of the Gospels. Nor can it be considered a coincidence that Paul's healing ministry, his welcoming of sinners, his life of poverty, and humble service closely paralleled Jesus' life and ministry as recorded in the Gospels. Paul practiced what he preached, and at the foundation of what he preached was a body of knowledge about the ministry and character of the Lord he served.[2]

Jesus' Miracles. Although Paul does not mention the miracles of Jesus per se, he does allude to them as a reflection of the power of God in his own

---

1. We hold that Paul wrote all thirteen letters attributed to him. See my defense in *The End of the Age Has Come: The Theology of Paul* (Grand Rapids: Zondervan, 1995), 34–40.
2. For these references, see Boyd and Eddy, *The Jesus Legend*, 209–10.

apostolic ministry. Here we rightly merge two concepts in the ministries of Jesus and Paul—miracles as a demonstration that the kingdom of God is present. This is transparent in the first written gospel. Mark 1:14–15 reports that Jesus announced the arrival of the kingdom of God in his ministry which is then connected to his miracles in Mark 1:21–3:6. Luke 11:20 makes explicit the association of the kingdom of God and miracles. Paul too speaks of the kingdom of God (see Rom. 14:17; 1 Cor. 4:20; 6:9–10; 15:24, 50; Gal. 5:21; Eph. 5:5; Col. 1:13; 4:11; 1 Thess. 2:2; and 2 Thess. 1:5). First Corinthians 4:20 explicitly ties the kingdom of God to power (miracles). And in Romans 15:18–19 Paul claims that Christ is working through Paul apostolic signs and wonders via the power of the Spirit (cf. Gal. 3:5; 1 Cor. 2:4; 2 Cor. 12:12; 1 Thess. 1:5). Taking these passages together permits us to say that Paul alludes to the miracles of Jesus.

Jesus' Death and Resurrection. Paul mentions the death and resurrection of Jesus quite often (Rom. 1:3–4; 3:21–25; 4:24–25; Gal. 1:1–3; 6:14; 1 Cor. 2:8; 15; 2 Cor. 5:14–15; 1 Thess. 4:14; Eph. 1:20–22; 1 Tim. 3:16; 2 Tim. 1:10; 2:8; Titus 2:11–14). For the apostle, the death/resurrection complex was the point in time when the age to come broke into this present age.

Jesus' Return. Paul draws upon the eschatological discourse of Jesus' return (the Olivet Discourse: Mark 13; Matt. 24/Luke 21) in 1 Thessalonians 4–5; 2 Thessalonians 2. Using Matthew 24 as a frame of reference we provide a chart containing the parallels with Paul's statements regarding the signs of the times of the parousia:[3]

OLIVET DISCOURSE (MATTHEW)	EVENT	PAUL
24:5	Warning about deception	2 Thessalonians 2:2
24:5, 11, 24	Lawlessness, delusion of the non-elect, signs and wonders	2 Thessalonians 2:6–11
24:12	Apostasy	2 Thessalonians 2:3
24:15	Antichrist in the temple	2 Thessalonians 2:4
24:21–22	Tribulation preceding the end	2 Thessalonians 1:6–10
24:30–31	Parousia of Christ, on clouds, at the time of a trumpet blast, with angelic accompaniment	1 Thessalonians 4:14–16
24:30–31	In power	2 Thessalonians 2:8

---

3. See Douglas Moo, in *The Rapture: Pre-, Mid-, or Post-Tribulational?* Gleason L. Archer, et. al (Grand Rapids: Zondervan, 1984), 194. David Wenham has made a compelling case that Paul utilizes a pre-canonical form of the Olivet Discourse; see his *Gospel Perspectives 4: The Rediscovery of Jesus' Eschatological Discourse* (Sheffield: JSOT, 1984).

OLIVET DISCOURSE (MATTHEW)	EVENT	PAUL
24:31	Gathering of believers	1 Thessalonians 4:16 2 Thessalonians 2:1
24:36, 42, 44, 50; 25:13	Unexpected and uncertain	1 Thessalonians 5:1–4
24:42–25:13	Exhortation to watch!	1 Thessalonians 5:6–8

Paul and the Teachings of Jesus

Following Seyoon Kim, we will divide the instances of Jesus' teaching in the Pauline material into two broad categories: certain/probable references and possible echoes. The first category includes Jesus' teaching on everything from divorce to the Lord's Supper to relating to government. The second category includes things like calling God "Abba," not judging others, and love of one's neighbor.[4]

Conclusion

In the past it was often said that Paul had no interest in the historical Jesus, but in this section we have seen that such a statement is grossly misinformed, for Paul alludes heavily to Jesus' life and teachings. But why then does Paul not explicitly quote the Jesus tradition? We will return to this question after examining the non-Pauline dependence on the gospel tradition.

Non-Pauline Letters and the Gospels

Now we turn our attention to the Gospels and the non-Pauline New Testament. What does this literature tell us about Jesus' life and teaching? We examine Acts, Hebrews, James, the Petrine letters, the epistles of John, Jude, and Revelation.

Acts

The most obvious material regarding the Jesus tradition that we find in Acts is the gospel of Luke (Luke's first work of his two-volume set—Luke–Acts) and Mark (behind which one can detect the voice of Peter, as we discussed earlier). The latter of these as utilized in Acts focuses upon the life of Jesus, while the former of these as found in Acts emphasizes the teaching of

---

4. See Kim's many references on this subject in the article below. Earlier we noted the occurrences of the kingdom of God in both Paul and Jesus, something Seyoon Kim also points out in the article we are following here, "Sayings of Jesus" in *DJG*, ed. Gerald F. Hawthorne, Ralph P. Martin, and Daniel G. Reid (Downers Grove, IL/Leicester, England, 1993), 474–92. David Wenham's book is an excellent work on Paul's usage of the Jesus tradition, *Paul: Follower of Jesus or Founder of Christianity?* (Grand Rapids/Cambridge: Eerdmans/University Press, 1995).

Jesus. We begin with the Markan material in Acts and then turn to the impact of the third gospel upon Acts.

1. Mark, the Speeches of Peter in Acts, and the Life of Jesus. Since C. H. Dodd's masterful treatment of the *kērygma* (the preaching of the early church) in Acts, it has been commonplace in New Testament studies to see in Peter's speeches in Acts the basic outline of the Jesus tradition as found in the Synoptic gospels.[5] We can do no better than to summarize Dodd's findings in this regards:

- First, the age of fulfillment has dawned.
- Secondly, this has taken place through the ministry, death, and resurrection of Jesus.
- Thirdly, by virtue of the resurrection, Jesus has been exalted at the right hand of God, as messianic head of the new Israel.
- Fourthly, the Holy Spirit in the Church is the sign of Christ's present power and glory
- Fifthly, the messianic age will shortly reach its consummation in the return of Christ.
- Finally, the *kērygma* always closes with an appeal for repentance, the offer of forgiveness and of the Holy Spirit, and the promise of "salvation," that is, of "the life of the Age to Come," to those who enter the elect community.

Moreover, Dodd argued that the basic outline of the *kērygma* as culled in Peter's speeches matches Mark 1:14–15, the summary statement of the preaching of the historical Jesus. Dodd writes of this:

> We may take it that this is what the author of Acts meant by "preaching the Kingdom of God." It is very significant that it follows the lines of the summary of the preaching of Jesus as given in Mark i.14–15: "Jesus came into Galilee preaching the gospel of God, and saying, 'The time is fulfilled, and the Kingdom of God has drawn near: repent and believe the gospel.'" This summary provides the framework within which the Jerusalem *kerygma* is set.[6]

Indeed, William Lane went on to argue that the outline of Mark is compressed in Peter's sermon in Acts 10:36–41.[7] Thus, we may say that the speeches of Peter in Acts as they are rooted in the gospel of Mark essentially

---

5. C. H. Dodd, *According to the Scriptures: The Sub-Structure of New Testament Theology* (London: Nisbet, 1952).
6. C. H. Dodd, "The Framework of the Gospel Narrative," in *New Testament Studies* 1 (Manchester: Manchester University, 1953), 396–400.
7. William L. Lane, *The Gospel According to* Mark (Grand Rapids: Eerdmans, 1974), 10–11.

present us with the life of Jesus, in particular that in his life, works, death, and resurrection the kingdom of God dawned.

2. *Luke, the Speeches of Paul in Acts, and the Teaching of Jesus.* While Luke no doubt utilizes Mark as one of his main sources in reporting the life of Christ (probably along with Q and Luke's special material), the third gospel accentuates a theme present in Mark but not as clearly stated as it is in the third gospel, namely, the teaching that the Old Testament predicts that the Messiah would first suffer and then be raised into his glory (Luke 2:34–35; 9:18–22, 44; 18:31–33; 22:14–22, 66–70; 24:26–27, 45–47). This Old Testament teaching of a coming suffering and resurrected Messiah is highlighted in Acts especially in Paul's speeches therein (Acts 13:16–41; 17:2–3; 26:22–23; 28:23–31; cf. 1:3–4; 8:32–35).[8]

Hebrews

The inspired author of Hebrews does not make much use of the Jesus tradition, but still one can identify allusions in Hebrews to the life and teaching of Jesus. A chart nicely illustrates the point:

	LIFE OF JESUS	SAYINGS/TEACHINGS OF JESUS
Incarnation	Hebrews 2:13	Hebrews 10:5–6
From Tribe of Judah	Hebrews 7:14	
Tested in wilderness	Hebrews 4:15	
Gethsemane	Hebrews 2:10; 5:7–9	
Crucifixion	Hebrews 13:12	
Exaltation		Hebrews 2:12

James

In James, one finds that the life and teachings of Jesus overlap. This connection between James and Jesus should not occasion surprise since James was the brother of Jesus (see James 1:1; Matt. 13:55; Mark 6:3; John 7:3–10; Acts 1:14; 1 Cor. 9:5; Gal. 1:19). Peter Davids has compiled a list of twenty-eight connections in James originating in Jesus' Sermon on the Mount and having to do with righteous suffering as proof one is in the kingdom of God. One can see from all of this that Jesus' life serves as the basis of James' teachings:

---

8. The speeches of Paul in Acts presume the Markan outline of the life of Jesus but add the new element of the teaching of Jesus' suffering and glory as predicted in the Old Testament. The commentaries do not seem to have noticed the above two-fold influence on Acts, namely, Mark informs Peter's speeches while Luke imprints Paul's speeches. Moreover, the deuteronomic tradition is also at work in the speeches of Acts, including Paul's; see my forthcoming commentary on Acts.

believers are to follow their Lord in his path of suffering which in turn gains them entrance into the Kingdom of God.[9]

1 Peter

Robert Gundry provides a list of proposed allusions to the Gospels in 1 Peter.[10] What we may say concerning Gundry's references is that 1 Peter, like James, also draws on the Sermon on the Mount and other of Jesus' sayings regarding the suffering of the righteous as the prerequisite for entering the kingdom of God.

In addition to the preceding observation we may call attention to other echoes of the Gospels in 1 Peter: Peter is one of the twelve apostles (1:1); Jesus was raised from the dead (1:3); Jesus will return (1:7); Jesus died, descended into Hades to announce judgment on the fallen angels,[11] and ascended into heaven (3:18–22).

2 Peter

There are not many references or allusions to the Gospels in 2 Peter. We list them below: Peter is one of the twelve apostles (1:1); the believer will enter into the kingdom of God (cf. the message of Jesus regarding the Kingdom of God) (1:11); Peter will soon die (1:14; cf. John 21:18–19); Peter was a witness of the transfiguration of Jesus (1:16–18; cf. Matt. 17:1–13; Mark 9:1–13; Luke 9:28–36); the latter fate of the one who commits apostasy is worse than his former state (2:20; cf. Matt. 12:45); the return of the Lord will be as a thief in the night (3:10; cf. Matt. 24:43; Luke 12:39; 1 Thess. 5:2). Even though these echoes to the gospel tradition are few, they nevertheless give evidence of the overlapping of the life and the teachings of Jesus.

Jude

The reference in v. 1 to James as Jude's brother indicates that Jude too is a brother of Jesus (recall the passages above listed for James). Beyond this there is only one possible allusion to the Gospels and that is vv. 17–18, which may allude to Matthew 24:10–12 and Jesus' prophecy of the coming eschatological apostasy, which Jude believes is being fulfilled in his day.

The Epistles of John

Here we can do no better than to turn to Raymond Brown's magisterial study on the epistles of John. There Brown makes two important contributions

---

9. Peter H. Davids, *The Epistle of James: A Commentary on the Greek Text,* NIGTC (Grand Rapids: Eerdmans, 1982). His charts are on 47–48.

10. Robert H. Gundry, "*Verba Christi* In 1 Peter," *NTS* (1966): 336–50 and "Further *Verba* on *Verba Christi* in First Peter," in *Biblica* 55 (1974): 211–32.

11. We will cover this much debated passage in a later question.

to the subject of the relationship of the epistles of John to the gospel of John. First, Brown outlines 1 John on the basis of the gospel of John:[12]

GOSPEL OF JOHN	1 JOHN
A. Prologue: 1:1–18 The word that was from the beginning entered the world in Christ.	A. Prologue: 1:1–4 Christ who was from the beginning was manifested to the disciples.
B. The Book of Signs: 1:19–12:50 The light shined in the darkness of Judaism but was rejected.	B. Part 1: 1:5–3:10 God is light, and like Jesus, we must walk in the light.
C. The Book of Glory: 13:1–20:29 Jesus cares for and loves his own (believers in him).	C. Part 2: 3:11–5:12 God is love, and those who know him must love one another.
D. Conclusion: 20:30–31 The purpose is to bring people to faith in Jesus the Christ, the Son of God.	D. Conclusion: 5:13–21 The purpose is to bring people to faith in Jesus the Christ, the Son of God.

Second, from Brown's extensive lists of parallels among the epistles of John and the fourth gospel what emerges is that the epistles of John draw both upon the life and the teachings of Jesus as presented in the gospel of John. Regarding the former of these, the epistles of John stress the historical reality of Jesus to make the point against the docetist opponents that Jesus was fully divine and fully human. And the latter theme—the teachings of Jesus in John—are adapted in the epistles of John to reinforce the fact that Jesus Christ has come in the flesh. Another way to put it is that the epistles of John rework the themes of light and love in the gospel of John to the effect that in the epistles of John, light means believing that Jesus Christ has come in the flesh and love means caring for true believers, that is, those who confess that Jesus Christ has come in the flesh.[13]

Revelation

Mark Wilson has provided a detailed list of the parallels between Revelation and the Gospels and Paul.[14] It is clear from these parallels that Revelation is the fulfillment of Jesus' predictions in the Olivet Discourse regarding his second coming to earth. The suffering servant is now the conquering lamb of God; his afflictions have given way to glory. Moreover, Jesus'

---

12. Raymond E. Brown, *The Epistles of John*, AB 30 (Garden City, NY: Doubleday, 1982), 124.
13. For these lists, see ibid, 755–59.
14. Mark Wilson, *Charts on the Book of Revelation: Literary, Historical, and Theological Perspectives* (Grand Rapids: Kregel, 2007), 36–39.

followers must also suffer for their faith in Christ if they are to experience his glory at the parousia. Another theme that emerges from comparing the gospel of John and Revelation is a literary one, namely, the numerous topics that connect these two books suggests that the author of the one (gospel of John) is the author of the other (Revelation), something many modern interpreters have overlooked in discussing the authorship of Revelation. In other words, the apostle John who wrote the fourth gospel seems to be the author of Revelation.

Conclusion

We are now in a position to answer the question that began this chapter: Why do the New Testament authors outside the Gospels frequently allude to the Jesus tradition but do not directly quote it that often? To be more specific, two pieces of data have surfaced in this chapter which, on first consideration, appear to be in contradiction. First, it is a fact that non-gospel authors of the New Testament draw frequently on the Jesus tradition, some two hundred times if our count is roughly accurate. Moreover, the usage of the Jesus tradition by Pauline literature and non-Pauline literature alike covers both the life and the teachings of Jesus. But, second, despite drawing heavily upon the Jesus tradition, the non-gospel authors predominantly prefer to allude to or echo the Jesus tradition rather directly quote it. This is true for New Testament material written before the Jesus tradition took canonical shape (the Pauline literature), that is the oral stage of the Gospels, during the writing down of the Gospels (Hebrews, James, 1, 2 Peter, Jude) and after the completion of the written process of the four gospels (the epistles of John and Revelation).

So, what accounts for this? Two explanations have been proposed, to which we would like to add a third. (1) Recent oral studies have identified the notion of "traditional referentiality" as a part of the reason for the above phenomenon. Thus, Homeric scholar John Miles Foley has noted that oral traditions typically allude to their histories with dense idiomatic expression that their audiences are well equipped to recognize.[15] Dale Allison applies this to the Bible in general when he observes that "much of the Bible is fundamentally elliptical. It says much in few words, in words that point beyond themselves, for the canonical writings are literature of inheritance, being deliberately interactive and full of allusive reciprocal discourse."[16] This would certainly pertain to the New Testament's usage of the Jesus tradition.[17] (2) What Michael Thompson says of Paul's allusions to the Jesus tradition applies equally as well to the non-Pauline New Testament. He argues that Paul's lack of citation of the Jesus tradition is

---

15. J. M. Foley, "What's in a Sign?" in *Signs of Orality: The Oral Tradition and Its Influence in the Greek and Roman World*, ed. A. E. MacKay (Boston: Brill, 1991).
16. Dale Allison, "Scriptural Allusions", 4, quoted in Boyd and Eddy, *The Jesus Legend*, 231.
17. Boyd and Eddy so argue in *The Jesus Legend,* 230–31.

readily understood if we keep in mind that the purpose of Paul's letters was primarily exhortation, not argumentation. "Where argument ceased and exhortation began, apostles had little need to cite sources."[18] Kim agrees, "In paraenesis, unlike in theological argument, one normally does not prove the truth of one's teaching, and so it is not required to cite its sources."[19] (3) To these suggestions we add a third, namely, reverence for Jesus explains both points of the aforementioned anomaly. Thus, the non-gospel New Testament authors make much use of the Jesus tradition because they obviously consider him to be the founder of Christianity and thus worth often mentioning it. Moreover, precisely because those inspired authors considered Jesus to be God, and not mere mortals like them, it was only with hesitancy that they actually quoted his sayings. One is reminded in this of how ancient Jews did not pronounce the name of Yahweh out of their reverence for God. And so it may well have been because of reverence for Jesus that the non-gospel New Testament authors make much of the Jesus tradition yet without often citing it verbatim.

REFLECTION QUESTIONS

1. What four areas of the historical Jesus does Paul touch upon?

2. What are the six components of the *kērygma* that occur in Acts?

3. What are the allusions to the historical Jesus in Hebrews?

4. How much does James draw on the Sermon on the Mount?

5. Why do the epistles of John draw heavily on the life of Jesus?

---

18. Michael Thompson, *Clothed with Christ: The Examples and Teaching of Jesus in Romans 12:1–15:13* (Sheffield: Sheffield Academic Press, 1991), 71.
19. Kim, "Sayings of Jesus," 489.

What Do We Learn About the Historical Jesus from Archaeology?

The question with which this chapter is concerned is, does archaeology teach us something about the historical Jesus. In other words, does archaeology confirm the Gospels' portraits of the Jesus of history? Our answer to the question is, "yes it does." So this chapter will summarize the key archaeological sites, inscriptions, etc. that tell us something about the historical Jesus. Here the problem is selecting the historical sites most connected to Jesus. We will proceed by classifying those places under four headings: (1) the birth and boyhood of Jesus, (2) the inauguration of Jesus' public ministry, (3) Jesus' public ministry, especially in Galilee, and (4) Jesus' ministry and last days in Jerusalem.

The Birth and Boyhood of Jesus

Two places occupy our attention under this point: Bethlehem and Nazareth.

Bethlehem

The place where Jesus was born has never been seriously disputed (Matt. 2:1; Luke 2:4). Jerome provides evidence that the cave in Bethlehem, under the present Church of the Nativity, was identified as the birthplace before the time of Emperor Hadrian (117–38).[1] Hadrian marked the site by planting a grove of trees there in honor of the Roman god Adonis. In the fourth century, Eusebius wrote that Emperor Constantine and his mother Helena built a church over the cave, adorning the place with lavish magnificence.[2] Excavations in Bethlehem in 1934 by William Harvey, and in 1948 to 1951 by

---

1. Jerome, Letter 58 "To Paulinus."
2. Eusebius, *Life of Constantine* 3.43.

the Franciscan Custody of the Holy Land unearthed the foundations of the Constantinian church.

Nazareth

Nazareth was the birthplace of Mary, Jesus' mother (Luke 1:26–27; cf. Matt. 2:23) and, after the holy family returned from Egypt, became the place of Jesus' boyhood (Luke 4:16). Later, during Jesus' public ministry he was expelled from the city, and his hometown even tried to kill him by throwing him off of a cliff. The precipice of the hill on which Nazareth was built has been confirmed archaeologically to be on the west side of the present-day Church of the Annunciation. Nazareth is located in the southern end of the hills of Lower Galilee at 1,200 feet above sea level.

The Inauguration of Jesus' Public Ministry

Here we examine the two key sites associated with the inauguration of Jesus' public ministry: His baptism by John the Baptist in the Jordan River and his temptations in the Judean Desert and at the Temple.

The Jordan River

According to Matthew 3:13–17, Jesus was baptized by John the Baptist at the Jordan River where it forms the eastern border (cf. Mark 1:4–5) of the desert of Judea (Matt. 3:1). The Judean Desert stretches some twenty miles from the Jerusalem-Bethlehem plateau down to the Jordan River and the Dead Sea. More specifically, the baptism of Jesus seems to have occurred between the mouth of the Wadi Farah and the site where the Jordan enters the Dead Sea, precisely in the environs of Qumran.

Jesus' Temptation in the Judean Desert and at the Temple

After his baptism, Jesus was taken into the wilderness to be tempted by Satan (Matt. 4:1; Mark 1:12–13; Luke 4:1–2). The traditional site of Jesus' temptations is the Judean Wilderness, as we described above. On top of the most imposing peak of these hills, are the walls and foundations of an unfinished church, which was evidently planned to replace the Byzantine church whose ruins stand on the summit. This hill is known by its Arabic name, *Jebel Quarantal* ("Mount of the Forty"), recalling the forty days of temptation Jesus endured there; however, the exact location of the temptation cannot be determined.

One of the three temptations of Jesus took place at the pinnacle of the Temple in Jerusalem (Matt. 4:5; Luke 4:9). This is the southeast corner of the Temple Mount, perhaps the Royal Porch's southeast corner, which stood on the Temple platform during Jesus' time. The pinnacle was probably either the corner of the building that stood on the platform or the corner of the retaining wall itself. The present platform of the Temple Mount cannot be the one involved in the gospel account because the platform of Herod's Temple was destroyed by the Romans in AD 70.

Jesus' Public Ministry

At Jesus' baptism, God the father set his seal of approval upon his son and anointed him with the Holy Spirit for his public ministry. After demonstrating his obedience to God in the Judean Desert, Jesus then began his public ministry. Numerous sites in Galilee especially call for comment here. But before discussing those, we first look briefly at Jesus' foray into Samaria.

Jacob's Well and Sychar

There is little recorded activity of Jesus in Samaria, given the hostility that existed between Jews and Samaritans. But Jesus did stop to converse with a woman from Sychar who was drawing water from Jacob's well. Jacob's Well is located in the eastern part of modern Nablus. The depth of the well has changed through the years as debris has accumulated in it. Moreover, one church has replaced the other in housing it—first Byzantine, then Crusader, and today the Greek Orthodox Church is building a new church over the site. But there is no doubt as to the authenticity of the well. Sychar, the woman's hometown, is located a half-mile north of the well, on the southern slopes of Mount Ebal; today it is called "Askar." Jesus mentioned the worship of the Samaritans in his conversation with the woman at Jacob's well (John 4:20), which refers to the Samaritan temple, the ruins of which are located not far from the area, on a northern spur of Mount Gerizim. The Samaritan temple was destroyed by the Hasmoneans.

Galilee

Under this category we cover Cana, the Sea of Galilee, Capernaum, Gergesa, Bethsaida, and Caesarea Philippi.

Cana. John 2:1–11 records that Jesus performed his first miracle in Cana of Galilee. The modern city named Kefr Kenna, Arabic for "City of Cana," does not seem to be the village in which Jesus changed water into wine. Rather, the recent excavations of Peter Richardson and Douglas Edwards have more likely identified Khirbet Qana as the place of the biblical Cana. This village sits on a hill on the north side of the Beth Netofa Valley at the Wadi Yodefat, and in sight of Nazareth. The town peaked during the early Roman and Byzantine periods. During Jesus' time it was without walls.

The Sea of Galilee. The Sea of Galilee provided the heart of the economy of Galilee: the salted fishing industry at Tarichaeae which made the export of fish possible on a wide scale, the grain industry (but which was mostly dominated by the imperial establishment), farming, and the easy access to various regions surrounding Galilee that the lake provided thus better facilitating exports.[3] Indeed, the "Jesus boat" reinforces the impression that the Sea of Galilee stimulated a thriving economy in the first century. The boat was found in 1986 by two brothers near Kibbutz Ginosar. It was built in the first century AD and was used until sometime around AD 70. It is 26.5 feet long, 7.5 feet wide and 4.5 feet high. The Jesus boat would have accommodated about fifteen fishermen. Originally it had a mast for sailing and two oars on each side.

Capernaum. Capernaum (*Tell Hum,* located on the north shore of the Sea of Galilee just west of the Jordan River), became the place of Jesus' residence for a time at the beginning of his public ministry in Galilee. Josephus refers to Capernaum (*Jewish Wars* 3.10.8; *Life* 72). An imperial road passed nearby. Perhaps the toll booth there (Mark 2:14) for taxing fishermen was manned by Matthew Levi. The large village of some fifteen hundred residents consisted of individual living quarters containing large families. Of particular archaeological interest in Capernaum are the synagogue remains and Peter's house. Concerning the synagogue remains, a debate once raged as to its date. At first, scholars thought that the limestone remains dated to the first century, but upon further review that synagogue structure was dated to the fourth or fifth century. But since 1975, archaeologists have discovered black basalt walls under the walls of the surface structure, along with a basalt cobblestone floor and pottery, all of which date to the time of Jesus. There is little doubt this is the synagogue built by a Roman centurion and in which Jesus preached (Luke 7:1–5; cf. Mark 1:21–29).[4]

Just across the way, eighty-four feet from the synagogue in Capernaum, is a Byzantine octagonal building with mosaic floors that stands in partial remains. After excavating those remains from 1968 to 1985, two Franciscan fathers, V. Corbo and S. Loffreda, claimed that they had discovered Peter's house.[5]

Gergesa. Gergesa (*El Kersi*) is located nine miles southeast of Capernaum on the east side of the Sea of Galilee. This is most likely the site where Jesus cast out the demons in a man into a herd of swine (Matt. 8:28; Mark 5:1; Luke 8:26). The remains of a Byzantine church were uncovered in 1970, three hundred yards from *El Kersi.* Nearby, lies a small bay of a well-constructed harbor. John McRay notes that the location of the town on the eastern side of the Sea of Galilee and the fact that Gergesa is the only town on the east side of the lake that has a steep bank coming out to the sea, not to mention the tombs nearby, match the biblical description of the demoniac episode.[6]

Bethsaida. Modern tourists are told that Jesus fed the multitudes at Tabgha on the west side of the Sea of Galilee where, in 1932, archaeologists

---

3. Sean Fryene, *Galilee, Jesus, and the Gospels: Literary Approaches and Historical Investigations* (Philadelphia: Fortress, 1988), 161–63.
4. See John McRay, *Archaeology and the New Testament* (Grand Rapids: Baker, 1991), 164–65.
5. V. Corbo, and S. Loffreday, *Cafarnao,* Studium Biblicum Franciscanum 19 (Jerusalem: Franciscan Printing Press, 1974).
6. McRay, *Archaeology and the New Testament,* 166–67.

discovered a fifth-century church. Yet, subsequent excavations have demonstrated that no earlier construction ever existed at that spot. Rather most scholars today locate Bethsaida on the eastern side of the Sea of Galilee primarily because that town matches the Gospels' account. Thus, Jesus fed the multitudes in Bethsaida (Luke 9:10) after which Jesus had the disciples go over to the other side (Matt. 14:22; Mark 6:45) to Gennesaret (on the west side of the lake; see Matt. 14:34; Mark 6:53).

Caesarea Philippi. The northernmost town in Galilee visited by Jesus was Caesarea Philippi. It is distinguished from Caesarea on the Sea by Josephus (*Jewish Wars* 3.9.7; 7.2.1). In Caesarea Philippi, Simon Peter made the confession of Jesus as the Christ, the Son of the living God (Matt. 16:13–20; cf. Mark 8:27–30 and Luke 9:18–21). The city was built by Philip, one of the sons of Herod the Great, who obviously named it after himself and Caesar. Josephus says that "Philip built Caesarea near the sources of the Jordan, in the district of Paneas" (*Jewish Wars* 2.9.1). In another place, he says that Philip "made improvements at Paneas" (*Antiquities of the Jews* 18.2.1). This reference is to a cave, located in the mountains due east of Dan, with a deep pool below it. Josephus calls the area "Panion" or "Paneion" (*Jewish Wars* 3.10.7; *Antiquities of the Jews* 15.10.3). The cave was sacred to the Roman god Pan, the god of the forest, whose name is preserved in an inscription beneath one of three niches cut into the stone mountain. A statue of the god stood in the niches; the words "to Pan and the Nymphs" are still discernible in the tabula ansata beneath the niche nearest the huge cave.[7] Thus, for Peter to have confessed Jesus to be the Messiah, the Son of the living God would have opposed the local worship of Pan and Caesar. We may also note that since Mount Hermon is just north of Caesarea that that may have been the location of the transfiguration of Jesus, which is recorded immediately after Peter's confession (Matt. 17:1–13; Mark 9:2–13; Luke 9:28–36).

Jesus' Ministry and Last Days in Jerusalem

In this last section we divide Jesus' time in Jerusalem into two categories: His ministry in Jerusalem and his last days in Jerusalem.

Jesus' Ministry in Jerusalem

Here we will briefly describe two key sites in Jerusalem connected with Jesus' miracles.

The Pool of Bethesda. The gospel of John records one of Jesus' visits to Jerusalem. At one of the festivals Jesus healed an invalid at the Pool of Bethesda (John 5:1–15). In digs conducted in the nineteenth century, a large tank situated about one hundred feet northwest of St. Anne's Church was discovered

---

7. The texts of the Greek inscriptions are collected in C. R. Conder and H. H. Kitchener, *Survey of Western Palestine*, 6 vols. (Jerusalem: Kedem, 1970), 1:112–13.

and identified as the Pool of Bethesda. Further archaeological excavations in the area in 1964 unearthed the remains of Byzantine and Crusader churches, Hadrian's (early second century emperor of Rome) Temple of Asclepius and Serapis (gods of healing), the small healing pools of the Asclepieion, the other two large pools, and the dam between them. The Twin Pools are today equated with the Pool of Bethesda.

The Pool of Siloam. Another pool in Jerusalem was immortalized when Jesus put clay on the eyes of a blind man and told him to wash his eyes in its water (John 9:1–41). In the gospel of John, that pool is called the "Pool of Siloam" (v. 7). *Shiloah* (Hebrew) was built by King Hezekiah in the eighth century BC at the southern end of a long tunnel he cut through solid rock to bring water from the Gihon Spring outside of the city walls to the Pool of Siloam inside the city walls (2 Kings 20:20). An ancient inscription depicts the stunning accomplishment of Hezekiah's workmen cutting from both ends of the tunnel until they met in the middle. A walk through the 1,749-foot tunnel is a popular tourist attraction today.

Jesus' Last Days in Jerusalem

Jesus had contact with numerous sites in Jerusalem during his passion week, places now famous tourist attractions. We will touch upon them in the chronological order of the biblical narrative.

Bethany. Six days before his final Passover, Jesus went to Bethany where he had earlier raised Lazarus from the dead (John 12:1; cf. 11:1–44). Bethany is to be identified with the modern village of *el-Azariyeh*, which is located two miles from Jerusalem on the eastern slopes of the Mount of Olives. The modern Church of Saint Lazarus (which stands over church ruins of previous constructions) marks the place where tradition says the tomb of Lazarus is to be located. The tomb is not large. A northern opening in the small vestibule leads through a narrow, five-foot long passage into the burial chamber, which is about eight feet square. Although it is difficult to date the tomb, the design of the tomb does seem to match those of other tombs built during the Roman period in general and during the time of Jesus in and near Jerusalem in particular. Such grave sites consisted of two-chambered tombs built one behind the other, a ledge around the rooms to hold sarcophagi, ongoing burials with bones placed in the sarcophagi or ossuaries on the ledges, beneath *arcosolia* (arch-shaped ceilings above the burial box). Such a burial site is associated with Jesus' burial (see below).[8]

Mount of Olives. Not only did Jesus predict the future of the world in a sermon he delivered on the Mount of Olives, but that site played a significant role in his passion week. There Jesus wept over Jerusalem, began his triumphant entry, and prayed in the Garden of Gethsemane. We will touch upon the first two of these moments now, leaving the last for later. During his last

---

8. See McRay's discussion, *Archaeology and the New Testament*, 206–10.

days, Jesus made a triumphal entry into Jerusalem from the Mount of Olives (Matt. 21:1–11; Mark 11:1–11; Luke 19:24–44; John 12:12–19). Coming from Bethany, Jesus passed through the probable location of Bethphage on the top of the Mount of Olives, and then upon his descent down the western slope of the Mount, Jesus wept over Jerusalem's coming destruction (Luke 19:37, 41). *Dominus Flevit* (the Lord wept) is a Franciscan chapel built in the shape of a tear drop in commemoration of that moment. The chapel is about half-way down the Mount of Olives on the descent into the Kidron Valley. In the construction of this chapel in 1953, excavations yielded hundreds of graves from two periods—135 BC to AD 70 and from the third and fourth centuries AD. Names on the ossuaries included familiar names to readers of the New Testament (Yeshua [Jesus], Miriam [Mary] , Martha, Eleazar [Lazarus], Simeon, Zechariah, etc.), written in Hebrew, Aramaic, and Greek.

Jesus' Cleansing of the Temple. Solomon first built the magnificent temple to God on Mount Moriah , just north of the Ophel Hill where Jerusalem was located (2 Chron. 3:1). Zerubbabel erected a new temple on the spot after the Solomonic one was destroyed by the Babylonians in 587 BC (Ezra 3:8–13). Herod the Great renovated and expanded the second temple, following a plan far more ambitious than either Solomon's or Zerubbabel's. Construction had already been in progress for forty-six years when Jesus was there (John 2:20). The temple mount or platform upon which the temple was situated was twice the size of the original temple grounds. The wall enclosing the temple platform measured 1,591 feet on the west (a portion of which is exposed today), 1,033 feet on the north, 1,542 feet on the east, and 918 feet on the south. This is roughly an area of thirty-five acres. The temple was built approximately on the spot where the Dome of the Rock sits today. The Jerusalem Temple was the capital of Israel, politically, religiously, and economically. Indeed, it was the center of Judaism. For Jesus to cleanse it was tantamount to attacking the nerve center of ancient Israel (Matt. 21:12–17; Mark 11:12–21; Luke 19:45–48; John 2:13–25). The cleansing may have taken place in the royal portico on the Temple's south side.

The Upper Room. Jesus celebrated the last Passover meal with his disciples in an "upper room" (Mark 14:15; Luke 22:12), which was also the place of the first gathering of the believers on the day of Pentecost (Acts 1:13). Today, the Holy Zion Church, situated above the so-called David's tomb in the southwest section of Old Jerusalem, is thought to be the site of the Upper Room. Indeed, tradition goes back to Byzantine times that such a spot was the hall of Jesus' Last Supper. Moreover, remains of a Jewish Christian synagogue dating from AD 73 to 135 have been discovered there as well. All indication is that this is the Upper Room mentioned in the Gospels and in Acts.

Gethsemane. The descriptions of the evangelists that Jesus and his disciples crossed the brook Kidron rules out any doubt regarding the general location of the Garden of Gethsemane (Matt. 26:36; Mark 14:32; John 18:1–2), which is on the western slope of the Mount of Olives. The name "Gethsemane" suggests an olive garden with an oil press. Today the Gethsemane Church of All Nations marks the spot venerated as the place of Jesus' agony since at least the fourth century. Tradition holds that, before his betrayal by Judas, Jesus prayed on the rock that is now in front of the apse (Matt. 26:36; Mark 14:32; Luke 22:40–41; John 18:1). The rock is referred to by the Bordeaux Pilgrim in 333.

The Palace of Caiaphas. After his arrest in Gethsemane, Jesus was taken to Annas (John 18:13), the former high priest and then to his son-in-law Caiaphas (John 18:24), who was high priest from AD 18 to 36. The Palace of Caiaphas, in which the proceedings against Jesus took place (Matt. 26:58; Mark 14:54; cf. Luke 22:54; John 18:24), stood on the hill west of the city according to Josephus (*Jewish Wars* 2.426). This site seems to have been located near Saint Peter of the Cockcrow Church. Stones on the north side of this church may have led to the Palace of Caiaphas.

Annas (or Ananus) the high priest, whose five sons and son-in-law Caiaphas served terms as high priest (Josephus, *Antiquities of the Jews* 20.198), is mentioned in the New Testament.[9] According to Josephus, the father of Annas was Sethi (*Antiquities of the Jews* 18.26). This is probably the priestly family excoriated in rabbinic tradition (*Babylonian Pesachim* 57a; *Midrash Keritot* 1.7).

The Praetorium. The official residence of the Roman prefect (*praitōrion/* governor), where Jesus' hearing before Pilate took place (Matt. 27:27; Mark 15:16; John 18:28), was in the Upper City not in the Antonia Fortress (the location of the Sisters of Zion today). The *lithostrōton* (Greek, John 19:13) denotes the public square in front of the Praetorium; it was paved with large stones. The Aramaic *Gabbatha* (John 19:13) denotes the high place or the setting of the Praetorium. This term probably denotes Herod's palace that is situated in the western elevated part of the city (see Josephus, *Jewish Wars* 5.4.3–4). Indeed, *Gabbatha* may be the rock cliff, still visible today, opposite the Wailing Wall. Such a location would also fit well with Mark's account, according to which the crowd "came up" presumably from the Temple (Mark 15:8).

The Church of the Holy Sepulchre. The most likely burial place of Jesus together with his empty tomb is identified by most biblical scholars and archaeologists with the Church of the Holy Sepulchre. Recent investigations show that this site lay outside the city wall (Matt. 28:11; John 19:17–42) in the vicinity of a gate (Heb. 13:12; cf. Josephus *Jewish Wars* 5.4.2).[10] Remains have also been found of the temple of Aphrodite, which Emperor Hadrian erected in AD 135 to displace a Jewish-Christian worship site. But Emperor Constantine's mother, Queen Helena, had a Christian church built in its place, the forerunner of the present edifice. Also, the area surrounding the Church of the Holy Sepulchre

---

9. Luke 3:2 ("the high-priesthood of Annas and Caiaphas"); John 18:13 ("they led him to Annas; for he was the father-in-law of Caiaphas"); Acts 4:6 ("Annas the high priest and Caiaphas and John and Alexander, and all who were of high-priestly family").
10. See James Charlesworth, *Jesus and Archaeology* (Grand Rapids: Eerdmans, 2006), 30–31.

was a huge limestone quarry, from which the name "Golgotha (skull) will have had its origin and rose as high as twelve meters (Luke 23:33; cf. Matt. 27:33; Mark 15:22; John 19:17). Moreover, John 19:20 mentions that the garden tomb Jesus was buried in was close to Golgotha, which is the case in the Holy Sepulchre. Mark 16:5 presupposes that the ledge on which Jesus' body was placed lay on the right side of the rock burial chamber, a detail corroborated by the tomb under the dome of the Church of the Holy Sepulchre. If one needed more evidence in favor of the Church of the Holy Sepulchre as the burial place and empty tomb of Jesus, in the 1970s beneath the Armenian Chapel of St. Vartan was revealed a second century drawing of a boat and an inscription, which seems to have read in English, "We have arrived." James Charlesworth agrees with many who interpret the boat and the inscription to mean that Christians from the West, perhaps Rome (the inscription is in Latin), saluted their arrival to the place where tradition had already made known was the place where Jesus was crucified, buried, and resurrected.[11]

Emmaus. Luke 24:13 says that the resurrected Jesus appeared to two disciples on the road to Emmaus. The most likely candidate for the village of Emmaus is Emmaus-Nicopolis (today the destroyed Arab village *Amwas*), which is twenty-three kilometers west of Jerusalem. There one also finds the warm springs which one would expect from the name Emmaus, which means "hot spring."

Conclusion

The archaeological sites that we have discussed in this chapter overwhelmingly confirm the historical reliability of the four gospels. Perhaps they also might motivate us to visit the places where Jesus walked.

REFLECTION QUESTIONS

1. What two places are associated with Jesus' birth and boyhood?

2. What two events occurred in connection with the inauguration of Jesus' public ministry?

3. What are some of the important sites associated with Jesus' ministry in Galilee?

4. What two miracles did Jesus perform in Jerusalem?

5. What are some of the places that are connected to Jesus' last days in Jerusalem?

---

11. Ibid., 35–36

PART 2

QUESTIONS ABOUT
JESUS' BIRTH AND CHILDHOOD

SECTION A

Questions Related
to the Birth of Jesus

When Was Jesus Born?

The reckoning of time in antiquity went through a variety of changes until Julius Caesar, on the basis of the Egyptian solar calendar, standardized a 365-day year with an extra day inserted on leap years. Both the church and the Western world followed this method of reckoning time until the reforms of Pope Gregory XIII promulgated on February 24, 1582. Since that time, the Gregorian calendar has been followed. In AD 525, when Pope John I asked a Scythian monk named Dionysius to prepare a standard calendar for the Western church that would be reckoned from the birth date of Christ, Dionysius relied both on the Julian calendar and on available information about the date of the founding of the city of Rome to compute the birth date of Christ. In Dionysius' calendar, AD 1 was set at 754 A. U. C. (*anno urbis conditae*, i.e., from the founding of the city of Rome), with Jesus' birthday being set as 25 December 753 A. U. C. Unfortunately, Dionysius miscalculated the birth of Jesus, for the Gospels state that Jesus was born during the reign of Herod the Great, who died before the turn of the era (estimates range from about 4 to 1 BC). Thus, historically, one arrives with the anomaly of Jesus being born several years BC.[1]

Several key factors in the Gospels provide information that enables one to more precisely date the birth of Christ: (1) Herod's death, (2) the census of Quirinius (Luke 2:1–2), (3) the beginning of John the Baptist's ministry (Luke 3:1) coupled with the mention of Jesus' age (Luke 3:23), and (4) the timing of the magi's visit to Jesus (Matt. 2:9–12) which is related to the star that guided them to Jesus. We now examine these four considerations.

Herod's Death

Two kinds of evidence help us determine the probable date of Herod the Great's death—literary and numismatic (i.e., coinage). Regarding the

---

1. See Ben Witherington III, "Birth of Jesus", in *DJG*, ed. Joel B. Green, Scot Knight, and I. Howard Marshall (Downers Grove/Leicester, England: InterVarsity Press, 1992), 60–74.

first of these, Josephus relates that Herod the Great was proclaimed King of Judea by the Romans when Calvinus and Pollio were proconsuls, in 40 BC (*Antiquities of the Jews* 14.381–85; *Jewish Wars* 1.282–85; cf. Tacitus *Historiae* 5.9). Josephus then adds that Herod reigned for thirty-seven years from the time of that proclamation (*Antiquities of the Jews* 17.191; *Jewish Wars* 1.665). The difference in years (40 and 37) stems from the fact that it took Herod from 40 BC until 37 BC to gain possession of Jerusalem and the rest of his domain. This then would place the death of Herod at approximately 3 BC.[2] However, Josephus also reports that an eclipse of the moon occurred shortly before Herod's death (*Antiquities of the Jews* 17.167), and in view of the fact that this is the only time Josephus mentions this sort of phenomenon, it is improbable that he fabricated this piece of data. There were no such eclipses in 3 BC, but there was one on March 12/13, 4 BC. He also mentions that Passover was celebrated shortly after Herod's death (*Antiquities of the Jews* 17.213; *Jewish Wars* 2.10). In 4 BC, the first day of Passover would have been April 11. Thus, it is likely Herod died between March 12 and April 11, 4 BC. Since Jesus was born during Herod's reign, this means that Jesus was born sometime before March of 4 BC.

The numismatic evidence centers on Herod's first coin, which was minted in "Year 3." No doubt this coin was minted shortly after his final capture of Jerusalem in 37 BC, thus backdating his reign to the time of 40 BC.

The Census under Quirinius

Luke 2:1–2 says that Caesar Augustus took an empire-wide census when Quirinius was governor of Syria and Palestine. This statement poses three historical problems. First, there is no evidence for an empire-wide census taken during the reign of Caesar Augustus. Second, Quirinius was sent by Augustus to be governor of Syria and Judea in AD 6 not 6 BC, the time of Jesus' birth (see our discussion below). And Quirinius did take a notable census in AD 6–7, according to Josephus (*Antiquities of the Jews* 18.1.1–2). Thus it has been suggested that Luke confused Quirinius with P. Quintilius Varus who was legate of Syria during 6–3 BC. Third, a Roman census would not have required Jews to travel to their ancestral home for registration. Moreover, would Rome have undertaken a census in a client state that already had its own ruler (Herod)?

Five responses counter the preceding doubts about Luke's reliability in the matter. (1) If there was a census that affected Judea during the reign of Herod the Great, it would probably proceed along the lines of a Jewish census, not a Roman one. In that case it is plausible that Jews would return to their ancestral homes and that both adults go (especially if Mary was also

---

2. There is a debate as to whether Herod's reign began in 40 BC when he was appointed client king over Judea by Antony, Octavian, and the Senate or when he took possession of Jerusalem in 37 BC.

of Davidic descent). (2) Elsewhere Luke demonstrates knowledge of the later census by Quirinius which prompted the revolt of Judas the Galilean in AD 6–7 (Acts 5:37). It is not likely that he would have confused this census, which he knew to be a later one, with one during the reign of Herod. (3) It is not certain that Luke in 2:1 means that Augustus took one enormous census of the whole empire. The language is general and could simply mean that the various parts of the empire were subject to various censuses during the time of Augustus. The Greek says that Caesar decreed that "all of the Roman world be enrolled." Both the present tense of *apographō* ("I enroll") and the use of *pas* ("all") suggest that Luke intended to say that Caesar Augustus decreed that the enrollment, which had been previously been going on in some parts of the empire, should now be extended to all parts, including client states like Judea. Indeed, the Roman historian A. N. Sherwin-White agrees, "A census or taxation-assessment of the whole provincial empire . . . was certainly accomplished for the first time in history under Augustus."[3] (4) There is some evidence of a census of Judea under Saturninus between 9–6 BC (cf. Tertullian, *Against Marcion* 4.19). We also know that Quirinius undertook more than one census during his governorship. (5)While Luke 2:2 could be translated as referring to the first census, *prōte* could also mean *former*. In other words, on this reading Luke would be saying that the census under Quirinius at the time of Jesus' birth was a former or prior one than the decree Luke mentions in Acts 5:37, the one in AD 6–7. Ben Witherington summarizes the impact of these five counter-responses:

> Thus it is more probable that Luke is referring to a census under Quirinius that took place prior to the famous one in AD 6–7. If so, we have no clear record outside Luke of such an action by Quirinius, though it is not impossible that it took place. Herod's power was on the wane at the time of Jesus' birth, and a census in preparation for the change of power could well have been forced on Herod since he had fallen into some disfavor with Augustus near the end of his life. We know also that Quirinius had been made consul in 12 BC and a person of his rank serving in the East frequently had far-reaching authority and duties. It is thus not improbable that, acting as Caesar's agent, he had Herod take a census. It is also possible he was governor more than once in Syria, though the possibility also remains that Luke may be identifying him by his later and, to his audience, more familiar office. It is less likely that Luke means that Quirinius started

---

3. A. N. Sherwin-White, *Roman Society and Roman Law in the New Testament* (Grand Rapids: Baker, reprint, 1978), 168–69.

a census in 6 BC and finished it in AD 6–7, for he says that this was the first census the governor took (distinguishing it from some later one). The upshot of all of this is that Luke's reference to the census does not suggest a different date for Jesus' birth than does the Matthean evidence.[4]

John the Baptist and Jesus' Public Ministry

Luke tells us that John the Baptist began his ministry during the fifteenth year of Caesar Tiberius' reign (Luke 3:1). Augustus died in the summer of AD 14, and that fall the Senate acknowledged Tiberius to be the new Caesar. Thus, John the Baptist began his ministry in AD 29. In Luke 3:23 the author says that Jesus was about thirty years old at that time. The word Luke uses here of Jesus is *hōsei* which should be taken as a round number. Thus, there is no real discrepancy between Luke and Matthew on this point. Jesus was born in about 6 BC (so Matthew as we saw above) and on this reckoning would have been thirty-five years old at the start of his ministry, which Luke conveniently rounds off to thirty.

The Magi's Visit

Three factors enter into the date of Jesus' birth and the magi's visit, two relative to the magi and one concerning church tradition: the star the magi saw, the timing of their visit, and the day of Jesus' birth. Regarding the first of these, various astronomical suggestions have been made concerning the

---

4. Witherington, *"Birth of Jesus,"* 68. I deal with the Quirinius census in my commentary on Luke. There I draw upon the findings of William Ramsay who, though writing a century ago, makes a plausible connection with the Lukan statement:

> The reference in Luke 2:1 to the first worldwide enrollment for taxes when Quirinius was governor of Syria has raised the eyebrows of historians because, while the birth of Jesus took place during the reign of Herod the Great (who died in 4 B.C.; see Matt. 1–2 and Luke 1:5), Quirinius was governor of Syria A.D. 6–9. Thus it was assumed that Luke had misinterpreted the chronology of the two. However, William Ramsay offered a very plausible explanation: Quirinius may well have been the military leader in Syria from ca. 9 to 4 B.C., in conjunction with the civil governor, Saturninus. Indeed, Ramsay pointed to the famous inscription, *titulus tiburtinus*, which contains the significant line, "as pro-praetorial legate of Divus Augustus, he received again the province of Syria and Phoenicia." This remark suggests that someone was Caesar Augustus's legate (governor) in Syria twice. Although the name of the person is lost from the manuscript, Ramsay suggested that, in light of Luke 2:1, Quirinius well fits the description. His first activity in Syria took place, along with the census, from 9 to 4 B.C., while his second contact with the area, this time as chief magistrate, stretched from A.D. 6 to 9 (William Ramsay, *The Bearing of Recent Discoveries on the Trustworthiness of the New Testament* [London: Hodder & Stoughton, 1915], 238–300; taken from my *Luke*, Moody Gospel Commentary [Chicago: Moody, 1995], 24–25).

star that guided the magi to Bethlehem: the star was the conjunction of Jupiter and Saturn in 7 BC; it was the conjunction of Venus and Jupiter from August 12, 3 BC onward; the astronomical phenomenon was Halley's comet, which took place in the region in 12 BC; the star was a super-nova or the birth of a new star, which Chinese astronomers recorded in 5/4 BC. But Matthew 2 provides information that makes the astronomical suggestions difficult to sustain, especially the facts that the magi saw the star at its rising which led them to Jerusalem and then to Bethlehem (but why would they need the star's leading for the short six mile journey from the former to the latter?) and then to the precise location in Bethlehem. Most likely, then, the star was the glory of God or an angel; in other words, something supernatural rather merely natural.

Concerning the second factor in ascertaining the date of the birth of Jesus, Matthew 2 reports that the magi arrived at the place of Jesus' birth when he was a child, not an infant. Thus, it seems that the magi arrived in Bethlehem about a year after Jesus' birth. This piece of information, plus the date of the death of Herod in 4 BC, indicates that Jesus was born in 6/5 BC.

The third factor related to determining the date of Jesus' birth is church tradition. As early as the church father Hippolytus (AD 165–235), it was said that Jesus was born on December 25, a date also set by John Chrysostom (AD 345–407), whose arguments prevailed in the Eastern Church and have been assumed in the Western Church. Some have argued that Luke mentions that shepherds were watching their flocks outside (which might favor a date between March and November, that is the spring-summer-fall, not the winter). But Rabbinic literature (the Mishnah, *Mishna Seqalalim* 7.4) suggests that sheep might also be outside in winter. Thus, we may say that December 25, the traditional date, and January 6, the date followed by the Armenian Church, are both possible. The celebration of the nativity is attested in Rome as early as AD 336 and this celebration also involved recognizing January 6 as Epiphany, the day the magi visited Jesus.

Conclusion

Taking into consideration the death of Herod the Great, the census by Quirinius, the ministry of John the Baptist and Jesus' public ministry, and the magi's visit leads one to the conclusion that Jesus was born in Bethlehem somewhere between 6–5 BC and in the winter, perhaps December 25.

REFLECTION QUESTIONS

1. When did Herod the Great die?

2. When was the census taken by Quirinius?

3. When did John the Baptist begin his public ministry?

4. When did the magi visit Jesus?

5. When, then, was Jesus most likely born?

Was Jesus Really Born of a Virgin?

The virgin birth of Jesus is a litmus test for conservative Christians: Was Jesus really born of a virgin? But before beginning our discussion we should offer a point of clarification concerning terminology. The matter at hand is more precisely Jesus' virginal *conception*, not virgin birth. The former term has to do with whether Jesus was conceived without the intervention of a human father (i.e., without male seed impregnating his mother Mary), while the latter relates to his manner of birth or the way Jesus came out of the womb. In post-biblical Christianity, there did develop a belief in virginal birth alongside virginal conception.[1] But, in fact, there is no such concept in the New Testament concerning Jesus. Rather, it is his miraculous conception that is taught. In what follows, we will make two broad points: the affirmation of the virgin birth by New Testament authors and the church fathers and a rebuttal to those denying the virgin birth.

Affirming the Virgin "Birth" (Conception) of Jesus

Here we consider two points in favor of the historicity of the virginal conception: the New Testament texts dealing with it and the witness of the church fathers.

The New Testament Treatment of the Virginal Conception of Jesus

The virgin "birth" of Jesus is explicitly taught in the infancy narratives of Matthew and Luke and is alluded to elsewhere in the New Testament. We take these considerations in order.

The Virginal Conception in Matthew and Luke. The virginal conception is explicitly presented in two New Testament texts: Matthew 1:18–25 and Luke 1:26–39. Four relevant statements meet the reader of the first passage,

---

1. That is, a miraculous and painless birth in which the hymen was not ruptured, something already hinted at in the second-century *Proto-Evangelium of James* 19–20.

which we simply list here. First, before Joseph and Mary were married they discovered that Mary was with child through the Holy Spirit (v. 18). Second, similarly it is said that what was conceived in Mary according to the angel that appeared to Joseph was from the Holy Spirit (v. 19). Third, this was in fulfillment of Isaiah 7:14, which predicted that the virgin would give birth to a son (vv. 22–23). Fourth, upon hearing the word of the angel, Joseph and Mary did not have sexual relations until after Jesus was born (v. 25).

But here we must ask the question, what led Matthew to see the Holy Spirit as the divine agent of the virginal conception of Jesus? W. D. Davies and Dale C. Allison Jr. see the confluence of some several factors to provide the answer: The coming of the Messiah constituted a "new creation" for the early church, one borne along by the work of the Spirit:

1. The Spirit was traditionally understood to be the source of (human) life.

2. Jesus was believed to be the Davidic Messiah and the suffering servant, and both of these figures were firmly associated with the Holy Spirit.

3. The virginal conception was a miracle, and in both Jewish and Christian texts the Holy Spirit is the power behind miracles.

4. Eschatological sonship and the Spirit were closely linked in early Christian thinking as they apparently already were in pre-Christian Judaism.

5. It was believed that messianic times would see a fresh and full coming of the Holy Spirit.

6. In Luke 1:15 it is said of John that he was "filled with the Holy Spirit from his mother's womb."

Davies and Allison conclude, "In view of the facts to which we have called attention, it is no surprise that the eschatological appearance of the Messiah and the resultant new creation were interpreted by the faithful as brought about by the Spirit of God."[2]

Luke 1:26–39 also relates the miraculous virginal conception of Jesus. The key remarks are in 1:34–35, "'How will this be,' Mary asked the angel, 'since I am a virgin?' The angel answered, 'The Holy Spirit will come upon you, and the power of the Most High will overshadow you. So the holy one to be born will be called the Son of God.'"

---

2. W. D. Davies and Dale C. Allison, *Matthew* [I–VII], ICC (Edinburgh: T&T Clark, 1988), 1:201–2.

Joseph Fitzmyer doubts that Luke's infancy narrative presents a virginal conception. We list here his four objections, responding to each as we go.[3] First, Mary's query in Luke 1:34, "How will this be, since I do not know a man?" should not be taken as historical. Rather, it was created by Luke to dramatize the identity of the child. But, as I. Howard Marshall observes, if that were the case, why did Luke not just omit v. 34, for v. 35 would have flowed logically from v. 33?[4] Perhaps the most accurate depiction of v. 34 is that Mary assumed that the conception was imminent, which confirms the fact that she had not yet had sexual relations with a man. Second, Fitzmyer denies that the language of Luke 1:35—"the Holy Spirit will come upon you, and the power of the Most High will overshadow you"—refers to a conception. But Manuel Miguens refutes Fitzmyer's objection noting the following points: the context indicates that Mary and Elizabeth are discussing the same subject, namely, conception; the whole point of the angel's dialogue with Mary indicates that her conception will not be typical; and the references to Mary not knowing (having sex) with a man and being overshadowed by God and the Spirit make it clear that a conception, even a supernatural conception, is in view.[5] Third, the detail in Luke 2:3 that Mary was betrothed to Joseph and was with child rules out a virginal conception. But Miguens rightly refutes this objection noting that whereas Elizabeth is introduced as the wife of Zechariah, Mary is only introduced as betrothed to Joseph and a virgin at that (Luke 1:27)! So it is clear that Mary is not pregnant with Joseph's child.[6] Fourth, if Jesus is portrayed by Luke as supernaturally conceived then why did Luke connect Jesus to Joseph's genealogy (Luke 3:23–37)? The attempt to distance Jesus from Joseph with the words, he "was supposed to be the son of Joseph" (Luke 3:23) do not prove that Joseph is not Jesus' father. But besides disregarding the clear intention of the preceding statement (which surely alludes to Jesus' virginal conception) Fitzmyer does not grasp that for Luke, the only alternative to Jesus' virginal conception is illegitimacy.[7]

It is clear from the infancy narratives in Matthew and Luke that the virginal conception of Jesus was non-sexual in that Mary was not impregnated by a male deity or element, but that the child was conceived through the creative power of the Holy Spirit. This fact has an important bearing when we later discuss possible parallels between the conception of Jesus and non-biblical famous characters.

---

3. Joseph A. Fitzmyer, "The Virginal Conception of Jesus in the New Testament," *TS* 34 (1973): 541–75.

4. I. Howard Marshall, *Commentary on Luke*, NIGTC (Grand Rapids: Eerdmans, 1978), 70.

5. Manuel M. Miguens, *The Virgin Birth: An Evaluation of Scriptural Evidence* (Westminster, MD: Christian Classics, 1975), 72–84.

6. Ibid., 64–70.

7. Miguens makes this point (ibid, 89). Fitzmyer's magisterial commentary on Luke fares no better in affirming the virginal conception of Jesus. Note his four points of dismissal of the virginal conception, *The Gospel According to Luke, 1–IX*, AB (New York: Doubleday, 1979), 341–42.

Possible Allusions to the Virginal Conception of Jesus in the Rest of the New Testament

Here we deal with three clusters of texts that some have argued allude to Jesus' miraculous conception: those passages using *ginomai* of Jesus' birth; the "son of Mary" references in Mark; and certain texts in John.

First, Galatians 4:4, Romans 1:3, and Philippians 2:7 use the Greek word *ginomai* ("to be born") of Jesus' birth rather than *gennaō* ("begotten"). Because Paul uses *gennaō* of Ishmael and Isaac in Galatians 4:23–24, 29, some have surmised that Paul uses *ginomai* of Jesus but *gennaō* of others to signal the virginal conception. Besides this grammatical note, these three Pauline passages accentuate the two natures of Christ, namely, his deity and his humanity, and that in one person. It is hard to imagine that Paul knew of Jesus the God-Man and not know that it was through his virginal conception that he acquired such a status.

Second, Mark never mentions Joseph by name but rather calls Jesus the "son of Mary" (Mark 6:3). Miguens has argued that the silence about Joseph on Mark's part here is deliberate because Mark knew that Jesus had no human father.[8] Moreover, in Mark 3:31–35 it is mentioned that Jesus' mother and brothers came to him but no mention is made of Joseph. Furthermore, in that same passage when Jesus redefines his family as those who follow him he mentions brother, sister, and mother, but conspicuous by its absence is a reference to father.[9] Probably, Joseph had died when Jesus was young.

Third, John 8:41 records the Jewish opposition to Jesus and their accusation that they are not illegitimate children, which looks very much like they were accusing Jesus of such, which was a common Jewish slander regarding Jesus' virginal conception (see below for further discussion). We should also mention that the gospel of John never mentions Joseph but only refers to Mary. Furthermore, John 1:14, like the preceding Pauline texts, accentuates Jesus as both God and human suggesting that the apostle John also knew of Jesus' virginal conception.

The Witness of the Church Fathers

Here we need only summarize the research of Thomas Boslooper, who has investigated the church fathers relative to the virgin "birth" of Jesus. He documents that the church fathers consistently from the second-century to Aquinas all believed in the virgin birth, though their discussions of the topic underwent changes in emphases: the virgin birth and atonement, the virgin birth and the incarnation, the virgin birth and the Logos, and the virgin birth and Mariology.[10]

8. Miguen, *The Virgin Birth*, 22. Raymond E. Brown disagrees, *The Birth of the Messiah: A Commentary on the Infancy Narratives in Matthew and Luke* (Garden City, NY: Doubleday, 1979), 519.

9. Miguen, *The Virgin Birth*, 22.

10. Thomas Boslooper, *The Virgin Birth* (Philadelphia: Westminster Press, 1962), 27–51.

Here then is consistent testimony to the historicity of the virgin birth from the witness of the church, a witness that is encapsulated in the Apostles' Creed.

Denying the Virgin "Birth" (Conception) of Jesus

From the beginning, there have been many detractors of the virginal conception of Jesus. We summarize their positions under three headings: (1) Jewish claims that Jesus' birth was illegitimate; (2) pagan parallels that are thought to invalidate the historicity of the virgin birth; and (3) naturalistic explanations of Jesus' miraculous conception.

Jewish Accusations That Jesus' Birth Was Illegitimate

The charge that Jesus was born illegitimately is hinted at in the Gospels (John 8:41; Mark 6:3) and came to full fruition in the second century by the rabbis.[11] The anti-Christian work of Celsus, written ca. AD 180, drew upon Jewish sources, and in it we find a fully developed tale of Jesus' birth which can be reconstructed as follows:

> It was Jesus himself who fabricated the story that he had been born of a virgin. In fact, however, his mother was a poor country woman who earned her living by spinning. She had been driven out by her carpenter-husband [*tekton*] when she was convicted of adultery with a soldier named Panthera. She then wandered about and secretly gave birth to Jesus. Later, because he was poor, Jesus hired himself out in Egypt where he became adept in magical powers. Puffed up by these, he claimed for himself the title of God.[12]

But first came the reality (Jesus' miraculous conception) and then came the Jewish slander of that event, not the reverse. In other words, the charge of illegitimacy did not prompt Matthew and Luke to come up with the story of Jesus' virginal conception.

Pagan Parallels That Are Thought to Invalidate the Historicity of the Virgin Birth

Among the parallels offered for the virginal conception of Jesus have been the conceptions of figures in world religions (the Buddha, Krishna, and the son of Zoroaster), in Greco-Roman mythology (Perseus and Romulus), in Egyptian and classical history (the Pharaohs, Alexander the Great, and Augustus), and among famous philosophers or religious thinkers (Plato and Apollonius of Tyana), to name only a few. But Raymond Brown rightly

---

11. See Origen, *Contra Celsum* 1.32; Tosephta *Hullin* II 22–23; the Jerusalem Talmud tractates *Aboda Zara* 40d and Sabbath 14d (Cited in Brown, *The Birth of the Messiah*, 536, number 8)
12. The text is taken from Brown, *The Birth of the Messiah*, 35.

questions that these examples are truly parallel to the birth account of Jesus. First, would such legends or traditions have been known to the New Testament authors? Second, would the New Testament authors and early Christians have countenanced comparing the conception of Jesus to such gross and immoral descriptions? Third, the purported parallels above all involve a type of *hieros gamos* (sacred marriage), where a divine male, in human or other form, impregnates a woman, either through normal sexual intercourse or through some substitute form of penetration. But does this manner of conception actually compare with the non-sexual virginal conception of Jesus by the Holy Spirit? Brown correctly answers these questions in the negative.[13]

Naturalistic Explanations of Jesus' Miraculous Conception

In recent scientific investigations two procedures are being considered as analogues to Jesus' virgin "birth": parthenogenesis (Greek for "virgin birth") and stem cell research. Was Jesus' conception more along these naturalistic lines than the supernatural explanation offered by the church for thousands of years? Parthenogenesis is a form of asexual reproduction where growth and development of embryos occur without fertilization. Parthenogenesis occurs naturally in many plants, some invertebrate animal species (including water fleas, some scorpions, some bees, etc.) and some vertebrates (some fish, amphibians, reptiles, etc.). This type of reproduction has been induced artificially in a few species including fish and amphibians.

John Morris of the Creation Institute responds to the relationship between these two procedures and the virgin "birth":

> But is this the same thing as the virgin birth? No, it would not
> [be]. In humans, the DNA in each egg's nucleus contains 23
> chromosomes, with the remaining 23 usually supplied by the
> father. In cloning, the original 23 chromosomes are stripped
> from an unfertilized egg, and a full complement of 46 from a
> donor is inserted. The child would possess identical DNA to
> the donor, with a minor exception—a small segment of DNA
> present in the cells' mitochondria is passed from mother to
> child, undiluted by the father. Is cloning a possible explana-
> tion of Christ's birth? If Mary's nuclear DNA was used, the
> resulting child would have been female. If another source
> was used, the offspring would have carried Mary's imper-
> fect mitochondrial DNA, mutated over the generations
> since Adam, and thus could not have been the perfect "lamb
> without blemish and without spot" (1 Peter 1:19). Cloning
> is not the answer. While much remains a mystery, the birth

---

13. Ibid., 522–23.

of Christ was a miracle in every regard. He said of God the Father, ". . . a body hast thou prepared for Me" (Hebrews 10:5), free from any genetic defect and thus qualified to be a perfect sacrifice. And then, "when the fullness of the time was come, God sent forth his Son, made of a woman . . . to redeem them that were under the law, that we might receive the adoption of sons" (Galatians 4:4–5).[14]

Not being a scientist prevents me from coming to a firm conclusion in the matter, but Morris' refutation of parthenogenesis as a vehicle of stem cell research as the means for Jesus' virginal conception seems accurate to me. At the end of the day, I prefer to view the virgin birth as a miracle, which as we noted in one of the beginning questions above, is no problem for the believer to accept.

Conclusion

In this chapter we have affirmed the belief in the virginal conception. The New Testament does so both explicitly (Matt. 1:18–25; Luke 1:26–39) and implicitly (Mark 3:31–35; 6:3; John 1:14; 8:41; Rom. 1:3; Gal. 4:4; Phil. 2:7). And the church fathers attest to their belief in the virgin birth as well. Next, we dismissed those arguments denying the virgin birth (Jewish accusations that Jesus' birth was illegitimate; pagan parallels that apparently invalidate it; and modern scientific explanations of Jesus' virgin birth (such as parthenogenesis and stem cell research). The virginal conception is a phenomenon that we can investigate, ponder, and try to explain, but ultimately it is a miracle to be believed.

REFLECTION QUESTIONS

1. What do Matthew and Luke have in common regarding their respective reports about the virgin birth of Jesus?

2. What passages in the rest of the New Testament may allude to the virgin birth?

3. What Jewish accusations have been made against Jesus' virgin birth?

4. What have critics of Jesus' virgin birth said about ancient pagan stories of virgin births?

5. What naturalistic explanations have been offered to explain away Jesus' virgin birth?

---

14. http://www.icr.org/article/cloning-virgin-birth/ (accessed March 1, 2014).

Why Does It Matter That Jesus Was Born of a Virgin?

Those who reject the virginal conception also tend to deny its theological importance. They usually say something like this, "the virgin birth is a myth that basically tries to communicate the truth that God is with us." And that's about it for their view. But those of us who do accept that Jesus' conception was indeed miraculous, in other words a virginal conception, wish to point out how theologically significant that teaching is. On my reckoning, at least nine cardinal Christian beliefs flow from the reality of the virgin "birth" of Jesus: the incarnation, trinity, sinlessness of Jesus, atonement, resurrection of Jesus and the believer, ascension, Jesus' heavenly intercession ministry, the second coming of Jesus, and the inspiration of the Bible. In this chapter we will develop how it is that Jesus' virginal conception impacts these highly important Christian beliefs.

The Incarnation

It is clear that the New Testament portrays Jesus as deity, especially in the titles applied therein to him: Messiah (used of Jesus in the New Testament some 531 times), the heavenly Son of Man (cf. Dan. 7 with Jesus' self-usage of that designation for himself throughout the Gospels), Wisdom (see John 1:1–18; Col. 1:15–20; Heb. 1:2–3), Logos (John 1:1–18), Son of God (see, for example, John 20:28), and Lord, that is Yahweh (John 8:58–59; 20:28; Phil. 2:9–11, etc.). It is also transparent that the New Testament portrays Jesus as human (see, e.g., John 1:14; Philippians 2:6–8; 1 John 1:1–4).

It seems clears that the virginal conception accounts for the doctrine of the Incarnation—Jesus is both God and human. Indeed, a number of New Testament passages intimately combine those two aspects of Jesus' person (Matt. 1:20–23; Luke 1:31–35; Gal. 4:4; Rom. 1:3–4; Phil. 2:6–11; 1 John 1:1–4; 4:2; 2 John 7). The reader will recall that several of these texts draw upon the virginal conception either explicitly (Matt. 1:20–23; Luke 1:31–35) or implicitly (Gal. 4:4; Rom. 1:3–4; Phil. 2:6–11).

But it would take the deliberations of the church after the close of the New Testament to arrive at the hypostatic union formula of Jesus the God-Man. The following diagram illustrates the decisions of the first four ecumenical councils regarding the matter:

The Hypostatic Union:
Jesus Christ is the God-Man in One Person, with Two Natures

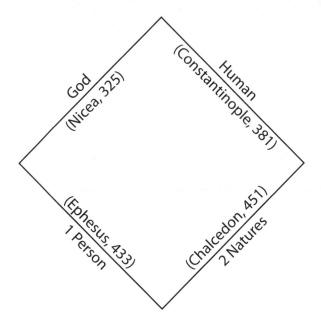

The Trinity

The concept of the Trinity is clearly taught in the New Testament (see Matt. 28:19; 2 Cor. 13:14; Eph. 1:3–14; and 1 Peter 1:2). Yet, the Trinity is not explained by the New Testament authors; that would be a mystery left to the church fathers with which to grapple. We can also rest assured that the New Testament, in holding to the doctrine of the Trinity, did not see that as opposed to monotheism. For our purposes, for the New Testament authors the equation of Jesus with God was the first step to propounding the Trinity.

Although the church fathers' deliberations are not inspired Scripture, they are nevertheless extremely helpful for us in grappling with the nature of the Trinity. We mentioned above that the first four ecumenical councils constructed the hypostatic union formula in pronouncing that Jesus is the God-Man. But it is interesting to note that the Eastern Church also applied that formula to the

Trinity, based on the Incarnation. To pursue this matter requires us to observe that the church fathers up through Augustine adapted Platonic and Neo-Platonic categories in understanding, or at least in further explaining, Christian doctrines. In particular, Neo-Platonists developed the idea that the essence of something or its substance is formless matter, and the Nicene Creed (AD 325) and the Chalcedonian Creed (AD 451) used such language of Jesus and the Trinity. In doing so, those statements of belief equated Jesus' essence or substance with formless matter using the image of wax while speaking of Jesus' divine and human natures as the seal. Note the following diagram of the hypostatic union:[1]

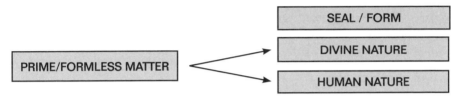

The same concept can be applied to the Trinity:

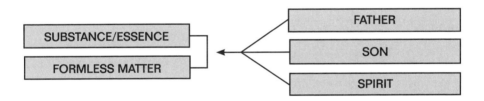

All this to say that Jesus the God-Man not only provided the impetus for delineating the Trinity but also for trying to understanding it, at least in the terms that the church fathers used to construct it. And it was the virginal conception that produced both Jesus' deity and humanity.

The Sinlessness of Christ

The New Testament is crystal clear that Jesus Christ was sinless (see, e.g., John 8:46; Rom. 8:3–4; 2 Cor. 5:21; Heb. 4:15; 7:26; 1 Peter 2:22; 1 John 3:5). But this begs the question, "Since Jesus was human how did he miss the sin nature born to all since Adam and Eve" (see Ps. 51:5; Rom. 5:12)? Throughout the years, four theories have been suggested to answer that quandary, only the last of which seems accurate. First, many Protestants have argued that Adam's sin nature continues in the human race via the male. But there is no biblical support for this,

---

1. See C. Marvin Pate, *From Plato to Jesus: What Does Philosophy Have to Do with Theology?* (Grand Rapids: Kregel, 2011), 117, 204 respectively for these charts.

and certainly no scientific evidence can be elicited to defend it either. And, in any event, Jesus had no human father, so the issue of whether or not sin is passed on via the father relative to Jesus is a moot point. Rather, it seems more likely that the sin nature proceeds from both male and female; in other words, both genders contribute the sin "gene" to their children. This reality refutes a second theory as to how Jesus missed out on the sin nature—the Roman Catholic view that Mary herself was virginally conceived and had no sin nature. But, again, there is neither biblical nor scientific evidence to support this cherished theory, though Catholics appeal to apocryphal gospels to make their point (see the second century AD document *Proto-Evangelium of James,* 19–20). Third, Christian laymen apparently have no problem suggesting that Jesus actually did inherit a sin nature (!) but that he did not give in to it. Indeed, one of my Sunday School teachers mentioned matter-of-factly that that was the case for Jesus and that we should follow in his obedient way. But to say that Jesus had a sinful nature surely goes against the grain of the passages above affirming the sinlessness of Jesus. Jesus was without spot and blemish; he knew no sin; he was only in the *likeness*—not the reality—of sin; etc. Fourth, the most promising theory regarding Jesus' sinlessness is that his divine nature overruled Mary's sin from entering his human nature at conception. Robert Glenn Gromacki sheds light on this statement:

> Evangelical theologians have debated whether Christ was able not to sin *(posse non peccare)* or not able to sin *(non posse peccare)*. Adam was created with an ability not to sin, but he chose deliberately to sin. Thereafter, he along with his descendants were *not* able *not* to sin (Eccles. 7:20). They were unable to keep themselves from sinning. Did Christ only have the original Adamic capacity? If so, then His sinlessness rested upon the obedience of His human will. The lack of ability to sin is a prerogative of the divine essence. Taken by themselves, the divine nature within the person of Christ was both intemptable and impeccable (Heb. 6:18; James 1:13) whereas the human nature was both temptable and peccable. Unfortunately, the debate reflects a lack of balance between the two natures. When Christ is viewed from the standpoint of His human nature, then proponents say that He was able not to sin. When He is viewed from the stance of His divine nature, then advocates state that Jesus was not able to sin.[2]

Now Gromaki's solution to viewing Jesus' two natures separately is that the two should be seen as united and that therefore the divine nature

2. Robert Glenn Gromacki, *The Virgin Birth: Doctrine of Deity* (Nashville/New York: Thomas Nelson, 1974), 123.

overruled Jesus' human nature such that he was not able to sin. But how is this any different from the heretic Eutyches who said that Jesus' divine nature swallowed up his human nature, something the Council at Ephesus rightly rejected? (I am not at all calling Gromaki, my brother in Christ, a heretic. I am merely concerned about his analogy.) Two pieces of evidence lead me to reject this view that Christ was not able to sin. (1) The struggle with his temptations, whether in the wilderness or in the Garden of Gethsemane, was so intense it is hard to deny that Jesus was in the battle of his life in resisting sin (Luke 22:42–44; Heb. 2:18; 4:15). (2) Philippians 2:7 is rightly understood as saying that Jesus emptied himself of his right to use his divine nature as an advantage over his humanity. In other words, in the union of Jesus' two natures he did not allow to happen precisely what Gromacki claims, namely, his divine nature to override his human nature. Therefore, I would rather suggest that the union of the two natures of Christ were united in the following way: at his conception the divine nature of Jesus prevented sin from entering his humanity and during his life the human nature of Jesus prevented the divine nature from removing anything human from his experience, including the temptation to sin. In other words, Jesus on earth was able not to sin. This to me seems to best explain the union of the two natures of Christ concerning his sinlessness.

The Atonement

Both Matthew and Luke associate Jesus' virginal conception with his salvific mission—to save his people from their sins (see Matt. 1:21–23; Luke 1:46–55). Other New Testament texts specify how this happened—Jesus died on the cross as God's perfect sacrifice to permanently atone for sin (e.g., Matt. 26:26–28; Mark 14:22–24; Luke 22:19–20; John 1:29; Rom. 3:24–26; 2 Cor. 5:21; Heb. 9:11–10:18; 1 Peter 1:19). We will not be far off the mark to suggest that the two natures bequeathed to Jesus at his miraculous conception account for Jesus' atoning sacrifice. Thus, in his divinity Jesus was the Son of God who in his humanity lived a sinless life and died as the perfect sacrifice to end all sacrifices. Jesus' divine nature pleased the heavenly Father at his crucifixion while Jesus' human nature identified with sinful humanity on the cross.

But no New Testament author understood that the atonement of Jesus was intimately tied into the incarnation better than the apostle John in his epistles. More particularly, the Epistles of John tie together the incarnation, atonement, and ethics in an amazing way. The following chart points out this dynamic:[3]

---

3. For this chart see C. Marvin Pate, *The Writings of John: A Survey of the Gospel, Epistles, and Apocalypse* (Grand Rapids: Zondervan, 2011), 298–99.

DOCTRINE	DENIERS OF CHRIST'S HUMANITY	JOHN AFFIRMS CHRIST IS HUMAN
Incarnation	Denied: Jesus (man)=Christ (1 John 2:22) Christ came in flesh (1 John 4:2; 2 John 7) therefore that together Jesus Christ is the Son of God (1 John 2:23)	Affirmed: Jesus=Christ (1 John 5:1) Christ has come in flesh (1 John 1–4; 4:2) Jesus Christ is Son of God (1 John 1:7; 2:23; 3:23; 4:9–10, 15; 5:6) Summary: the eternal Son of God, second member of the trinity in eternity past, became human=Jesus (via Mary) and deity=Christ (via God). Thus, Jesus Christ=the God-Man at birth, baptism, ministry, death, resurrection
Atonement	Implicitly denied atonement: Sufficiency of atonement=Jesus died not Christ; therefore death of mere man not deity Need for the cross=human dilemma is ignorance (so Gnostics) not sin (1 John 1:8, 10)	Affirmed Atonement: Sufficiency of atonement: Christ died (1 John 2:1–2; 4:10) Need for the cross: 1 John 1:8, 10=if no sin, that makes God to be a liar, when what we need to do is confess sin, v. 9
Ethics/Sanctification	Denied that Christian life should impact the body: sinless (1 John 1:8, 10) elite (1 John 2:20, 27=special anointing)	Affirmed that Christian life should impact the body: confess sin; otherwise walk in darkness (1 John 1:8–10) love brethren; otherwise liar (1 John 2:9; 3:11–18; 4:20)

So the Epistles of John perceive the intimate association between the incarnation and the atonement and, beyond that, with ethics.

The Resurrection of the Body of Jesus and Believers

The virginal conception produced the God-Man and the two components comprising the God-Man contributed to the nature of Jesus' resurrection body and that of his followers. First Corinthians 15 is Paul's great chapter on the resurrection of Jesus and of his followers. After Paul discusses the reality of the bodily resurrection of Jesus Christ (vv. 1–34), he engages in a treatise on the resurrection of the believer. The two resurrections are obviously connected. Verses 42–44 get at the heart of the nature of the resurrection:

> So it is with the resurrection of the dead. What is sown is perishable, what is raised is imperishable. It is sown in dishonor, it is raised in glory. It is sown in weakness, it is raised in power. It is sown a physical body, it is raised a spiritual body. If there is a physical body, there is also a spiritual body.

The key construct that governs this paragraph is the notion that Jesus' body now and the believer's resurrection body later is characterized by continuity and discontinuity. It will be corporal and personal but it will also be spiritual. The words, "spiritual body," pinpoint this reality. Note the contrasts between the mere physical body and the resurrection body: perishable/imperishable; dishonor/glory; weak/power; physical/spiritual. Thus, Jesus' present resurrection body and the Christian's future resurrection body will be corporal but spiritual, that is completely controlled by the Spirit. So we can make the following correlation between Jesus the God-Man and the resurrection body:

Jesus' humanity	Jesus' deity
Corporal aspect of the resurrection body	Spiritual aspect of the resurrection body

And because Christians are united to Jesus, their future resurrection bodies will correspond to his: corporal and spiritual. One can see, then, how significant the virgin "birth" is for the resurrection of the body for it contributed to Jesus his status of the God-Man, which will be the pattern for the believer's resurrection body.

The Ascension

We might mention in passing that the virginal conception that produced Jesus the God-Man also informed his ascension to heaven forty days after his resurrection. Luke-Acts alone records Jesus' ascension (see Luke 24:50–53; Acts 1:9–11; and our later discussion). The Acts description assures the readers that the same Jesus who ascended to heaven in a spiritual body will return to earth in the same manner. More specifically, just as Jesus ascended to heaven personally, corporally, and visibly in a spiritual body so will he return at his parousia. And the same manner of existence awaits the believer with the resurrection body, according to the Acts passages that deal with the resurrection (e.g., 1:1–4; 2:24–36; 3:15–26; 4:8–10; 7:59–60; 13:23–37; 23:6–8).

Jesus' Heavenly Intercession

Hebrews 4:14–16 describes Jesus as the believers' high priest in heaven. As such he has experienced all that humanity experiences, being tempted as they are tempted, yet without sin. Because Jesus is our great high priest, believers may come boldly to the throne of grace to receive help in time of need. Hebrews 7:25 encapsulates Jesus' high priestly ministry when it exclaims of him, "He ever lives to make intercessions for us." But how is this so? Paul uses a little phrase in 1 Corinthians 15:48 that is pregnant with meaning when he declares of Jesus that he is "our man from heaven." In light of our earlier discussion of the resurrection of Jesus and the believer based on 1 Corinthians 15, we realize that Paul is saying that Jesus in his heavenly spiritual body as the God-Man is our representative in heaven. In other words, Jesus did not cease being divine and human when he returned to heaven. And it is in that capacity that Jesus is the Christian's high priest. Because Jesus is human, he deeply identifies with our hurt and as God he is able to do something about it.

Beyond that truth the Scripture does not go, though Lutherans and Calvinists have enjoyed a delightful debate concerning the matter. Luther taught the ubiquity of the body of Christ (i.e., that Jesus' spiritual body is omnipresent—on earth and in heaven at the same time). This colors the Lutheran understanding of the Lord's Supper, claiming that the real presence of Christ is present at the observance of that sacrament. Calvinists, on the other hand, do not hold to the omnipresence of Christ's heavenly body, arguing instead that Christ is localized in heaven and it is his Spirit that represents him on earth, even at the Lord's Supper. While one can only speculate on this issue, the paraclete passages in John that make much of the presence of the Holy Spirit in Jesus' absence might favor the Calvinist viewpoint.

The Parousia

What we learned of Jesus' resurrection, ascension, and intercession applies to his parousia as well, namely, his God-Man status will constitute the nature of his return. Thus, just as Jesus arose with a spiritual body and ascended to heaven in that glorified body and intercedes for the church in that perfect body so he will return in that dynamic body. His humanity correlates with the physicality of his body while his deity correlates with the glorified composition of that body, and in that status he will make himself visible at his second coming to earth (see again Acts 1:9–11).

The Inspiration of the Bible

Since a student in college, I have thrilled to hear of the analogy between Jesus the God-Man and the inspiration of Scripture. Thus, just as Jesus is fully divine and fully human yet without sin, so the Bible in its authorship is fully divine and fully human yet without error. Indeed, I have devoted a whole chapter to this analogy elsewhere.[4] We may express this truth in chart form:

JESUS CHRIST THE GOD-MAN	THE BIBLE
Fully God	Was inspired by God
Fully human yet without sin	Was written by humans yet without error

Obviously this analogy of the God-Man status of Jesus accentuates the divine-human nature of the inspiration of the Bible.

Conclusion

As it turns out, the teaching of the virginal conception that produced Jesus the God-Man is a vital doctrine of the Christian faith. It impinges on important orthodox doctrines such as: incarnation, trinity, sinlessness of Jesus, atonement, resurrection of Jesus and the believer, ascension, Jesus' heavenly intercession, the second coming of Jesus, and the inspiration of the Bible. We as evangelicals do well, then, to hold dearly to the virgin "birth" of Jesus. For to discard that doctrine would be to throw out the baby with the bathwater, so to speak. Therefore, on a theological note, we confess with the church that the pre-existent Son of God, the second member of the Trinity, through the virginal conception became none other than Jesus the God-Man.[5]

But is the New Testament the only biblical witness to the virgin birth? In other words, does the Old Testament predict such a phenomenon? We believe that it does and we address that fascinating topic in the next question.

REFLECTION QUESTIONS

1. How does the virgin birth of Jesus relate to the doctrines of the incarnation and the Trinity?

---

4. See Pate, *From Plato to Jesus*, chapter 8.
5. We disagree with W. Pannenberg's statement in this regard, "In its content, the legend of Jesus' virgin birth stands in an irreconcilable contradiction to the Christology of the incarnation of the preexistent Son of God in Paul and John" (*Jesus—God and Man* [Philadelphia: Westminster, 1968], 143). Brown rightly also takes issue with Pannenberg in the matter: "Two points should be remembered. First, in orthodox Christian belief, Jesus would be God's Son no matter how he was conceived. Second, for ordinary Christians the virginal conception has proved an effective interpretative sign of that eternal divine sonship; and we should not underestimate the adverse pedagogical impact on the understanding of divine sonship if the virginal conception is denied" (*The Birth of the Messiah: A Commentary on the Infancy Narratives in Matthew and Luke* [Garden City, NY: Image Books, 1977], 529).

2. How does the virgin birth of Jesus relate to the doctrines of his sinlessness and to his atoning death?

3. What does the virgin birth of Jesus have to do with the resurrection of Jesus and believers, and to Jesus' ascension?

4. How does the virgin birth of Jesus relate to his heavenly intercessory ministry and to the doctrine of the second coming?

5. How might the inspiration of Scripture compare to the virgin birth in terms of the two natures of Jesus Christ?

Did Isaiah 7:14 Predict That Jesus Would Be Born of a Virgin?

When the Revised Standard Version of the Bible was published in the mid-twentieth century, its translation of Isaiah 7:14 ("a woman [not a virgin] will conceive and bear a son") sparked a firestorm of reaction from conservative Christians. As a young teenager, I well-remember my pastor foaming at the mouth as he preached against the Revised Standard "Perversion!" Much of the criticism of that translation centered on the claim that the RSV denied the virgin birth. Though some of the criticism against that translation has abated (now being replaced by the heated debate over inclusive or genderless translations of the Bible), many conservative Christians are still suspicious of the RSV's rendering of the Hebrew word *alma* as "young woman" not "virgin." This discussion raises the significant question: Does Isaiah 7:14 predict the virgin birth? Isaiah 7:14 is the only Old Testament text that clearly is interpreted in the New Testament (Matt. 1:22–23) as being fulfilled by the virgin "birth" of Jesus. We detect that there are four stages to the issue of whether or not Isaiah 7:14 is a prophecy of the virginal conception of Jesus: (1) the Hebrew text of Isaiah 7:14; (2) the Septuagint text of Isaiah 7:14; (3) the earliest Christian interpretation of the Septuagint of Isaiah 7:14, the possible sources of Matthew 1:22–23 and Luke 1:26–35; and (4) Jewish criticism of the Septuagint translation of the Hebrew *alma* as the *parthenos*. We now proceed with an examination of these four stages of interpretation/translation.

The Hebrew Text of Isaiah 7:14

The Hebrew text of Isaiah 7:14 states, "Behold the young girl [*'alma*] is (will be) with child and will give birth to a son, and she will call his name Emmanuel." Our understanding of the Hebrew of Isaiah 7:14 is that it is messianic but not in and of itself a prophecy of the virginal conception of Jesus. These two statements are the two points of interest in this section. We will

begin with the latter point first. Raymond Brown has in our judgment correctly grasped the accurate interpretation of the Hebrew of Isaiah 7:14 as it
related to the original audience. We summarize Brown's argumentation here:

- It was to the wicked King Ahaz (ca. 753–715 BC) that Isaiah spoke the
  oracle involved in 7:14. It was intended as a sign to this disbelieving
  monarch during the Syro-Ephraimite war of 734 BC and must refer to
  something that took place during that year or shortly thereafter.
- The child to be born was not *the* Messiah, for messianism had not yet
  developed to the point of expecting a single future king. Scholars are
  not agreed on the identity of the child, but *at most* it may refer to the
  birth of a Davidic prince who would deliver Judah from its enemies. An
  ancient Jewish interpretation, known to Justin (*Dialogue* 67:1) identified the child as Hezekiah, Ahaz' son and successor, one of the few truly
  religious monarchs of the House of David.
- The word 'alma, used to describe *the woman*, normally describes a
  young girl who has reached the age of puberty and is thus marriage-
  able. It puts no stress on her virginity, although *de facto*, in the light of
  Israelite ethnic and social standards, most girls covered by the range of
  this term would be virgins.
- The presence of the definite article, "the young girl," makes it likely that
  Isaiah was referring to someone definite whose identity was known to
  him and to King Ahaz, perhaps someone whom the king had recently
  married and brought into the harem. The proposal that the 'alma was
  Isaiah's own wife, "the prophetess" mentioned in 8:3, is most unlikely;
  for the fact that she had already borne Isaiah a son old enough to walk
  with him (7:3) makes such a designation for her implausible.
- From the Hebrew participial construction it is not possible to know
  whether Isaiah meant that the 'alma was already pregnant or would
  become pregnant. The birth, however, was almost certainly future; yet
  even in that judgment we are hampered by the temporal vagueness of
  the Hebrew conjugations.
- In summary, the MT of Isaiah 7:14 does not refer to a virginal conception in the distant future. The sign offered by the prophet was the imminent birth of a child, probably Davidic, but naturally conceived, who
  would illustrate God's providential care for his people. The child would
  help to preserve the House of David and would thus signify that God
  was still "with us."[1]

But even though the virgin birth reading of Isaiah 7:14 does not seem
to be on target, the messianic reading of this verse is quite correct (*contra*

---

1. Raymond Brown, *The Birth of the Messiah* (Garden City, NY: Doubleday, 1977), 147–48.

Brown, who not only denies the verse as forecasting the virgin birth of Jesus, but also discredits any messianic reading of the verse). In the Old Testament prophets, the Davidic covenant and Davidic dynasty are infused with messianic expectations. This mix of royal ideology (Davidic king) and messianic hope provided the fertile soil in which messianism developed. The promised child who will signify that Immanuel is with Judah is to be connected with the Davidic messiah/king prophesied in Isaiah 9:1–7 and 11:1–9. Isaiah 9 is a prediction of a child to be born during a period of national threat (probably Hezekiah's reign), and it is said of him: "There shall be endless peace for the throne of David and his kingdom," and "He will establish and uphold it with justice and with righteousness" (9:7). The child is also to be called "Mighty God" and "Everlasting Father" (9:6; cf. 7:14). While this might reflect nothing more than throne names of ancient Near East monarchs, such honors clearly transcend language used in divine worship of Yahweh. Another prophetic oracle reflecting a similar royal ideology is found in the opening of Isaiah 11:

> A shoot shall come out from the stump of Jesse, and a branch shall grow out of his roots. The Spirit of the Lord shall rest on him. The spirit of wisdom and understanding, the spirit of counsel and might, the spirit of knowledge and the fear of the LORD. His delight shall be in the fear of the LORD. He shall not judge by what his eyes see, or decide by what his ears hear; but with righteousness he shall judge the poor, and decide with equity for the meek of the earth; he shall strike the earth with the rod of his mouth, and with the breath of his lips he shall kill the wicked. (Isa. 11:1–4)

The figure envisaged clearly stands in the Davidic line and is endowed with the "Spirit of the Lord" in a particular way (cf. Isa. 61:1). He has a special relationship with Yahweh, executes judgments justly and effectively, and is able to dominate all that lies in his path.[2] Thus, a messianic understanding of the Hebrew of Isaiah 7:14–16 when compared with Isaiah 9:1–7 and 11:1–9 is quite plausible in our estimation.

The Septuagint Text of Isaiah 7:14

The Greek translation of Isaiah 7:14 (ca. 100 BC) is as follows, "Behold the virgin [*parthenos*] will conceive [*en gastri lēpsetai*] and will give birth to a son, and you will call his name Emmanuel." Two noticeable changes occur in the LXX of Isaiah 7:14: (1) any ambiguity concerning the timing of the birth of the child in the MT (will be conceived or is being conceived) is made clear

---

2. So Michael F. Bird, *Are You the One Who Is To Come? The Historical Jesus and the Messianic Question* (Grand Rapids: Baker, 2009), 38.

in the LXX as "will be conceived"; and (2) most notably the young woman is translated as a virgin (*parthenos*). In this section we make two points about the LXX of Isaiah 7:14—its messianic significance and its affirmation of a virginal conception.

The Messianic Significance of the LXX of Isaiah 7:14

In an intriguing article, Joachim Schaper has convincingly argued for a messianic theme running through the LXX of Isaiah 7:14–25, 8:23–9:6, 11:1–9 and 19:16–25.[3] Of the first two texts Schaper concludes:

> Thus, if Isa 8,23b–9,6 LXX is read as a whole, and especially if it is read in conjunction with Isa 7,14–16 LXX, it is beyond reasonable doubt that here we encounter a strong messianic belief, centered on the expectation of an upright Davidic ruler supposed to have Israel restored through the announcement of the *megalē boulē* [great counsel] of the Lord.[4]

The contents of the divine "counsel" (*boulē*) unfold in Isaiah 11:1–9 and 19:16–25, namely that the Davidic child to become king will execute God's counsel on earth by smiting Israel's enemies, in good messianic fashion. Indeed, this is similar to how the Aramaic (Targum) translation of Isaiah 11:1 reads, "And a king shall come from the sons of Jesse, and the Messiah shall be exalted from the sons of sons."[5] The LXX of Isaiah 19:16–25 continues this messianic theme, "and the Lord will send to them a man who will save them."[6] This connection of the divine counsel with the mighty execution of God's power upon Israel's enemies through the Davidic messiah seems to be more closely tied together than in the Hebrew of Isaiah 7:14–25; 8:23–9:6; 11:1–9; and 19:16–25.

The Affirmation of a Virginal Conception in the LXX of Isaiah 7:14

In a previous question we decried the liberal attempt to show that the virginal conception of Jesus was but one of numerous mythological stories of virgin births of heroes. Instead we argued that the supernatural conception of Jesus was a historical event, a miracle. We affirm that again here. But this is not to say that pagan parallel virgin birth stories were not known to the biblical authors. For that is most likely the case for the Greek translation of Isaiah 7:14, seeing that ancient Egypt of all places "birthed" some of

---

3. J. Schaper, "Messianism in the Septuagint of Isaiah and Messianic Intertextuality in the Greek Bible," in *The Septuagint and Messianism,* ed. Michael A. Knibb (Leuven: Leuven University Press, 2006), 371–80.
4. Ibid., 374.
5. Ibid., 375–76.
6. Ibid., 377.

the most well-known virgin birth stories and the Septuagint was produced in Alexandria, Egypt, in ca. 100 BC. We call attention to three of those stories here: the Egyptian Queen Pharaoh Hatshepsut, the Greek conqueror Alexander the Great, and the Roman emperor Augustus.

One of the oldest virgin birth stories in ancient Egypt concerned the god Amon (Re) who had sex with the mortal Queen Ahmose to produce the divine-human child Hatshepsut. Thomas Boslooper elaborates on this myth that dates as early as 3350 BC, based on reliefs and an inscription on the Der el-Bahri temple which tell about the birth of Queen Hatshepsut:

> The inscription opens with Amon (Re) prophesying the birth of Hatshepsut with the promise of great power. An interview between Amon and Thoth follows in which Thoth mentions that Queen Ahmose's husband is an old man, and that while his majesty is away is the time to go to her. In the next scene Amon and Queen Ahmose are seated facing each other and the god extends to her the symbols of life. Amon-Re "made his form like the majesty of this husband, the king Okheperkere [Thutmose I]. He found her asleep in the beauty of her palace. . . . He went to her immediately . . . he imposed his desire upon her, he caused that she should see him in his form of a god." Then the Queen exclaimed, "It is splendid to see thy front; thou hast united my majesty with thy favors, thy dew is in all my limbs." Then Amon did all that he desired with her.[7]

This story contributed to the ancient Egyptians belief that Pharaoh was divine. In later times, a similar account of the virgin birth of Alexander the Great (ca. 330 BC) was told in order that he might gain recognition in Egypt as the god's son. Only in this way could Alexander become the legitimate king of Egypt. Thus it was that Alexander journeyed to the Oasis of Amen in order that he might be recognized as a god and therefore king of Egypt.[8]

The Roman emperor Augustus (ca. 9 BC) was also thought to be virgin born. Thus, Suetonius writes in his *The Lives of the Caesars*:

> When Atia had come in the middle of the night to the solemn service of Apollo, she had her litter set down in the temple and fell asleep, while the rest of the matrons also slept. On a sudden a serpent glided up to her and shortly went away. When she awoke, she purified herself, as if after the embraces of her

7. Thomas Boslooper, *The Virgin Birth* (Philadelphia: Westminster, 1962), 163–65.
8. Ibid., 179.

husband, and at once there appeared on her body a mark in colors like a serpent, and she could never get rid of it; so that presently she ceased ever to go to the public baths. In the tenth month after that Augustus was born and was therefore regarded as the son of Apollo. Atia too, before she gave him birth, dreamed that her vitals were borne up to the stars and spread over the whole extent of land and sea, while Octavius dreamed that the sun rose from Atia's womb. (book II, chapter 94)

Suetonius learned from Gaius Drusus that when Augustus was still an infant, he was placed by his nurse at evening in his cradle on the floor. The next morning he disappeared. Later he was found lying on a lofty tower with his face toward the rising sun. Quintus Catulus dreamed that he saw the boy in the lap of Jupiter of the Capitol and that when he ordered that he be removed, the god warned him to desist, "declaring that the boy was being reared to be the saviour of his country. When Catulus next day met Augustus, whom he had never seen before, he looked at him in great surprise and said that he was very like the boy of whom he had dreamed" (*Suetonius,* vol. 1, 269).

It seems inconceivable that the LXX translator of Isaiah 7:14 was unaware of some of these famous and pervasive pagan parallel virgin births, especially since they originated in Egypt, his homeland. It seems quite plausible to suggest, therefore, that our author in choosing the term *parthenos* ("virgin") did so precisely to show that Israel's future earthly Davidic messiah would be supernaturally conceived as the son of God (cf. Ps. 2:6–7 and the divine king; Dan. 7:13–14 and the heavenly son of man). He would be both divine and human, like Pharaoh, Alexander, and later Augustus were (incorrectly) perceived to be. But it would take Matthew and Luke to set the record straight regarding Jesus' virginal conception—it was not in any way sexual or sensual in nature.

Early Christian Interpretations of the LXX of Isaiah 7:14

In this stage we detect two steps of Christian interpretation of the LXX of Isaiah 7:14—the earliest Christian interpretation of the LXX of Isaiah 7:14 and Matthew and Luke's interpretation of that Old Testament text.

The Earliest Interpretation of the LXX of Isaiah 7:14

M. J. J. Menken is one of a number of scholars who argues that the infancy narratives of Matthew and Luke draw on an earlier (Jewish?) Christian interpretation of the LXX of Isaiah 7:14. We list in chart form the parallels between the LXX of Isaiah 7:14 and Luke's infancy narrative:[9]

---

9. Maarten J. J. Menken, "Messianic Interpretation of Greek Old Testament Passages in Matthew's Fulfillment Quotations," in *The Septuagint and Messianism,* 457–86; my chart is

LXX OF ISAIAH 7:14 AND CONTEXT	LUKE
parthenos	*parthenos* (1:26–27)
syllambanein (will conceive)	*syllambein* (1:31)
The son will be born to the house of David (7:13)	The son will be born to the house of David (1:27)

Because Matthew and Luke relate independently of each other's respective infancy narratives, Menken correctly argues that both must be using an earlier Christian interpretation of Isaiah 7:14. Thus, this text may well be the first to apply Isaiah 7:14 to Jesus, from which Matthew and Luke build their material.

Matthew and Luke's Interpretation of the LXX of Isaiah 7:14

Here we simply suggest that besides conveying the fact that Jesus is the fulfillment of the LXX of Isaiah 7:14, these two gospels are concerned to distance the account of Jesus' conception from the sexual/sensual stories that accompanied the parallel pagan virgin birth stories noted above. We observed earlier that the key distinction between the biblical accounts of Jesus' virginal conception and pagan parallel virgin birth stories is that the latter are steeped in immoral portraits of the supposed deities, whereas Matthew and Luke make it clear that Jesus' conception was not born out of sexual act or sensual desire. Their statements about the Holy Spirit overshadowing Mary are as simple as they are pure. This is confirmed by the fact that the same word used of the Holy Spirit coming upon Mary is the same word used of the Holy Spirit coming upon the disciples on the day of Pentecost (cf. Luke 1:35 [*epeleusetai* epi] with Acts 1:8 [*epelthontos eph*]). Moreover, we also noted earlier that Matthew and Luke combat the slanderous rumor that Jesus was born illegitimately, so it is no surprise that they may also refute the rumor that Jesus' conception was like that of the pagan parallels.

Early Jewish Criticism of Translating *'alma* with *parthenos*

Here we observe the well-known fact that post-LXX translations of the Hebrew Bible into Greek (Aquila, Symmachus, and Theodotion) chose to translate the Hebrew *'alma* with *neanis* (young woman) because they disagreed with the earlier LXX choice of *parthenos*. Indeed, the Jewish opponent of Justin Martyr tried to tell him that the Christians were misunderstanding Isaiah 7:14, insisting that *neanis* and not *parthenos* was the correct rendering

---

based on his pages, 465–66. Other scholars taking this view include J. M. Court's chapter, "The Birth of Jesus Christ According to Matthew and Luke," in *New Testament Writers and the Old Testament: An Introduction* (London: SPCK, 2002), 13–25 (especially 19–20). For more bibliography, see Menken, *Messianic Interpretation*, 466n. 14.

(see *Dialogue* 13:8; 67:1; 84:3). We should also add here that Justin's Jewish opponent never denies that *parthenos* (virgin) is the LXX reading and so it cannot be said that the presence of *parthenos* in the LXX manuscripts (which were copied by Christians) is an interpolation from Matthew 1:23. All of this indicates that the choice of *parthenos* by the early LXX and as quoted by Matthew and Luke convey the meaning that the Davidic messianic king would not only be human but he would also be divine, compliments of his supernatural conception.

Conclusion

This chapter has suggested a four-stage process in the interpretation of Isaiah 7:14 relative to the virgin birth of Jesus. First, the Hebrew text (MT) offers a messianic interpretation of the promised Immanuel. Second, the Greek (LXX) adds to the previous understanding the idea that the Messiah would be virginally born or conceived. No doubt the famous and pervasive stories of the virgin births of notables like Pharaoh, Alexander the Great, and Augustus that emerged out of Egypt fostered a similar interpretation concerning the LXX of Isaiah 7:14. Third, the early, perhaps earliest, Christian interpretation represented in Matthew 1 and Luke 1 was apparently the first to equate Jesus with the fulfillment of Isaiah 7:14. Among other things, Matthew's and Luke's contribution to the subject was to dispel any idea of sensuality accompanying the virginal conception of Jesus. That is, they distanced Isaiah 7:14 from any pagan association that the LXX might have opened the door to. This was important because, fourth, that was precisely the later rabbinic accusation of the LXX and the early Christian application of a virginal conception to Jesus.

REFLECTION QUESTIONS

1. What does the Hebrew text of Isaiah 7:14 teach?

2. What does the Septuagint text of Isaiah 7:14 teach?

3. What is the possible evidence of a Christian interpretation of LXX Isaiah 7:14 upon which Matthew and Luke were based?

4. What reservations did Matthew and Luke introduce into the LXX Isaiah 7:14?

5. How did the later Greek Jewish translations render Hebrew text of Isaiah 7:14?

Questions Related to the
Childhood of Jesus

Did Jesus Have Brothers and Sisters?

In this chapter, we answer the question, "did Jesus have brothers and sisters?" We will cover three points in doing so: (1) the three views regarding the question in particular; (2) one of which is supported by the apocryphal gospel, *the Proto-Evangelium of James*; and (3) the recent ossuary discovered connecting Jesus with his brother James which, if genuine, would decidedly tip the scales for another view of Jesus' family. The last two points deal with James because he was the most prominent of Jesus' siblings.

Three Views of Jesus' Siblings

The earliest references to Jesus' brothers are found in Mark 6:3 and Matthew 13:55. Four brothers are named, and the sisters are referred to as a group. James heads the list, suggesting that he was the next eldest to Jesus. But the question of the relationship between Jesus and his siblings arises from those verses. In the history of the church, three views compete for the interpretation of these gospel verses. All three ancient views of this matter are still alive today in the three main branches of Christianity worldwide.

Jesus' Cousins

Jerome (the fourth-century father and great translator of the Latin Bible) taught that James and the other brothers were actually cousins of Jesus, sons of some woman and man other than the biblical Mary and Joseph. This is the most frequently enunciated position of the Roman Catholic Church proceeding from the belief that Mary was a perpetual virgin. Jerome argued for the cousin view because the Greek word *adelphos* could connote the sense of spiritual brother rather than only physical brother. But, as Ben Witherington III observes, there is a Greek word for cousin (*anepsios*) and that term is not used of Jesus' family. Also, it is rather clear that Jerome was an ascetic and

therefore viewed sexual relations with contempt. This might explain why
Jerome advocated the perpetual virginity of Mary.[1]

Jesus' Brothers and Sisters

Helvidius, a contemporary and critic of Jerome, maintained that James
and the other brothers were in fact the children of Mary and Joseph, and so he
denied the idea of the perpetual virginity of Mary. This is the usual Protestant
view today. We learn of Helvidius' critique of the cousins theory from Jerome's
quotations: (1) Matthew 1:18, 25 imply that Joseph did "know" Mary (that is,
have sexual relations with her) after the birth of Jesus because it says he did
not know her until then. The reference to Mary being found with child "prior
to when they came together" refers to prior to when they had sexual relationship, not merely prior to when they lived in the same house. (2) The reference
to Jesus as Mary's firstborn son (Luke 2:7) implies she had others later. (3)
Various passages mention Jesus' brothers and sisters. (4) Tertullian agreed
with this view, as did Victorinus of Pettau. (5) It was no dishonor that Mary
was a real wife to Joseph, as the patriarchs all had wives.[2]

Jesus' Step-Brothers and Sisters

Epiphanius (AD 366) popularized the view that Jesus' brothers originated
from Joseph's prior marriage, and therefore were step-brothers. This is the
Orthodox position today.[3] It is anticipated in *Proto-Evangelium of James* (9.2;
17.1–2; 18.1), an apocryphal work we look at below. But there are problems
with the view of Epiphanius, as Witherington points out:

> (1) There is no mention of the brothers of Jesus in the in-
> fancy narratives or in Luke 2:41–52. (2) Matthew 1:25 does
> not prohibit Mary and Joseph from having a sexual rela-
> tionship after the birth of Jesus. (3) The absence of Joseph
> from accounts of Jesus' ministry does not mean he had to
> be older or that he was previously married. (4) The fact that
> the brothers of Jesus are often associated with Mary in all
> four gospels suggests she is their mother. (5) Most important,
> there is nothing arising in the gospel texts to push us in this

---

1. See Hershel Shanks and Ben Witherington III, *The Brother of Jesus: The Dramatic Story and
   Meaning of the First Archaeological Link to Jesus and His Family* (New York: HarperCollins,
   2003), 79–80.
2. These statements are culled from Jerome's response to Helvidius in *Against Helvidius* and
   DeCarne Christi 7; see ibid., 203. Jerome argued that the James under discussion was James
   the Little, a son of Mary Clopas, a sister-in-law to Joseph (Mark 15:40; John 19:25). This
   would make James Jesus' cousin. For a refutation of this identification, see ibid., 200–4.
3. See Shanks and Witherington, *The Brother of Jesus,* 79.

interpretive direction. This scenario has to be brought from outside and imposed on the biblical texts.[4]

On balance the position of Helvidius, that the Gospels intend to tell us that Jesus had younger siblings born of Joseph and Mary, seems to be accurate.

The *Proto-Evangelium of James*

Proto-Evangelium means proto or first gospel, as related by James, most likely the brother of Jesus. The author of this Greek manuscript tells his readers that he wrote an early history of Jesus' infancy and especially regarding his mother Mary (25.1).[5] James would know because he was son of Joseph by a former marriage (9.2). The author asserts that he wrote his book right after the death of Herod Antipas (Herod the Great's son), which occurred in AD 44. In fact, *Proto-Evangelium of James* dates no earlier than AD 150, for it clearly draws on Jesus' infancy accounts in Luke (ca. AD 70–80) and Matthew (ca. AD 80–90). We know it was written by mid-to late second century AD, though, because there are indications that Clement of Alexandria (second century) and Origen (second/third century) probably knew of *Proto-Evangelium*.[6]

The story of *Proto-Evangelium of James* begins by telling of the sadness of Joachim and his wife, Anna, because they could not have children (1.1–3.2). But, reminiscent of God's answer to Hannah's cry for a child (1 Sam. 1), the angel of the Lord told Anna that she would give birth to a baby girl (4.1–4). Shortly after that, Anna miraculously conceived (nothing is said of Joachim's part in the conception) and nine months later delivered Mary. In grateful response, Anna promised that she would take her baby girl to the Jerusalem temple to be raised unto God (5.1–6.1). Then, at the age of two, Anna and Joachim took little Mary to the temple where she was raised by the priests as a virgin, separated unto the Lord (6.2–8.2) When Mary reached the age of twelve, God told the priests that she should be married to Joseph, a widower with children (9.1–10.2). "And the priest said to Joseph: 'Joseph, to you has fallen the good fortune to receive the virgin of the Lord; take her under your care'" (9.1). But some time later, Joseph discovered with horror that his wife Mary was pregnant. Like the account of Matthew, Joseph struggled to know what do with Mary, but an angel of the Lord assuaged his fears by telling him Mary's conception was by the Holy Spirit of God (9.2–16.2).

---

4. Epiphanius' work is entitled *Panarion*; the quotations come from section 29.3.8–29.4.4; see Shanks and Witherington, *The Brother of Jesus*, 204.

5. The text of *Proto-Evangelium of James* occurs in Wilhelm Schneemelcher, ed., *New Testament Apocrypha*, trans. R. McL. Wilson, vol. 1 of *Gospels and Related Writings* (Cambridge, England: James Clarke and Company; Louisville: John Knox Press, 1962), 426–37. For *Proto-Evangelium's* usage of the infancy narratives in Luke and Matthew, see 437–38.

6. See Oscar Cullmann's discussion in Schneemelcher, *New Testament Apocrypha*, 423.

Following the account in Luke, *Proto-Evangelium of James* then relates Augustus's census and the holy couple's journey to Bethlehem (17.1–19.1). Unique to *Proto-Evangelium*, however, Mary rested in a cave, where the glory of the Lord appeared and then a brilliant light, which prevented the onlookers from seeing the actual birth of Jesus. The light left that cave after Jesus was born (19.2–3). Then there follows the story about the midwife who was with Mary, who convincingly testifies to others that Jesus was virgin born (19.3–20.3). At that point, the story closely follows Matthew's infancy account, relating the incidents of the magi's visit to Jesus and Herod the Great's failed attempt to kill Jesus (21.1–4). In retaliation Herod had Jewish males under two years old killed, as well as Zechariah, father of John the Baptist (22.1–24.4).

There are two motives for the writing of the *Proto-Evangelium of James*. First, it is a defense of the virgin birth of Jesus, perhaps in contrast to Jewish accusations that Jesus was the illegitimate child born out of Mary's supposed sexual relations with a Roman soldier by the name of Panthera. Second, it purports that Mary was also virgin born and she remained a perpetual virgin. Oscar Cullman writes of this work:

> All the future themes of Mariology are already propounded: the "immaculate conception" of the mother of Jesus is not indeed yet taught, but her birth, in itself miraculous, is recorded. The virgin birth of Jesus, in contrast to the more unbiased views of Tertullian and Origen, is already understood as implying Mary's perpetual virginity. This is harmonized with the existence of brothers of Jesus in the primitive tradition by postulating an earlier marriage of Joseph, an explanation which was accepted as plausible down to the time of Jerome. Yet this very assumption provoked Jerome, who wished to have the brothers of Jesus regarded as his cousins, into a sharp polemic against the *Protev. of James*, which was then taken up by the popes.[7]

The belief in Mary's perpetual virginity continues to be cherished doctrine in Roman Catholicism.

The Ossuary of James, the Brother of Jesus

In the fall of 2002, an ossuary (bone box used for burial) bearing the inscription, "James, son of Joseph, brother of Jesus" created an uproar among academics and popular audiences alike. For scholars the controversy centered on the fact that the ossuary had not been excavated by qualified archaeologists. Apparently, it had come to its dealer via the antiquities (underground)

---

7. Ibid., 425.

market. For the general public, the debate focused on the relationship between James (the leader of the Jerusalem church from AD 40s to 62) and Jesus.

Hershel Shanks, the editor of *Biblical Archeology Review,* first broke the story on October 21, 2002, at a press conference held in conjunction with the Discovery Channel. The next morning, a color picture of the ossuary appeared on the front pages of the *New York Times, Washington Post,* and numerous other major newspapers around the world. Shanks appeared on the evening news with Peter Jennings, Tom Brokaw, and Jim Lehrer. Voice of America and CNN broadcasted the story around the globe.[8]

Shanks registered a number of questions that accompanied the discovery. But the initial excitement was followed by a barrage of questions. Where did it come from? How did the collector get it? Is it fake? How do we know that it refers to Jesus of Nazareth? Did Jesus have a brother? Who, really, was James, and why is he so significant in understanding the earliest forms of Christianity? And what are the theological implications of this extraordinary find? Does it cast doubt on the doctrine that Mary was a perpetual virgin? Does it challenge the Roman Catholic identification of James as only a cousin of Jesus?

These questions reveal how significant the ossuary of James is. Thus, on the book cover of Shanks and Ben Witherington's book, *The Brother of Jesus,* the *New York Times* said of this discovery, "This could well be the earliest artifact ever found relating to the existence of Jesus." Newsweek chimed in on the back cover: "Although Jesus of Nazareth is a universally recognized figure, no one has ever found any evidence for his existence apart from texts. Now, in the form of a twenty-inch long limestone ossuary, a box used by first-century Jews to hold the bones of the dead, biblical archeologists may have found their holy grail." To those who doubted the authenticity of the ossuary, the *Wall Street Journal* asserted this on the back cover: "The simplest explanation is the likeliest . . . the James ossuary is what it seems, the earliest recorded reference to Jesus of Nazareth."

It would also confirm that James, originally of Galilee, continued to live in or near Jerusalem, where the ossuary was discovered. This coincides with the data on James found in Acts 15:13–21, Galatians 2:9–13, and 1 Corinthians 15:7. Those New Testament writings provide a composite picture of James's role in the Jerusalem church. It seems that, after Jesus' post-resurrection appearance to his younger brother, James in AD 30 became the leader of the church in Jerusalem. James's leadership skills were showcased when, along with the guidance of the Holy Spirit, he helped the early church to recognize at the Jerusalem Council in AD 49 that both Jew and Gentile were justified before God through faith in Christ alone, apart from the works of the Old Testament law. This was a historic decision for early Christianity, for had Gentiles been expected to obey the Torah, the gospel may have never reached the non-Jews *en masse.*

---

8. See Shanks and Witherington, *The Brother of Jesus,* xi–xiv, 3–22.

Tradition has it that James was known for his holiness, hence his nickname, "James the Just." As such, he led the Jerusalem church to be faithful to Christ. This stance on James's part brought him into disfavor with the religious leaders in Jerusalem, especially the Sadducees. In AD 62, between the death of Festus, the Roman governor of Palestine (see Acts 25), and his replacement (Albinus) arrived, the Jewish high priest plotted to kill James. We recall from an earlier chapter that Josephus, the Jewish historian, reports the incident:

> The younger Ananus, who as we have said, had been appointed to the high priesthood, was rash in his temper and usually daring. He followed the school of the Sadducees, who are indeed more savage than any of the other Jews, as I have already explained, when they sit in judgment. Possessed of such a character, Ananus thought that he had a favorable opportunity because Festus was dead and Albinus was still on the way. And so he convened the judges of the Sanhedrin and brought before them a man named James, the brother of Jesus, who was called the Christ, and certain others. He accused them of having transgressed the Law and delivered them up to be stoned. Those of the inhabitants of the city who were considered to be the most fair-minded and who were strict in observance of the Law were offended at this. They therefore secretly sent to King Agrippa urging him, for Ananus had not even been correct in his first step [of convening the Sanhedrin without Albinus' permission], to order him to desist from any further such actions. Certain of them even went to meet Albinus who was on his way from Alexandria, and informed him that Ananus had no authority to convene the Sanhedrin without his consent. Convinced by these words, Albinus angrily wrote to Ananus threatening to take vengeance upon him. King Agrippa, because of Ananus' action, deposed him from the high priesthood which he held for three months. (Josephus, *Antiquities of the Jews* 20.199–203)

It is clear from Josephus' account that James was the spokesperson of the Jerusalem church, hence the high priest wanted to do away with him in particular. It is also remarkable that strict law-abiding, non-Christian Jews protested Ananus' action against James. Elsewhere, we learn from Hegesippus, a second-century Christian leader, more details about James' life and death. Of this holy reputation, Hegesippus writes:

> Control of the church passed together with the apostles, to the brother of the Lord, James, whom everyone from the

Lord's time till our own has named the Just, for there were many Jameses, but this one was holy from his birth; he drank no wine or intoxicating liquor and ate no animal food; no razor came near his head; he did not smear himself with oil and he took no baths. He alone was permitted to enter the Holy Place, for his garments were not of wool, but of linen. He used to enter the Sanctuary alone, and was often found on his knees beseeching forgiveness for the people, so that his knees grew hard like a camel's from his continually bending them in worship of God and beseeching forgiveness for the people. Because of this unsurpassable righteousness he was called the Just and Oblias [in Greek, "Bulwark of the people and Righteousness"] fulfilling the declarations of the prophets regarding him.[9]

All of this to say that the ossuary of James, discovered as it seems to have been in Jerusalem, reaffirms the impression conveyed by certain New Testament books that James did not return to his home in Galilee, but remained in Jerusalem after Jesus' post resurrection appearance to him.

Related to the last consideration, the James ossuary may confirm that James died in Jerusalem, as early church tradition maintains. If the ossuary was indeed discovered in Silwan, near the Temple Mount, then Hegesippus's account (similar to Josephus) would be strengthened. In a famous passage detailing the motive for, and the means of, James's death, he writes:

Representatives of the seven sects already described by me asked him what was meant by "the door of Jesus" and he replied that Jesus was the Savior. Some of them came to believe that Jesus was the Christ: the sects mentioned above did not believe either in a resurrection or in who is coming to give every man what his deeds deserve, but those who did come to believe did so because of James. Since therefore, many even of the ruling class believed, there was an uproar among the Jews and scribes and Pharisees, who said there was danger that the entire people would accept Jesus as the Christ. So they collected and said to James: "Be good enough to restrain the people, for they have gone astray after Jesus in the belief that he is the Christ. Be good enough to make the facts about Jesus clear to all who come for the Passover Day. We all accept what you say: we can vouch for it, and so can all the people, that you are a righteous man and take no one at his face value. So make

---

9. Hegusippus, quoted in Eusebius, *Ecclesiastical History* 2.23.4–8.

it clear to the crowd that they must not go astray as regards Jesus: the whole people and all of us accept what you say. So take your stand on the Temple parapet, so that from the height you may be easily seen, and your words audible to the whole people. For because of the Passover all the tribes have come together, and the Gentiles too."

So the scribes and Pharisees made James stand on the Sanctuary parapet and shouted to him: "Just one, whose word we all are obliged to accept, the people are going astray after Jesus who was crucified; so tell us what is meant by 'the door of Jesus.'" He replied as loudly as he could: "Why do you question me about the Son of man? I tell you, he is sitting in heaven at the right hand of great power, and he will come on the clouds of heaven." Many were convinced, and glorified in James's testimony, crying: "Hosanna to the Son of David!" Then again the scribes and Pharisees said to each other: "We made a bad mistake in affording such testimony to Jesus. We had better go up and throw him down, so that they will be frightened and not believe him."[10]

And the Jewish leaders did precisely that. Having survived the fall, James was then stoned and beaten to death by a club. If bones had been found in the ossuary, it would have been fascinating to see if the condition of the bones (most specifically if there was a skull fracture) corroborated this account of his death.

Ossilegium burial was a Jewish custom. If the bone box is authentic, it would simply imply that James, though a follower of Jesus and part of a movement that became more and more oriented toward Gentiles, continued to live as a Jew and so was buried as a Jew. Thus, James' Christianity was not something separate or opposed to the Jewish faith because he strictly obeyed the law of Moses.

Finally, if the inscription on the ossuary is authentic—"James, son of Joseph, brother of Jesus"—then the Protestant case that Jesus had natural brothers and sisters would be assured.

However, since the public appearance of the James ossuary, the Israeli courts have entered into the fray of debate. While no official word has been announced yet, more and more, the James ossuary appears to be a fraud. Yet, even if it does not prove to be genuine, to us the theory that best accounts for the data regarding Jesus' family is that Jesus did indeed have younger brothers and sisters born from Mary and Joseph.

---

10. Ibid., 2.23.9–18.

Conclusion

This chapter has surveyed three considerations regarding Jesus' siblings: (1) the views of the various religious traditions in terms of whether or not Jesus had brothers and sisters; (2) the testimony of *Proto-Evangelium of James*; and (3) the discovery of a bone box purporting to contain the bones of James the brother of Jesus. Our discussion weeded out the last two points questioning the historical reliability of the apocryphal text and raising questions about the authenticity of the ossuary. But based on the first point in which we evaluated the three religious traditions, as well as garnering the witnesses of the New Testament, Josephus, and Eusebius, we arrive at the Protestant conclusion: Jesus had brothers and sisters born of Mary and Joseph. Of these, James took on significant importance in the early leadership of the church and wrote his own canonical epistle, as did Jesus' brother Jude.

REFLECTION QUESTIONS

1. What did Jerome claim about the relatives of Jesus?

2. What did Helvidius claim about the relatives of Jesus?

3. What did Epiphanius say about the relatives of Jesus?

4. What is the Ossuary of James?

5. How was James, the brother of Jesus, looked upon by the early church and by Josephus?

Was Jesus' Family Rich or Poor?

According to the Gospels, we know that Jesus associated with the poor and the disadvantaged in Palestine; indeed that was an essential component of his ministry (see Luke 4:18–20). But was Jesus himself poor? Or was he wealthy? Or was he somewhere in between? This chapter seeks to answer the question, what was Jesus' family's socio-economic status as compared to Palestine's living standard? Three possibilities present themselves, which we will consider: (1) Jesus was wealthy; (2) Jesus was poor; (3) Jesus was somewhere in between. We will see that the last option is the most viable.

Jesus Was Wealthy

In a petty, dependent princedom like Galilee, the truly rich were a very small group that would have included Herod Antipas, his powerful court officials (cf. Mark 6:21), the owners of large estates (at times absentee landlords like Jesus' parables presume), highly successful merchants, and a few overseers of the collection of taxes and tolls (cf. Zacchaeus in Luke 19:2, though the city involved is Jericho in Judea).[1] Did Jesus fit into this group since he was a wood maker (translation of *tektōn*)? A few scholars say so. According to them, both Joseph and Jesus were master builders who traveled extensively, worked sometimes in cities like Sepphoris and Jerusalem, and were relatively well to do.[2] Richard Batey contended that this was the background of Jesus' socio-economic level.[3] George Wesley Buchanan argued that Jesus' teachings were largely directed to the upper class, with whom Jesus associated. Jesus was a business administrator who supervised craftsmen. This background

---

1. See John P. Meier, *A Marginal Jew,* vol. 1: *The Roots of the Problem and the Person* (New York: Doubleday: New York, 1991), 1:282.
2. So according to W. F. Albright and C. S. Mann, *Matthew,* AB 26 (Garden City, NY: Doubleday, 1971), 21–22, 172–73. But see Meier's devastating critique of this argument in *A Marginal Jew,* 313.
3. Richard A. Batey, "Jesus and the Theatre," *NTS* 30 (1984): 563–74.

makes Jesus' challenge to give one's possessions away to the poor all the more radical.[4] Rainer Riesner asserted that Jesus was a carpenter, a profession that was devoted to scholarly study of the Scriptures, which placed Jesus in the upper echelons of Palestine.[5]

But the above suggestions are not convincing. The problem with Batey's thesis is that the Gospels do not support his interpretation. They never present Jesus preaching in or even talking about the strongly Hellenistic urban centers of Galilee. As far as we know, within Galilee, Jesus' ministry was restricted to traditional Jewish villages and towns: Nazareth, Capernaum, Cana, Nain, and Chorazin. Within Galilee proper, the Hellenistic cities of Sepphoris and Tiberias (only mentioned in passing in John 6:23) are notable by their absence on Jesus' itinerary. This general picture of Jesus' activity in Galilee, consistent throughout the four gospels, does not favor early and influential contact with Hellenistic centers like Sepphoris.[6] Meier put it well, "Jesus spent those [early] years as a citizen of Nazareth in Galilee, plying the trade of a woodworker."[7] The problem with Buchanan's view is that he makes the texts say what they do not say. For example, he states the miracles done for the centurion's servant, Jairus' daughter, and the Syro-Phoenician's daughter show that Jesus directed his teachings to the upper classes.[8] And the problem with Riesner's thesis is that the sources he relies on to connect the carpenter's trade in Palestine with scholarly study of the Scriptures come from the Mishnah, which is dated to the second century AD.

Jesus Was Poor

The sentimental favorite of the three views overviewed here relative to Jesus' socio-economic status is that he was poor and thereby appealed to the masses because he was one of them. Sean Freyne includes in the poor, peasants with their ancestral and largely unchanging rural way of life and tenant farmers.[9] James C. Scott quotes a famous remark of R. H. Tawney to this effect: "There are districts in which the position of the rural population is that of a man standing permanently up to the neck in water, so that even a ripple is sufficient to drown him."[10]

---

4. George Wesley Buchanan, "Jesus and the Upper Class," *NovT* (1964–65): 195–209.
5. Rainer Riesner, *Jesus als Lehrer*, WUNT (Tübingen: Mohr [Siebeck]), 1981.
6. Recall our earlier comments regarding the supposed Hellenization of Galilee in Jesus' day. For further discussion the reader is referred to the appendix at the end of this chapter.
7. Meier, *A Marginal Jew*, 1:314–15.
8. Ibid., 310, 313.
9. Sean Freyne, *Galilee from Alexander the Great to Hadrian, 323 B. C. E. to 135 C. E.: A Study of Second Temple Judaism* (Notre Dame, IN: Michael Glazier/University of Notre Dame Press, 1980), 196–97.
10. James C. Scott, *The Moral Economy of the Peasant: Rebellion and Subsistence in Southeast Asia* (New Haven, CT/London: Yale University Press, 1976), 1.

Tawney was speaking of China in 1931, but the remark fits at least some of the Galilean peasants remarkably well. Freyne goes on to say of the peasants in Galilee that they were largely uninvolved in the wider commercial activity and thus less influenced by Hellenism than other groups. Their focus was village life with its closed patterns of kinship and loyalty that could remain relatively unchanged while empires came and went.[11] The poor may have comprised as much as ninety percent of Palestine.[12] John D. Crossan makes much of this background arguing that Jesus was a peasant cynic, who offered an egalitarian kingdom to his fellow Jews.[13] Douglas E. Oakman also places Jesus in the category of the poor peasant based on the agrarian setting of Jesus' parables.[14]

There are, however, at least three reasons why other scholars do not think Jesus fits the category of a poor peasant. First, as Craig Keener notes, while it is certain that Jesus' audiences were the poor masses, it is not a given that Jesus was poor, especially since leaders of movements do not always arise from the same socio-economic status as most of their followers.[15] Second, as Martin Hengel observes, the disciples of Jesus were not peasants. Thus, Zebedee, the father of James and John, employed day-laborers in his family business as well as his sons (Mark 1:20). Levi (Matthew?) was summoned from the seat of custom to follow Jesus (Mark 2:14). Moreover, well-to-do women followed Jesus (Luke 8:2), as did Zacchaeus (Luke 19:2).[16] Third, the term used for Jesus' occupation, *tektōn*, points rather to a socio-category other than poor peasant. This leads us to the third possibility of Jesus' background socioeconomically.

Jesus Was Somewhere in-between the Upper Class and the Lowest Class

The key to determining Jesus' socio-economic level is to investigate the word used of his occupation, *tektōn* (used of Jesus in Mark 6:3, used of Joseph in Matt. 13:55). We will do so in two steps. First, we will describe the occupation itself and then we will see how such an occupation was classified socio-economic ally.

A Description of Tektōn

A better translation of this term is woodworker rather than carpenter, because the latter term has acquired a more restricted sense in the contemporary

---

11. Freyne, *Galilee from Alexander the Great to Hadrian,* 197.
12. Craig Keener, *The Historical Jesus of the Gospels* (Grand Rapids: Eerdmans, 2009), 19.
13. John Dominic Crossan, *The Historical Jesus: The Life of a Mediterranean Peasant* (San Francisco: HarperSanFrancisco, 1991).
14. Douglas E. Oakman, "Was Jesus a Peasant? Implications for Reading the Samaritan Story," *BTB* 22 (1992): 117–25.
15. Keener, *The Historical Jesus of the Gospels,* 21.
16. Martin Hengel, *Property and Riches in the Early Church: Aspects of Social History of Early Christianity* (Philadelphia: Fortress, 1974), 27.

American workplace. Today a carpenter is a workman who builds or repairs wooden structures or their structural parts.[17] Thus, we tend to think of carpenters in terms of building houses or crafting the major wooden parts thereof. We do not go to a carpenter for a piece of furniture and certainly not for plows or yokes to use on oxen. Yet, the ancient Greek term *tektōn* encompassed that and much more. The term *tektōn* could be applied to any worker who plied his trade, "with a hard material that retains its hardness throughout the operation, e.g., wood and stone or even horn or ivory."[18] More specifically, the term was often applied to a woodworker. Meier writes of this ancient occupation:

> Some of Jesus' work would have been carpentry in the narrow sense of the word [*tektōn*], i.e., woodwork in constructing parts of houses. But in Nazareth the ordinary house would have had walls of stone or mud brick. Wood would be used mostly for the beams in the roof, the space between beams filled in with branches along with clay, mud, and compacted earth. The people of Nazareth could not have afforded the use of wood to build whole houses, or even the floors in them. However, doors, door frames, and locks or bolts were often made of wood, as at times the lattices in the (few and small) windows. Beyond carpentry in this sense, Jesus would have made various pieces of furniture, such as beds, tables, stools, and lampstands (cf. 2 Kgs. 4:10), as well as boxes, cabinets, and chests for storage. Justin Martyr claims that Jesus also made plows and yokes.[19]

Archaeology and written sources tell us that a large number of tools were used in ancient woodworking, tools—as well as techniques—not too different from those employed as late as colonial America. Paul Hanly Furfey lists the following list of tools of the *tektōn*: hammer, mallet, chisel, saw, hatchet, ax, adz, gimlet, drill, knife, plane, rasp, lathe, the square, straightedge and ruler, chalk line, plumb line, level, and compasses. Furfey notes that most of these instruments appeared very early in the ancient Near East and were widespread throughout the ancient Mediterranean world. One poignant detail is that nails were expensive and so less freely used than today.[20] Moreover, Furfey points out that it is unlikely that a village like Nazareth could have supported more than one woodworking establishment.[21]

---

17. *Webster's Ninth Collegiate Dictionary* (Springfield, MA: Merriam-Webster, 1983), s.v.
18. Richard A. Batey, "Is Not This the Carpenter?" *NTS* 30 (1984): 249–58, especially 257n. 2.
19. Meier, *A Marginal Jew*, 1:281.
20. Paul Hanly Furfey, "Christ as *Tektōn*," *CBQ* 17 (1955): 204–15, especially 204.
21. Ibid., 209.

The Socioeconomic Classification of Tektōn
A sample list of biblical scholars reveals that a consensus is emerging today regarding the class status of Jesus' wood making trade, though it is only a general opinion. Thus, Martin Hengel says Jesus was of the middle class.[22] Meier is a little more specific, arguing that Jesus was in the lower middle class.[23] Keener thinks Jesus was in the upper middle class.[24] Bruce Longenecker has calculated the most detailed socio-economic classification of the ancient Greco-Roman world (including Palestine) to date, grouping it into seven categories, which he labels "poverty scale" (PS):

- PS 1: Imperial elites
- PS 2: Regional or provincial elites
- PS 3: Municipal elites
- PS 4: Moderate surplus
- PS 5: Stable near subsistence level
- PS 6: At subsistence level (and often below minimum level to sustain life)
- PS 7: Below subsistence level[25]

Longenecker places the artisan (another way to describe Jesus' occupation) in categories PS 4, 5, and 6. If we may use the label "middle class" (which really does not translate into ancient Palestine's economy), then we might place Jesus somewhere from above the poor peasant level (PS 7) but no higher than the middle rung of the middle class. Putting this another way, Jesus was neither from the bottom of the lower class nor from the upper class, but somewhere in between.

Conclusion
Theologians and sociologists of religion have long been interested in Jesus' socio-economic status. In this chapter, we have located that level between the rich and the abject poor. And, yet, Jesus interacted well with all three levels identified above—wealthy, poor, and somewhere in between. He truly was a man for all people.

Appendix: The Jewish Ethos of Galilee at the Time of Jesus
During the twentieth century a debate raged over whether or not Galilee, at the time of Jesus, was Hellenized and pagan or faithful to Judaism. Three views have dominated the discussion. We simply mention the first two of

---

22. Hengel, *Property and Riches*, 27.
23. Meier, *A Marginal Jew*, 282.
24. Keener, *The Historical Jesus of the Gospels*, 21.
25. Bruce W. Longenecker, *Remember the Poor: Paul, Poverty, and the Greco-Roman World* (Grand Rapids: Eerdmans, 2010), 45.

these letting the evidence speak on behalf of the third view. First, earlier scholars (such as Ernest Renan, David Strauss, and, in the twentieth century Walter Grundmann) argued that after the Assyrian invasion of Israel in 721 BC, Samaria and Galilee were paganized by the influx of Assyrians into those areas. Consequently, these scholars and others did not think that one should even label Jesus a "Jew." But later research by Martin Hengel, and especially Sean Freyne, have exposed such thinking for what it was—the imposing on the data of an anti-semitic mentality popular in Europe at that time.[26] Yet, scholars like Dominic Crossan and others have not been able to shake the vestiges of the pagan view of Galilee in their portraits of Jesus as a Cynic sage.[27]

Second, Richard Horsley has argued that Galilee was in the throes of a virtual civil war, with Hellenized aristocrats imported by the Herods ruling over the Galilean poor masses.[28] But with the most recent archaeological evidence now available, a third view has attained something of a consensus among scholars. Two pieces of data in particular have surfaced. (1) The data indicate an almost complete abandonment of the region, painting a picture of a totally devastated and depopulated Galilee in the wake of the Assyrian campaigns of 733/732 BC. (2) The sudden burgeoning of data around the end of the second century BC (architecture, pottery, and Hasmonean coins) indicates that there was a rapid rise in new settlements in the wake of the Hasmonean conquest, attesting also economic and political ties between Galilee and Jerusalem. These data simultaneously refute the other two views above about the composition of Galilee.[29]

To this has to be added what Jonathon Reed calls four indicators of Jewish religious identity in the Galilee contemporaneous with Jesus: stone vessels, attesting a concern for ritual purity (recall John 2); plastered stepped pools, that is, Jewish ritual baths (*mikvaot*); burial practices (placing ossuaries inside horizontally shafted underground family tombs, a distinctively Jewish phenomenon at the end of the Second Temple period); bone profiles that include no pig bones, indicating conformity to Jewish dietary laws.[30] These finds have been made across Galilee, whereas they are lacking at sites outside Galilee and the Golan. In the light of such evidence, we can hardly

---

26. Sean Freyne's studies have done much to clarify the Jewishness of Galilee, including, *Galilee, Jesus, and the Gospels: Literary Approaches and Historical Investigations* (Philadelphia: Fortress, 1988).
27. Recall our earlier discussion regarding the proper milieu in which to place Jesus.
28. Richard A. Horsley, *Galilee: History, Politics, People* (Valley Forge, PA: Trinity, 1995).
29. See James D. G. Dunn's study, "Did Jesus Attend the Synagogue?" in *Jesus and Archaeology*, ed. James H. Charlesworth (Grand Rapids: Eerdmans; Cambridge: Cambridge University Press), 206–22; see again Freyne, *Galilee from Alexander the Great to Hadrian*.
30. Jonathan L. Reed, *Archaeology and the Galilean Jesus* (Harrisburg, PA: Trinity, 2000), 28–35; recall again our discussion earlier regarding Sepphoris.

do other than speak of the characteristically Jewish population of Galilee in the late Second Temple period.

As James Dunn notes, this archaeological picture of Galilee is confirmed by the literary data. His comments are worth quoting in full:

> Galilean regard for the Jerusalem Temple is fairly well attested. During the reign of Herod Antipas (which covers the adult life of Jesus), there are indications that Galileans were expected to pay tithes and other dues to the priest and Temple, even if in the event they were notably slack in doing so. According to Mk 1:44 (pars.), there were priests in Galilee, who could expect to benefit from the tithes due to priests. Galilean participation is also attested in the great pilgrim festivals (in Jerusalem); following the death of Herod the Great, Josephus speaks of "a countless multitude" from Galilee and elsewhere that flocked into Jerusalem at Pentecost (*War* 2.43; *Ant.* 17.254); later on he notes "the custom of the Galileans at the time of a festival to pass through the Samaritan territory on their way to the holy city" (*Ant.* 20.118; *War* 2.232); and the tradition of some Galilean participation in the pilgrim festivals echoed in Lk. 2:41–43 and Jn. 7:10 is no doubt soundly based. In addition, the reference to Pilate mingling the blood of Galileans with their sacrifices (Lk. 13:1) suggests that at least some Galileans did participate in the Temple cult; and according to Mk. 7:11 and Mt. 5:23–24, Jesus assumed similar participation for his hearers. As for Galilean loyalty to the Torah, we need simply note here that Jesus' own knowledge and use of the Torah presumably implies that schooling in Torah was practiced in Galilee. Some of the issues confronting Jesus were matters of Torah and Torah interpretations (including fasting and Sabbath, purity laws, and Temple offerings) and a similar breadth of concern regarding the Law. As attested by Mk. 1:44 (pars.), the local priests would be responsible for administering the Law. Beyond the gospel accounts, and over against later rabbinic disdain for "the people of the land", we should note Josephus' account of Eleazar, "who came from Galilee and who had a reputation for being extremely strict with regard to the ancestral laws" (*Ant.* 20.43–44). And we should certainly recall the striking episode occasioned by Emperor Caligula's order for a statue of himself to be erected in the Jerusalem Temple (39–40 BC). It evidently triggered just as vehement a response among the Galilean peasantry in Tiberias as it would have in Judea, the

mass protest before the Roman legate (Petronius) declaring, "We will die sooner than violate our laws" (*Ant.* 18.271–272). The pillars of Second Temple Judaism—Temple, monotheism, and Torah . . . were evidently as deeply embedded in Galilean as in Judean soil.[31]

The cumulative effect of the most recent archaeological evidence coupled with the literary data speaks overwhelmingly of a Jewish Galilee during the time of Christ, which reinforces the view that Jesus was from the lower classes (but not the lowest) of Judaism.

REFLECTION QUESTIONS

1. What are the problems with the view that Jesus came from a wealthy family?

2. What might suggest that Jesus did not come from the poorest level of society?

3. Where should we locate Jesus between the upper class and the lowest class?

4. What might the word *tektōn* suggest about Jesus' socio-economic level of living?

5. What was the ethos of Galilee at the time of Jesus?

---

31. Dunn, "Did Jesus Attend the Synagogue" 210–11. Matthew 4:15 calls Galilee, "Galilee of the Gentiles." Earlier scholarship misinterpreted this to mean that Galilee was thoroughly Hellenized, but we have seen that such an interpretation is an overstatement, for Galilee before AD 70 was strongly Jewish in perspective though heavily populated by Gentiles, as the Matthean statement calls attention to.

Did Jesus Do Miracles as a Child?

In an earlier chapter, we were introduced to the New Testament Apocryphal Gospels. Here we draw on them once again because it is in this literature that we find the claim that the boy Jesus performed miracles. Four stages of Jesus' life before his public ministry will be highlighted from those fascinating, but dubious, works: (1) infancy (the *Proto-Evangelium of James*); (2) two-year stay in Egypt after his birth (the *Arabic Infancy Gospel* and the *Gospel of Pseudo-Matthew*); (3) childhood from ages five to twelve (the *Infancy Gospel of Thomas*); and (4) teenage years and early adulthood (*The Unknown Life of Jesus Christ: from Buddhistic Records*). We will discover that these materials reveal their respective motives for their stories about Jesus. After summarizing the contents of these works, we will critique them in the next section.

Jesus' Infancy: *The Proto-Evangelium of James*

Here we simply recall an earlier chapter that examined this New Testament apocryphal gospel in its two-fold claim that both Jesus and his mother Mary were virgin born. We found that Mary's own virginal birth is highly suspect when compared with the canonical gospels.

Jesus' Stay in Egypt: *The Arabic Infancy Gospel* and *Pseudo-Matthew*

If *Proto-Evangelium of James* is a defense of one aspect of Jesus' infancy (his and his mother's virgin births), the next two works are born out of concerns to present Jesus as solely God. *The Arabic Infancy Gospel* and *Pseudo-Matthew* claim that Jesus as a young child during his sojourn in Egypt was every bit the supernatural Son of God that he was in adulthood, performing miracles that were sometimes bizarre in nature.

The first of these, the *Arabic Infancy Gospel*, is an Arabic work probably based on a Syriac text, which does not date any earlier than the fifth century AD. The first edition of the Arabic translation appeared in 1697 and became familiar to Muslims.[1] We will only comment on the part of the text that speaks of Jesus' stay in Egypt. (The other part of the work deals with miracles of Jesus as a boy in Israel, but because these are also recorded in the *Infancy Gospel of Thomas*, which we will soon discuss, we will not treat that section here.)

The *Arabic Infancy Gospel* relates several legends associated with Jesus' childhood in Egypt.[2] Jesus' bath water cleansed a girl of leprosy (17–22). In an Egyptian desert, Joseph, Mary, and Jesus came upon a band of robbers, led by two thieves, Titus and Dumachus. Titus took compassion on the holy family and granted them safe passageway. When Dumachus objected, Titus paid him forty drachmae to let them go, which he did. After the family safely left, the young Jesus prophesied to his mother that in thirty years he would be crucified between those very two men. And Titus would be taken to paradise because of his kindness to Jesus and his parents (23). After that incident, the holy family stopped under a sycamore tree and Jesus caused a spring to gush forth from it. Mary then washed his shirt in the water, and the sweat wrung out from the shirt caused balsam to appear in that place (24).[3] The last miracle recorded in this document has Jesus change children into three-year-old goats because they hid from him. But Jesus showed mercy on the children by changing the goats back into children, after which they played with Jesus. The onlookers thereby proclaimed Jesus to be the good shepherd and the Lord (40).

The second work which highlights Jesus' childhood in Egypt is *Pseudo-Matthew*. This work was probably written in the eighth or ninth century, but rumor had it that the great Latin translator, Jerome, identified it as being written by Matthew. But no scholar today believes that to be true; hence the name *Pseudo* (false) *Matthew*. This writing, too, ascribes supernatural miracles to the young Jesus, moving from one legend to the next.

After his birth in the cave at Bethlehem, Mary moved Jesus to a manger in the stable, where an ox, donkey, and other beasts worshipped him (14.1–2).[4] In Egypt, Jesus cast out dragons from a cave so Mary and Joseph could rest in it (18.1). Lions and leopards were tamed by Jesus. In his presence, wild beasts walked peacefully with domesticated animals (18.2–19.2). In the hot Egyptian desert, little Jesus commanded high palm tree branches to bend down and give its fruit to Mary to nourish her, which they did, only resuming their upright posture at Jesus' command. Next, Jesus commanded the roots of the tree to spring forth water to drink (20.1–2). The next day, Jesus commanded

---

1. See A. K. Tebecis, *Mahikari: Thank God for the Answers at Last* (Tokyo: Yoko Shuppansha, 1982), 456.
2. According to Matthew 2:13–14, Joseph fled to Egypt with Mary and Jesus to escape Herod the Great's wrath at the birth of a rival king. If Jesus was born in 6 BC (as we argued earlier) and since Herod died in 4 BC, then the holy family stayed in Egypt approximately two years.
3. This place is identified as *Matarea* in the text.
4. Is this perhaps the legend behind the beloved Christmas carol, "The Drummer Boy"?

that an angel take one of the palm branches to be in heaven's paradise (21). Because the desert was so hot and Mary and Joseph were dehydrated, Jesus miraculously fast-forwarded their journey to the city of Hermopolis, compressing a thirty-day trip into one day (22.1). When the holy family reached that pagan Egyptian city, the 365 idols in its temple fell and shattered on the ground as Jesus passed by. This prompted the governor, the priests, and all of the people of Hermopolis to worship Christ (22.2–24). After these things, an angel told Joseph to go back to Judea because Herod was dead (25).

Jesus from Age Five to Twelve: *The Infancy Gospel of Thomas*

Second in popularity only to *Proto-Evangelium of James,* the *Infancy Gospel of Thomas* (not to be confused with the *Gospel of Thomas*) has attracted much attention throughout the centuries. Knowledge of this work goes as far back as Irenaeus (*Against Heresies* 1.13, second century), who criticizes it. It has come to us in various languages, including Greek (probably the original language of the text), Syriac and Latin. The *Infancy Gospel of Thomas* has a distinct purpose—to prove that Jesus was a child prodigy. Oscar Cullmann notes of this:

> All the miracles he was later to perform are here anticipated in a particularly blatant fashion. There is, however, a great difference between those miracles and those reported in the canonical Gospels. Here the extraneous material is simply imported into the story of Jesus, without the slightest attempt to make it fit, even remotely, the portrait of Christ. If the name of Jesus did not stand alongside the description "child" or "boy," one could not possibly hit upon the idea that these stories of the capricious divine boy were intended to supplement the tradition about him. Parallels from the legends of Krishna and Buddha, as well as kinds of fables, can here be adduced in particular quantity. The cruder and more startling the miracle, the greater the pleasure the compiler finds in it, without the slightest scruple about the questionable nature of the material. In this respect there is a vast difference also between the [infancy] Gospel of Thomas and the *Proto-Evangelium of James.*[5]

Not only Christ the miracle-worker but also Christ the teacher is foreshadowed in the boy Jesus. He possessed all the wisdom of this age and was

---

5. Cullmann in Wilhelm Schneemelcher's, ed. *New Testament Apocrypha*, trans. R. McL. Wilson, vol. 1 of *Gospels and Related Writings* (Cambridge, England: James Clarke and Company; Louisville: John Knox Press, 1991), 442.

highly esteemed as a Gnostic teacher.[6] This is why he could confound the Jewish sages in his temple visit at age twelve (19.1–5).

Here is a list of the miracles and teachings of Jesus from ages five to twelve, as portrayed in *The Infancy Gospel of Thomas:*

Age 5

- **2.1:** Jesus miraculously gathered the water of a ford into pools, and purified them by his word.
- **2.2–5:** Jesus made twelve live sparrows from soft clay on the Sabbath. Jesus clapped his hands and the sparrows flew away.
- **3.1–3:** The son of Annas the Scribe was disturbed with this happening on the Sabbath, so he stirred up the pools of water. Jesus curses the lad and he withered up like a tree.
- **4.1–5.2:** Jesus pronounced a death curse on a boy who inadvertently ran into Jesus. The boy died. When the parents of the deceased boy rebuked Jesus, he struck them blind.
- **6.1–8.2:** The teacher Zacchaeus saw in Jesus great promise, so he tried to teach him the Greek and Hebrew alphabet. But Jesus confounded the teacher by providing an allegorical interpretation of the alphabet.
- **9.1–3:** Jesus raised to life a child who fell off a roof and died.
- **10.1–2:** Jesus healed the foot of a young man who split it with an axe.

Age 6

- **11.1–2:** Jesus fell and broke a pitcher of water, but he supernaturally gathered the water in his cloak and brought it to his mother.
- **12.1–2:** Jesus miraculously multiplied one kernel of wheat into a hundred-fold.
- **13.1–3:** The six year-old carpenter miraculously caused a crossbeam of a bed to grow.
- **14.1–3:** Another teacher attempted to teach Jesus Hebrew and Greek, but Jesus again told mysteries about the languages, angering the instructor. The teacher rebuked Jesus, only to have Jesus curse the teacher, who then died.
- **15.1–4:** A third teacher attempted to teach Jesus. But this instructor marveled at Jesus' wisdom. Jesus rewarded that man by bringing to life the second teacher cursed by Jesus.

---

6. This perspective is clear in the longer version of the *The Infancy Gospel of Thomas* (6.2) in Schneemelcher, ibid., 449–50. There, the boy Jesus utters a long discourse on his superior wisdom to his teachers.

- **16.1–2:** A poisonous snake bit Jesus' brother, James, but Jesus breathed on the bite and his brother was healed.
- **17.1–2:** Jesus raised a child from the dead who had been sick.
- **18.1–2:** Jesus raised a construction worker from the dead who had met with an on-site accident.

Age 12

- **19.1–5:** Jesus appeared in the temple and amazed the teachers with his knowledge of the law and the prophets.

So what we find in the *Infancy Gospel of Thomas* is a rather misbehaved miracle-working boy who possessed knowledge that confounded the teachers of Israel. Two Gnostic themes inform this portrait. First, Jesus did not (like Luke 2:52 says) grow in wisdom; he had it instantly. The Docetics held that Jesus only appeared to be human, that he was really only God from the start. One will recognize in this description the aversion that Gnostics had for human flesh. Second, Jesus possessed special knowledge (gnosis) that set him apart from even the brightest in ancient Israel. Later forms of Gnosticism would connect these two ideas: thus Gnostics believed true knowledge recognized that spirituality resides in the soul not the body. Thus, the *Infancy Gospel of Thomas* was propaganda for Gnosticism.

From Jesus as a Teenager until His Public Ministry (Age 30): *The Unknown Life of Jesus Christ: From Buddhistic Records*

In the early twentieth century, Nicholas Notovich published his work *The Unknown Life of Jesus Christ: From Buddhistic Records*. In that book, the author claims that on his trip to Tibet he found numerous sermons by Jesus. Supposedly, Jesus had delivered these sermons in India while a teenager. News of Notovich's claim attracted much attention in the 1920s.[7]

Notovich's work is but one of a number of twentieth-century books that want to demonstrate that Jesus' teaching ultimately is not Judeo-Christian in orientation but rather is permeated by Asian thinking, even New Age-like teaching. As such, the movement's motive is polemical in nature: that the orthodox, established church has until recently managed to suppress the "authentic" sources of the life and work of Jesus. For Notovich, the authentic source is clear: Jesus was Buddhist.

Elaine Pagels herself, in *The Gnostic Gospels*, accepts the supposed connection between Jesus and Buddha, basing it in *The Gospel of Thomas*, which we examined in an early chapter. Pagels writes, "One need only listen to the

---

7. Nicholas Notovich, *The Unknown Life of Jesus Christ: From Buddhistic Records* (New York: G. W. Dillingham, 1894), 155–218.

words of the *Gospel of Thomas* to hear how it resonates with the Buddhist tradition . . . these ancient gospels tend to point beyond faith toward a path of solitary searching to find understanding, or *gnosis.*" She asks, "Does not such searching—the identity of the divine and human, the concern with illusion and enlightenment, the founder who is presented not as Lord but as spiritual guide-sound more Eastern than Western?" She suggests that we might see an explicitly Indian influence in Thomas, perhaps via the Christian communities in southern India, the so-called Thomas Christians.[8]

Never mind that Notovich's work was exposed as a forgery; the seed had been planted and the twenty-first century is experiencing its harvest of ideas.[9]

A Response to New Testament Apocryphal Gospels

Two damaging pieces of evidence have emerged in our discussion of New Testament apocryphal gospels that claim to fill in the missing pieces of Jesus' silent years. First, the late dating of these works prohibits their inclusion in the New Testament canon, the latter of which was completed by AD 100. *The Arabic Infancy Gospel* dates no earlier than the fifth century AD. *Pseudo-Matthew* only goes back to the eighth or ninth century AD. Assertions in the *Unknown Life of Christ* that sermons Jesus preached in India have been found are recognized by all biblical scholars to be forgeries dating to the early twentieth century. That leaves us with the *Infancy Gospel of Thomas* and *Proto-Evangelium of James.* They date to the mid-second century AD, but even these were written fifty years after Revelation, the last book of the Bible. Furthermore, the church fathers from the second century up to the fifth century AD have left us their sermons and quotations of the books considered by the early church to be inspired, and they are our current twenty-seven books of the New Testament, referenced over 36,000 times. The only time they mention the New Testament Apocrypha, such as we discussed in this chapter, is for the purpose of criticizing them. In other words, it is clear that books like those we have analyzed in this chapter were never highly regarded in early Christianity.

Second, it has also become clear that the writings evaluated in this chapter are driven by agendas other than historical fact. Thus, *Proto-Evangelium of James* obviously plays loose with the truth when it attempts to defend the perpetual virginity of Mary, the mother of Jesus. The author's claim that Joseph was a widower who had children from a first marriage fares no better to convince the reader than those who say the brothers and sisters of Jesus were only his cousins, not his natural siblings. The Gospels (see Mark 3:31–33 and its parallel passages) and Paul (1 Cor. 15:7) are quite clear on the matter: Mary

8. Elaine Pagels, *The Gnostic Gospels* (New York: Random House, 1979), xx–xxi.
9. See Ross Clifford and Philip Johnson, *Jesus and the Gods of the New Age: A Response to the Search for True Spirituality* (Colorado Springs: Victor, 2003), 218–27.

and Joseph had children after the virginal conception and birth of Jesus. Mary was a human being who later gave birth to other children.

The repeated, and sometimes bizarre, miracle stories in the *Arabic Infancy Gospel* and *Pseudo-Matthew* are obviously born of motives to portray Jesus as solely God, not at all human. While we certainly agree that Jesus was God in all phases of his life, one is left with the distinct impression that these two writings are Docetic in perspective; that is, they will not let Jesus be human as well. This is in contrast to Luke 2:52, which tells us that Jesus grew in wisdom and knowledge and in favor with God and humans. He was divine as a child but undeveloped; he had to grow and mature like all other humans. Likewise, the propaganda conveyed in the *Infancy Gospel of Thomas* plays down the human nature of young Jesus in typical docetic fashion, while its portrayal of Jesus as an ethereal, mystic teacher combines to portray him as the first Gnostic. Such a picture demeans the Gospels' message that Jesus was fully God and fully human.

And the agenda behind *The Unknown Life of Christ*—that orthodox Christianity has not been able to suppress the true message that Jesus was a Buddha—has no place in serious biblical study.

Conclusion

We conclude this chapter by giving a quiz. Which of the following are not in the canonical gospels?

1. Jesus was born in a cave.

2. Mary placed the baby Jesus in a manger.

3. Animals such as an ox, donkey, and other beasts worshipped the infant Jesus.

4. A small child played a musical instrument for the infant Jesus and was rewarded with a smile.

5. A bright light surrounded both the face of the infant Jesus and his mother Mary.

6. Jesus was virgin born.

7. Mary was also a virgin born and remained a perpetual virgin.

8. Jesus astounded the religious authorities in his visit to the temple at age twelve.

9. Jesus' bath water as a child cleansed a girl of leprosy.

10. A child fell off a roof and died. The boy Jesus raised the child from the dead.

11. Jesus, as a child, tamed lions and leopards.

12. As Jesus, Mary, and Joseph traveled together during his childhood, they were attacked by two robbers. Jesus told Mary that one day he would be crucified between those very two men.

REFLECTION QUESTIONS

1. What does the *Proto-Evangelium of James* suggest about Jesus' infancy?

2. According to the *Arabic Infancy Gospel* and *Pseudo-Matthew* what miracles did Jesus perform as a young child?

3. What does the *Infancy Gospel of Thomas* say Jesus did from ages five to twelve?

4. According to the author, Nicholas Notovich, what was Jesus' relationship with Buddhistic teachings?

5. What facts make the above New Testament apocryphal gospels and Notovich's claim highly dubious?

What Language(s) Did Jesus Speak?

Before we can answer this question, we must first ask what languages were spoken in ancient Israel. Since the discovery of the Dead Sea Scrolls and their publication from 1947 until the 1990s, we now know the answer to that question—assuming the authors of the Scrolls are an indication of what ancient Jews in Israel spoke (and in some cases may have written). The evidence suggests three languages: Hebrew, Aramaic, and Greek. For this reason, Stanley E. Porter can correctly assert, "Jesus would probably be best described as productively multilingual in Greek and Aramaic, and possibly Hebrew, though only Aramaic would have been his first language, and Greek and Hebrew being second or acquired languages."[1] We fill out the details of these three languages spoken by Jesus and perhaps many of his Jewish compatriots by tracking their usage in ancient Palestine.

Hebrew

Obviously Hebrew is the language of the Old Testament, though the Old Testament never refers to the Hebrew language by that name, calling it instead "the language of Canaan" or "Judean."[2] But by the time of the United Monarchy the various dialects of Israel gave way to Hebrew as the official language of the empire. Michael Wise labels this, "Standard Biblical Hebrew" and it was the language of the Old Testament (though not its only dialect of Hebrew). But with the rise of Assyrian and Babylonian empires from the eighth to sixth centuries, imperial Aramaic (a sister language to Hebrew) became the official spoken language of the Ancient Near East. Indeed, many Jews who were exiled to those countries adopted Aramaic as their *lingua franca*

---

1. Stanley E. Porter, *The Criteria for Authenticity in Historical-Jesus Research: Previous Discussion and New Proposals*, JSNTSupp 191 (Sheffield: Sheffield Academic Press, 2000), 134.
2. Michael O. Wise, "Languages of Palestine," in *DJG*, ed. Joel B. Green, Scot McKnight, I. Howard Marshall (Downers Grove, IL/Leicester: InterVarsity Press, 1992), 433–35.

while the transporting of those foreign people groups to Israel facilitated the process of converting the language of Israel from Hebrew to Aramaic. By post-exilic times, many Jews in Israel no longer knew Hebrew, as is indicated in Nehemiah 8:8 and Nehemiah 13:24. The first passage narrates that Ezra the scribe had to have the Hebrew Old Testament translated into Aramaic so that gathered Israel could understand the Word of the Lord, since they no longer spoke in Hebrew but Aramaic.[3] The second passage mentions that Nehemiah had to contend with a situation in which, because of intermarriage with neighboring peoples especially at the northern and western borders of Palestine, many of the Jews spoke Aramaic not Hebrew. Aramaic would remain the spoken language of Jews in Israel during the time of Jesus. As such, Aramaic would no doubt have been Jesus' first language (see below).

But one must not judge from the preceding discussion that the Hebrew language was a dead language for all Jews in the post-exilic and Second Temple periods, for literary, inscriptional, and numismatic evidence reveals otherwise. Thus, the Dead Sea Scrolls were mostly written in Hebrew (both their copies of the Old Testament and their own writings (ca. 150 BC—AD 68). And documents and inscriptions at both Masada during the First Jewish Revolt against Rome (AD 66–73) and at the caves at Murabba'at during the Second Jewish Revolt against Rome (AD 132–135) were written in Hebrew. Earlier, from the time of the reign of the Hasmoneans (134–37 BC), coins were minted in Hebrew. The reader might have detected a connection among the usage of the Hebrew language in the preceding data, namely, Jews in revolt against occupiers of Israel, Judea in particular, tended to draw upon the Hebrew language, their ancestral language, as a language of protest.[4] Indeed, Wise suggests from this that upper class Jews living in Judea continued to speak Standard Biblical Hebrew while the lower classes of Judean Jews spoke Mishnaic Hebrew, a less polished form of Hebrew.

We might add to the preceding discussion two observations. First, as one trained in Jerusalem to be a Pharisee, Paul no doubt spoke Hebrew (see Phil. 3:5). Second, earlier we noted that Jesus could read the Hebrew Bible, which would be stored in all synagogues, as Luke 4:16–22 indicates. Moreover, since many of Jesus' debates took place with the Pharisees—who spoke Hebrew—he too undoubtedly did so in Hebrew, if he was to hold his own in those arguments. Furthermore, a handful of Hebrew loanwords in the Gospels attributed to Jesus are Hebrew, for example "Gehenna" and "rabbi."

---

3. This is the basis of the Aramaic translations (*Targumim*) of the Hebrew Bible, the first of which is the *Targum on Job* in the Dead Sea Scrolls (ca. 150–100 BC). These translations most likely originated in the synagogues and were codified from the second century AD on, though the beginnings of the Aramaic translations continue to be highly debated among scholars.

4. Wise, "Languages of Palestine," 436–37.

Aramaic

As mentioned above, by the period of Second Temple Judaism, which encompassed the time of Christ, Aramaic was the *lingua franca* of Israel. Wise well summarizes the development of Aramaic into the spoken language of Jesus' day:

> The widespread use of Aramaic in Palestine apparently began in the late-Assyrian period (c. 720 BC), when the language began to function as an international language of diplomacy. As there existed numerous different dialects of Aramaic within the broad expanse of Assyrian hegemony, a standardized form intelligible to all began to develop. This process led ultimately to Imperial Aramaic, the language of government during the Persian period (c. 538–332 BC). The Jews of Palestine were, of course, part of the Persian Empire, and thus the upper levels of their society acquired a functional knowledge of the *lingua franca*.[5]

Wise goes on to say that the general population in Israel began to speak various dialects of Aramaic after the Assyrians resettled Aramaic speakers in Gaza and Samaria. With the passage of time, Aramaic became the most widely spoken language in Syria and Palestine among Jews, with the possible exception of the Jews of Judea.[6] "Thus by the time of Jesus there had come to be a standard written Aramaic language, usually called *Standard Literary Aramaic* and various spoken dialects."[7]

Evidence for the prevalence of Aramaic in ancient Israel can be found in those books of the Dead Sea Scrolls written in Aramaic (for example, the *Genesis Apocryphon*, the *Prayer of Nobonidus*, the *New Jerusalem* text, the *Testament of Levi*) as well as Aramaic contracts and the letters of the leader of the Second Jewish Revolt, *Bar Kokhba*, found at *Murabba'at*, not to mention Daniel 2–7 and Ezra 4:8–6:18; 7:12–26. Moreover, although it is much debated, the *Targumim* (Aramaic translations of the Hebrew Bible preached in the synagogues) may well have been written down during the Second Temple period (they were certainly codified by the second century AD). Of particular importance to Christians are the Aramaic nouns and sentences Jesus used. For the former see, for example, *amen, rabbi, abba* in such places as Mark 5:41; 7:34; 15:34=Matthew 27:46. For the latter, see Mark 5:41 ("little girl, arise!"); Mark 7:34 ("Be opened"); and Mark 15:34 ("My God, my God, why have you forsaken me?"). Thus it is that the vast majority of New Testament scholars believe that

---

5. Ibid., 437.
6. Ibid.
7. Ibid.

Jesus' first language was Aramaic, which at times is preserved even in the Greek New Testament. This should not lead one to assume, however, that the Gospels were first written in Aramaic. Attempts to translate the Greek text back into a supposed Aramaic original have failed again and again.[8]

Greek

Even before the exploits of Alexander III (the Great, 332 BC), Greek mercenary soldiers fighting in the Levant (Syria and Palestine) as well as trade between Palestine and Greece or Greek-speaking regions have left their archaeological remains in Palestine. But when Alexander the Great conquered much of the then-know world, Classical Greek merged with the various languages of those defeated people groups to replace Aramaic as the *lingua franca* of the day. The hybrid language that was formed is known today as *Koine*, or common, Greek. After young Alexander's death, his empire was divided among his leading generals, and Palestine first fell to the lot of Ptolemy of Egypt. Egyptian rule governed Palestine for the next century. As Wise remarks, "The Ptolemaic administration of Palestine was involved in every detail of life. Bureaucrats were installed in every village and hamlet and, as the Zeno papyri of c. 250 BC indicate, this administration was conducted in Greek."[9] Thus, both the upper and lower levels of society spoke, or were at least familiar with, *Koine* Greek. The Seleucids of Syria wrested control of Palestine from Egypt in the next century but continued the practice of conducting their government in Greek. Even when Hebrew was advanced for ideological reasons (i.e., Jewish uprisings), many of the same coins minted with Hebrew inscriptions by the Hasmoneans also bore Greek inscriptions.

Thus, from 200 BC to AD 135 (the end of the Second Jewish Revolt), *Koine* Greek had made its presence felt in ancient Israel. The following data amply attests to such a fact. (1) While three out of every four Jews lived outside of Israel from the Babylonian exile on and spoke mostly Greek, even in Jerusalem

---

8. Such a thesis was championed by C. F. Burney, *The Aramaic Origin of the Fourth Gospel* (Oxford: Clarendon, 1922); M. Black, *An Aramaic Approach to the Gospels and Acts* (Oxford: Clarendon, 1946); C. C. Torrey, *The Four Gospels: A New Translation* (New Haven, CT: Yale University Press, 1958); and J. Jeremias, *New Testament Theology*, vol. 1 (*The Proclamation of Jesus*), trans. J. Bowden, NTL (London: SCM Press; New York: Charles Scribner's Sons, 1971). But the failures to show that the earliest texts in the Synoptic tradition, such as the Lord's prayer, the sermon on the mount, or Q are translations from Aramaic originals have not bode well for the theory that the present Greek New Testament Gospels can be retroverted back into Aramaic. See Porter, *The Criteria for Authenticity in Historical-Jesus Research*, 95. See also Joseph P. Meier's critique of the Aramaic hypothesis, *A Marginal Jew*, vol. 1: *The Roots of the Problem and the Person* (New York: Doubleday, 1991), 1:178–80. But see James D. G. Dunn's more recent defense of an Aramaic substructure to the Gospels as well as Aramaic serving as a criterion of authenticity, in *Christianity in the Making*, vol. 1: *Jesus Remembered* (Grand Rapids: Eerdmans, 2003), 225–38.

9. Wise, "Languages in Palestine," 43.

ten to fifteen percent of Jerusalemites spoke Greek as their first language.[10] (2) Hellenistic linguistic and cultural character pervaded lower Galilee surrounded as it was by the Decapolis (ten Gentile cities). (3) Indeed, *Koine* Greek at the time of Jesus was the spoken language of the eastern half of the Roman Empire (Latin was the official language of the western half of the Roman Empire). (4) Palestinian books advocating the Jewish way of life were nonetheless written in Greek—for example, *Jubilees,* 2 Maccabees, and 1 Esdras. (5) Although the Septuagint (the Greek translation of the Hebrew Bible, ca. 250–100 BC), was used pervasively by Jews outside Palestine, the fact that the early church consisted of both widows who spoke in Aramaic (Hebrew?) and those who spoke in Greek (see Acts 6:1) permits one rightly to conclude that the LXX was available to be read in Palestine. Eventually, so would the Greek New Testament. (6) The Jewish historian Josephus, who lived in Israel and watched as Jerusalem fell to the Romans in AD 70, spoke Hebrew as his mother tongue but nevertheless wrote his works in Greek (see his comment about this in *Antiquities of the Jews* 20.263–66). (7) Even more interesting perhaps is the fact that *Bar Kokhba* had to resort to having his letters written in Greek because his followers did not speak Hebrew (letter 5/6 *Nahal Hever* [caves where Jews of the Second Revolt hid]). Indeed a Greek copy of the Minor Prophets has also been found at *Nahal Hever.* (8) More germane to our point, Stanley E. Porter has convincingly argued that Jesus was conversant in Greek, which he used in dialogue with Gentiles in Palestine. Porter identifies seven episodes in the Gospels where Jesus used Greek in speaking with non-Jews or upper class Jews:

1. Jesus' conversation with the centurion or commander (but the Johannine account diverges in terms of wording; Matt. 8:5–13 = John 4:46–54).

2. Jesus' conversation with the Samaritan woman (John 4:4–26).

3. Jesus' calling of Levi/Matthew (Mark 2:13–14 = Matt. 9:9 = Luke 5:27–28).

4. Jesus' conversation with the Syrophoenician or Canaanite woman (Mark 7:25–30 = Matt. 15:21–28).

5. Jesus' conversation with the Pharisees and Herodians over the Roman coin of Caesar (Mark 12:13–17 = Matt. 22:16–22 = Luke 20:20–26).

6. Jesus' conversation with his disciples at Caesarea Philippi (Mark 8:27–30 = Matt. 16:13–20 = Luke 9:18–21).

---

10. Martin Hengel with C. Markschies, *The "Hellenization" of Judaea in the First Century after Christ,* trans. J. Bowden (London: SCM Press; Philadelphia: Trinity Press International, 1989), 10.

7. Jesus' trial before Pilate (Mark 15:2–5 = Matt. 27:11–14 = Luke 23:2–4 = John 18:29–38).[11]

This stands to reason since Jesus was a craftsman who did business in Galilee with Gentiles.[12]

Conclusion

We are on firm ground when we say, with many New Testament scholars and classicists, that three languages were spoken in Palestine: Aramaic mostly, but also some Hebrew and Greek. Jesus too was conversant with the same three. He probably read and taught in Aramaic as his first language, but he could also understand and speak in Hebrew and Greek. (We should also note that Jesus may have known Latin due to the presence of the Roman occupation of Israel). So could the inspired authors of the four Gospels, who translated Jesus' Aramaic and Hebrew words into Greek, although sometimes they decided to leave some Aramaic and Hebrew words of Jesus in those original languages along with some conversations he had in Greek. Interestingly enough, many modern day Israelis and Palestinian Arabs also understand three languages, which are placed on all road signs: modern Hebrew (which is European in derivation), Arabic, and English.

REFLECTION QUESTIONS

1. How do we know that exilic Jews who returned to Israel did not speak the nation's original Hebrew language?

2. What was the *lingua franca* of Israel at the time of Jesus?

3. When did Greek become the common spoken language of the world in general and Israel in particular?

4. What three languages may Jesus have spoken?

5. In what seven episodes in the Gospels did Jesus possibly speak in Greek?

---

11. Porter, *The Criteria for Authenticity in Historical-Jesus Research*, 158.
12. We offer here two caveats: (1) This is not to gainsay our earlier argument that Galilee was still Jewish to the core; it is just to say that Jesus a Jew knew enough Greek to speak with non-Jews for business. (2) Porter's overall thesis is controversial—Greek should be a criterion of authenticity for words of Jesus (Greek words, Greek textual variants, and Greek discourse; see ibid., 126–237). This challenges the older view that Aramaic is a criterion for determining Jesus' words. Time will tell if Porter's hypothesis stands.

PART 3

Questions About Jesus' Life and Teaching

Questions Related
to the Life of Jesus

Why Are There Four Different Accounts of Jesus' Life?

We may summarize this issue by answering two questions which are but two sides of the same coin: Why are there *four* gospels? Why are there *only* four gospels?

Why Are There Four Gospels?

We will develop our answer to this primary question by addressing two topics: the four gospels and the one gospel of Jesus Christ.

The Four Gospels

To begin with, we briefly outline the process of how the four gospels came to be accepted as a canonical collection. First, already in the second century AD, the four gospels were being recognized as inspired. Papias (ca. AD 160), Justin Martyr (ca. AD 160), Tatian (ca. AD 170), Irenaeus (ca. AD 180), and the Muratorian Canon (ca. AD 170) are some of the earliest witnesses to this fact.[1] These four writings were labeled "Gospels" because they presented the "gospel" of Jesus Christ. Moreover, as Martin Hengel has argued, the superscriptions, "The gospel according to . . ." were added to each gospel early on because of their apostolic origin.[2] This conviction goes against the liberal view that the

---

1. For Papias, see Eusebius' *Ecclesiastical History* 3.39.4, 15, 16; for Justin Martyr, see *First Apology* 67; *Against Trypho* 100.4; 101.3; 102.5; 103.6, 8; 104.1; 105.1, 5, 6; 106.1, 3, 4; 107.11; Tatian wrote the first harmony of the Gospels, calling it the *Diatessaron* ("though four"); Irenaeus provided an elaborate rationale as to why the Gospels about Jesus were four and only four (*Against Heresies* 3.11.8); and the Muratorian Canon (a list of the New Testament books beginning with the present order of the four gospels in our Bibles today that was discovered by L. A. Muratori).
2. Martin Hengel, *The Four Gospels and the One Gospel of Jesus Christ: An Investigation of the Collection and Origin of the Canonical Gospels* (Harrisburg, PA: Trinity Press International, 2000), chapter 3.

four gospels were first written anonymously and then only later in the second century were the superscriptions added. Second, collecting the four gospels into one document occasioned using the codex, a book made of papyri sheets. This was cheaper and easier read than the scroll, the type of material containing the Hebrew Bible. This was so because the codex was easier to handle and cheaper to make (the second century church did not have the financial means to afford using the scroll as a writing material). Third, by the end of the second century, the four-fold gospel collection was a well-known and accepted fact. The Church Father Tertullian (died, ca. 220) acknowledged this reality (*Against Marcion* 4.2.2). Fourth, the Council of Carthage in AD 397 recognized the four gospels and the rest of the New Testament as canonical.

With that as background, we now answer the question, why four gospels? It is rather simple—one portrait of Jesus Christ was not sufficient to fully represent him. And who better to share their respective inspired portraits of Jesus than the apostles (Matthew and John, two of the twelve disciples, and the leading apostle Peter via Mark and to some degree through Luke)? Thus, Matthew relates to his Jewish Christian audience that Jesus is the Messiah, Son of David, the new Moses. Mark presents Jesus as the suffering Son of Man. Luke presents Jesus as the Savior of the world. John reveals that Jesus is the Son of God who fulfilled Israel's deepest longings. So it turns out that the explanation as to why there are four different accounts of Jesus' life is rather straightforward, as we have now seen.

The One Gospel of Jesus Christ

But these four inspired portraits do not contradict each other as Celsus, the first pagan literary critic of Christianity (third century), contended (see Origen's *Against Celsus*). Rather, the four gospels present the one gospel of Jesus Christ. We see witness of this in the New Testament itself and in the church fathers. Thus, the apostolic *kērygma* (gospel message) in Acts and Paul's writings testify to the one gospel of Jesus Christ in the four gospels, as we saw in an earlier chapter. We see this also in the way the second church fathers preferred to use the singular "gospel" (*euangelion*), not the plural "gospels" (*euangelia*), from Justin Martyr to Augustine.[3] Moreover, Tatian's *Diatesseron* fundamentally was a statement to the effect that there was only one gospel represented in the four gospels. Finally, Augustine's work, *De consensu evangelistarum* (AD 397–400), defended the inerrancy of the four gospels, which was another expression of the unity of the gospel in the midst of the diversity of the four gospels.

Why Only Four Gospels?

Here we necessarily enter the troubled waters of debate over the delimitation of the New Testament canon, especially the four gospels. Our second

---

3. Ibid., 3–5.

major point deals with a timely subject; one that has recently captured the imagination of both popular audiences due to *The Da Vinci Code* as well as stirred up old controversies in the academy, thanks to scholars like Elaine Pagels, Karen King, John Dominic Crossan, Bart Ehrman, along with the Fellows of the Jesus Seminar. So the topic is, "Current Challenges to the Christian Canon." Or, to state it another way, "Should the New Testament canon be augmented to include alternate expressions of early Christianity, most notably Gnosticism?" Our purpose here is to update the debate over the relationship between the Christian canon, that is the New Testament, and orthodoxy. Should the two be equated, or not? Perhaps the best way to proceed would be to summarize the subject by highlighting three stages in the debate: (1) the traditional understanding of the Christian canon (i.e., the New Testament is rightly equated with orthodoxy); (2) the liberal challenge to the traditional view (i.e., the New Testament canon should be expanded to include alternative expressions of early Christianities); and then, (3) the traditional counter-responses to the liberal challenge. (By the way, in using the title "Christian canon" I do not intend to restrict its contents to the New Testament; I believe it also includes the Old Testament/Hebrew Bible).

The Traditional Understanding of the Christian Canon: The New Testament Is Rightly Equated with Orthodoxy[4]

James D. G. Dunn provides a helpful summary statement of the traditional view of Christian orthodoxy and, by implication, its relationship to the New Testament canon:[5]

> The classical view of orthodoxy is that there always has been a single, pure faith reaching right back to the apostles, that the Church has kept the teaching of Jesus and the apostles undefiled. In the fight against heresy from the latter decades of the second century onwards the typical picture presented by orthodoxy was that heresy was a corrupt offshoot from the true faith; in all cases the pure teaching of orthodoxy had been established first; only at a later stage did the wolves and false teachers appear to disturb the flock and distort the faith. Thus, for example, Eusebius quotes Hegesippus to the effect that "godless error" only began to penetrate into the Church in the second century when all the apostles had passed on, before which time the Church "had remained a virgin, pure, and uncorrupted"

---

4. The following material comes from my article, "Current Challenges to the Christian Canon," in *CTR* 3, no.1 (Fall 2005): 3–10.

5. James D. G. Dunn, *Unity and Diversity in the New Testament: An Inquiry into the Character of Earliest Christianity*, 2nd ed. (Harrisburg, PA: Trinity Press International, 1990).

(*HE*, III.32.7–8). Similarly, Tertullian, one of the earliest and doughtiest champions of this view of orthodoxy and heresy: "Were Christians found before Christ? Or heresy before true doctrine? But in everything truth precedes its counterfeit. It would be absurd to regard heresy as the prior doctrine since it is prophesied that heresy should arise (*prae. Haer.*, 29)." And the same writer castigates and characterizes Marcion as "a deserter before he became a heretic" (*adv. Marc.* 1.1).[6]

We can say that there are three key words or assumptions driving the preceding perspective: authority, unity, and continuity.

1. **Authority.** The four canonical gospels are reliable and therefore provide the correct interpretation of the historical Jesus. This is so because of their apostolic *imprimatur*: Matthew and John were two of the original twelve disciples who passed on eyewitness accounts of the earthly Jesus. Mark was Peter's interpreter and Luke received his information from Peter, Mary (the mother of Jesus), Paul, and others in the know about Christ. The upshot of this assumption is that these four gospels equate the historical Jesus with the Christ of faith.

2. **Unity.** The rest of the New Testament concurs with the accounts of the Gospels, taking their testimonies one step further by making the one gospel of the four gospels the basis of Christian orthodoxy.

3. **Continuity.** Such orthodoxy continued to be championed in the second through the fifth centuries AD thanks to the efforts of Irenaeus, Athanasius, and even Emperor Constantine, and was objectively recorded by Eusebius. And this rule of faith, or orthodoxy, guided the church in its formation of the New Testament, weeding out all other contenders for the faith.

The Liberal Challenge to the Traditional View: The New Testament Canon Should Be Expanded to Include Alternate Expressions of Early Christianities
    The rise of the historical critical method called the aforementioned assumptions into question, offering instead a different paradigm for grasping the relationship between the New Testament canon and orthodoxy. Notable scholars advocating this new construct include: Hermann Reimarus (1694–1768), Ferdinand Christian Baur (1792–1860), and Walter Bauer (1877–1960).

1. **Authority.** H. Reimarus' "The Intention of Jesus and His Disciples" (published posthumously by G. E. Lessing) assaulted the reliability, and thus

---

6. Ibid., 2–3.

the authority, of the canonical gospels. As we saw earlier, according to Reimarus, Jesus preached the coming of a political kingdom of God, one that would liberate ancient Jews from Roman enslavement. Such an inflammatory message brought about Jesus' demise at the hands of the Roman officials. But the disciples, intent on perpetuating the cause, invented the idea that Jesus was a suffering Messiah who had been raised from the dead. To prevent the refutation of their claims, the disciples stole Jesus' body from the tomb. Now, no scholar today agrees with Reimarus' reconstruction of the historical Jesus. But, as Albert Schweitzer noted in his classic study, *The Quest of the Historical Jesus*,[7] more than anyone else Reimarus began the critical quest to establish what really happened in Jesus' life, based on the premise that the gospel narratives are not reliable, but later, embellished stories written by believers with a vested interest in them. Bart D. Ehrman, in his book, *Lost Christianities: The Battles for Scripture and the Faiths We Never Knew*, pinpoints the significance of this train of thought that began with Reimarus and continued down to Rudolph Bultmann and to the Jesus Seminar today:

> But once we begin to suspect the historical accuracy of our Gospel sources, and find evidence that corroborates our suspicions, where does that lead us? With regard to our questions about the nature of orthodoxy and heresy in early Christianity, it leads us *away* from the classical notion that orthodoxy is rooted in the apostles' teaching as accurately preserved in the New Testament Gospels and *to* the realization that the doctrines of orthodox Christianity must have developed at a time later than the historical Jesus and his apostles, later even than our earliest Christian writings. These views are generally held by scholars today, based on in-depth analyses of the gospel traditions since the days of Reimarus.[8]

2. **Unity.** If Reimarus and others questioned the authority of the four gospels, it would be F. C. Baur who jettisoned the supposed unified voice of the rest of the New Testament. According to him, not one gospel, but two, permeate the New Testament writings: on the one hand, Paul and his gospel of justification by faith alone and, on the other hand, Peter and James with their gospel of justification by faith plus the Jewish Law. Consequently, a

---

7. Albert Schweitzer, *The Quest of the Historical Jesus: A Critical Study of Its Progress from Reimarus to Wrede*, trans. W. Montgomery (New York: MacMillan; London: Black, 1910), chapter 2.

8. Bart D. Ehrman, *Lost Christianities: The Battles for Scripture and the Faiths We Never Knew* (Oxford: Oxford University Press, 2003), 170.

theological civil war was unleashed in the early church that runs rampant throughout the Christian canon, suppressed only by Acts' idealistically sanguine portrait of Peter and Paul. And even though later scholars un-masked Baur's construct for what it was—the application of the Hegelian dialectic to first-century texts—the damage to the perceived unity of the message of the New Testament had been done.

3. **Continuity.** Thus far in this second point, we have seen the apparent dis-mantling of the apostolic authority of the four Gospels and the seeming disintegration of the unity of the one gospel message in the New Testament. And, according to many, the result was that no longer could we pit the "or-thodoxy" of the New Testament against the "heresies" of later centuries. Rather, the two—orthodoxy and heresy—commingle within the pages of the Christian canon itself. In other words, earliest Christianity was plural-istic from the beginning.

It would be left to Walter Bauer to argue that the same diversity to the point of contradiction characterized the second century church. In his, *Orthodoxy and Heresy in Earliest Christianity*, Bauer tried to demon-strate that second century Christianity was a very mixed bag. There was no "pure" form of Christianity that existed in the beginning which can properly be called "orthodoxy." In fact, there was no uniform concept of orthodoxy at all—only different forms of Christianity competing for the loyalty of believers. In many places, particularly Egypt and eastern Syria, it is more likely that what later churchmen called heterodox Christianity was the initial form of Christianity, the dominant force in the early decades of Christianity's establishment in these areas. The concept of orthodoxy only began to emerge in the struggle between different viewpoints—the party that won claimed the title "orthodoxy" for itself. Our viewpoint today is distorted because we hear the voice of only one of the parties—Clement, Ignatius, Polycarp, Irenaeus, etc.—and only echoes and quotations from the Ebionites, Marcion, the Montanists, etc.[9]

So, now, in place of a continuous stream of orthodoxy flowing from the first century New Testament writers to the second-century church, when orthodoxy was challenged by heresy, Bauer introduced the idea of the "his-torical winners." A ready-to-hand analogy for grasping this concept of "his-torical winners" in early Christianity can be found in the idea of Rabbinic Judaism which, through Talmudic sources, claims Pharisaism to have been the monolithic view of first century Jews, an argument no longer plausible since the discovery of the Dead Sea Scrolls, not to mention the existence of the New Testament itself.

---

9. See Dunn, *Unity and Diversity*, 3.

All of this is the background for the current challenge to the Christian canon, which comes most notably in the writings of Elaine Pagels, John Dominic Crossan, Bart Ehrman, the Jesus Seminar, made palatable to the masses by *The Da Vinci Code*. Their combined thesis is that non-canonical gospels like the Gospels of Thomas, Peter, Mary Magdalene, Philip, and the Nag Hammadi Gnostic works in general have just as much right to be considered canonical as the four gospels; more particularly that Gnosticism is just as valid a form of Christianity as orthodoxy, because the two coexisted in the first century.

The Traditional Counter-Arguments to the Liberal Challenge

Some well-known European scholars, or at least European trained scholars, have, of course, recognized the liberal challenge to the New Testament canon for what it really is, an unbridled and uncritical embrace of Bultmannian assumptions—assumptions such as the unreliability of the oral transmission of the gospel tradition, the divorce of the historical Jesus from the Christ of faith, and the naïve belief in a pre-Christian Gnosticism. These European scholars carefully argue that Bultmann's intellectual descendants have rushed to judgment in their condemnation of the exclusivity of the New Testament canon. Consider again our three terms: authority, unity, and continuity.

1. **Authority.** Martin Hengel, no ranting raving fundamentalist, has devoted a lifetime of scholarship to demonstrating the basic reliability, and thus authority, of the four gospels. His book, *The Four Gospels and the One Gospel of Jesus Christ*, may turn out to be his *magnum opus* in that regard. After providing an insightful defense of the antiquity of the superscriptions of the Gospels (i.e., the labels "The gospel according to Mark, Luke, etc."), Hengel makes the following points: (1) Mark is indeed Peter's interpreter and therefore places us in direct contact with an eyewitness account of the historical Jesus. (2) Luke's gospel does the same, according to his prologue. This argument would be strengthened if Hengel is correct (as I suspect he is) that Luke's two writings are connected with the Stephen circle, Hellenist Jews with whom Jesus had contact. (3) Matthew, though according to Hengel not one of the twelve disciples, is certainly dependent on Mark and most likely follows Luke, thus also basing Matthew squarely on eyewitness accounts of Jesus. (4) John, for Hengel, is the Elder, not the apostle John, but was a Palestinian Jew who knew early traditions about Jesus and, as such, became the guarantor of Papias' testimony (see Eusebius, *Ecclesiastical History* III.39,4). You will recognize from these points that Hengel has engineered a rather brilliant campaign for the antiquity and the authority of the four gospels *without* relying on the traditional attempt to equate the authors of those Gospels with the actual apostles. In doing so, Hengel (and others like him) has pulled the rug out from beneath the liberal stance, such that

no longer can it be said that *non-apostolic* authorship of the four Gospels equals *non*-reliable accounts of the historical Jesus.[10]

2. **Unity.** James D. G. Dunn is another European scholar to address the issue of the unity of the New Testament. The title of Dunn's work, *Unity and Diversity in the New Testament*, indicates the thesis of his book. That is, though each New Testament author has his own theological agenda, which is sometimes at odds with other parts of the Christian canon (i.e., Paul and James in their presentations of the gospel, or John and Matthew in their perspectives on the Jewish Law), nevertheless there is a basic unity in the New Testament. And that unity is the equation of the historical Jesus with the exalted Christ. In terms of the New Testament canon, Dunn expresses that unity in the midst of diversity thusly:

> It [the New Testament] canonizes the range of acceptable di-versity but also the *limits* of acceptable diversity. It recognizes the gospel of Matthew, but not the *Gospel of the Ebionites*, the gospel of John but not the *Gospel of Thomas*, the Acts of the Apostles but not the *Acts of Paul*, the Apocalypse of John but not the *Apocalypse of Peter*. If the conviction that God meets us now through the one who was Jesus of Nazareth marks the beginning and heart of Christianity it also marks the limits and edge of Christianity.[11]

In other words, it is a falsehood when revisionist historians like Crossan, Pagels, and Ehrman claim that there was no core belief system, no critical mass of agreement, in first-century Christianity that could be called ortho-doxy against which aberrant teachings could be measured.

---

10. And, speaking of Hengel, I am still looking for one reference to any of his fifty or more works in the writings of Crossan, the Jesus Seminar, Pagels, and Ehrman. I have to as-sume that either they have not read his research or, more likely, Hengel's dismantling of Bultmann's agenda is too threatening for them to acknowledge. I just discovered two refer-ences to Hengel by Ehrman in *How Jesus Became God: The Exaltation of a Jewish Preacher from Galilee* (San Francisco: Harper One, 2014), 158, 320–21. Yet these two references are not enough to salvage Ehrman's argument!

11. Dunn, *Unity and Diversity in the New Testament*, 387. Compare the recent work of I. Howard Marshall, *New Testament Theology: Many Witnesses, One Gospel* (Downers Grove, IL: InterVarsity Press, 2004); see also his bibliography for those supporting an essential unified theme in the New Testament (707–32). I believe Marshall has correctly established that the unified core of the New Testament encompasses more than Dunn allows. Thus, Marshall rightly adds such components as Jesus' announcement of the Kingdom of God and the subsequent overlapping of the two ages, salvation by faith, and the community of faith's experience of the Spirit.

3. **Continuity.** The last point about there being a unified message in the New Testament undermines Walter Bauer's argument that orthodoxy and heresy existed side by side from the beginning and only later at the councils did orthodoxy win out. Thus, Ben Witherington points out three flaws with this approach. First, there is no evidence that any system of heresy existed in the first century—not Marcionism; not Ebionism; and not Gnosticism. Second, with regard to second-century Gnosticism in particular, there never was a time when any known Christian church recognized Gnostic texts as legitimate representatives of the Christian faith. This can be seen from the fact that no Gnostic texts were included in any of the early canon lists. (Related to this, I might add that the church fathers quote or allude to the twenty-seven books of the New Testament as inspired some 36,000 times; it must count for something that those fathers do not do the same for Gnostic works.) Third, in reality, Gnosticism could have never enamored the early church for very long because Gnosticism rejected the Old Testament (the Hebrew Bible), which was the foundation of the Christian faith, especially so concerning the goodness of creation.[12]

Thus, the reaffirmation of the authority, unity, and continuity of the Christian canon by the traditional view leads this interpreter to agree with Witherington:

> The Gnostic documents were not deleted from the canon, rather they were never serious contenders for inclusion in it in the first place. . . . These documents were not recognized as having the same worth or authority as the canonical documents. . . . For some time certain scholars have distained the notion of an authoritative canon of Scripture. This idea is said to be offensive because it privileges certain documents over others. Sometimes this complaint takes the form of urging that we consider all the evidence in all the documents, a perfectly legitimate complaint. But sometimes it arises out of a distaste for the notion of exclusivity—the idea that the twenty-seven books of the New Testament tell the truth and have the truth, and one need not look elsewhere for salvation.[13]

---

12. Ben Witherington III, *The Gospel Code: Novel Claims About Jesus, Mary Magdalene and Da Vinci* (Downers Grove, IL: InterVarsity Press, 2004). For a more detailed, point-by-point critique of Bauer's *Orthodoxy and Heresy*, see H. E. W. Turner's *The Pattern of Christian Truth*. In that insightful collection of essays, Turner argues persuasively against Bauer that there was indeed a core of belief that distinguished Christian orthodoxy from its inception and continued into the second century and beyond under the rubric of "the rule of faith."
13. Ibid., 109, 126.

Conclusion

This chapter has attempted to answer two fundamental questions about the biblical gospels: Why four gospels, and why only four gospels? Our conclusions are that there are four gospels because one would not have been sufficient to portray the life, death, and resurrection of Jesus Christ. Yet, these four divinely inspired accounts agree on the one gospel of Jesus Christ. That is to say, the four Gospels are not contradictory to each other; neither should we collapse them into one reading and miss the fullness of who Jesus was. Furthermore, we agree with those who say that the church got it right in restricting the canonical Gospels to the four we accept today; these four, no more and no less.

REFLECTION QUESTIONS

1. How did the four gospels become accepted as canonical?

2. Why did it take four separate accounts to provide the life of Jesus?

3. How did authority, unity, and continuity account for admitting the four gospels into the New Testament?

4. What did liberal theologians say about the three terms above relative to the four gospels?

5. How have conservative scholars countered the liberal theologians' criticisms of the authority, unity, and continuity of the canonical gospels?

When Did Jesus Begin His Earthly Ministry?

We briefly touched upon this question when we attempted to determine the date of Jesus' birth when we considered Luke 3:23 (Jesus was about thirty years old when he began his ministry). Now we need to look more at a related passage, Luke 3:1–2, the time of the beginning of John the Baptist's ministry. We will proceed along three lines: (1) the basic time frame of Jesus' ministry (AD 26–36); (2) the specific time frame of Jesus' ministry (AD 28–33); and (3) the most likely years of Jesus' ministry (AD 28–30).[1]

The Basic Time Frame of Jesus' Earthly Ministry: AD 26–36

The Four Gospels, the Acts of the Apostles, Josephus, and Tacitus agree that Jesus was crucified during the rule of Pontius Pilate, governor of Judea. The works of Josephus, Philo, Tacitus, Suetonius, Cassius Dio, and Eusebius confirm that Pilate held his office from AD 26–36. We can be fairly sure that Jesus was not crucified toward the end of Pilate's term in office (AD 36). Data from Paul's letters, Acts, and the Delphi inscription mentioning Gallio as proconsul of Achaia (Acts 18:12–17) indicate that Paul's arrival in Corinth on his second missionary journey (Acts 18:1) must have occurred around AD 49–51. Joseph P. Meier correctly observes:

> When we consider all the events that had to take place in
> early Church history between the death of Jesus and Paul's

---

1. The following is indebted to Joseph P. Meier, *A Marginal Jew*, vol. 1: *The Roots of the Problem and the Person* (Doubleday: New York, 1991), 1:372–86. For other works on the chronology of Christ's life, see Jack Finegan, *Handbook of Biblical Chronology* (Princeton, NJ: Princeton University Press, 1964) and Harold W. Hoehner, *Chronological Aspects of the Life of Christ* (Grand Rapids: Zondervan, 1977).

arrival in Corinth ca. AD 50 (e.g., the spread of Christianity in Palestine, the persecution and scattering of the Hellenists, the founding of the church in Antioch, the conversion of Paul and his years of seclusion and activity before he joined the church at Antioch, his first missionary journey and the so-called "Council of Jerusalem"), it is almost impossible to place Jesus' execution as late as AD 36. It must be pushed back at least a few years in Pilate's governorship. Jesus therefore died sometime in the late twenties or early thirties of the 1st century AD. In addition, Josephus tends to confirm an idea often taken for granted but made explicit in Luke 3:1, namely, that Jesus' entire ministry occurred during Pilate's rule. Hence the whole ministry of Jesus lasted somewhere between AD 26 and the early 30s.[2]

We are also on good grounds in saying that Jesus' crucifixion was not toward the beginning of Pilate's rule, especially when we take into consideration Luke 3:1–2. There Luke correlates the beginning of the ministry of John the Baptist with various rulers. We offer here an annotated translation of Luke 3:1–2:

> Now in the fifteenth year of the reign of Tiberius Caesar [who reigned as sole ruler AD 14–37], when Pontius Pilate was governor of Judea [AD 26–36] and Herod [Antipas] was tetrarch of Galilee [4 BC–AD 39], and his brother Philip was tetrarch of the region of Iturea and Trachonitis [4 BC–AD 33/34], when Lysanius was tetrarch of Abilene [dates unknown], and during the high priesthood of Annas and Caiaphas [Caiaphas was high priest AD 18–36], the word of the Lord came to John the son of Zechariah in the desert.[3]

The mention of Pilate places the beginning of John's ministry within the decade of AD 26–36 and indicates that Jesus' ministry began after Pilate had already assumed his office in Judea. The mention of Philip, who died in AD 33 or 34, also suggests that Jesus did not begin his ministry at the end of Pilate's tenure.

But the key reference in Luke 3:1–2 is to Tiberius. The reader will recall that we earlier noted that Tiberius co-reigned with Augustus in AD 12 but did not become sole emperor until after the latter's death on August 19, AD 14. The issue is, from which of these dates did Luke count? I. H. Marshall

---

2. Meier, *A Marginal Jew*, 1:373–74. The Josephus reference is *Antiquities of the Jews* 18.3.
3. Meier supplies these dates (ibid, 373–74).

and Harold W. Hoehner make a convincing case that Luke has in mind AD 14, for two reasons. First, there is abundant evidence that Tiberius reckoned the first year of his reign from the death of Augustus, AD 14. Second, all the major Roman historians who calculate the years of Tiberius' rule (i.e., Tacitus, Suetonius, and Cassius Dio) count from AD 14, the year of Augustus' death.[4] Thus, John the Baptist began his ministry in AD 29. Yet, technically it may be that Luke counted the *de facto* regnal years of Tiberius (i.e., the first year was August 19, AD 14 to August 18, AD 29). The fifteenth year would have run from August 19, AD 28 to August 18, AD 29. Meier suspects that Luke then calculated the beginning of the fifteenth year of Tiberius's sole reign to have begun in AD 28.[5] Assuming that to be the case, then Jesus began his ministry in the same year as John the Baptist, in AD 28. Thus, the beginning of Jesus' earthly ministry was not at the beginning of Pilate's rule over Judea.

The Specific Timeframe of Jesus' Earthly Ministry: AD 28–33

Now we attempt to be more specific about the dates of Jesus' ministry. We have just argued that AD 28 was most likely the year Jesus began his ministry. But when did it end? To determine that we must factor in two considerations: 1) the Synoptics' and the gospel of John's respective calculations of the number of years Jesus ministered; 2) the date of Jesus' death.

The Synoptics' and the Gospel of John's Respective Calculation of the Number of Years of Jesus' Ministry

Simply put, Matthew, Mark, and Luke only speak of one observance of Passover by Jesus, whereas the gospel of John mentions at least two, and maybe more. Which one are we to go by? The majority of gospel scholars, rightly in my opinion, recognize that the reason the Synoptics only mention one journey of Jesus to Jerusalem to observe the Passover is because they want to focus only on Jesus' last journey to Jerusalem and observance of Passover; the one that resulted in his death. Therefore, most interpreters prefer the gospel of John's record of multiple trips to Jerusalem by Jesus for the purpose of celebrating Passover (John 2:13; 4:4; 9:55). Beyond that, it is difficult to determine whether Jesus went to Jerusalem to celebrate Passover twice or three times.[6] If two times, then Jesus' ministry ended in AD 30; if three times, then his ministry ended in 31. So which was it? The next point reveals the probable answer.

---

4. I. Howard Marshall, *Commentary on Luke,* NIGTC (Grand Rapids: Eerdmans, 1978), 133; Hoehner, *Chronological Aspects,* 31–32.
5. Meier, *A Marginal Jew,* 385.
6. Most commentators believe the Jesus of the Synoptics observed Passover but there is a difference of opinion whether the meal celebrated before his death in John was Passover. I believe it was; see C. Marvin Pate, *The Writings of John: A Survey of the Gospel, Epistles, and Apocalypse* (Grand Rapids: Zondervan, 2011), 142–43.

The Date of Jesus' Crucifixion

The key here is to understand the timing of Passover in Jewish custom:

> According to the rules of Exodus 12 as interpreted by "mainstream" Jews at the time of Jesus, the Passover lambs were slain in the Jerusalem temple on the fourteenth day of the month of Nisan (March/April). Exodus 12:6 directs that the killing of the lambs is to take place "between the two evenings," which perhaps originally meant "during the evening twilight." In the 1st century AD, however, the sacrifice took place between 3 and 5 p.m., according to Josephus (*J.W.* 6.9.3 §423), though the hour may have been moved up some when the fourteenth of Nisan fell on a Friday. Exodus 12:8 goes on to direct that the Passover lambs be eaten "on that night," which, in the context, must mean after sundown on the day the lambs were slain. Now, according to the Jewish way of calculating liturgical days at the time of Jesus, sundown would mark the beginning of a new day, the fifteenth of Nisan, Passover Day proper. This type of calculation for liturgical days is already witnessed in the OT (e.g., for the Day of Atonement in Lev 23:27, 32) and is explicitly applied to Passover in the *Book of Jubilees* 49:1 (written in the 2nd century BC): "Remember the commandment that the Lord commanded you concerning Passover, that you observe it in its time, on the fourteenth of the first month [Nisan], so that you might sacrifice it before it becomes evening and so that you might eat it during the night on the evening of the fifteenth from the time of sunset."[7]

According to the tables drawn up by Joachim Jeremias, within the range of AD 29–34, the only years in which the fourteenth of Nisan probably fell on a Friday are AD 30 (Friday, April 7) and AD 33 (Friday, April 3).[8] Meier concludes from this:

> In my opinion, AD 30 is the more likely date. To begin Jesus' ministry in AD 28 (which seems to me the most probable year) but to put off his death until AD 33 would result in a ministry of some four to five years. While this is not impossible, it goes beyond what either the Synoptics or John indicate. As a tentative conclusion, then, I suggest that Jesus

---

7. Meier, *A Marginal Jew*, 1:388–89.
8. J. Jeremias, *The Eucharistic Words of Jesus* (London: SCM, 1966), 39–40.

began his ministry soon after that of John the Baptist in AD 28 and that he was executed on the cross on April 7, 30.[9]

The Most Likely Years of Jesus' Ministry: AD 28–30

Following John's chronology, Jesus attended multiple Passovers; how many we do not know. But while Jesus visited Jerusalem more than once, it is not likely that he celebrated five Passovers—that is, that his ministry lasted five years, which is the number that would be required if he were crucified in AD 33. Therefore, we seem to be on firm footing to say that Jesus engaged in ministry here on earth from AD 28–30. As we noted earlier, Luke 3:23 says that Jesus began his ministry at about thirty years of age. If he was born in about 6 BC, as we argued above, then Jesus will have been thirty-four years old at the inception of his ministry and about thirty-six years old when he was crucified.

Conclusion

This chapter has narrowed the circle of the possible years of Jesus' earthly ministry by moving from AD 26–36 to AD 28–33 to AD 28–30. It is remarkable that in such a short time of two years and a few months that one individual could have accomplished so much, not only on earth but also for eternity. But then again, Jesus of Nazareth was no ordinary man; he was the Son of God.

REFLECTION QUESTIONS

1. Why can we be fairly sure that Jesus' ministry did not occur at the beginning of Pilate's governorship in Israel in about AD 26?

2. Why can we be fairly sure that Jesus' ministry did not occur at the end of Pilate's governorship in Israel in about AD 36?

3. How do the Synoptics and John compare with the number of Jesus' trips to Jerusalem?

4. What are the two best candidates for the last Passover that Jesus celebrated before his death?

5. What were the most likely years of Jesus' earthly ministry?

---

9. See Meier, *A Marginal Jew*, 1:402.

What Did the Baptism of Jesus Signify?

The baptism of Jesus is written about in Matthew 3:13–17; Mark 1:9–11; Luke 3:21–22.[1] Although their accounts are different from each other (Matthew adds the new Moses nuance to Jesus' baptism; Mark's story is shorter than the other Synoptics; Luke has the Baptist in prison before Jesus' baptism), these three gospels nevertheless share some seven portraits of Jesus which are thoroughly rooted in the Old Testament and Second Temple Judaism. These seven portraits of Jesus, plus the new Moses theme of Matthew, reveal to us what the baptism of Jesus signified. In discussing these themes, we will reference them in their most probable chronological order of writing—Mark, Luke, and Matthew (though it is difficult to know which came first—Luke or Matthew; see the temptations of Jesus in the next chapter). Also, in recounting the aforementioned portraits, we will necessarily consider the context of Jesus' baptism, namely, the ministry of John the Baptist. Thus, the following verses govern our discussion below: Mark 1:1–11; Luke 3:1–22; Matthew 3:1–17.

Jesus' Baptism and the New Exodus

In serving as the forerunner of the Messiah, John the Baptist quoted Isaiah 40:3, a prophetic text predicting that the return of Israel to her land out of exile would be nothing less than a new exodus (Mark 1:2; Luke 3:4; Matt. 3:3). Indeed, commentators have often called attention to the heavens being ripped open at the baptism of Jesus as signifying a new exodus (Mark 1:10; cf. Luke 3:21; Matt. 3:16). It is interesting in this regard that the Qumran community also quoted Isaiah 40:3 as indicating that it constituted the new exodus (see 1QS 8:12–16).

---

1. The gospel of John does not record the baptism of Jesus by John the Baptist but it does imply it.

Jesus' Baptism and the New Restoration

But in drawing upon Isaiah 40:3 as the introduction to the second half of Isaiah, John the Baptist signaled that the new exodus would culminate in the new restoration of Israel. This pattern would have reminded Jews of their first exodus which led to the possession of their promised land. In fact, the term "gospel" (Mark 1:1, 14–15; Matt. 4:23) is itself taken from the LXX of Isaiah 40–66 which signified the good news of the coming restoration of Israel out of her exile to Assyria and Babylonia especially (Isa. 40:9; 52:7–10). No doubt the references to the kingdom of God (Mark 1:1) or the kingdom of heaven (Matt. 3:2; the two are synonymous) conveyed, among other things, the rule of God over his people, the Jews. Moreover, according to the Old Testament prophets, before such a renewal could take place, Israel would need to repent of her sin and return to the Lord. This was precisely the meaning behind John the Baptist's call to submit to his baptism of repentance (Mark 1:4; Luke 3:7–14; Matt. 3:4–11). Those who responded positively to the Baptist's message continued the Old Testament tradition of the remnant, those who repented and therefore returned to Israel out of exile.

But, as N. T. Wright has convincingly argued in his writings, when Israel returned to her homeland in ca. 539 BC under the decree of King Cyrus the Persian, she discovered that she was still in exile even after returning to her land. This was so because the Jews continued to be ruled and occupied by the nations—Greece, Egypt, Syria, and now Rome. Consequently, various religious groups in Israel offered their respective spiritual remedies as to how they could motivate God to rid the land of Israel of their enemies.[2] And the message of the Jesus movement joined the shrill of competing voices, arguing that the true restoration of Israel was spiritual, not geographical (at least for the moment; see our chapter on the ascension as recorded only in Luke-Acts), and that it centered on Jesus the Messiah and one's relationship with him.

Jesus' Baptism as the New Conquest

It is not without significance that John the Baptist chose to baptize his converts in the Jordan River (Mark 1:9; Luke 3:3; Matt. 3:5), for it was there that ancient Israel staged the conquest of Canaan. Indeed, Josephus (the first century Jewish historian) records that some ten would-be messianic movements gathered at the Jordan River for the purpose of invading Canaan again and ridding Israel of the Roman occupation (*Antiquities of the Jews* 20.97; *Jewish Wars* 20.169–70). Moreover, Jesus' defeat of Satan in the Judean wilderness (into which the Jordan River emptied), followed by Jesus' expulsion of demons, also signified the new conquest of Canaan land.

---

2. The books by N. T. Wright that programmatically put forth this notion are *The New Testament and the People of God* (Minneapolis: Fortress, 1992), *Jesus and the Victory of God* (Minneapolis: Fortress, 1996), and *Paul and the Faithfulness of God* (Minneapolis: Fortress, 2013).

Jesus' Baptism and The New Covenant

John the Baptist preached a baptism of repentance, but he prophesied that the coming Messiah would baptize with the Holy Spirit and fire (Mark 1:8 [which only predicts the baptism of the Spirit]; Matt. 3:11 and Luke 3:16 add the baptism with fire). The baptism of the Spirit would be the fulfillment of the Old Testament prophecy of the arrival of the new covenant (Ezek. 36:25–28 [note the connection of water, repentance, and the Spirit therein]; Joel 2:28–32). There is a debate regarding the baptism with fire: does it mean that believers in Jesus will be baptized with the Spirit and non-believers baptized with the fire of divine judgment or will believers experience both baptisms? Perhaps one need not choose between these two options. Rather, if the baptism with fire alludes to the messianic woes, the end-time tribulation that was expected to fall on the world but purge Israel before the coming of the Messiah, then one has the answer. Indeed, both the Old Testament and Second Temple Judaism envisioned that the covenant curses that rested on Israel would intensify into the messianic woes which would in turn purge Israel in preparation for the appearance of the new covenant.[3] A powerful analogue to such an expectation is pervasive in the Dead Sea Scrolls writings, the only other group in Second Temple Judaism besides early Christianity that identified itself as the "new covenant."[4]

In addition, there are at least four reasons why some scholars have argued that John the Baptist acquired his baptism of repentance from the Qumran community. First, geographically, both the Qumran community and John the Baptist lived in the Judean Desert (cf. Mark 1:5; Luke 3:2; Matt. 3:1 with 1QS 8:13). Second, as we noted above, textually, both based their ministries on Isaiah 40:3 (cf. Mark 1:2–3; Luke 3:4–6; Matt. 3:3 with 1QS 8:12–16). Third, both proclaimed their messages with an eschatological fervency (cf. Mark 1:1–8; Luke 3:1–20; Matt. 3:1–12 with, e.g., 1QS 3–4). Fourth, both adhered to a type of baptism or repentance for *Jews* (see especially Luke 3:7–9 with 1QS 4:20–21). In light of these similarities, it is possible that John the Baptist may have been associated with the Qumran Jewish sect at one time; nevertheless, he later separated from the group to pursue his own calling.

Jesus' Baptism as the New Israel

All three Synoptic gospels report that at his baptism, God the Father proclaimed Jesus to be his son (Mark 1:11; Luke 3:22; Matt. 3:17). In doing so, the Gospels quote Psalm 2:7 and Isaiah 42:1, passages well-known for identifying Israel as the son of God. Moreover, as our next chapter on Jesus' temptations

---

3. See C. Marvin Pate and Douglas K. Kennard, *Deliverance Now and Not Yet: The New Testament and the Great Tribulation* (New York: Peter Lang, 2004).
4. See C. Marvin Pate, *Communities of the Last Days: The Dead Sea Scrolls, the New Testament, and the Story of Israel* (Downers Grove, IL: InterVarsity Press, 2000), 207–8.

in the wilderness will demonstrate, Jesus there passes the tests whereas ancient Israel failed her tests/temptations in the wilderness. Thus, the baptism and temptations of Jesus served to reveal that he was the true, new Israel.

Jesus' Baptism as the New Creation

It is common among Christians to see the Trinity at work during Jesus' baptism: the Holy Spirit like a dove descends upon Jesus at his baptism while the Father declares his pleasure with his son. But the careful reader will also hear in the references to the three members of the Trinity allusions to Genesis 1 and the creation of the world. God creates the world (Gen. 1:1), the Spirit broods like a dove over the newly created cosmos (Gen. 1:2), and together they create Adam in the image of God (Gen. 1:26–27). In the next point, we will specify how Christ relates to the creation of Adam, but here we note that the Synoptic authors may well have interpreted Jesus' baptism as the beginning of a new creation.

Jesus' Baptism as the New Adam

Furthermore, we can make several statements that clarify what Jesus' baptism seems to have said regarding his relationship to the first Adam. First, Genesis 9:1–3 presents Noah embarking on the new world after the flood as the new Adam. Moreover, it was the dove that signaled to Noah that he and his family could now safely step onto that new creation (Gen. 8:8–12; cf. Gen. 1:2). Second, Adam's role plays a significant role in the temptation narratives of the Synoptic Gospels (see our next chapter for full documentation of this point). Furthermore, Luke takes Jesus' genealogy all the way back to Adam (Luke 3:38). The point the three gospel authors make is that Jesus is the true, new Adam who obeyed the Father whereas the first Adam did not. Third, if we may bring the apostle Paul into this discussion we can now clarify how it was that Jesus was related to the creation of the first Adam. According to 1 Corinthians 15:21–22, 45–49, Adam was created in the image of the Son of God, the second member of the Trinity. Pulling these two considerations together—the new creation and the new Adam—we may now say that our gospel authors may well have interpreted the creation of the world as recorded in Genesis 1 as the workings of the Trinity: the Father created the world, the Spirit like a dove crafted the world, and the Son made the first man in his (the Son's) image. Thus, the baptism of Jesus reflects the Trinity in the making of the new creation.

Jesus' Baptism and the New Moses

Only Matthew records Jesus' overcoming John's resistance to baptize Jesus by asserting that he (Jesus) must be baptized in order to fulfill all righteousness (Matt. 3:13–15). When we compare this statement with Matthew 5:17–20 and Jesus' pledge to fulfill every bit of the Torah, we realize that Jesus is thereby proclaiming himself to be the new Moses. Indeed, that Matthew presents Jesus as the new and greater Moses is a theme dear to the first gospel.[5]

Conclusion

So we see that the Synoptic Gospels present the baptism of Jesus as multi-faceted involving the new exodus, restoration, conquest, covenant, Israel, creation, Adam, and for Matthew, the new Moses. All of these new beginnings that are associated with the baptism of Jesus remind us that Jesus associated with sinful humanity while still being the spotless Son of God. Therefore, it is appropriate for followers of Jesus to publicly identify with him by being baptized in the name of the Father, the Son, and the Holy Spirit.

REFLECTION QUESTIONS

1. How was Jesus' baptism a new exodus?

2. How did Jesus' baptism relate to the new restoration of Israel?

3. How did Jesus' baptism relate to the new conquest of Canaan?

4. What was the relationship between Jesus' baptism and the new covenant of the new Israel?

5. How does Genesis 1 relate to Jesus' baptism?

---

5. See W. D. Davies' treatment of this subject, *The Sermon on the Mount* (Cambridge: Cambridge University Press, 1966), 10–32.

What Is the Significance of Jesus' Temptations in the Wilderness?

The temptations of Jesus in the wilderness prepared him for his public ministry. The reader might be surprised that there are five, not just three, biblical sources for the telling of Jesus' temptations: Mark 1:12–13; Q 4:1–13,[1] Matthew 4:1–11; Luke 4:1–13; and the gospel of John. Q (the sayings of Jesus) and the gospel of John are not normally factored into the topic by general readers, but scholars have long noted the importance of Q and John as important sources for the temptations of Jesus as well. Below, we will summarize each of these five sources of the temptations narrative, which will be followed by a consideration of the individual meanings of the respective temptations as well as the overriding theme of the temptations as a whole.

The Five Sources of the Wilderness Temptations of Jesus

Many scholars agree that Matthew and Luke used Mark and Q as two of their main sources in telling the story of Jesus, and this applies to the temptation narrative as well. In addition, years ago Raymond Brown identified the gospel of John to also be a source for Jesus' temptations. We now summarize the five sources in the following order, which most likely is the order of their composition: Mark 1:12–13; Q 4:1–13; Matthew 4:1–11; Luke 4:1–13; and the gospel of John.

---

1. "Q" stands for the hypothetical document *Quelle*, which supposedly consisted of the common 235 sayings of Jesus in Luke and Matthew. Although we accept the theory that there was a "Q" document, until such an actual document is found we can only refer to it as a theory not as a fact. So even though I refer to such a document by name, chapter and verse, I recognize the uncertainty that such a manuscript ever existed.

Mark 1:12–13

This account of Jesus' temptation in the Judean wilderness reads as follows:

> At once the Spirit sent him out into the desert, and he was in the desert forty days, being tempted by Satan. He was with the wild animals, and angels attended him.

Mark presents Jesus as the new Adam who was obedient to God in the desert in contrast to the first Adam who was disobedient to God in paradise. Moreover, Jesus tames the animals made wild by Adam's sin (cf. Gen. 1:19–20; Isa. 11:6–9; 65:25; Jubilees 3:27–9; *2 Baruch* 73:6–7; etc). After passing his test appropriately, Jesus eats of the manna that Adam once ate and dwells with and is served by the angels (cf. Ps. 78:25; 2 Esdra 1:19; *Babylonian Sanhedrin* 59b; etc.).[2]

Q 4:1–4, 9–12, 5–8, 13[3]

The Q passage on Jesus' temptations in the wilderness runs as follows:

> [1]And Jesus was led [into] the wilderness by the Spirit [2][to be] tempted by the devil. And "he ate nothing" for forty days . . . he became hungry. [3]And the devil told him: If you are God's Son, order that these stones become loaves. [4]And Jesus answered [him]: It is written: A person is not to live only from bread.

> [9][The devil] took him along to Jerusalem and put him on the tip of the temple and told him: If you are God's Son, throw yourself down. [10]For it is written: He will command his angels about you, [11]and on their hands they will bear you, so that you do not strike your foot against a stone. [12]And Jesus [in reply] told him: It is written: Do not put to the test the Lord your God.

> [5]And the devil took him along to a [very high] mountain and showed him all the kingdoms of the world and their splendor, [6]and told him: All these I will give you, [7]if you bow down before me. [8]And [in reply] Jesus told him: It is written: Bow down to the Lord your God, and serve only him.

> [13] And the devil left him.[4]

---

2. For support of this statement, see W. D. Davies and Dale C. Allison's *Matthew* [I–VII], ICC (Edinburgh: Scotland, T&T Clark, 1988), 1:356–57.

3. Refer again to footnote 1 for reference to the "Q" document.

4. James M. Robinson, Paul Hoffmann, and John S. Kloppenburg, eds., *The Sayings Gospel Q in Greek and English with Parallels from the Gospels of Mark and Thomas* (Minneapolis: Fortress, 2002), 79–80.

Three items emerge in the supposed Q's version of the temptations of Jesus in the Judean wilderness: (1) It delineates the general statement in Mark about Jesus' temptations into three specific temptations. (2) It presents Jesus as the true Israel, the Son of God, who passes the tests in the wilderness against the backdrop of Israel's failures in the Sinai wilderness. (3) It gives the order that Matthew follows. So Mark 1:12–13 presents Jesus as the new Adam while Q 4:1–13 portrays Jesus as the new Israel.

Matthew 4:1–11

Matthew's record of Jesus' temptations runs as follows:

> ¹ Then Jesus was led by the Spirit into the desert to be tempted by the devil. ² After fasting forty days and forty nights, he was hungry. ³ The tempter came to him and said, "If you are the Son of God, tell these stones to become bread." ⁴ Jesus answered, "It is written: 'Man does not live on bread alone, but on every word that comes from the mouth of God.'" ⁵ Then the devil took him to the holy city and had him stand on the highest point of the temple, ⁶ "If you are the Son of God," he said, "throw yourself down. For it is written: 'He will command his angels concerning you, and they will lift you up in their hands, so that you will not strike your foot against a stone.'" ⁷ Jesus answered him, "It is also written: 'Do not put the Lord your God to the test.'" ⁸ Again, the devil took him to a very high mountain and showed him all the kingdoms of the world and their splendor. ⁹ "All this I will give you," he said, "if you will bow down and worship me." ¹⁰ Jesus said to him, "Away from me, Satan! For it is written: 'Worship the Lord your God, and serve him only.'" ¹¹ Then the devil left him, and angels came and attended him.

Matthew combines the themes of Jesus as the new Israel and as the new Adam, with the former receiving the greater emphasis. We can do no better than quote W. D. Davies and Dale C. Allison regarding the new Israel theme in Matthew's account of the temptations:

> . . . in each temptation Jesus quotes from Deuteronomy, from Deut 8.3 in 4.4, from Deut 6.16 in 4.7, and from Deut 6.13 in 4.10. This is the key to the narrative: we have before us a haggadic tale which has issued forth from reflection on Deut 6–8. Jesus, the Son of God, is repeating the experience of Israel in the desert (cf. Tertullian, *De bapt.* 20). Having passed through the waters of a new exodus at his baptism (cf.

1 Cor 10.1–5), he enters the desert to suffer a time of testing, his forty days of fasting being analogous to Israel's forty years of wandering. Like Israel, Jesus is tempted by hunger. And, like Israel, Jesus is tempted to idolatry. All-important for a right understanding of our pericope is Deut 8.2–3: "And you shall remember all the way which the Lord your God has led you these *forty* years *in the wilderness,* that he might humble you, *testing you* to know what was in your heart, whether you would keep his commandments, or not. And he humbled you and let you *hunger.*"[5]

But the new Adam theme can also be detected in Matthew's account. Davies and Allison observe this:

> As God once miraculously gave Israel manna in the desert, so now he feeds his Son who, unlike Adam, did not succumb to temptation and so received the food which the first man ate in paradise before the fall. Perhaps we should also think of the tradition according to which God sent the angels to guard Adam and pay him homage (LAE 12–17, 33; Apoc. Sed. 5; Gk. Apoc. Ezra 2; cf. Heb 1.14). What Adam forfeited by his disobedience, namely, the ministration of angels, Jesus regained by his obedience (cf. Phil 2.5–11; Heb 1.6). (Eden was on a mountain according to some Jewish texts [see on 5.1]. This would fit in with seeing Jesus as the counterpart of Adam. So too would the identification of Adam as "son of God"; see Philo, *Virt.* 203–5; Lk 3.38; Sophia of Jesus Christ 3.105.22–3).[6]

But why does Matthew combine the new Adam theme of Mark with the new Israel theme of Q? We will postpone our answer to this question until the point to follow on Luke.

Luke 4:1–13
Luke's account of Jesus' wilderness temptations runs as follows:

> [1] Jesus, full of the Holy Spirit, returned from the Jordan and was led by the Spirit in the desert, [2] where for forty days he was tempted by the devil. He ate nothing during those days, and at the end of them he was hungry. [3] The devil said to him,

---

5. Davies and Allison, *Matthew*, 1:352.
6. Ibid., 1:374.

"If you are the Son of God, tell this stone to become bread."
[4] Jesus answered, "It is written: 'Man does not live on bread
alone.'" [5] The devil led him up to a high place and showed
him in an instant all the kingdoms of the world. [6] And he said
to him, "I will give you all their authority and splendor, for
it has been given to me, and I can give it to anyone I want to.
[7] So if you worship me, it will all be yours." [8] Jesus answered,
"It is written: 'Worship the Lord your God and serve him
only.'" [9] The devil led him to Jerusalem and had him stand on
the highest point of the temple. "If you are the Son of God,"
he said, "throw yourself down from here. [10] For it is written:
'He will command his angels concerning you to guard you
carefully; [11] they will lift you up in their hands, so that you
will not strike your foot against a stone.'" [12] Jesus answered,
"It says: 'Do not put the Lord your God to the test.'" [13] When
the devil had finished all this tempting, he left him until an
opportune time.

Many scholars think that Luke here has altered Matthew's order of the
temptations rather than the reverse, primarily because Luke's interest in the
temple seems to have motivated him to place that temptation last.

We will now answer the question of why Matthew and Luke combine the
new Adam and new Israel traditions in their narratives of Jesus' temptations.
Second, we will offer an exposition of Luke's narrative, which will set the stage
for grasping the meaning of the temptations.

The Combination of the New Adam and New Israel Traditions in the Temptations of Jesus

Our theory here in Luke also applies to Matthew. Commentators of Luke
4:1–13 have reached an impasse in identifying the Old Testament backdrop
for that narrative. Many prefer to view the scene of Jesus' temptation in light
of Israel's temptations in the wilderness. This is quite understandable because
of: the desert setting (v. 1); the forty days (cf. the forty years of wilderness
wandering, Deut. 8:2); the three quotations from the wilderness wandering
setting in Deuteronomy (Luke 4:4/Deut. 8:3; Luke 4:8/Deut. 6:13; Luke
4:12/Deut. 6:16); and the reference to Jesus as the Son of God, the same title
applied to Israel (Deut. 14:1). The interpretation arrived at with the preceding
data in mind is that Jesus is the true Son of God, who passed his temptations,
in contrast to Israel's failure.

Others play down the wilderness-wandering theme and argue for an
Adamic context of Luke 4:1–13. They marshal the following pieces of evidence in support of their position: the explicit reference to Adam (3:38)
specifies Luke's intended background; Luke's transposition of the genealogy

of Jesus from the beginning of Matthew's gospel (Matt. 1:1–17) to its intervening spot between the baptism (Luke 3:28–38) and temptations (4:1–13) of Jesus sheds critical light on how Luke wants it interpreted—Jesus' temptations in the desert are to be perceived against the foil of Adam's temptation in the Garden of Eden; the three temptations of Jesus by the Devil are best grasped by comparing them with Genesis 3 (see the exposition that follows); and the reference to Adam as the Son of God is the backdrop for understanding Jesus' title Son of God, in Luke 4:3, 9. The interpretation advocated, then, by this school of thought is that Jesus is the obedient Son of God, in contrast to Adam's past disobedience.

We suggest, however, that the aforementioned impasse is removed when one realizes that both the Old Testament and early Judaism cherished the belief that Israel, the true son of God, was intended to be the divine replacement of Adam, the son of God whose sin deprived him of his intimate relationship with God. N. T Wright has insightfully and thoroughly documented this belief elsewhere,[7] though he does not apply it to Luke 4:1–13. We maintain that such a belief wonderfully furthers our understanding of Luke 4:1–13: Israel, in its disobedience to God in the wilderness, showed itself to still be in Adam, whereas Christ, in his obedience in the desert, showed himself to the replacement of Adam, who is the true Israel, the Son of God.[8]

Exegesis of Luke 4:1–13[9]

- **4:1** Endued with the Holy Spirit from his baptism at the Jordan River, Jesus was led by the same Spirit into the Jordan wilderness, an area that can still be seen today by looking southwest from Jericho or east from Jerusalem. In light of the reference to Adam in 3:38, it seems that Luke invites the reader to contrast Adam's temptation in the Garden, a perfect environment (but which did not prevent him from succumbing to sin) with Jesus' temptation in the wilderness, a desolate location (but which did not hinder his obedience). Two other pieces of data support this Adamic reading of the text. First, the mention of the Spirit (v. 1) reminds one of Genesis 1:2 and 2:7, references to the Spirit's involvement in the old creation. Jesus, however, filled with the Spirit, launched a new creation. Second, bringing Mark 1:13 and the mention of the wild beasts with Jesus in the desert (undoubtedly one of Luke's sources for the temptation account) to bear on Luke 4:1 is enlightening—as animals

---

7. N. T. Wright, "Adam in Pauline Christology," *Society of Biblical Literature 1983 Seminar Papers*, ed. K. Richards (Chico, CA: Scholars Press, 1983), 358–89; reprinted as "Adam, Israel, and the Messiah," N. T. Wright in *The Climax of the Covenant: Christ and the Law in Pauline Theology* (Minneapolis: Fortress, 1993), 18–40.

8. See C. Marvin Pate, *Luke* (Chicago: Moody Press, 1995), 113–14.

9. Ibid., 114–17.

in the garden honored Adam (see Gen. 2:19–20; cf. Gen. 9:1–2), so even the wild beasts did to Jesus.[10]

- **4:2** But the background of the temptations of Jesus should not be restricted to Genesis 3. It is clear that the mention of the wilderness (v. 1) in conjunction with the forty days (v. 2) typify Israel's forty years of wilderness wandering and its attendant temptations (*peirasmos*). Furthermore, Jesus' fast of forty days recalls Moses' forty-day fast as he 'interceded for Israel's sin of worshiping the golden calf (Ex. 34:28; Deut. 9:9). However, the identification of the Devil as the source of the temptation is not similar to the wilderness temptations; it is more reminiscent of Satan's allurement of Eve and Adam in the Garden. Luke's point is that, unlike the parents of the human race who ate the forbidden food and Israel which ate the manna from heaven but still sinned, Jesus, who did not eat, was nevertheless obedient.
- **4:3** The first of three temptations was posed to Jesus by the Devil. The Devil's temptation did not consist of denying that Jesus was the Son of God (he conceded that, "If you are the Son of God"). Rather, the point of temptation was to get Jesus to use his power as the Son of God for his own purpose (fill his hunger by turning a stone into bread) instead of being obediently dependent on the Father for his needs.
- **4:4** Jesus resisted the Devil's play by quoting Deuteronomy 8:3, a passage describing God's provision for Israel with manna from heaven while, at the same time, reminding the nation that it should be dependent on the word of God, which alone could ultimately nourish one's life. Israel, however, did not obey God's word. Neither did Adam and Eve heed the warning of the word of God (Gen. 3:1–7). In contrast, Jesus, the Son of God, the replacement of Adam and the true Israel, demonstrated himself to be totally reliant upon his Father. It was more important to him to submit to the will of God, even if it entailed hunger and suffering.
- **4:5** Verses 5–8 constitute the second temptation of Jesus. In v. 5, we are told that the Devil led Jesus up, though the location is not specified by Luke. According to Matthew 4:8, it was a high mountain from which the Devil showed Jesus all the kingdoms of the inhabited world. This last remark probably infers that it was on a high mountain that Jesus was given a vision of the panorama of the enemy's power and domain, since the world obviously cannot be seen from one mountaintop. Jesus was about to be presented with a choice between two kingdoms, God's or the Devil's.
- **4:6** The Devil offered to Jesus the authority and glory that accompanied his kingdoms of the world. The meaning of the words "for it has been handed over to me, and I give it to whomever I will" is difficult to pin down, but the comparison of this temptation to the Adam/Eve

---

10. See again footnote 2 above.

narrative clarifies the situation. Adam and Eve were given dominion over all things (Gen. 1:26–30), yet Satan offered them more—they could become like God (Gen. 3:5). But in obeying Satan, the first couple lost their authority and became subject to death. In some way, the dominion of the world devolved onto Satan (John 12:31; 2 Cor. 4), that is, until the seed of the woman, the Messiah, would one day crush the head of the serpent (Gen. 3:15–16; cf. Rom. 16:20; Rev. 12:17).

- **4:7** The condition for receiving the Devil's kingdom was that Jesus worship him. The strategy was probably to get Jesus to accept the glory of this world without first going to the cross.

- **4:8** Jesus rebuffed the Devil by again quoting Scripture, this time from Deuteronomy 6:13. Deuteronomy 6 is the classic Old Testament text on monotheism, called the *shemah* (the Hebrew word for "hear"—hear Israel, the Lord our God is one, Deut. 6:4). Jesus affirmed his allegiance to God alone. As Luke's narrative later shows, Jesus obeyed the divine directive to go to the cross and, in so doing, served his God.

- **4:9** Verses 9–12 describe Jesus' third temptation, which may be placed last in the list by Luke because of its locale in Jerusalem, the divine destiny of Jesus (9:51); in Matthew it is listed as the second temptation. The Devil led Jesus to the pinnacle of the temple, identified variously as the royal colonnade of the temple on the court (Josephus, *Antiquities of the Jews* 15.410–20) or as the southeast corner of the temple mound, which overlooked the Kidron Valley (a tradition dating back to Byzantine times). From the pinnacle, the Devil presented his greatest challenge yet—"if you are the Son of God, throw yourself off of here." It may be that the later rabbinic text (*Babylonian Pesachim* 36[32a]), informs the Devil's temptation. It reads, "Our teachers have taught, 'When the king, the Messiah, reveals himself, he will come and stand on the roof of the temple.'" If so, then the Devil's temptation consisted of enticing Jesus to cater to popular messianic expectations.

- **4:10** The Devil's bait included an appeal to Scripture. He quoted Psalm 91:11–12 in vv. 10–11, respectively. If Jesus truly was the Son of God, then the angels would protect him during his fall.

- **4:11** Continuing his quotation of Psalm 91:12, the Devil assured Jesus that the angels would undergird his body with their own hands so as to prevent him from being hurt by the stones on the ground.

- **4:12** Jesus' reply to the Devil was quick and decisive, as he countered the enemy's perversion of Scripture by quoting Deuteronomy 6:16—you shall not tempt the Lord your God! Jesus would not presume on his Father's power, nor would he swerve from his will. He will go to the cross; first suffering, then glory (cf. Luke 24:26, 46). In the third temptation, we hear the echo of ancient Israel's putting God to the test by its murmuring disobedience (cf. Deut. 6:12–16). We also hear therein the

Serpent's temptation to Adam that he will not die if he eats of the forbidden fruit (Gen. 2:17; 3:3–4). Jesus, too, was tempted to defy the sure death that would result from leaping off the temple. His gallantry would be rewarded with angelic protection. Behind this temptation, then, lay the subtle suggestion that Jesus need not die in Jerusalem in order to be proclaimed the Son of God. Unlike Israel and Adam, however, Jesus obeyed God; he chose the way of the cross.

- **4:13** From Luke's words "all temptations," we are apparently to gather that the three recorded were illustrative of others that occurred during the forty-day span, and that Jesus successfully withstood all such diabolic schemes. As a result, the Devil left him until an opportune time.

The Gospel of John

Readers of the Synoptic Gospels' narratives of the temptations of Jesus might be surprised that they seem to be alluded to in the gospel of John, as Raymond Brown noted in the following chart:[11]

JOHN	SYNOPTIC TRADITIONS
6:15: The people would make him king	Satan offers him the kingdoms of the world
6:31: The people ask for miraculous bread	Satan invites him to turn the stones into bread
7:3: The brothers want Jesus to go to Jerusalem to show his power	Satan takes Jesus to the Jerusalem Temple and invites him to display his power by jumping from the pinnacle

The Meaning of Jesus' Temptations in the Wilderness

The meaning of the three wilderness temptations of Jesus seems to be as follows:

1. The temptation to turn the stones into bread was Satan's attempt to get Jesus to use his supernatural power to spare himself of hunger, in other words, not to suffer.

2. The temptation to jump off the pinnacle of Jerusalem was Satan's attempt to get Jesus to declare himself the Messiah in a miraculous way so that the Jewish crowd would accept him as their king without Jesus first going to the cross to suffer.

---

11. Raymond E. Brown, *The Gospel According to John I–XII*, AB 29 (Garden City, NY: Doubleday, 1966), 308.

3. The temptation on the mountain top to worship Satan and thus transfer Jesus' allegiance from God to the devil was Satan's attempt to get Jesus to receive the kingdom of this world without going to the cross.

One can readily see from these individual explanations of the temptations that the tie that binds them together is the temptation for Jesus to be a non-suffering Messiah, not the suffering Messiah he was called to be as the suffering servant of the Lord. But because Jesus was obedient to the Father as the new Adam and the new Israel, he was now prepared to enter his public ministry with the proper focus, namely, for Jesus first would come the cross and only then the crown; first suffering and then glory; first the rejection of this world's hegemony in order to reign in the kingdom of God.

Conclusion

This chapter has highlighted the five temptation narratives associated with the four gospels. Mark provided an Adamic nuance to Jesus' temptation in the Judean wilderness while Q presented Jesus' temptation as three-fold and as the new Israel. Matthew and Luke brought those two views together under the tradition that Israel was supposed to be the replacement of the first Adam but failed at doing so. Jesus, however, by his obedience to God became the new Adam and the new Israel. John possibly alludes to the three temptations as occurring not only in one setting but during Jesus' life as well. In conclusion, we remember from an earlier question that Jesus really could have succumbed to the Devil's wiles, but thank God he did not!

REFLECTION QUESTIONS

1. How does Mark 1:12–13 compare Jesus' temptations in the wilderness to the temptation of Adam?

2. What theme governs the temptation of Jesus in Q 4:1–13?

3. How do the themes of the new Adam and the new Israel relate to each other according to Matthew 4:1–11 and Luke 4:1–13?

4. How does the gospel of John parallel the three temptations of Jesus?

5. What was the overlying theme that informed the three temptations of Jesus?

Who Were the Twelve Disciples, and Why Did Jesus Choose Twelve?

This fundamental question concerning the historical Jesus divides into two obvious questions, but perhaps not-so-apparent answers: Who were the twelve disciples? And why did Jesus choose twelve?

Who Were the Twelve Disciples?

To answer this question we need to cover four points: (1) the disciples' names; (2) a profile of each; (3) their role; and (4) their fate. The last point is important because it forms a fitting conclusion to the picture of the Gospels that Jesus' disciples did not always follow their master while he was on earth but later each of them, except of course Judas, was faithful to Jesus to the end of their lives.

The Names of the Disciples

The following chart supplies the lists of the disciples' names from the Synoptic Gospels and Acts[1]:

MATTHEW 10:2–4	MARK 3:16–19	LUKE 6:13–16	ACTS 1:13
Simon Peter	Simon Peter	Simon Peter	Simon Peter
Andrew	James	Andrew	John
James	John	James	James
John	Andrew	John	Andrew
Philip	Philip	Philip	Philip

---

1. See Eckhard J. Schnabel, *Early Christian Mission: Jesus and the Twelve* (Downers Grove, IL: InterVarsity Press; Leicester, England: Apollos, 2004), 1:263.

MATTHEW 10:2–4	MARK 3:16–19	LUKE 6:13–16	ACTS 1:13
Bartholomew	Bartholomew	Bartholomew	Thomas
Thomas	Matthew	Matthew	Bartholomew
Matthew	Thomas	Thomas	Matthew
James b. Alphaeus	James b. Alphaeus	James b. Alphaeus	James b. Alphaeus
Thaddaeus	Thaddaeus	Simon the Zealot	Simon the Zealot
Simon Cananaeus	Simon Cananaeus	Judas b. James	Judas b. James
Judas Iscariot	Judas Iscariot	Judas Iscariot	[vacancy]

A Profile of the Disciples[2]

Peter. Simon/*Symeōn* (Hebrew)/*Cephas*=rock (Aramaic)/Peter (*Petros*, the Greek equivalent of rock) are all names of the leading disciple of Jesus. Peter was a native of Galilee, where he grew up making his living as a fisherman along with his father (Jonah, Matt. 16:17) and his brother Andrew (Mark 1:16–18; John 1:35–42). Peter had a house in Capernaum (recall our chapter on archaeology) and he was married (Matt. 8:14–17; Mark 1:29–38; Luke 4:38–39; 1 Cor. 9:5). Peter occurs first in all of the lists of the disciples (including Acts 1:13), indicating that he was the most prominent of the disciples. Moreover, Peter was the spokesman for the disciples (e.g., Matt. 14:28; 15:15; 18:21; 26:35, 40; Mark 8:29; 9:51 10:28; John 6:68) and was the "rock" upon which Jesus founded his church in that he first preached the gospel after Pentecost (Matt. 16:17–19; cf. Acts 1:8; 2:14–41; 8:14–25; 10:34–48). However, one need not conclude from this that Peter was the beginning of the tradition of apostolic succession. Though the leading disciple, Peter failed his Lord at least twice: when he denied Jesus three times (Matt. 26:69–75; Mark 14:66–72; Luke 22:55–62; John 18:16–18, 25–27) and when he reneged on Paul's message of justification by faith alone (Gal. 2:11–21); but he was reclaimed by the grace of God (John 21; 2 Peter 3:15–16). Two New Testament books are attributed to Peter—1 and 2 Peter. Moreover, Peter provided much material for Mark's gospel, and maybe for Matthew's and Luke's gospels as well (recall our earlier discussion).

Andrew. Andrew is best known as the brother of Simon Peter. Originally a disciple of John the Baptist, Andrew is the first follower of Jesus to be identified by name. He told Peter about Jesus (John 1:35–42), and he and Peter left their fishing business to follow Jesus. It was Andrew who brought to Jesus

---

2. For the following descriptions of the disciples, see Michael J. Wilkins, "Disciples," in *DJG*, ed. Joel B. Green, Scot McKnight, and I. Howard Marshall (Downers Grove, IL/Leicester: InterVarsity Press, 1992), 176–82; 179–81; "Discipleship," 182–89; Schnabel, *Early Christian Mission*, 1:262–69.

the boy with the loaves and fishes in John's account of the feeding of the five thousand (John 6:8) and who with Philip brought the inquisitive Greeks to Jesus (John 12:22). Andrew and his brother were from Bethsaida (John 1:44), on the northern shore of the Sea of Galilee.

James and John. James and John, the sons of Zebedee, were also from Bethsaida. Their family was not poor; they owned a boat and employed wage laborers (Mark 1:20) and the wife of Zebedee supported Jesus during his ministry (Matt. 27:55–56; cf. Luke 8:3). Jesus called James and John "the sons of thunder" probably owing to their fiery temperaments (Mark 3:17; cf. Mark 9:38; 10:35–40; Luke 9:54). James was the first of the twelve disciples to be killed on account of his allegiance to Jesus: Herod Agrippa I ordered his execution by sword in AD 41 (Acts 12:2). Though debated, it is likely that John is to be identified with "the disciple whom Jesus loved" (John 13:23; 19:26–27; 20:2; 21:7, 20; 21:4; cf. 1:40; 18:15; 19:35) and the author of the fourth gospel.[3] John was the only disciple from the group of the Twelve that directly witnessed the crucifixion of Jesus (John 19:25–26), and he was the first disciple to see the empty tomb (John 20:2–5). John, along with Peter and James, formed the inner circle of Jesus' disciples. He later belonged to the leadership of the Jerusalem church, being one of the pillar apostles (Gal. 2:9). According to early Christian tradition, John lived in Ephesus in his later years, founding churches there and writing the five books associated with his name (the gospel of John, the epistles of John, and the Revelation of John).

Philip. Philip also hailed from Bethsaida (John 1:44; 12:21) and was originally a disciple of John the Baptist. He brought Nathanael (John 1:45–46) to Jesus as well as the Greeks who wanted to meet Jesus (John 20:21–22), and he played an important role in the multiplication of the bread by Jesus (John 6:5–7). In a conversation with Jesus, Philip elicited the immortal words, "I am the way, and the truth, and the life" (John 14:6; cf. 14:8–14). This Philip, whose name along with Andrew's is Greek, is not the same Jewish Christian Philip in Jerusalem mentioned in Acts who preached the gospel in Samaria and in Caesarea (Acts 8:4–40).

Bartholomew. Bartholomew appears in all four lists of the twelve disciples (the Synoptics and Acts), but he is otherwise not mentioned in the New Testament. From the ninth century on Bartholomew has been frequently identified with Nathanael. This is based on the conjecture that Nathanael's surname was Bartholomew, so that his full name would have been Nathanael Bar-Tholami. Since the Synoptic Gospels never mention Nathanael, while John never mentions Bartholomew, the juxtaposition of the names Philip and Bartholomew in the Synoptic lists of the Twelve (not in the list in Acts) suggests the close relationship between Philip and Nathanael depicted in

---

3. See C. Marvin Pate, *The Writings of John: A Survey of the Gospel, Epistles, and Apocalypse* (Grand Rapids: Zondervan, 2011), 17–23.

John 1:43–51. All of Nathanael's companions are apostles (John 1:35–51), he appears as a member of a group of apostles (John 21:1–2) and Christ's promise to him suggests an apostolic status (John 1:50–51). If Bartholomew is indeed Nathanael, Philip brought Bartholomew (Nathanael), a native of Galilee (John 21:2) to acknowledge Jesus as the Messiah (John 1:45–46). Jesus called Nathanael "a true Israelite, without guile" and revealed to him that his dream of Jacob's ladder ultimately referred to the heavenly Son of Man, Jesus Christ (John 1:47–51). But if Bartholomew should not be equated with Nathanael, then we have no other information about Bartholomew except that his name is mentioned in the disciples' lists.

Thomas. Thomas the "twin" (*didymus*; John 11:16; 20:24; 21:2), is popularly known as "doubting Thomas" because he had misgivings about Jesus' resurrection (John 20:24) and imperceptions about Jesus' destiny. Beyond that, however, Thomas had some high moments: when he challenged the other disciples to go to Jerusalem with Jesus so that they might die with him (John 11:6); when he showed his faithfulness by gathering with the other disciples in Galilee after the resurrection (John 21:2); and when he confessed that Jesus was Lord and God (John 20:28). But as we saw above, the apocryphal *Gospel of Thomas* is not authentic and neither was Thomas Jesus' twin. Indeed, the *The Gospel of Thomas* was not written before AD 170; recall our earlier argumentation to that effect.

Matthew. Matthew was called to leave his job as tax collector to follow Jesus (Matthew 9:9). When referring to that account, Mark and Luke call him Levi, suggesting that he had two names—Matthew Levi. His tax collector's booth was probably located on one of the main trade highways near Capernaum, where he collected tolls for Herod Antipas from the commercial traffic flowing through that area. After his call to follow Jesus, Matthew Levi hosted a banquet for Jesus at his home, to which a crowd of tax collectors and sinners was invited (Luke 5:29–30). Little else is known of Matthew except for the widely attested tradition from the second century that he was the author of the first gospel.

James, son of Alphaeus. James, son of Alphaeus (Mark 2:14), is mentioned only in the disciples' lists. He often is identified with "James the younger" (Mark 15:40), the brother of a certain Joses, whose mother was a certain Mary. The appellation "younger" could be used to distinguish him from James the disciple and from James the brother of Jesus, or to note his younger age, or to his smaller stature, or to his lesser renown.

Thaddaeus/Judas Brother of James. Thaddaeus is most likely to be identified with "Judas brother of James" (Luke 6:16; Acts 1:13). Apart from the disciples' lists he is mentioned only in connection with Jesus' last Passover, during which Judas, not Iscariot, asked, "Lord, how is it that you will reveal yourself to us, and not to the world?" (John 14:22). This disciple is not to be equated with Judas (Jude) the brother of Jesus and the author of the Epistle of Jude.

Simon the Zealot. Simon has the surname, "the Cananean" (Mark 3:18/Matt. 10:41), a Greek transliteration of the Aramaic word for "zeal/zealot" (*qanānā*), or Simon the Zealot (Luke 6:15; Acts 1:13). The expression indicates that this Simon was a zealous nationalist prior to his call to follow Jesus (and perhaps the nature of his temperament). Later, the term *zealot* was used to designate the religiously motivated Jewish revolutionaries who helped stir up the first Jewish Revolt against Rome (AD 66–73).

Judas Iscariot. "Iscariot" most likely identifies this Judas' place of origin since his father is described as "Simon Iscariot" (John 6:71; 13:2, 26). Judas Iscariot was the treasurer for the apostolic band (John 12:4–6; 13:29). John relates that Judas became a thief, pilfering from the treasury funds (John 12:6). Judas is infamous for betraying Jesus for thirty pieces of silver (Matt. 26:14–16; Mark 14:10–11; Luke 22:3–6). Luke and John portray Judas as being led by Satan (Luke 22:3; John 13:2) to do so. This act of betrayal took place in connection with the Last Supper (Matt. 26:20–25; Mark 14:17–21). Securing a band of soldiers from the chief priests and Pharisees (John 18:3), Judas led them to the garden of Gethsemane at night and kissed Jesus to identify him for the soldiers (Matt. 26:47–56; Mark 14:43–52; Luke 22:47–53; John 18:2–12). Later, after Jesus was arrested, Judas was filled with remorse and tried to give the silver back to the priests, who used the blood money to purchase a burial plot for strangers. Then Judas committed suicide (Matt. 27:3–10; Acts 1:18–19). It seems that Judas hung himself (Matt. 27:3–10) and then his body fell onto the field below bursting asunder (Acts 1:18–19). The disciples chose Matthias to replace Judas (Acts 1:26). Nothing is known about Matthias. William Klassen's suggestion that Judas was not a failure since he handed Jesus over to the Jewish authorities with Jesus' full knowledge and consent, contributing to the final fulfillment of Jesus' mission, is not plausible.[4] Similarly, the recently publicized *Gospel of Judas* fares no better in its attempt to exonerate Judas by portraying Judas and Jesus as Gnostics; thus Judas' handing Jesus over to be crucified so that he could be delivered from the evil body and taken into heaven as a good soul is clearly a later Gnostic revision of the act of betrayal by Judas.

The Two-fold Role of the Twelve

The Twelve had a two-fold role: they were called to be disciples and they represented Jesus as his apostles. We now look at these two roles, which essentially come together in Jesus' two-fold call: follow me (as disciples) and become fishers of men (as apostles): Matthew 10:1–4; Mark 3:13–19; Luke 6:12–16. As such, following Jesus (disciple) and representing Jesus (apostle) are two sides of the same coin, complementing one another.

---

4. William Klassen, *Judas: Betrayer or Friend of Jesus?* (Minneapolis: Fortress, 1996).

The Twelve as Disciples. The term *mathētēs* ("disciple") already enjoyed a rich background before the time of Jesus. Before Jesus, "disciple" was used in the Greek philosophical schools of those who associated themselves with a famous philosopher (e.g., Sophists, Socrates, Plato, Aristotle, Pythagoras). Although the Hebrew equivalent for *mathētēs* (i.e, *talmîd*) occurs only once in the Old Testament (*mathētēs* does not occur at all in the LXX), in 1 Chronicles 25:8, the relationships between Moses and Joshua, Elijah and Elisha, and the associate of the prophets as well as the school of the prophets all confirm a master-disciple relationship.[5] After Jesus, Rabbinic literature is famous for its master-disciple relationships. The commonality of these backgrounds is that the disciple would find a teacher/master to live with and learn from. Jesus, however, was unique in that he called the disciples to follow him rather than the customary approach of the disciples seeking out a teacher. The twelve disciples of Jesus were to follow him, learn from his lifestyle, and emulate him. As Michael Wilkins puts it, "the twin prerequisites of discipleship [were] paying the cost and committing themselves to the cause."[6] This explains why many who started following Jesus did not stay the course (e.g., John 6:60). The Twelve that Jesus issued a call to personally answered the challenge (though, for the most part, they all failed him at the end of his life). But there was also a group of genuine disciples whom Jesus did not ask to follow him but rather to stay home and bear witness to him (Matt. 8:19, 21; 10:24–25, 42; 27:57). Indeed, as we will see below, Luke knows of a mission of 70/72 disciples (Luke 10:1–16).[7]

Eckhard J. Schnabel lists six aspects of Jesus' calling of the Twelve: (1) Jesus called the disciples by his own divine authority. (2) Jesus called some of the disciples out of their own personal helplessness (Simon, Andrew, James, John; Luke 5:1–11). (3) Jesus' commissioning call was an action of God. (4) Jesus called his disciples to leave their work and follow him full time. (5) Jesus called them first to follow him, after that came their commissioning [as apostles]. (6) Jesus' call necessitated them leaving their family and possessions as well.[8]

The Twelve as Apostles. Not only were the Twelve called to be disciples of Jesus, they were also called to be sent forth as his witnesses, apostles. *Apostolos*, the noun, and *apostellein*, the verb, relate to the apostolic calling of the disciples: as Jesus' representatives they were to carry the message of Jesus and the kingdom of God (see below) throughout Galilee and beyond. Karl Heinrich Rengstorf made famous the thesis that the office of apostle derived from the ancient Jewish legal institution of *šaliah,* whereby a person's

---

5. See Wilkins' discussion, "Disciples," 176.
6. Ibid., 177.
7. For the historicity of the Twelve, see Schnabel, *Early Christian Mission,* 1:264–65.
8. Ibid., 1:273–75.

representative or agent is like to himself (*Midrash Berakoth* 5.5).[9] But three criticisms have been raised against this thesis that *šaliah* is the basis of Jesus' sending out the disciples. First, such an institution did not arise until after AD 70 in the sense of official commissioners of the great Sanhedrin who collected dues in the Diaspora for the central agency, who undertook inspection journeys, who gathered collections for the Palestinian sages, etc. Second, the Jewish institution of *šaliah* did not encompass religious acts, for example, concerning Jewish missionaries. Third, the sending of envoys was also well-known in Greco-Roman circles, so to restrict apostleship to one tradition—Jewish—is unwise.[10] These criticisms seem valid.

Schnabel provides a helpful summary of the nuances of *apostolos* in the New Testament:

> The following nuances of meaning of *apostolos* can be distinguished in the New Testament: (1) "envoy," as a courier sent by a church; (2) "messenger of Christ (Jesus)," as designation of a task; (3) "apostle," as designation of an office (without subsequent genitive); (4) "apostle," as a class of early Christian leaders; (5) "apostle," as a numerically limited group, sometimes identified with the Twelve. The evidence from the Synoptic Gospels shows that the term "apostle" is sometimes limited to the group of Jesus' twelve disciples, but on occasion it designates the wider group of Jesus' followers. Several passages connect *apostolos* or *apostellein* with a specific process of sending.[11]

As Jesus' apostles, the Twelve represented Jesus to Israel and beyond, so much so that how the various audiences responded to the apostles was how they in effect responded to Christ himself (Matt. 10:11–15).

Their Fate

Scripture and Church tradition combine to tell us the fate of the apostles:

1. Peter was crucified head down in Rome, AD ca. 64 during Emperor Nero's persecution of Christians in Rome.

2. Andrew preached until his death in AD 74, when he was bound and crucified to death.

---

9. K. H. Rengstorf, *"apostolos"* in TDNT, ed. G. Kittel, trans. Geoffrey W. Bromily (Grand Rapids: Eerdmans, 1964), 1:407–45.
10. Schnabel provides these three criticisms, *Early Christian Mission*, 1:282.
11. Ibid., 283.

3. James, son of Zebedee, was beheaded in Jerusalem by Herod Agrippa the First in AD 44.

4. John was banished to the Isle of Patmos in AD 96 by Emperor Domitian.

5. Phillip was crucified at Heirapole, Phryga in AD 52.

6. Bartholomew was beaten, crucified, then beheaded by the command of a king in AD 52.

7. Thomas was run through by a lance at Corehandal, East Indies, in AD 52.

8. Matthew was slain by the sword in the city of Ethiopia in ca. AD 60.

9. James, son of Alphaeus, was thrown from a pinnacle then beaten to death in AD 60.

10. Thaddeus was shot to death by arrows in AD 72.

11. Simon the zealot was crucified in Persia in AD 72.

And so, even though the disciples of Jesus may have failed their master while he was on earth, they rebounded and followed him to their deaths.

Why Did Jesus Choose Twelve Disciples/Apostles?
Two answers present themselves in responding to this question. First, the number twelve indicated that the disciples were restoring the twelve tribes of Israel. Second, the disciples also represented the remnant. These two answers complement one another.

The Restoration of Israel
The fact that Jesus chose twelve disciples was a programmatic action—it represented the hope of Israel's eschatological restoration. One of the central concerns of Jewish eschatology was the restoration of the twelve tribes of Israel.[12] Thus, Jesus' choice of twelve disciples corresponds to the twelve tribes of Israel (Matt. 19:28/Luke 22:29–30), even though Israel at the time of Jesus only consisted of Judah, Benjamin, and the priests from Levi. In Matthew 10, the twelve disciples were commissioned by Jesus to go throughout Galilee

---

12. See Isaiah 49:5–6; 56:1–8; 60:3–7; 66:18–24; Jeremiah 31:10; Ezekiel 34, 37; Zephaniah 8:7–8; Tobit 13:5; 14:6–7; 2 Maccabees 1:27–29; 2:7, 18; *Jubilees* 1:15–17; *Testament Benjamin* 9:2; Philo (*Praem.* 94–97, 162–72); Baruch 4:37; Sirach 36:11; 48:10; *Psalms of Solomon* 11; 17.28–31, 50; Dead Sea Scrolls (11 Q Temple 18:14–16; 1 QM 2:2–3, 7–8).

spreading the good news that in Jesus Christ the kingdom of God had dawned. To prove that this was so, the disciples were empowered by Jesus to heal the sick and drive out demons (Matt. 10:7–8).

But there was more: the Old Testament also predicted that in the last days when Israel is restored, the Gentiles would be converted to Yahweh (Isa. 45:15; 60:15–17; Mic. 4:13; cf. Tobit 3:11). Although both Jesus and the Twelve concentrated their missionary activity on the house of Israel, still both reached out to Gentiles in fulfillment of the Old Testament prophecy just noted.[13] Especially to be noted was Jesus' sending of the seventy/seventy-two disciples other than the Twelve to preach the gospel of the kingdom in Luke 10:1–16.[14] The number seventy/seventy-two alludes to Genesis 10–11 where in the Hebrew text there are seventy nations that comprise the world and the LXX text has seventy-two as comprising the world. Either way, Jesus anticipated the full-scale outreach to the nations/Gentiles such as is recorded in Acts by sending seventy/seventy-two disciples to proclaim the presence of the kingdom.

Thus, Jesus chose twelve disciples/apostles to signify that in him the restoration of Israel and the conversion of the Gentiles were in the process of becoming a reality.

The Remnant of Israel

But the kind of Messiah Jesus offered and the type of kingdom he preached were not what Israel expected. Instead of a political Messiah, Jesus offered a suffering Messiah and the kingdom Jesus presented was not geographical but one of God's reign in the hearts of the followers of Jesus. Such a message did not impress the Jews, so they rejected Jesus and his kingdom. Thus, the restoration of Israel would have to wait until Jesus' parousia. In the meantime, the twelve disciples constituted the remnant. The following self-explanatory chart highlighting the remnant places the disciples in their proper conceptual framework.

---

13. See, e.g., the summaries of the progress of the gospel (Matt. 4:24–25; Mark 3:7–8; Luke 6:17–18); the centurion in Capernaum (Matt. 8:5–13/Luke 7:1–10; cf. John 4:46–54); the demon-possessed man in Gadara (Matt. 8:28–34/Mark 5:1–10; Luke 8:26–30); the woman in Syro-Phoenicia (Matt. 15:21–29/Mark 7:24–31); the deaf-mute in the Decapolis (Mark 7:32–37); the four thousand people east of the sea of Galilee whom Jesus miraculously fed (Matt. 8:1–10/Mark 15:32–39); Jesus' cleansing of the temple which had prohibited Gentiles from worshipping God (Matt. 21:12–13/Mark 11:15–17/Luke 19:45–46).

14. Luke 10:1 has a famous text variant which is equally supported by strong witnesses: Sinaiticus and Alexandrinus read "70" disciples while p75 and Vaticanus have "72" disciples. It seems that "72" is the preferred reading on the grounds that a scribe mostly likely changed "72" to a more popular number in Jewish tradition, "70" (see Schnabel's discussion, *Early Christian Mission*, 318–19).

Conclusion

This chapter has attempted to answer the two-fold question: who were the disciples, and why did Jesus choose twelve of them? The disciples followed Jesus and became his apostles to Israel and ultimately to the world. On the one hand, the Twelve represented the restoration of Israel and, yet, on the other hand because most Jews in Jesus' day rejected him, the disciples constituted the remnant, the faithful few who awaited the Kingdom of God. Moreover, although the Twelve abandoned Jesus during his most difficult hour, nevertheless, except for one, they became faithful to Jesus unto death.

The Remnant:

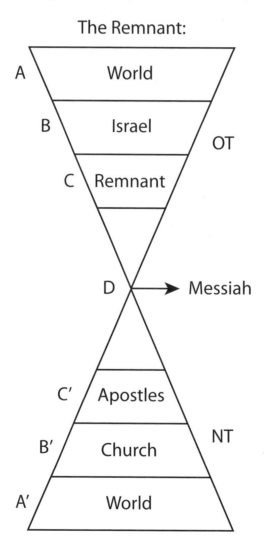

REFLECTION QUESTIONS

1. What were the names of the twelve disciples?

2. What is the common denominator of the portraits of the twelve disciples?

3. What was the two-fold role of the twelve disciples?

4. What was the fate of the twelve disciples?

5. What is the relationship between the twelve disciples and the remnant?

What Does It Mean That Jesus Was Transfigured?

Jesus' transfiguration is recounted in Matthew 17:1–13; Mark 9:2–13; and Luke 9:28–36. It is also mentioned in 2 Peter 1:16–18. There is a basic story line to the Gospels' account of Jesus' transfiguration: Jesus took his inner circle of disciples (Peter, James, John) up a high mountain (probably Mount Hermon since Peter's confession in Caeserea Philippi, which is at the base of Mount Hermon, had just happened). There Jesus' body suddenly shone brightly as he conversed with two heavenly personages—Moses and Elijah (the former representing the Law and the latter representing the Prophets). Peter suggested that they build three booths (replicating the Feast of Tabernacles) to preserve the glory of the moment. But God responded that the disciples should honor only his Son. Furthermore, no tabernacles or booths should be built at all because before receiving permanent glory, Jesus first had to endure the sufferings of the cross. The two heavenly visitors suddenly disappeared. While this is the basic storyline of the Transfiguration, each gospel shapes the event to convey their respective messages about that experience. Therefore, we will attempt to capture the nuances of the Transfiguration by discussing each account in their probable chronological order: Mark, Luke, and Matthew. Afterwards, we will make a brief comment regarding 2 Peter 1:16–18. After summarizing these passages, we must dispel a once-popular theory among gospel scholars, namely, that the Transfiguration story is a misplaced resurrection account.

Mark 9:2–13

Mark uses the Greek term, *metamorphoō*, which is translated in the Latin Vulgate as, *transfiguratus est*. Mark recognizes that the Transfiguration of Jesus was modeled after Moses' encounter with Yahweh on Mount Sinai

(Ex. 24 and 34). Note the parallels between Mark 9:2–13 and Exodus 24, 34:

- The setting is the same: a high mountain (Ex. 24:12, 15–18; 34:3; Mark 9:2).
- There is a cloud that descends and overshadows the mountain (Ex. 24:15–18; 34:5; Mark 9:7).
- A voice comes from the cloud (Ex. 24:16; Mark 9:7).
- The central figures, Jesus and Moses, become radiant (Ex. 34:29–30, 35; Mark 9:2–3).
- Those who see the radiance of the central figure become afraid (Ex. 34:30; Mark 9:6).
- The event takes place "after six days" (Ex. 24:16; Mark 9:2).
- A select group of three people is mentioned (Ex. 24:1; Mark 9:2).[1]

Mark presumes that background, but shapes his account to emphasize the suffering aspect of Jesus' mission. Thus: (1) Elijah occurs before Moses, thus assigning to the prophet a dominant role in the episode (*contra* Matthew's account). More specifically, Elijah is equated with John the Baptist whose sufferings prefigure the sufferings of Jesus on the cross. (2) The three-fold pattern that occurs in Mark 9:9–13, and in the central section of Mark as a whole, highlights Jesus' upcoming sufferings in Jerusalem as well as the disciples' misunderstanding of the necessity of Jesus' death. We supply that three-fold pattern below in chart form.

	MARK 8:31–38	MARK 9:2–13	MARK 9:30–37	MARK 10:32–45
PASSION PREDICTION	Jesus predicted his (the Son of Man's) upcoming death in Jerusalem and his resurrection (8:31).	Jesus said that he was going to rise from the dead (9:9).	Jesus predicted that he was going to Jerusalem to be killed but he would arise on the third day (9:30–31).	Jesus explicitly predicted his upcoming death in Jerusalem and resurrection (10:32–34).

---

1. See Davies and Allison, *Matthew* [VIII–XVIII], ICC (Edinburgh: T&T Clark, 1991), 2:686–87.

	MARK 8:31–38	MARK 9:2–13	MARK 9:30–37	MARK 10:32–45
DISCIPLES' MISUNDER-STANDING	Peter rebuked Jesus because Peter wanted Jesus to be a political, delivering Messiah, not a suffering Messiah (8:32).	The disciples did not understand why Jesus would need to rise again because they did not expect him to die in the first place; the disciples pointed out that Elijah's presence with Jesus indicated that the Messiah Jesus was here to deliver Israel (9:10–11; cf. Malachi 3:1; 4:5–6).	The disciples did not understand what Jesus meant and they argued about which of them was the greatest on the "way" (to Jerusalem to die; note the irony) (9:32–34).	James and John wanted to be Jesus' right- and left-hand men when he established the kingdom of God in Jerusalem; the rest of the disciples were angry that James and John beat them to Jesus to make the request (10:35–41).
JESUS' CORRECTION	Jesus rebukes Satan who is working through Peter to get Jesus to avoid the cross; but Jesus will go to the cross and all of his followers must be willing to do the same (8:33–38).	Jesus responded that Elijah did come but in the person of John Baptist who was killed just as Jesus the Son of Man would suffer the same fate (9:12–13).	Jesus held up a child as an example of the last being first (9:35–37).	Jesus offers himself—the Son of Man—as the example *par excellence* of what it meant to serve others (10:45).

So it is clear that the emphasis of the Transfiguration narrative in Mark is on Jesus' suffering, death, and resurrection. His suffering would come before his glory. And the disciples would have to embrace the same order if they wished to follow Jesus. Moreover, in Mark's account the disciples are portrayed in a negative light as they keep misunderstanding Jesus' mission.

Luke 9:28–36

Luke omits the word, *metamorphoō*, perhaps because he wanted to avoid the connotation that such a word had in the mystery religions, which portrayed humans as undergoing a metamorphosis and becoming divine. To the contrary, for Luke, Jesus' Transfiguration occurred the moment his inward supernatural glory transformed his outward natural body into brilliant light. Luke's account differs from Mark. From the Markan account, Evans proceeds to observe several noteworthy modifications in Luke's version of the Transfiguration, modifications which only enhance and strengthen the connection between the Transfiguration and Moses.

- In v. 30, Luke reverses the order of the names of the two heavenly visitors by mentioning the name of Moses first. This reversal is likely designed to place more emphasis upon the Law-giver.
- That Luke intends such emphasis is confirmed when he notes in v. 31 that the two visitors speak with Jesus of "His departure." The word "departure" translates the Greek word *exodus,* the very word that gives the Book of Exodus its name.
- Only Luke mentions Jesus' "glory" seen by his disciples (v. 32). Luke may very well intend this to recall Moses' request to see God's glory (Ex. 33:18–23). Also, in Exodus 24:16 we read that the "glory of the Lord rested on the mount." This glory not only looks back to the glory manifested upon the mount in Exodus, but also anticipates the glory into which the Messiah will enter at his resurrection (see Luke 24:26).
- Luke notes in v. 29 that Jesus' face was changed, which may recall more specifically the change in Moses' face (Ex. 34:30, 35).
- Luke introduces the episode by saying "about eight days after" (v. 28), instead of Mark's "six days later" (9:2). There is seemingly only one plausible explanation for this alteration. The rules for observing the Feast of Booths are laid down in Leviticus 23:33–44. According to Leviticus 23:36, there are to be offerings for seven days and then on the eighth day there is to be "a holy convocation" or gathering. During this time the people are to dwell in booths (tents or tabernacles, Lev. 23:42), the purpose of which is to remind the people of the Exodus long ago (Lev. 23:43).
- Finally, Luke has slightly modified the wording of the heavenly voice in v. 35. Instead of Mark's "My beloved Son" (9:7), Luke has "My chosen Son." This modification is likely meant to recall the chosen servant of Isaiah 42:1.

Evans concludes from this that Luke has taken the raw materials that he found in the Markan version of the Transfiguration and has enriched the parallels in such a way as to enhance the presentation of Jesus as God's Son (and Servant) whose authority and significance greatly surpass those of Moses and

Elijah. Luke shows his readers that the two greatest Old Testament figures appeared in order to discuss with Jesus his own impending "exodus." Moses, who may represent the Law, and Elijah, who may represent the prophets, bear witness to Jesus' identity and to his destiny awaiting him at Jerusalem. Even the heavenly voice is probably meant to allude to both major parts of the Old Testament. The first part of the voice's declaration, "This is my Son whom I have chosen," echoes Isaiah 42:1 and so represents the prophets. The second part, "listen to him," is a phrase taken from Deuteronomy 18:15 (where Moses commands the people to listen to the great prophet that God will someday raise up) and so would represent the Law. This idea of the "Law and the Prophets" bearing witness to Jesus is seen explicitly in Luke 24:27 and 24:44. Moses and Elijah bear witness to Jesus and then fade away from the scene, leaving Jesus "alone," because the era of the "Law and the Prophets" is over (Luke 16:16a). Now is the era of the "good news of the kingdom of God" (Luke 16:16b). Just as God's glory appeared on Mount Sinai, so now God's Son, in all of his glory, has appeared on the mount (cf. John 1:14–18). Whereas only the face of Moses shone, Jesus' entire personage is transfigured. Finally, because the disciples wish to build "three shelters" (i.e., "tents" or "booths") for Jesus and the two visitors, Luke has likely seen the connection with the Feast of Booths, a festival in commemoration of the Exodus. Hence, Luke begins his episode on the eighth day, the day on which a "holy convocation" was to take place (Lev. 23:36, 42). Undoubtedly, in the evangelist's mind, there could be no holier convocation than the meeting of Moses, Elijah, and Jesus; God's Law-giver, Prophet, and Son.[2]

Luke's main theme is that the Messiah will first suffer (his *exodus*) and then be glorified. This truth according to Luke was predicted by the law (hence Moses' appearance with Jesus) and the prophets (hence Elijah's appearance with Jesus). Indeed, that is a key concern to Luke-Acts.[3]

Matthew 17:1–13

Davies and Allison note the distinct additions in Matthew's Transfiguration narrative compared to Mark's:

- Moses comes before Elijah, thus indicating the importance of Moses to the scene.
- Matthew adds to Mark's story that Jesus' face shone like the sun, an obvious allusion to the glory of the Lord shining on Moses' face (see Ex. 34:29–35).

---

2. Craig Evans, *Luke* (Peabody, MA: Hendrickson, 1990), 211–12.
3. See Luke 24:25–27, 44–46 (where the Psalms/Writings are included in that prediction thus completing the three divisions of the Hebrew canon: law, prophets, writings, the first of which is Psalms). Compare this to those passages in Luke-Acts that root Jesus' suffering in Old Testament prophecy (Acts 2:22–36; 8:32–35; cf. Luke 9:22, 44; 17:25; 18:31–33; 22:37).

- Matthew adds that the cloud enveloping Jesus was bright thus creating a paradox, namely, a bright cloud which alludes to the Shekinah glory that, along with the cloud, led Israel in the wilderness.
- "In Mark the heavenly voice declares to the disciples, 'This is my beloved Son'. In Luke this becomes, 'this is my Son, my Chosen'. In Matthew we find this: 'This is my beloved Son, with whom I am well pleased'. These variants are interesting, especially that in our gospel. 'With whom I am well pleased' also occurs in the narrative of Jesus' baptism, but originally it is from Isaiah 42.1, where it refers to the suffering servant of Deutero-Isaiah. Matthew appears to have added the phrase in order to signify Jesus as the one who is destined to bring his law to the nations (Isa. 42.4). Such a suggestion is supported by the following words, 'listen to him', in their broader Matthean context point to Jesus as an ethical teacher, like Moses. Moreover, it is possible, even probable, that *akoute autou* ["listen to him"] is to be interpreted in the light of Deuteronomy 18.15: 'the Lord your God will raise up for you a prophet like me from among you, from your brethren—him you shall listen to.'"[4]

The authors conclude from these additions in Matthew, "there is scarcely room for doubt that Matthew has modified Mark for the deliberate purpose of presenting Jesus after the manner of Moses."[5] Indeed, Jesus is the greater Moses.

2 Peter 1:16–18

Peter adapts the Transfiguration narrative to his situation, which was the need for the apostle to refute those skeptics who denied that the parousia of Jesus would occur. So Peter, an eyewitness of the Transfiguration, makes the following connection: the glory that he saw at Jesus' transfiguration will attend Jesus at his parousia. If the former happened, then certainly the latter will occur as well.

Is the Transfiguration a Misplaced Resurrection Account?

Since Rudolph Bultmann, it has been popular among scholars to claim that the Transfiguration narrative is a misplaced resurrection account.[6] They point (1) to the use of *ōphthē* ("was seen") in the Transfiguration narrative (Mark 9:4; Luke 9:31; Matt. 17:3) and in the resurrection report in 1 Corinthians 15:5–8; (2) to the luminousness of Jesus (cf. Acts 26:13; Rev. 1:13–16); and (3) to the use of "after six days"=seventh, that is, Sunday; and 2 Peter 1:16–18 is a post-Easter statement. But against this theory, what resurrection account

---

4. Davies and Allison, *Matthew*, 2:686.
5. Ibid.
6. Rudolf Bultmann, *The History of the Synoptic Tradition* (New York: Harper & Row, 1963), 259.

in the New Testament included Old Testament saints, a heavenly voice, Jesus referred to as "Rabbi," and Jesus saying almost nothing? In our opinion, then, the Transfiguration is not to be confused with a resurrection account.[7]

Conclusion

This chapter has tried to answer the question, "what did it mean for Jesus to be transfigured?" While all the gospel accounts agree that Jesus' inward supernatural glory momentarily shone through Jesus' humanity on the mountain of the Transfiguration, each author conveys his own nuance. Thus, Mark emphasizes that Jesus must first suffer and then be glorified. Luke heightens that theme by rooting it in the three-fold division of the Hebrew Bible, which in one accord, predicted that the Messiah would suffer before entering into his glory. Matthew adapts Mark's narrative to portray the theme that Jesus is the greater Moses. For the Christian, two truths emerge from this chapter on the Transfiguration: First, we must suffer by taking up the cross and following Jesus. Second, that will result one day in our own glorious body, one likened unto Jesus' glorified body. And that day will come in the future as surely as it was prefigured at the Transfiguration (2 Peter 1:16–18).

REFLECTION QUESTIONS

1. What are the parallels between Mark 9:2–13 and Exodus 24 and 34 in terms of the transfiguration of Jesus?

2. What is the pattern in the central section of Mark that illuminates Jesus' transfiguration?

3. What is the unique word that Luke 9:28–36 uses of Jesus' transfiguration?

4. How does the transfiguration of Jesus, according to Matthew 17:1–13, emphasize that Jesus is the new Moses?

5. How do 2 Peter 1:16–18 relate Jesus' transfiguration to Jesus' second coming?

---

7. See the thorough refutation of the transfiguration as a misplaced resurrection narrative by Robert H. Stein, "Is the Transfiguration (Mark 9.2–8) a Misplaced Resurrection-Account?" *JBL* 95 (1976): 79–96.

Did Jesus Really Perform Miracles as an Adult?

In an earlier question, we were introduced to legends about miracles Jesus supposedly performed as a child, yet we found no credible evidence supporting such reports. But it is a totally different matter when we ask the question, "did Jesus really perform miracles as an adult?" because the Gospels record some thirty-five miracles that Jesus did indeed perform in his ministry. To better appreciate those miracles, this chapter covers five points: (1) miracles in the ancient Greco-Roman and Jewish settings; (2) the unified ancient reports regarding Jesus' miracles; (3) the types of miracles Jesus performed; (4) the purposes of his miracles, and (5) the secret accompanying Jesus' miracles.[1]

Miracles in the Ancient Greco-Roman and Jewish Settings

Miracles in the Ancient Greco-Roman Settings
 Belief in and reports of miracles were widespread in Greco-Roman antiquity, two kinds in particular: healing sanctuaries and pagan miracle workers.[2]
 Healing Sanctuaries. Healing sanctuaries especially included Asclepius, the most popular healer in ancient Greco-Roman society. As the Asclepius myth goes, he was originally a mortal whom Zeus struck dead for raising too many fellow mortals. But it was widely believed that Asclepius himself was raised from the dead from which vantage point he continued to heal the sick, often through dreams in his temples. The Asclepius shrines were scattered

---

1. Because we earlier dealt with the anti-supernatural bias of western mentality that discredits miracles in general, we will not re-enter that philosophical and scientific discussion.
2. This section is indebted to Craig S. Keener, *Miracles: The Credibility of the New Testament Accounts* (Grand Rapids: Baker, 2011), 1:35–65.

throughout the ancient world: Epidauros, Cos, Triccê, Pergamum, Corinth, etc. The rather usual format of a miracle story regarding Asclepius (whose symbol was a snake) involved three components: a description of the circumstances of the healing, the healing itself, and its confirmation or effects on the audience.[3] Comparing the Asclepius miracle reports reveals that, other than the rather stereotyped three-fold components, the content of the miracles do not parallel Jesus' miracles in the Gospels.

Pagan Miracle Workers. Apollonius of Tyana (late first century AD) was probably the most famous pagan miracle worker in Greco-Roman history, often compared to Jesus Christ. We learn of Apollonius from the writings of Philostratus' *Life of Apollonius* (second century AD). Like Jesus, Apollonius performed multiple healings and exorcisms. Moreover, like Jesus, Apollonius was branded a "magician" by his critics. Yet, it is certain that the stories about Apollonius' miracles circulated later than the writing of the Gospels and therefore have no direct bearing on Jesus' miracles.

Miracles in the Jewish Setting

Judaism exalted Moses, Elijah, and Elisha as great miracle workers of the one true God in the Old Testament. Nearer to Jesus' day were two notable Jewish miracle workers—Honi and Hanina ben Dosa. The former lived earlier than Jesus. He was well known for getting answered prayer regarding rain. The latter lived in the first century and in Galilee. It was reported that Hanina ben Dosa healed the sons of the Jewish sages of Johanan ben Zakkia (who led the way in reconstituting Israel after the fall of Jerusalem to the Romans in AD 70) and Gamaliel II. Geza Vermes goes so far as to claim that men like Hanina ben Dosa dominated first-century Galilean religious experience more than the priests or scribes did.[4]

Thus, we see that miracles were rather rampant in Greco-Roman and Jewish settings and that people were also informed enough to know the distinction between a bona fide miracle and magic. In other words, the ancients were not near as naïve as moderns have made them out to be.

Unified Ancient Reports Regarding Jesus' Miracles

The canonical evidence for Jesus as a miracle worker is substantial: the Synoptic Gospels, John (the four Gospels record some thirty-five miracles of Jesus), Acts, the Epistles, Revelation (11:6; 11:18; 19:10), and Paul (Rom. 15:19; 1 Cor. 12:8–10; 2 Cor. 12:12; Gal. 3:5). But the non-canonical sources also attest to the fact that Jesus was a miracle worker. Darrell Bock writes of this:

---

3. See ibid., 41. Rudolph Bultmann popularized the forms associated with miracles in the Gospels and in Greco-Roman literature (*The History of the Synoptic Tradition*, trans. John Marsh [New York: Harper & Row, Publishers, 1963], 218–43).

4. Geza Vermes, *Jesus and the World of Judaism* (Philadelphia: Fortress, 1983), 5.

> [O]ur ancient sources are consistent in not challenging that
> Jesus performed unusual works. What was debated by Jesus'
> opponents was the source of those acts. The Jewish retort
> that Jesus' power was either a reflection of magic, sorcery or
> of satanic power is not a denial that these activities took place
> but an effort to place their origin in a sphere outside God's
> benevolent activity. This theme runs through the centuries,
> whether it be in the Beelzebul controversy of the gospel tra-
> dition, the debates Justin Martyr had with Trypho or in the
> Talmudic tradition.[5]

On a more positive note, the reader will recall Josephus' report that Jesus performed wondrous works (*Antiquities of the Jews* 18.63).

Ironically, modern radical critics, Jewish scholars, and conservative theologians agree that Jesus performed miracles. Note the following sample:

> Thus, from the standpoint of the gospels, the mighty deeds of
> Jesus, healings and exorcisms alike, were the product of the
> power which flowed through him as a holy man. His powers
> were charismatic, the result of his having become a channel
> for the power of the other realm, that which Jesus and his
> contemporaries also called Spirit.[6]

> I hold, in summary, that Jesus, as a magician and miracle
> worker, was a very problematic and controversial phenom-
> enon not only for his enemies but even for his friends.[7]

> A powerful healer of the physically and mentally sick . . . he
> was . . . unconditionally given over to the rescue, not of com-
> munities, but of persons in need.[8]

---

5. Darrell L. Bock, "The Historical Jesus: An Evangelical View," in *The Historical Jesus: Five Views*, ed. James K. Beilby and Paul Rhodes Eddy (Downers Grove, IL: InterVarsity Press, 2009), 249–81; Bock follows here Graham Stanton, "Jesus of Nazareth: A Magician and a False Prophet Who Deceived God's People," in *Jesus of Nazareth Lord and Christ: Essays on the Historical Jesus and New Testament Christology*, ed. Joel B. Green and Max Turner (Grand Rapids: Eerdmans, 1994), 164–80.
6. Marcus Borg, *Jesus: A New Vision* (San Francisco: HarperSanFrancisco, 1987), 67 (modern radical scholar).
7. John Dominic Crossan, *The Historical Jesus: The Life of a Mediterranean Jewish Peasant* (San Francisco: Harper-SanFrancisco, 1991), 311 (modern radical scholar).
8. Giza Vermes, *The Religion of Jesus the Jew* (Minneapolis: Fortress, 1993), 206 (Jewish scholar).

[Jesus] probably saw his miracles as indications that the new age was at hand. He *shared the evangelists' view that he fulfilled the hopes of the prophets—or* at least that these hopes were about to be fulfilled.[9]

[Jesus'] healings and exorcisms were an intrinsic part of his proclamation of the kingdom (or rule) of God. The mighty deeds and the proclamation must go together; neither can be understood without the other.[10]

Types of Miracles Jesus Performed

As we mentioned, the Gospels record some thirty-five miracles Jesus performed. We list them below under their respective category: (1) healings/exorcism; (2) miracles over nature; (3) bringing the dead back to life:

HEALING/ EXORCISMS	MATTHEW	MARK	LUKE	JOHN
Man with leprosy	8:2–4	1:40–42	5:12–13	
Roman centurion's servant	8:5–13		7:1–10	
Peter's mother-in-law	8:14–15	1:30–31	4:38–39	
Two men from Gadara	8:28–34	5:1–15	8:27–35	
Paralyzed man	9:2–7	2:3–12	5:18–25	
Woman with bleeding	9:20–22	5:25–29	8:43–48	
Two blind men	9:27–31			
Man mute and possessed	9:32–33			
Man with a shriveled hand	12:10–13	3:1–5	6:6–10	
Man blind, mute and possessed	12:22		11:14	
Canaanite woman's daughter	15:21–28	7:24–30		
Boy with a demon	17:14–18	9:17–29	9:38–43	
Two blind men (one named)	20:29–34	10:46–52	18:35–43	

9. E. P. Sanders, *The Historical Figure of Jesus* (London: Penguin, 1993), 168; emphasis original (an open-minded liberal scholar).

10. Craig Evans, *Fabricating Jesus*, 141 (conservative scholar).

HEALING/ EXORCISMS	MATTHEW	MARK	LUKE	JOHN
Deaf mute		7:31–37		
Man possessed, synagogue		1:23–26	4:33–35	
Blind man at Bethsaida		8:22–26		
Crippled woman			13:11–13	
Man with dropsy			14:1–4	
Ten men with leprosy			17:11–19	
The high priest's servant			22:50–51	
Official's son at Capernaum				4:46–54
Sick man, pool of Bethesda				5:1–9
Man born blind				9:1–7

NATURE MIRACLES	MATTHEW	MARK	LUKE	JOHN
Calming the storm	8:23–27	4:37–41	8:22–25	
Walking on the water	14:25	6:48–51		6:19–21
5,000 people fed	14:15–21	6:35–44	9:12–17	6:5–13
4,000 people fed	15:32–38	8:1–9		
Coin in the fish's mouth	17:24–27			
Fig tree withered	21:18–22	11:12–14, 20–25		
Catch of fish			5:4–11	
Water turned into wine				2:1–11
Another catch of fish				21:1–11

RESURRECTION MIRACLES	MATTHEW	MARK	LUKE	JOHN
Jairus' daughter	9:18–19, 23–25	5:22–24, 38–42	8:41–42, 49–56	
Widow's son at Nain			7:11–15	
Lazarus				11:1–44

Moreover, John 20:30–31 proclaims that Jesus performed many more miracles than are recorded about him.

The Purposes of Jesus' Miracles

We may gather that Jesus performed miracles to serve at least three purposes. First, Jesus performed miracles to alleviate human suffering. His compassion for others, especially those who were sick and disadvantaged, runs right though all four gospels. Second, Jesus' miracles served to demonstrate that the kingdom of God had indeed dawned in connection with his ministry. Third, Jesus' miracles also authenticated the perception that he was the Messiah. It is interesting that Josephus talks about some ten messianic claimants in the first century, two of whom at least attempted to perform miracles to show that they were the Messiah. One name Theudas expected the Jordan River to part so that he and his followers could invade Canaan (Israel) to expel the Romans (*Antiquities of the Jews* 20.97). Another, "the Egyptian," expected the walls of Jerusalem to fall down before his followers (*Jewish Wars* 2.261; *Antiquities of the Jews* 20.169–70). Josephus called these attempts "sign miracles." Both efforts failed. Such attempted miracles, however, suggests that common expectation of the Jewish masses seems to have been that the Messiah would perform miracles (cf. Luke 4:18–21 with Isaiah 61 and The Dead Sea Scrolls [4Q 521]). Thus, Jesus' miracles would have helped to confirm the impression that he was truly the Messiah.

The Messianic Secret

In 1901, William Wrede advanced the theory that Mark's gospel contains the Messianic secret. That is to say, on a number of occasions in Mark, Jesus commands his disciples, and those he heals, to keep as a secret his actions on their behalf (Mark 1:34, 44; 3:12; 5:43; 7:36–37; 8:26, 30; 9:9). For Wrede, this meant that Jesus never actually claimed to be the Messiah, but after his death his followers made that assertion. So to compensate for the fact that Jesus never claimed to be the Messiah, whereas the disciples did, Wrede argued that the disciples made up the commands to silence in Mark as a way to cover their tracks. In other words, the messianic secret (Jesus' commands to silence) supposedly stemmed from Jesus' attempt to keep the idea that he was the Messiah as a secret, when in fact the disciples made up those commands to secrecy.[11]

Wrede's thesis has been largely rejected by gospel scholars for a couple of reasons. First, even though Jesus called for silence, that silence was broken by those he healed or even by demons he exorcised. If Mark's purpose was to show that nobody knew about Jesus' messiahship during his life, then Mark did a poor job of it. Second, it seems more accurate to suggest that the overall reason Jesus swore some of his audience to silence was because he did not want to be presented as a political Messiah, but rather as the Suffering Servant/Messiah.

---

11. W. Wrede, *The Messianic Secret*, trans. J. C. G. Greig (Edinburgh: T&T Clark; Greenwood, SC: Attic Press, 1971).

Conclusion

This chapter on miracles performed by Jesus as an adult covered five topics: miracles in the ancient Greco-Roman and Jewish settings; the unified ancient reports regarding Jesus' miracles; the types of miracles Jesus performed; the purposes of his miracles; and the secret accompanying Jesus' miracles. All of this to say, the historical Jesus of the Gospels surely performed miracles.

REFLECTION QUESTIONS

1. Who was a near-contemporary of Jesus, was a famous Gentile, and supposedly performed miracles?

2. What near-contemporary of Jesus was a famous Jew who supposedly performed miracles?

3. What reports converged to confirm that Jesus performed miracles as an adult?

4. What three types of miracles did Jesus perform?

5. What were the purposes of Jesus' miracles?

Questions Related
to the Teachings of Jesus

What Was the Focus of Jesus' Teaching?

Practically all biblical scholars agree that the focus of Jesus' teaching was the theme of the kingdom of God. Preceding Jesus' message of the kingdom of God is its place in the Old Testament, where the emphasis falls on God's kingship. God is king of Israel (Ex. 15:18; Num. 23:21; Deut. 33:5; Isa. 43:15) and of all the earth (2 Kings 19:15; Ps. 29:10; 99:1–4; Isa. 6:5; Jer. 46:18). Juxtaposed to the concept of God's *present* reign as king are references to a day when God will *become* king over his people (Isa. 24:23; 33:22; 52:7; Zeph. 3:15; Zech. 14:9). This emphasis on God's kingship continues throughout Judaism and takes on special significance in Jewish apocalypticism, which abandoned any hope for present history. Only at the end of the age will the kingdom of God come. With this as background, we make the following points regarding Jesus' message of the kingdom of God: (1) three major views of Jesus' message of the kingdom of God; (2) the already/not yet aspects of the kingdom of God in Jesus' ministry; and (3) miracles, parables, and the kingdom of God in Jesus' ministry.

Three Views Regarding Jesus' Message of the Kingdom of God

Although biblical scholars are nearly unanimous that the major emphasis of Jesus' message was the kingdom of God, three conflicting views emerged during the twentieth century as to how we are to understand that kingdom in Jesus' life and teachings. They are consistent eschatology, realized eschatology, and inaugurated eschatology.

Consistent Eschatology

"Consistent Eschatology" is a label applied by New Testament scholars to the works of Albert Schweitzer, a late nineteenth to early twentieth century biblical scholar.[1] "Consistent" means futurist, with reference to how

---

1. See especially his *The Quest of the Historical Jesus: A Critical Study of Its Progress from Reimarus to Wrede*, trans. W. Montgomery (New York: MacMillan, 1968) and *Paul and His*

Schweitzer interpreted the message of Jesus. Judaism at the time of Christ divided history into two periods: this age of sin (when sin rules) and the age to come (when the Messiah is expected to bring the kingdom of God to earth). Schweitzer concluded that an apocalyptic understanding of the kingdom was not only foundational for Christ's teaching, but also to understanding his life. Thus, Schweitzer maintained that Jesus believed it was his vocation to become the coming Son of Man. Initially, Jesus revealed this messianic secret only to Peter, James, and John. Later, Peter told it to the rest of the Twelve. Judas told the secret to the high priest who used it as the ground for Jesus' execution (Mark 14:61–64; cf. Dan. 7:13).

According to Schweitzer's interpretation, when Jesus sent out the Twelve on a mission to proclaim the coming kingdom of God, he did not expect them to return. The Twelve were the "men of violence" (Matt. 11:12) who would provoke the messianic tribulation that would herald the kingdom. Whereas some earlier scholars believed that one could only wait passively for the kingdom, Schweitzer believed that the mission of Jesus was designed to provoke its coming. When this did not happen, Jesus determined to give his own life as a ransom for many (Mark 10:45), and so cause the kingdom to come.

According to Schweitzer, Jesus took matters into his own hands by precipitating his death, hoping that would be the catalyst for causing God to make the wheel of history turn to its climax—the arrival of the kingdom of God. But, said Schweitzer, Jesus was wrong again, and he died in despair. So, for Schweitzer, Jesus never witnessed the dawning of the age to come, it lay in the distant future, separated from this present age.

Evangelical New Testament scholars today generally reject most of Schweitzer's conclusions regarding his "consistent eschatology," especially his disregard for the reliability of the Gospels. On the positive side, he did call attention to the fact that the message of Jesus is rooted in the concept of the kingdom of God, a connection that is still foundational to a proper understanding of biblical prophecy and the Gospels today, even though most modern New Testament scholars interpret that connection quite differently than Schweitzer did.

Realized Eschatology

In contrast to futurist eschatology where the kingdom of God awaits a final consummation at the end of history, realized eschatology views the kingdom of God as already realized in the person and mission of Jesus. The futurist aspects of Jesus' teaching are reduced to a minimum and his apocalyptic language is viewed as symbolic of theological truths.

Interpreters: A Critical History, trans. W. Montgomery (New York: MacMillan, 1956); *The Mysticism of Paul the Apostle,* trans. W. Montgomery (New York: Seabury Press, 1968).

The person most responsible for advocating this position is British scholar C. H. Dodd. In his 1935 book *Parables of the Kingdom*,[2] he focused on Jesus' teachings that announced the arrival of the kingdom with his coming. For instance, in Luke 11:20 Jesus says, "But if I drive out demons by the finger of God, then the kingdom of God has come to you" (cf. Luke 17:21; Matt. 13). Eschatology becomes a matter of the present experience rather than any kind of future event. The kingdom has come in the messianic ministry of Jesus.

Most interpreters have criticized Dodd's realized eschatology for ignoring Jesus' teachings that point to a future consummation of the kingdom (e.g., Mark 13; Matt. 24–25). When all of Jesus' teachings are considered, futurist eschatology balances realized eschatology. To be sure, the kingdom arrived with Jesus, but Jesus himself taught that history still awaits a final completion. The kingdom of God is both "already" and "not yet."

Inaugurated Eschatology

"Inaugurated Eschatology" is a concept commonly connected with the twentieth-century Swiss theologian Oscar Cullmann.[3] Like others before him, Cullmann realized that the Jewish notion of two ages formed an important background for understanding the message of Jesus. According to Judaism, history is divided into two periods: this age of sin and the age to come (i.e., the kingdom of God). For Jews, the advent of the Messiah would affect the shift from the former to the latter. In other words, Judaism viewed the two ages as consecutive. According to Cullmann, Jesus Christ announced that the end of time, the kingdom of God, had arrived in history (see Mark 1:15 and parallels; especially Luke 4:43; 6:20; 7:28; 8:1, 10; 9:2, 11, 27, 60, 62; 10:9, 11; 11:20; 13:18, 20; 16:16; 17:20, 21; 18:16, 17, 24, 25, 29; Acts 28:31). Yet, other passages suggest that, although the age to come had *already* dawned, it *was not* yet complete. It awaited the second coming for its full realization (Luke 13:28–29; 14:15; 19:11; 21:31; 22:16, 18; 23:51; Acts 1:6). Hence the name "inaugurated" eschatology. Such a view is pervasive in the New Testament besides in the Gospels (see, e.g., Acts 2:17–21; 3:18, 24; 1 Cor. 15:24; 1 Tim. 4:1; 2 Tim. 3:1; Heb. 1:2; 1 John 2:18). So, for inaugurated eschatology, the two ages are simultaneous: the age to come exists in the midst of this present age. Christians therefore live in between the two ages until the parousia (second coming of Christ). As Russell Moore has shown, the already/not yet aspect of the kingdom of God is the hermeneutical tie that binds evangelicals together these days.[4]

---

2. See C. H. Dodd, *The Parables of the Kingdom* (London: Nisbet, 1935; New York: Scribner's, 1936).
3. See especially Oscar Cullmann, *Christ and Time: The Primitive Christian of Time and History*, trans. Floyd V. Filson (Philadelphia: Westminster, 1950).
4. Russell D. Moore, *The Kingdom of Christ: The New Evangelical Perspective* (Wheaton: Crossway, 2004).

The Already/Not Yet Aspects of the Kingdom of God in Jesus' Ministry

The term "the kingdom of God" occurs over hundred times in Mark, Luke, and Matthew (where kingdom of heaven is a synonym for kingdom of God). Mark, perhaps the first gospel to be written, records Jesus' programmatic statement in 1:15, "The time is fulfilled, and the kingdom of God is at hand." That gospel, along with Luke and Matthew, then goes on to demonstrate that Jesus' miracles, teachings, death, and resurrection inaugurated the kingdom of God. Yet, it is also clear from Matthew, Mark, and Luke that the final manifestation of the kingdom has not yet happened. Luke indicates that the kingdom was present in Jesus (Luke 7:28; 8:10; 10:9–11; 11:20; 16:16; 17:20–21), but it also awaited the return of Christ for its completion (Luke 6:20–26; 11:2; 12:49–50, 51–53; 13:24–30; 21:25–29; 22:15–18, 30). The same dual aspect of the kingdom pertains to Luke's second volume, Acts. The kingdom was present in Jesus' ministry and, now, through his disciples (Acts 1:3; 8:12; 19:8; 20:25; 28:23–31); but it will not be completed until Christ comes again (Acts 1:6; 14:22).

There are only three references to the kingdom of God in John's gospel. Nicodemus is told by Jesus that he needed to be born again to enter the kingdom of God (3:3–5). Yet, Jesus' kingdom was not worldly in nature, but spiritual—one of the heart (18:36). John's emphasis on the present aspect of the kingdom of God is portrayed as the gift of eternal life which believers already possess (John 3:15–16, 36; 6:47, 51, 58; 8:51–52; 11:24–26; 10:28; cf. 1 John 2:25; 3:14; 5:11–13). But John still leaves room for a future aspect to the kingdom (see John 5:26–30 [which is juxtaposed to the present aspect of the kingdom in 5:16–25]; 14:1–4).

Miracles, Parables, and the Kingdom of God in Jesus' Ministry

Miracles and the Kingdom

As we saw above, Jesus' mighty works inaugurated the kingdom of God in his ministry. It was one thing for Jesus to claim to bring the kingdom but it was something else for Jesus to prove he brought the kingdom, and this he did in his miracles.

Parables and the Kingdom

But it is in Jesus' parables that we find the bulk of Jesus' teaching regarding the kingdom of God. There is a consensus among gospel scholars that the parables of Jesus are intimately connected to his message of the kingdom of God. However, Jesus' offer of the kingdom differed radically from then current Jewish expectations. There are six central aspects pertaining to the kingdom of God as reflected in the parables of Jesus: (1) the inauguration of the kingdom; (2) the recipients of the kingdom; (3) the requirements of the kingdom; (4) the growth of the kingdom; (5) the rejection of the kingdom; and (6) the consummation of the kingdom.

1. The inauguration of the kingdom of God. One need only to examine the characteristics of the teaching of Jesus to discover that in him the kingdom of God was being inaugurated. One such characteristic was that he taught with authority. Another characteristic of his teaching was that he taught with a compassionate, keen sense of wisdom. Last, but not least, Jesus taught in parables; in fact, one third of his teachings consisted of parables. It was this characteristic alone that should have hinted at his Messiahship, for one of the Old Testament prophecies foretold that the Messiah would come as the originator of parables (Ps. 78:2).

The Jewish people, however, for the most part, missed the hints. The kingdom they anticipated lay in the distant future, not in the present. Yet, Jesus came teaching his people that the kingdom of God had already come; it came with the arrival of the King. This is implied in several parables, two of which are the Parable of the Wineskins and Patch (Matt. 9:16–17; Mark 2:21–22; Luke 5:36–38) and the Parable of the Divided Realm (Matt. 12:25–29; Mark 3:23–30; Luke 11:17–28). In the Wineskins and Patch parable, the basic point of Jesus is that a whole new age has arrived, and that the old is finished having served its purpose. Now someone greater than just another prophet had arrived, the Messiah himself. In the Parable of the Divided Realm, Jesus answered his critics by pointing to his miracles as validation and testimony to his messiahship and thus his deity. This was so because, like the man who overcomes the owner of the house, Jesus had invaded and defeated the kingdom of Satan, namely, this world.

2. The recipients of the kingdom of God. The contrast in the two concepts of the kingdom between Judaism and Jesus becomes apparent again relative to the recipients of the kingdom. The Jews at the time of Jesus felt that they would be the exclusive participants in the coming kingdom of God. One can imagine their horror in discovering that the true recipients would be Jewish sinners and Gentiles. In numerous parables, Jesus makes it quite clear as to who the true recipients would be. In the Parable of the Lost Sheep (Luke 15:3–7) as well as in the Parable of the Lost Son (Luke 15:11–32), Jesus identifies non-observant Jews as being recipients, people who are despised by the ultra-observant Pharisees. Jesus declares not only that they were recipients, but that God actually delights in their entrance into the kingdom. In the Parable of the Two Debtors (Luke 7:36–50), Jesus offers the kingdom of God to women, even "sinful" women. In the Parable of the Great Banquet, the kingdom is offered to sinners (harlots and tax-collectors, Luke 13:28–29), and to those who were outcasts from society. Indeed, the Jewish understanding of the recipients of the kingdom of God and Jesus' conception were diametrically opposed.

3. The requirements of the kingdom of God. Once again, the distinction in the two concepts of the kingdom of God becomes visible through Jesus' parables in regard to the requirements for entrance into the kingdom. The Jewish people were taught that acceptance into the kingdom of God involved embracing the Shema (the unity of God) and the Torah as a whole. Jesus' requirements, however, went to the heart of the matter. One requirement for entrance into the kingdom of God is illustrated in the very purpose of Jesus' parables. To those who repented, the parables *revealed* truth, but for those who did not repent, the parables *concealed* truth (Matt. 13:13–15). This need for *repentance* is also illustrated in the Parable of the Royal Wedding (Matt. 22:1–4), where those who were clothed in the garments of "repentance" were invited in while those who were not were cast out. A second requirement was the element of *risk*, as is revealed in the Parable of the Hidden Treasure and the Parable of the Pearl of Great Price (Matt. 13:44–46). A third requirement was *faith*, as is attested to in the Parable of the Two Debtors, where the woman was "saved because of her faith" (Luke 7:50) and in the Parable of the Dishonest Steward (Luke 16:1–15) whose only hope lay in his master's grace. Another requirement for entrance into the kingdom of God, as Jesus presented it, was *counting the cost*. This can be seen in the Parable of the Tower Builder (Luke 14:25–30). A fifth requirement was *humility*, as can be seen in the publican (i.e., tax collector) in the Parable of the Pharisee and the Publican (Luke 18:9–14), where humility is redefined by Jesus as an honest assessment of oneself before God. One might say that these requirements for entering the kingdom of God can be reduced to two components—repentance and faith.

4. The growth of the kingdom of God. Jesus' thoughts on the growth of the kingdom are found in various parables, the first of which is the Parable of the Leaven (Matt. 13:33). Here the leaven was hidden in the three pecks of meal symbolizing the secret, inward growth of his kingdom. The same truth is portrayed in the Parable of the Mustard Seed (Matt. 13:31–32; Mark 4:30–32; Luke 13:18–19) and the Parable of the Seed Growing Secretly (Mark 4:26–29). All of these parables illustrate the mysterious growth of the kingdom, as well as the lack of human work involved in it. The truth of these parables, however, stood in direct opposition to ancient Jewish thinking on the subject. The Jews (particularly the Zealots) believed that the kingdom of God would come through the use of force. They felt that the growth of the kingdom would come through a revolutionary upheaval of the existing political system. The Zealots sought to bring about the messianic deliverance by forcibly throwing off the Roman yoke. Another parable that illustrates Jesus' thoughts on the growth of the kingdom is the Parable of the Sower (Matt. 13:1–23; Mark 4:1–20; Luke 8:4–15) where, despite the insignificant beginning, a bumper crop is promised. This brings with it great assurance concerning the success of the kingdom.

5. The rejection of the kingdom of God. Despite the open invitation of Jesus, the Jews, and particularly the religious leaders of his day, rejected his kingdom. There were several reasons for this rejection, none the least of which were covetousness and the love of money. Jesus points this out in the Parable of the Rich Fool (Luke 12:16–21) and the Parable of the Rich Man and Lazarus (Luke 16:19–31). In addition, there was prejudice against the

Gentiles, as the Parable of the Talents (Matt. 25:14–30) reveals, where the religious leaders had been hoarding the Law for themselves, refusing to share it with the Gentiles. The logical conclusion of this rejection is emphasized in the Parable of the Empty House (Luke 11:25–26) and the Parable of the Wicked Husbandman (Matt. 21:33–46; Mark 12:1–12; Luke 20:9–19), where judgment is pronounced on the nation of Israel, a pronouncement which was fulfilled in AD 70 when Jerusalem was destroyed. In reality, these reasons for rejecting Jesus can be summarized in one word—power! Jesus' critics did not want to share their power, so they crucified him.

6. **The consummation of the kingdom of God.** While Jesus announced the inauguration of the kingdom of God at his first coming, he also made numerous references to the future consummation of the kingdom. In the Parable of the Tares (Matt. 13:24–30), the main thrust of the parable is that there is coming a day of separation; a separation of the authentic from the inauthentic. However, Jesus' primary concern here was not with the forceful division of the two kingdoms here and now but with the weeding out that will come at the great eschatological consummation. In the Parable of the Persistent Widow (Luke 18:1–8), encouragement to continue in prayer is given in light of the return of Christ. In the Parable of the Ten Virgins (Matt. 25:1–13) the certainty and the suddenness of this consummation is emphasized. And lastly, in the Parable of the Sower the great assurance of this consummation is revealed. Even though the kingdom of God began with an insignificant beginning, its ending will be triumphant!

Conclusion

This chapter reflects the importance of the kingdom of God in Jesus' ministry. We have seen that of the three interpretations of the kingdom of God in Jesus' ministry, that inaugurated eschatology has the best claim on the data. That is, the kingdom of God began with the first coming of Christ, but it will not be completed until the second coming of Christ. Moreover, the miracles of Jesus proved that the kingdom of God did dawn in Jesus, while in the parables, we find the focus of Jesus' teaching on the kingdom of God.[5]

REFLECTION QUESTIONS

1. What does consistent eschatology mean with regard to the focus of Jesus' teaching?

---

5. For this discussion and more, see J. Daniel Hays, J. Scott Duvall, C. Marvin Pate, *An A to Z Guide to Biblical Prophecy and the End Times* (Grand Rapids: Zondervan, 2012), 325–28; formerly titled *Dictionary of Biblical Prophecy and End Times* (Grand Rapids: Zondervan, 2007).

2. What does realized eschatology mean with regard to the focus of Jesus' teaching?

3. What does inaugurated eschatology mean concerning the focus of Jesus' teaching?

4. What do the miracles of Jesus say about the kingdom of God in Jesus' ministry?

5. What is the message of the parables of Jesus relative to the kingdom of God in Jesus' ministry?

QUESTION 28

What Is the Main Message of Matthew About Jesus?

Though some doubt that Matthew, one of Jesus' twelve apostles, actually wrote the first gospel, it looks very much like Matthew's testimony is behind Matthew 9:9–13 (the calling of Levi the tax collector to follow Jesus) and Matthew 13:47–52 (the parable of the net, which emphasizes the scribal background of Matthew). Furthermore, the early church fathers were unanimous in holding that Matthew was indeed the author of this gospel.

The Jewish nature of Matthew's gospel suggests it was written in Palestine or perhaps in Syrian Antioch. Many scholars believe Matthew was written to counter the emergence of Rabbinic Judaism in the AD 80s, after the fall of Jerusalem to the Romans nearly annihilated the various branches of Judaism. Above all, the first gospel demonstrates that Jesus is the Messiah, drawing heavily on the promise-fulfillment theme (see below). The book, therefore, is steeped in biblical prophecy. Matthew especially emphasizes four unique features of prophecy related to Jesus the Messiah: (1) Jesus is the fulfillment of Old Testament prophecy; (2) he is the savior of the Jewish people (and the Gentiles); (3) he will build the church; and (4) the already/not yet aspects of the kingdom of God.

Jesus Is the Fulfillment of Old Testament Prophecy

Matthew follows Mark's major points regarding biblical prophecy. Thus, Jesus the Christ inaugurated the kingdom of God (Matt. 4:12–17 ["kingdom of heaven" for Matthew]); the parables record the small beginning but big projected ending of the kingdom (Matt. 13); the paradox of the kingdom means that Jesus first suffered and then entered heavenly glory (Matt. 16:21–28; 17:22; 20:17–19); at the Transfiguration, the inner three disciples witnessed the foretaste of the coming kingdom of God (Matt. 16:28–17:7); the nation as a whole rejected Jesus (Matt. 12:1–12, for which Matthew especially blames the Pharisees, the founders of Rabbinic Judaism); and Jesus' death and resurrection underscore his triumph over his enemies (Matt. 28).

But there are added features in Matthew that reveal the depth of influence of biblical prophecy on the first gospel. It is clear in Matthew's infancy narratives (chapters 1–2) that Jesus is the Messiah who fulfills Old Testament prophecy in two ways. First, Jesus is the new Moses who is going to bring about a new exodus, one spiritual in nature (Matt. 1:21; 2:13–15). Second, Jesus is the long-awaited Davidic Messiah (Matt. 1:23 and Isa. 7:14 [the Messiah will be called Immanuel]; Matt. 2:1–8 and Mic. 5:2 [the prediction of the Messiah's birth in Bethlehem]; Matt. 2:9 and Num. 24:17 [the star of the Davidic dynasty rising]).

In addition, Matthew announces fourteen times that Jesus is the fulfillment of Old Testament biblical prophecy, especially related to the restoration of Israel. In Matthew 1:22–23 and Isaiah 7:14, Jesus is called the Immanuel of God because he will save his people from their sins. Matthew equates Jesus with the Messiah who will deliver his people (Matt. 2:5–6; cf. Mic. 5:1; 2 Sam. 5:2). In Matthew 2:14–15, Jesus' return to Israel from Egypt after Herod the Great's death is portrayed as a type of Exodus which, in light of Matthew 3:3, should be understood as his vocation to deliver Israel from the bondage of sin (cf. Hos. 11:1). Matthew also perceives in Jesus' ministry the fulfillment of Jeremiah's prophecy of Israel's restoration (Matt. 2:17–18; cf. Jer. 31:5).

The text of Isaiah 11:1 (cf. Isa. 4:2), envisions the coming of the Davidic deliverer, called the Branch. If *Nazarene* refers to *Nezer* (Branch), then Matthew 2:23 can also be viewed as equating Jesus with the Davidic Messiah. Isaiah 9:1–2 foretells of Israel's future restoration and the Gentiles' conversion, which Matthew sees as resulting from Jesus' miracles (Matt. 4:14–16). In both Matthew 8:17 and Isaiah 53:4, healing as a metaphor for Israel's restoration is applied to Jesus' dealings with the masses.

Obviously, the first gospel perceives in Jesus the suffering servant who will be the catalyst for Israel's restoration to God (Matt. 12:17–21; cf. Isa. 42:1–4). In Matthew 13:14–15, Israel's rejection of Jesus is interpreted as indicating that the nation's sin and exile persist (cf. Isa. 6:9–10). The overriding theme of Psalm 78 is the story of Israel—sin—exile—restoration—and for that reason is drawn on Matthew 13:35. Isaiah 62:11 and Zechariah 9:9 predict that God will send a messianic deliverer to Israel, which is applied by Matthew to Jesus at his triumphal entry (Matt. 21:4–5). The smiting of the shepherd and the scattering of the nation is applied in Matthew 26:56 (cf. v. 31) to Jesus' death and the disciples' subsequent departure, perhaps as an allusion to the continuing exile of Israel (cf. Zech. 13:7). The purchasing of a field by Jeremiah (Jer. 32:6–15) was promissory of the coming restoration of Israel, even though that nation was about to go into exile. Perhaps Matthew (Matt. 27:9–10; cf. Zech. 11:12–13) understands the purchase of the field with Judas' blood, and at the expense of Jesus' death, to have conveyed a divine irony: that which cost Jesus his life (the cross) was the basis for the true restoration of Israel.

The dominant theme, then, in all of these Matthean fulfillment texts is the restoration of Israel inaugurated by Jesus. Not to be overlooked in all of this is the historical situation necessitating the writing of Matthew's gospel, which is commonly thought to have been the post-AD 70 debates between the Matthean community and the Pharisees. Both of these groups were touting their respective devotees as the true Israel to emerge after the fall of Jerusalem. Matthew portrays the Jesus movement as restored Israel over against the Pharisees, hence his use of the Old Testament as a witness to the truth of that message.

Jesus Is the Savior of the Jewish People and the Gentiles

Matthew 1:21 applies the prophecy of Isaiah 7:14 to Jesus—Jesus has come to save his people, the Jews. We saw in the first point above that Matthew focuses on how it is that Jesus is fulfilling the Old Testament prophecies of the coming restoration of Israel. We now cast our net wider by observing how the restoration of Israel theme is developed throughout Matthew under the two-fold topic of the salvation of both Jews and Gentiles.

Jesus Is the Savior of the Jewish People

I suggest the following outline for Matthew:

1:1–17	Introduction: Genealogy
1:18–2:23	The New Moses
ch. 3	The New Exodus
ch. 4	The New Israel
chs. 5–25	The New Covenant Described
chs. 26–27	The New Covenant Inaugurated
ch. 28	Conclusion

The overriding theme of these sections is the sin-exile-restoration paradigm of Israel, with the emphasis falling on the third of these components.

N. T. Wright has demonstrated that the threefold division of the Matthean genealogy centering on Abraham, Moses, and Christ is designed to evoke the story of Israel:

> Abraham is the start . . . [which] is the story of Israel. The next focal point is ... on Jesus as the true David, the Messiah. The third focal point is unexpected: the exile. This is not so regular a marker within Jewish schemes but for Matthew it is crucial. . . . [M]ost Jews of the second-temple period regarded themselves as still in exile, still suffering the results of Israel's age-old sin. Until the great day of redemption dawned, Israel was still "in her sins," still in need of rescue.

The genealogy then says to Matthew's careful reader that the long story of Abraham's people will come to its fulfillment, its seventh seven, with a new David, who will rescue his people from their exile, that is, "save his people from their sins." When Matthew says precisely this in 1:18–21 we should not be surprised.[1]

Looming behind the introduction and making his explicit appearance in Matthew 1:18–2:23 is Moses and in particular Jesus, the New Moses. As such, Jesus the deliverer inaugurates a new exodus, according to chapter 3. More than this, in Matthew 4 we learn that Jesus is the true Israel who obeys God in the wilderness, whereas ancient Israel did not. One begins to sense from these early chapters in the first gospel that Jesus' redemption of his people constitutes the fulfillment of the long-awaited restoration of Israel.

This is confirmed by the heart of the Matthean material, chapters 5–25, wherein Jesus presents the New Covenant to Israel, Deuteronomic blessings included. Wright correctly points out that the five blocks of teaching material occurring in this major section are designed by Matthew to elicit Deuteronomy 27–30 (esp. Deut. 30:15–20). The first and last blocks draw on the Deuteronomic blessings, including the Beatitudes (Matt. 5–7) and the curses on the Pharisees (Matt. 23–25). The dominant theme informing Matthew in all of this is the new covenant.[2] Figure 3.1 shows a chiastic structure of the five teaching blocks, along with brief comments on each, reflecting this understanding of Matthew.[3]

A. Deuteronomic blessings (5–7)

    B. Deuteronomic blessings and curses on those who follow or reject Jesus, respectively (10–11).

        C. The above two choices are by divine design (13).

    B'. Deuteronomic blessings and curses on those who follow or reject Jesus, respectively (18).

A'. Deuteronomic curses (23–25).

---

1. N. T. Wright, *The New Testament and the People of God* (Minneapolis: Fortress, 1992), 385–86.
2. Ibid., 386–87.
3. Ibid., 387.

Points A and A', as observed above with Wright, contrast the destinies of those who follow Jesus and those who do not. Thus according to A (Matt. 5–7), those who obey Jesus' teaching are blessed and inherit the kingdom of God, the epitome of the Deuteronomic blessings. Those who reject Jesus (most notably the Pharisees), however, bring on themselves and the nation of Israel the Deuteronomic curses, as presented in A' (Matt. 23–25).

Actually, the careful reader will detect in Matthew 23–25 the presence of the four tenets of the Deuteronomistic tradition: (1) Israel has been continuously disobedient to God in the past and now in the present due to the Pharisee's warped teaching (Matt. 23:1–28); (2) God sent his prophets to call Israel to repentance (Matt. 23:29–30, 34); (3) Israel has rejected God's messengers, culminating in its crucifixion of Jesus, instigated by the Pharisees (Matt. 23:31–34, 37); (4) God consequently will judge the nation in the future, and the city of Jerusalem will be destroyed (by the Romans) as it was in the past by the Babylonians (Matt. 23:35–36; amplified in Matt. 24–25). All of this bespeaks the actualization of the Deuteronomic curses on those who reject Jesus.

Points B (Matt. 10–11) and B' (Matt. 18) envision two responses. Those who accept Jesus' followers receive the Deuteronomic blessings, while those who reject them heap on themselves the covenantal curses. Point C (Matt. 13), the central concern of the five blocks of Matthean teaching, presents the truth via parables that one's reaction to Jesus—acceptance or denial—is by divine design (cf. Matt. 13:14–15 with Isa. 6:9). Such knowledge (*pesher?*) supplies the disciples the key to unlocking the mystery (*r'z?*) of the kingdom of God (Matt. 13:11).[4]

Having portrayed the new covenant (in Matt. 5–25), Matthew then describes Jesus' inauguration of such through his death and resurrection (Matt. 26–27). Chapter 28 (especially vv. 16–20) concludes Matthew's story of Israel. Comparing this to Deuteronomy 31–34 and Moses' final blessing on the people and his ascent of the mountain to see the land Israel would possess, Wright notes, "After his resurrection, Jesus, like Moses, goes up the mountain and departs from his people, leaving them with a commission to go in and possess the land, that is the entire world."[5]

Jesus Is the Savior of the Gentiles

The following nine points show that Jesus also reached out to Gentiles:

(1) The first gospel begins with Jesus' genealogy, tracing it back to Abraham, the father of all nations (1:1). (2) Four Gentile women are mentioned as among the ancestors of Jesus (Tamar, Rahab, Ruth, and Bathsheba [wife of Uriah]). (3) The birth narrative records Gentile magi traveling to

---

4. These two Aramaic terms occur throughout the Aramaic section of Daniel, chapters 2–7. The first is the interpretation of the dream while the second is the dream or mystery itself.
5. Ibid., 388.

Bethlehem to pay homage to the infant Jesus (2:1–12). (4) Two of Matthew's formula quotations—4:15–16 (Isa. 9:1–2) and 12:18–19 (Isa. 42:1–4)—state that Jesus is the light to the Gentiles. (5) At Capernaum, Jesus heals the servant of a Roman centurion, praising the soldier's faith as superior to that of anyone in Israel. In that context, Jesus announced that many Gentiles will eat at the messianic banquet while many Jews will be excluded (8:5–13). (6) Jesus traveled in the Gentile areas of Gadara (8: 28–34), Tyre and Sidon (15:21–39), performing miracles there. In the latter region, he healed a Canaanite woman, and praised her faith in similar manner as he did for the Roman centurion (15:22–28). (7) That the Gentiles have a place in the kingdom of heaven is made clear in the parabolic material of 21:28–22:14, especially 21:43 where Jesus emphasized that the kingdom would be taken from the Jews and given to a nation producing proper fruits—the Christian church composed of Jews and Gentiles. (8) At the cross of Jesus, the Gentile centurion and the other guards confess Jesus as the Son of God (27:54). (9) After the resurrection of Jesus, he challenges his disciples to take the Great Commission to all nations (28:19–20).

Jesus Will Build His Church

Only Matthew of the four gospels records Jesus' words about the church, in 16:16–19 and 18:15–20. These are hotly debated verses among various Christian denominations but we will offer what we think is the best reading of these passages. Three topics govern these two texts.

Christ as the Foundation of the Church

It is Peter's confession that Jesus is the Christ, the Son of the living God (v. 16) that elicits Jesus' following remarks regarding the church. So we may draw from verse 16 the conclusion that whatever vv. 17–19 may mean, Jesus is the ultimate foundation of the church (see also Eph. 2:20).

Christ's Representative in the Church

There are three views of what Jesus means when he says to Peter that he will build his church upon the rock. First, some Protestants say that Peter's confession that Jesus is the Christ is the foundation upon which Christ will build his church. This position is understandable in light of verse 16. Second, other Protestants say that the rock is Christ. This perspective is based on the assumption that Jesus engaged Peter in a pun on his name: You are Peter (*petros,* masculine) but upon this rock (*petra,* feminine, Christ) I will build my church. While the sentiment driving this view is correct—that Christ is the foundation/rock upon which the church will be built, it probably reads a word play into the text that is not intended. Rather, the more straightforward reading of the passage is this: Peter is the rock (*petros*), and upon this rock (*petra,* Peter), Christ will build his church. The former reading has no explanation as to why the feminine form is applied to Christ but the latter reading does: the feminine, *petra,* anticipates the feminine gender of *ekklēsia* (church) which follows *petra.* The third view of this passage is the Roman Catholic view, which equates the rock with Peter and thereby goes on to argue for apostolic succession (Peter was the first pope). We accept the first part of this view (that Peter was the rock upon which Christ started the building of the church), but we reject the accompanying apostolic succession view.

All in all, it is better, then, to understand this passage as teaching that Peter was Christ's representative for starting the church. And to him, Christ made two promises. (1) The gates of Hades shall not prevail against the church. This may well indicate that the church will be victorious over its enemies even to the end of the age (v. 18). (2) That Peter will have the keys of the kingdom which offers forgiveness of sin to those who respond and denial of forgiveness to those who reject the gospel. Here we must bring into the discussion Matthew 18:15–18, for there Jesus applies the same language of loosing/forgiveness of and binding/non-forgiveness to the church. This indicates to us that Peter's authority is no greater than that of the congregation and, further, it was fulfilled in Peter's preaching on the day of Pentecost (Acts 2:14–41).

Christ's Presence in the Church
Matthew 18:19–20 assures the church that the presence of Christ is in the gathered congregation even if there are no more than two or three present. Two background matters surface regarding these verses. First, the term church—*ekklēsia*—draws upon the LXX term that translated Israel's gathering to worship as *qahal* (Hebrew). Second, the quorum to qualify for the presence of Jesus in the gathering of the church (two or three) may play off the Jewish quorum of ten men needed to gather to worship in the synagogue (*Melkita* on Ex. 20:24; *Mishnah Abot* 3:6).

The Already/Not Yet Aspect of Matthew' Message

Matthew contains unique material that is stamped by the already/not yet eschatological tension: Matthew 5–7; 10; and 24. We now summarize each of these passages in terms of the already/not yet dynamic undergirding them.

1. Matthew 5–7 records Jesus' Sermon on the Mount, which presents the ethics that should characterize the citizens of the kingdom of God. Two modern interpretations of the Sermon on this point compete with one another. One school of thought (held by some Dispensationalists) argues that, because the requirements set forth in Matthew 5–7 are too unrealistic to follow in this present evil age, it will only be in the Millennium (the 1,000-year reign of Christ on earth after his second coming) that Christians will be able to live up to these noble standards. Most scholars, however, reflect a different school of thought believing that the already/not yet eschatological tension governs the Sermon. Because the kingdom of God has already dawned, believers should live now by the ethics of the kingdom as detailed in Matthew 5–7. But, because the kingdom is not yet complete, the full realization of the standards of the Sermon await the parousia and its aftermath.

2. The content of Matthew 10, which is not found in Mark, describes the mission of the twelve apostles to Israel before the passion of Christ. It is clear that the same language found in Mark 13:9–13 (the Olivet Discourse) is applied to the disciples' mission (see particularly Matt. 10:17–22), thus stamping it with prophetic import. The apostles' struggles and triumphs in preaching the gospel respectively testify to both the presence of the kingdom of God now in terms of Israel's rejection of its Messiah and yet the promise of her future acceptance. This paradoxical circumstance will continue until the parousia (Matt. 10:23).

3. Matthew's account of Jesus' Olivet Discourse (Matt. 24) agrees with Mark 13, except for one critical point. In Mark 13:3, the question of the disciples about the coming fall of Jerusalem to the Romans equates that with the end of the age. But in Matthew 24:3, the disciples' question separates the fall of Jerusalem (see Matt. 24:4–20) from the second coming of Christ (Matt. 24:21–31). The former is the backdrop of the latter. Here again is the already/not yet tension: already Jerusalem has fallen, but not yet has the end of the age come. This approach understands the first half of the Olivet Discourse as having been fulfilled at the fall of Jerusalem in AD 70 (the already aspect) with the second half of the discourse awaiting final completion at the second coming of Christ at the end of history (the not yet aspect). According to this view, the fall of Jerusalem in AD 70 serves as the backdrop for the future return of Christ. Moreover, the already side of the signs of the times will intensify until they are completed at the parousia (see Question 32).

4. Another matter raised in Matthew 24 is the identity of the elect who will be gathered together to be delivered at the Second Coming of Christ (cf. Matt. 24:31 with Mark 13:27). Those who are pre-tribulationists think the elect is Israel, who will convert to Jesus the Messiah during the Great Tribulation. Post-tribulationists, however, see the reference to be Christians (i.e., the church) who will endure the Great Tribulation. One's interpretation of the elect in Matthew 24:31 governs one's perspective toward the sheep and goats judgment, which is unique to Matthew 25. Pre-tribulationists think the sheep are Jews while the goats are the nations of the world who mistreat Israel in the Great Tribulation. But post-tribulationists believe the sheep are Christians of all ages, who are persecuted by the enemies of God (the goats), and the two will meet with opposite fates at the divine judgment that will conclude the Great Tribulation.[6]

---

6. For more, see J. Daniel Hays, J. Scott Duvall, C. Marvin Pate, *An A to Z Guide to Biblical Prophecy and the End Times* (Grand Rapids: Zondervan, 2012), 274–77; previously published as *Dictionary of Biblical Prophecy and End Times* (Grand Rapids: Zondervan, 2007).

One can also see eschatological value in Matthew 27:54—the group of Roman soldiers who confess Jesus to be the Son of God is the beginning of the salvation for the Gentiles predicted in the Old Testament that will occur after the Great Tribulation (e.g., Isa. 2:2–3; 11:9–10; 25:6–7; 45:20–25; Zech. 8; *Tobit* 13:11). Two considerations are offered by Dale C. Allison that suggest this interpretation. (1) The conversion of the Gentiles in 27:54 (cf. 28:19) can be seen to balance out the conversion of Jews (10:5–6); the latter characterizes the pre-Easter period with the former depicting the post-Easter era. Put another way, the conversion of the Gentiles that was expected to occur at the end of history (Matt. 8:11–12; 12:41–42) has already begun with the death and resurrection of Jesus (Matt. 8:27–54; 28:19). (2) The confession of the Gentiles (27:54) occurs in connection with the eschatological events of 27:51b–53. All of this to say that Jesus' death and resurrection set in motion for him the triumph of the Kingdom of God over the nations (see the Great Commission, Matt. 28:18–20).[7]

Conclusion

The major message of Matthew is four-fold. Jesus is portrayed as inaugurating the restoration of Israel, saving both Jews and Gentiles, building his church, and presenting the kingdom of God as already present but not yet complete.

REFLECTION QUESTIONS

1. What does Matthew say about the restoration of Israel?

2. What is the undergirding motif informing Matthew's fourteen Old Testament quotations?

3. What does Matthew say about the salvation of Jew and Gentile?

4. What does Matthew say about Jesus and the church?

5. What does Matthew say about the already/not yet aspects of the kingdom of God?

---

7. Ibid.; Dale C. Allison, *The End of the Ages Has Come: An Early Interpretation of the Passion and Resurrection of Jesus* (Philadelphia: Fortress Press, 1985), 46–47.

What Is the Main Message of Mark About Jesus?

Many New Testament scholars believe that Mark wrote his gospel under Peter's auspices right before the fall of Jerusalem to the Romans in AD 70, around AD 68. I concur with this conclusion. That would mean that the second gospel may well have been the first of the four gospels written. If so, the original readers of Mark faced a shocking presentation of Jesus of Nazareth, namely, he was a subversive Messiah compared to what Second Temple Judaism expected in a messianic figure. Indeed, if we are correct in our interpretation of the gospel of Mark, Jesus challenged at least six actions of the traditional Messiah expected by ancient Israel: (1) he conquered Jews in the land of Israel not her oppressors; (2) appointed twelve ordinary men, not political officials, to reconstitute the twelve tribes of Israel; (3) was not Torah abiding, at least not in the way the Pharisees were; (4) was the suffering Son of Man, not the political Messiah; (5) came to announce the destruction of the temple not the rebuilding of it; (6) was the suffering servant, not Israel. We now examine these six subversive actions on the part of Jesus the Messiah.

Jesus Messiah Conquered Jews, Not Her Oppressors

Although the purpose for Jesus' coming to Israel is surprisingly clear in Mark 1:1–15, it is often missed by interpreters. According to the preceding passage, Jesus came to restore Israel, the same restoration the Old Testament prophets anticipated (see esp. Isaiah, Jeremiah, Ezekiel, Zechariah, and Malachi). There are four indicators in Mark 1:1–15 that place Jesus' message in the same vein as the prophets. First, the word "gospel" (*euaggelion*) forms an inclusio around Mark 1:1–15, signaling it to be the key concept in this opening statement of Mark. When Jews in Jesus' day heard the word "gospel" it meant to them the promised restoration of Israel predicted by the Old Testament prophets (esp. Isa. 40 and following). The LXX of Isaiah uses *euaggelizomai* as a descriptor of the future restoration of Israel to her land out of exile (Isa. 40:9 [2x]; 52:7–10 [2x]; 61:1). Second, Malachi predicted that Elijah would be the forerunner of the Messiah calling Israel back to God, thereby setting in motion the restoration of Israel (Mal. 3:1; 4:5–6), which is applied to John the Baptist in Mark 1:2–11. Third, indeed Mark 1:2–3 quotes Isaiah 40:3 as John the Baptist's message to his fellow Jews. Isaiah 40:3 is a prediction of the restoration of Israel. Fourth, the baptizing activity of John the Baptist took place at the Jordan River in simulation of ancient Israel's crossing of the Jordan to conquer Canaan land. As we mentioned in an earlier chapter, a number of messianic movements began at the Jordan River in imitation of the conquest of Canaan, but now directed against the Romans. Furthermore, the Roman military quickly put any such attempt to the sword. All of this informs Mark 1:15 and Jesus' announcement that the kingdom of God is near. Even if the meaning of the verb, *ēggiken* (Mark 1:15), is not clear ("arrived" or "at hand"), the parallelism it forms with the phrase, "the time is fulfilled" (1:15) is clear: the kingdom of God has arrived, or dawned. And this is called by Jesus "the good news/gospel." In other words, the rule of God over the restoration of Israel was now present.[1]

But strangely, the story of the conquest of Canaan land takes a surprising turn in the ministry of Jesus, namely, he conquers the Jews in Israel not the Romans. More particularly, Jesus exorcized many demon-possessed Jews (see Mark 1:23–27, 32–34, 39; 3:10–11, 14, 20–30; 5:1–20; 6:7–13; 7:24–30; 9:14–29; 16:18 [if original to the text]). To put this in Old Testament language, Jesus cast out Canaanite influence within Jews in Israel. This may explain Mark's usage of the name Beelzebub, a Canaanite god, for Satan and his minions (see again 3:20–30). It is interesting in this regard that Deuteronomy 32:17 indicted Israel for worshipping demons in the wilderness wanderings, while Psalm 106:37 laments the fact that Israel in her land sacrificed her children to demons. These two passages suggest that a part of the covenant curses that will fall on Israel will involve an intimate association with demons. So the pervasive demonic possession of Jews at the time of Jesus may well have been one sign that the covenant curses still created havoc for Israel. All of this against the expectation of pious Jews at the time who longed for God's messiah to break the Roman occupation of the land of Israel.

According to N. T. Wright, Jesus retold the story of Israel (sin → exile → restoration) in a way that redefined Israel's enemy. Three passages highlight this reality.[2] The Beelzebul controversy (Matt. 12:22–32; Mark 3:20–30; Luke 11:14–23) reflects the fact that the Jewish leadership, in attributing to Jesus' miracles the power of Satan, accused him of dishonoring the covenant with Yahweh, particularly in his dismissal of the boundary markers of the Torah

---

1. Other Old Testament traditions occurring in Mark 1:1–15 are the new exodus and the wilderness temptation.

2. N. T. Wright, *Jesus and the Victory of God* (Minneapolis: Fortress, 1996), 451–56.

(Sabbath-keeping, dietary laws, circumcision) and later with his cleansing of the temple. This was perceived as nothing less than being in league with Israel's enemies, now personified in Rome—tantamount to being in cahoots with Satan. In effect, Jesus' refutation of such an accusation redefined Israel's real enemy: his miracles were by the power of God, not Beelzebul, and in actuality were defeating the evil one, the ultimate source of Israel's struggles. To miss this was to invite natural disaster because such a misperception would inexorably lead Israel into battle with Rome, the wrong opponent. Similarly, Luke 12:4–7 (cf. Matt. 10:28–31) suggests that Israel's enemy was not Rome (the one who had the power to kill the body), but rather Satan (the one who had the power to cast the nation into Gehenna).[3] So also the story of the attempted exorcism and the returning of seven demons (Matt. 12:43–45; Luke 11:24–26) makes the point that Israel needed to be delivered from Satan. That is, the nation's restoration would not come about by revolting against her physical enemies, something regrettably attempted since the Maccabeans, but rather by the expulsion of Satan.

The point we wish to make from this is that Jesus' exorcisms of Satan and his demons focused on Jews, not Romans.

Jesus Reconstituted the Twelve Tribes of Israel from Ordinary Men, Not the Political Leaders of the Nation

In an earlier chapter, we noted that Jesus chose twelve men/apostles to build the New Israel. Indeed, Second Temple Judaism expected that when the Messiah comes in the end times he will restore the twelve tribes of Israel to her land out of exile. We also observed in that chapter that the twelve disciples not only represented the twelve tribes (i.e., the new Israel), but they also represented the remnant, the faithful few who responded positively to God. They accepted Jesus as God's Messiah when the majority of Jews did not. Here we add one more point to this discussion: if the institution of Shaliah (the legal process whereby the Sanhedrin appointed their representatives to disseminate the decisions of that body politic to the public) did indeed exist at the time of Jesus, then his choice of the twelve disciples was notable in that Jesus did not include in that number any officials from the Sanhedrin (not that he would have been perceived to have had the authority to do so in any event). Rather, the men that Jesus appointed seemed to replace the official political leaders of Israel. To the apostles, Jesus gave representative power in his name to preach and heal, and the audiences' response to the disciples was tantamount to being their response to Jesus. It is patently clear in Mark, and in all of the Gospels, that the Jewish leadership overwhelmingly rejected Jesus as their Messiah and his apostles as his authoritative emissaries. We will see why the leaders reacted so negatively to the Jesus movement in the next point.

---

3. Ibid., 455, number 48.

Jesus Was Not the Law-Abiding Messiah the Leaders of Israel Expected Him To Be

From the beginning, Jesus did not teach or obey the Torah as the Jewish leadership expected the Messiah to do. Thus, Mark 1:21–22 states that Jesus taught with authority God's Word, not like the teachers of the law of Moses. The latter based their authority on what rabbis and eminent theologians said, not on what God was saying directly to them. In contrast, Jesus proclaimed what God directly revealed to him. More than that, Jesus seemed to go against the Torah. Thus, Mark 2:1–3:6 records a number of controversies that ensued between Jesus and the Pharisees, the teachers of the law of Moses. Mark 2:1–12 records Jesus as forgiving and healing a paralytic, which the Jewish leaders took as blasphemy on Jesus' part. Mark 2:13–17 relates that Jesus hung out with sinners and ate with tax collectors. Mark 2:18–22 says that Jesus did not fast like the Pharisees did, and 2:23–27 relates that Jesus defended his disciples against the Pharisees' accusation that they broke the Sabbath. Mark 3:1–6 records Jesus healing a man's hand on the Sabbath. Mark 5:1–43 relates three miracles in which Jesus broke kosher requirements by: contacting a demoniac, touching a woman with a hemorrhage, and raising up a dead girl. All of these marvelous works involved Jesus in coming into direct contact with the ceremoniously unclean. In Mark 7:1–30 Jesus rejected the Pharisees' clean and unclean categories and had contact with a Gentile woman. In Mark 9:14–29 Jesus had another encounter with a demoniac (as indeed much of Jesus' ministry was to the demonically possessed). According to Mark 10:1–12, Jesus trumped Moses's permission of divorce by rooting lifelong marriage in the beginning of creation (Gen. 2:24). In Mark 11:12–18, Jesus cleansed the temple, which was an act of desecration of the law in the eyes of the Jewish leadership (cf. Jesus' prophecy of the coming destruction of the temple). Mark 12:28–31 reports Jesus reducing the whole of the Torah to loving God and one's neighbor. Whether Jesus actually transgressed the Torah or, more likely, cut against the grain of the oral tradition of the Pharisees is a matter of debate. But, in any case, Jesus' posture toward the interpretation of the law of Moses was not countenanced by the Jewish leadership of his day. Surely, no Messiah would do that!

Jesus Was the Suffering Son of Man, Not a Political Messiah

The central section of Mark's gospel (Mark 8:22–10:45) is concerned above all to demonstrate that Jesus was the suffering Son of Man not a political messiah. Thus, these chapters record the following pattern: Jesus predicts that he, as the Son of Man, is going to Jerusalem for the purpose of suffering and dying; his disciples misunderstand him on that point; Jesus proceeds to correct their misunderstanding. This happens four times in Mark's central section. The reader will recall that chart from an earlier chapter.

The concept of the Son of Man dying and rising again is rooted in Daniel 7, obviously an apocalyptic text. In comparing Daniel 7 with Jesus' words "Son of Man" in his passion predictions, three observations can be made: (1) According to Daniel 7, the Son of Man is a corporate figure—he is identified with the saints of the Most High (Dan. 7:17–18, 21–22, 26–27). Jesus' application of this concept to himself and his followers proceeds from these texts. (2) Jesus, like the Son of Man in Daniel, is a suffering figure in that both are identified with the afflictions of the saints (Dan. 7:21, 25). (3) The Son of Man of Daniel 7 was considered to be a heavenly figure; that is, supernatural in nature. Indeed, such a title was Jesus' favorite designation for himself, not Messiah. In other words, in claiming to be the Son of Man Jesus was placing himself on par with God, as did the term "Messiah." And Jesus was certainly the Messiah, but he chose the title "Son of Man" because it did not have the political connotation that Messiah did. Thus, Jesus presented himself as the suffering Son of Man, not a political Messiah.

Jesus Messiah Called for the Destruction of the Temple, Not the Messianic Rebuilding of It

There are some Jewish traditions in which the eschatological Messiah is expected to rebuild the temple of Jerusalem. This expectation may be rooted in the prophecy of Zechariah 6:12, "The man whose name is Branch . . . he shall build the temple of the Lord." The *Targum* Zechariah 6:12 reads, "Behold, the man whose name is Messiah will be revealed, and he shall be raised up, and shall build the Temple of the Lord." The Dead Sea Scrolls seem to tap into this belief, "And he told them to build for him a sanctuary of man" (4 Q Florilegium 1:6–7; cf. 11Q Temple 29:7–10; *2 Baruch* 4:3).

However, Mark 14:58, along with Jesus' prediction of the coming destruction of the temple (Mark 13) as well as his cleansing of it (Mark 11:12–19), signaled that Jesus approved its demise, a notion contrary to what the Messiah was expected to do, namely, rebuild the temple in the end times.

Jesus Was the Suffering Servant, Not Israel

Mark clearly equates Jesus with the suffering servant of Isaiah 52:13–53:12, as the following chart shows:[4]

MARK	SUFFERING SERVANT
10:45	Isaiah 52:13–53:12
14:24	Exodus 24:8/Isaiah 52:13–53:12
14:27	Zechariah 13:7/Isaiah 53:4–6
14:61	Isaiah 53:7
15:15	Isaiah 53:6

---

4. Mark also draws on the righteous sufferer tradition as reflected in Psalms 22, which is applied to Jesus on the cross: cf. Mark 15:24 with Psalm 22:18; Mark 15:29 with Psalm 22:7; Mark 15:34 with Psalm 22:1.

But there is a long-standing tradition in Judaism that equated the suffering servant with Israel. See, for example, the suffering servant songs of Isaiah (42:1–9; 49:1–6; 50:4–11; 52:13–53:12),[5] the Talmud (Berachot 5a), the Midrash Rabbah, Numbers 13:2) the Zohar (Chadash, p. 15a), the Targum on Isaiah 53. We conclude from this data that Jesus is presenting himself as the suffering servant, not Israel (although Jesus probably considered himself to be the new, true Israel who replaced Old Testament Israel). Moreover, in making such an identification, Jesus seems to have been the first to speak of a suffering Messiah.

Conclusion

This chapter on Mark has argued that Jesus presented himself to Israel as a subversive Messiah, at least in terms of what most Jews expected of the coming Messiah to be: (1) Jesus Messiah conquered Jews, not her oppressors; (2) Jesus reconstituted the twelve tribes of Israel from ordinary men, not the political leaders of the nation; (3) Jesus was not the law-abiding Messiah the leaders of Israel expected him to be; (4) Jesus was the suffering Son of Man, not a political Messiah; (5) Jesus Messiah called for the destruction of the temple, not the messianic rebuilding of it; (6) Jesus was the suffering servant, not Israel.

REFLECTION QUESTIONS

1. Who did Jesus Messiah conquer in contrast to what Judaism expected he would do?

2. Who constituted Jesus Messiah's leadership?

3. What was Jesus Messiah's relationship with the Old Testament law?

4. What is the number-one piece of evidence in Mark that Jesus was not a political Messiah?

5. What was the eschatological temple that Jesus Messiah came to build?

---

5. Not that there were no other identifications of Isaiah's servant songs: Moses, Jeremiah, an ideal figure, the Messiah, etc. But on the messianic interpretation of Isaiah 53, recall our earlier note that there is no pre-Christian text that unequivocally equates the Messiah with the suffering Messiah.

What Is the Main Message of Luke About Jesus?

If Mark is the first canonical gospel to portray Jesus as the suffering Messiah against commonly held expectations in Second Temple Judaism, the gospel of Luke emphasizes that the Old Testament from beginning to end predicts that the Messiah would first suffer and then enter into his glory (see esp. Luke 24:7, 25–26, 44–47). In other words, even though Judaism at the time of Jesus did not read of a suffering messiah in the Hebrew Bible, Luke (quoting Jesus) declares that such a concept is loud and clear in the Torah, the Prophets, and the Writings (the three-fold division of the Hebrew Bible).

But what exactly does Jesus have in mind when he speaks of the message of the suffering and glory of the Messiah that runs right through the Old Testament? This chapter attempts to answer that question by suggesting that Jesus draws on four types of suffering/glory constructs that occur in the Old Testament: (1) the Deuteronomic tradition in the Torah, (2) the suffering servant theme in the Prophets, and (3) the messianic king and (4) heavenly Son of Man motifs in the Writings. Having demonstrated that those four suffering/glory traditions occur in Luke, we will then argue that it is the book of Daniel that combines all four of the preceding traditions into one grand picture, which is the catalyst for Jesus' integrating the preceding traditions in his ministry. Finally, we will see that Daniel subsumes the Deuteronomic tradition, the suffering servant theme, and the messianic king motif under the category of the heavenly Son of Man. The reason for this is that the first three constructs present an earthly kingdom, while the Son of Man emphasizes the heavenly aspect of the kingdom of God. And this is why Jesus embraces the identification of the heavenly Son of Man. We now unpack the preceding steps relative to the message of Luke.

The Four Suffering/Glory Traditions in the Gospel of Luke

As mentioned in the Introduction, Jesus attracts to himself in Luke four suffering/glory traditions that emerge in the Old Testament.

The Deuteronomic Tradition in Luke

The Deuteronomic tradition or the story of Israel is hinted at in the first four books of Moses, but explicitly presented in the book of Deuteronomy. That tradition consists of about five components: (1) Israel is disobedient to the Lord. (2) God sent his prophets to call Israel to repentance. (3) But Israel rejected the prophets. (4) Consequently, God will judge Israel by sending her away into exile. (5) Yet, if Israel will repent, God will restore her to her land. While I believe the Deuteronomic tradition occurs throughout Luke's gospel, it is especially compressed in the central section of Luke's gospel: 9:51–19:44. David P. Moessner has caught the way the story of Israel (sin, sending of the prophets, rejection of the prophets, and exile) underlines Luke 9:51—19:44, as the following chart notes:[1]

"THIS GENERATION" "STIFF-NECKED" LIKE THEIR "FATHERS"	JESUS SENT AS A VOICE TO MEDIATE GOD'S WILL, IN-STRUCT, ADMONISH, AND WARN	"THIS GENERATION" REJECTS JESUS AS PROPHET AND KILLS HIM	THEREFORE GOD WILL RAIN DESTRUCTION ON THE WHOLE CROOKED NATION
	9:51, 52–56, 57–62	9:51, 52–56, 57–58	
	10:1–12, 13–15, 16, 17–20, 21–24, 25–28, 29–37, 38–42	10:3, 10–11, 13, 16, 25	(10:12, 14–15)
11 :29–32, 49–52	11:1–4, 5–8, 9–13, 14–23, 24–26, 27–28, 29–32, 33, 34–36, 37–54	11:14–23, 24–26, 29–32, 47–54	11:31–32, 50–51
12:54–56, 57–59	12:1, 2–9, 10, 11–12, 13–15, 16–21, 22–32, 33–34, 35–48, 49–53, 54–56, 57–59	12:49–50, 54–56	12:57–59

---

1. David P. Moessner, *Lord of the Banquet: The Literary and Theological Significance of the Lucan Travel Narrative* (Minneapolis: Fortress, 1989), 211. See also C. Marvin Pate, *Communities of the Last Days: The Dead Sea Scrolls, the New Testament and the Story of Israel* (Downers Grove, IL: InterVarsity Press, 2000).

"THIS GENERATION" "STIFF-NECKED" LIKE THEIR "FATHERS"	JESUS SENT AS A VOICE TO MEDIATE GOD'S WILL, IN-STRUCT, ADMONISH, AND WARN	"THIS GENERATION" REJECTS JESUS AS PROPHET AND KILLS HIM	THEREFORE GOD WILL RAIN DESTRUCTION ON THE WHOLE CROOKED NATION
13:1–9, 22–30, 34	13:1–9, 10–17, 18–19, 22–30, 31–33, 34–35	13:1–9, 14–17, 25–30, 31–33, 34	13:24–30, 35
	14:1–6, 7–14, 15–24, 25–33, 34–35	14:1, 24	14:24
	15:1–7, 8–10, 11–32	15:1–2	
16:27–31	16:1–9, 10–12, 13, 14–15, 16–17, 18, 19–31	16:14–15, 16, 27–31	(16:27–31)
17:25–30	17:1–4, 5–6, 7–10, 11–19, 20–21, 22–37	17:25–30	17:26–30
18:8	18:1–8, 9–14, 15–17, 18–23, 24–30, 31–34, 35–43	18:8, 31–34	
19:41–42, 44	19:1–10, 11–27, 28–40, 41–44	19:7, 14, 39–40	19:27, 41–44

But even though Moessner does not call attention to the fifth component of the story of Israel—the future restoration of Israel—that component also occurs in Luke: see 1:11–17 (the birth of John the Baptist signaled the restoration of Israel); 1:26–38 (the birth of Jesus will spell the restoration of Israel); 1:46–56 (Mary's praise to God is for the deliverance that Jesus will bring to Israel); 1:67–80 (Zechariah's praise to God is for John the Baptist, who will be the forerunner of Jesus the savior of Israel); 2:1–20 (Jesus' birth sets the restoration of Israel in motion) 2:25–38 (Simeon recognizes that Jesus is the long awaited Messiah who will restore Israel); 7:18–50 (the report to John the Baptist concerning the miracles Jesus performs should confirm for John that Jesus is the Messiah who is in the process of restoring Israel); 21:24–38 (Jesus predicts that God will restore Israel); 22:1–39 (Jesus institutes the new covenant long awaited by Jews and he promises that the twelve apostles will one day rule over a restored Israel). Thus, the sin, exile (components 1–4), restoration (component 5) of the story of Israel correlate to the suffering/glory pattern Jesus called attention to in Luke 24 as pertaining to the Torah: the suffering of the Messiah leading to glory theme is conveyed in the Torah by the Deuteronomic message now applied to Jesus.

The Suffering Servant Theme

Luke 1–9:50 emphasizes the fact that Jesus' ministry will fulfill the predictions of the Old Testament prophets concerning the restoration of Israel. But Jesus will do so as the suffering servant. Therein, we find again the pattern of suffering/glory (restoration). We now discuss these two points: Jesus fulfills the prophetic promise of the restoration of Israel in his role as the suffering servant. In other words, the role of the suffering servant in effecting the restoration of Israel that predominates Luke 1:1–9:50 correlates with the suffering/glory theme Jesus said occurs in the Prophets (both former and latter) section of the Hebrew Bible.

Here we make three points from Luke 1:1–9:50: by way of a self-explanatory chart we identify the Old Testament references from the prophets division of the Hebrew Bible that correspond with Jesus the restorer of Israel; that restoration occurs for Gentiles as well; the restoration is based on the fact that Jesus is the suffering servant, the one through whom the Old Testament prophets predicted the restoration will come. The first point, the chart, accentuates that Luke 1:1–9:50 is greatly informed by the Prophets division of the Hebrew Bible, with reference to Jesus being the restorer of Israel:

LUKE 1:1–9:50	PROPHETS SECTION OF THE HEBREW BIBLE
1:16–17a (Elijah, the forerunner of the Messiah)	Malachi 4:5–6
1:17b (preparing the way for the restoration)	Isaiah 40:3
1:31(messianic Davidic king)	2 Samuel 7:11–16
1:46–55, 67–79 (restoration of Israel)	Micah 7:20; Jeremiah 31:34; Isaiah 9:2; 59:9
2:11–14 (the good news of restoration through the Son of God)	Isaiah 7:14; 9:6; 52:7; 53:5; 40
2:25 (consolation/restoration of Israel)	Isaiah 40; 52:9
2:30 (salvation)	Isaiah 40:5
2:31 (preparing the way of the Lord)	Isaiah 40:3
2:32 (the rejected/stumbling stone)	Isaiah 8:14–15/28:16; 42:6
3:4–6 (preparing the way of the Lord)	Isaiah 40:3; Ezekiel 36:24–28
4:17–21 (the servant of the Lord)	Isaiah 61:1–2; cf. Isaiah 42:7; 49:8, 9; 58:6
4:31–9:50 (messianic miracles of restoration)	Isaiah 61:1–2; Jeremiah 30–33; cf. Dead Sea Scrolls (4Q 521)

Second, the restoration of Israel includes Gentiles as well. The Old Testament prophets also predicted that when Israel is restored to God and her land, then the nations of the world will come to believe in Israel's God and stream into Jerusalem to worship him (see Isa. 45:15; 60:15–17; Mic. 4:13; etc.).

Luke taps into this theme of Gentiles coming to faith in the true God through Jesus Christ in both of his volumes. In the third gospel, Jesus offers salvation to the Samaritans (Luke 10:29–37; cf. Acts 8:14–25) and to Gentiles (Luke 10:1–9). And Acts 1:8 famously targets Gentiles for salvation in the light of the beginnings of the restoration of Israel (cf. Acts 1:8 with Acts 10:1–28:31).

Third, the restoration of Israel prophesized in the Prophets section of the Hebrew Bible envisions that such a renewal will come because of the atoning sufferings of the Servant of the Lord. This is especially clear in Luke 4:17–21, where Jesus explicitly identifies himself as the suffering Servant of the Lord. His suffering is bringing about the longed for restoration of Israel. Such suffering predicted by the prophets find its fulfillment in the rejection of Jesus by his own home town, Nazareth, Luke 4:28–30, and will culminate in Jesus' death at the hands of his own people (for this topic, see our later chapter on who killed Jesus).

The Opposed Messianic King

Luke 19:51–24:53 portrays Jesus as Israel's messianic king. Indeed, Jesus' triumphal entry into Jerusalem signaled as much (Luke 19:28–38). It continues with Jesus' application of Psalm 110:1 to himself in Luke 20:41–44, and culminates with Jesus' ascension (Luke 24:44–52/Acts 1:1–11). We will save the last chapter of this work on the ascension to delve more deeply into the theme of the opposed messianic king in the Writings section of the Hebrew Bible, but here we note that in the last third of Luke's gospel Jesus applies that theme to himself. Thus, the messianic or royal psalms that proclaim Yahweh's chosen one to be king over Israel but who is opposed by the nations (Pss. 2; 16; 22; 69; 72; 110; 118) undergirds Luke's passion narrative.

LUKE	MESSIANIC/ROYAL PSALMS
23:34	Psalm 22:18
23:35	Psalm 22:17; 69:21
23:36	Psalm 22:7
24:44	Psalms 2; 16; 22; 69; 72; 110; 118

The point to be made from these verses is that Jesus the messianic king was opposed by his own people, the Jews. This is another rendition of the suffering/glory contrast that constitutes Luke's hermeneutic throughout his third gospel.

The Heavenly Son of Man

The fourth type of suffering/glory construct that informs Luke's statements in 24:7, 25–27, 44–49 is that of the heavenly Son of Man. Taking his cue from Mark, Luke also records Jesus' statements in which the latter identifies himself as the heavenly Son of Man who suffers and then is raised to glory (Mark 8:31/Luke 9:22; Mark 9:31/Luke 9:44; Mark 10:33–34/Luke 18:31–33). The important point to be gleaned from this is that these predictions of Jesus draw upon Daniel 7:13–14, 18, 21–22, 25–27. These verses correlate the heavenly Son of Man and the saints of God/Israel in the following way:

vv. 13–14: Heavenly Son of Man receives the kingdom from God	vv. 25–27: The saints of God receive the heavenly kingdom from God
Implied, the Son of Man correlates with the saints of God in their suffering just as he correlates with the saints in receiving the kingdom of God	vv. 18, 21–22: The saints suffer for the kingdom of God

This is to say that the heavenly Son of Man correlates with the saints of God/Israel both in terms of their suffering for and glory in the kingdom. So when Jesus draws on the heavenly Son of Man in Daniel 7, he applies to himself the preceding suffering/glory construct.

Daniel 7 and 9 and the Four Suffering/Glory Traditions

Here we demonstrate that the above four suffering/glory traditions occur in Daniel, particularly in Daniel 7 and 9.[2]

The Deuteronomic Tradition in Daniel 9

The Deuteronomic tradition dominates Daniel 9. Thus:

1. Israel repeatedly sinned against God (v. 5).

2. God sent his prophets to call Israel to repentance (v. 6).

3. Israel repeatedly rejected God's prophets (vv. 7–11).

4. God judged Israel by exiling her to Babylonia (vv. 12–14).

5. Israel now repents and hopes in the future restoration (vv. 15–27).

Numbers 1–4 correspond with suffering, while number 5 corresponds with glory.

---

2. As far as I can tell, only Daniel in the entire Old Testament combines all four of these suffering/glory traditions.

The Suffering Servant Tradition in Daniel 9

The careful reader of Daniel 9 will notice that in the promise of the restoration section of Daniel 9:24–27, two allusions to the Suffering Servant occur. First, the anointed one is "cut off" (v. 24) = Isaiah 53:10 and second, "atone" (v. 24) = Isaiah 53:8. Thus, the suffering of the Servant of the Lord is the basis of the coming restoration of Israel.[3]

The Opposed Messianic King in Daniel 9

The preceding two allusions to the Suffering Servant is applied to the "anointed one" (v. 25), Israel's Messiah.[4] Herein we have an allusion to the opposed messianic king.

The Heavenly Son of Man in Daniel 7

We saw above that the suffering/glory contrast imprints the heavenly Son of Man: who joins the saints of God in their suffering while they participate in the Son of Man's glorious kingdom. It seems that Daniel subsumes the first three types of the suffering/glory constructs—Deuteronomic tradition, suffering servant, opposed messianic king—under the heavenly Son of Man theme. This is so because Daniel's overall message is that any earthly kingdom (for example, Maccabean, or in Jesus' day, Zealot) will not result in lasting restoration because they are earthly in orientation. But the kingdom of the heavenly Son of Man is not earthly and, indeed, one day will crush the kingdoms of this world (Dan. 2:44–45). So we might say that Daniel both integrates the three suffering/glory traditions in his heavenly Son of Man theme as well as transcends them in that the latter presents a heavenly kingdom, whereas the former do not.

Jesus and the Heavenly Son of Man

It is common knowledge among gospel scholars that Jesus preferred the title, "Son of Man" over "Christ/Messiah" or, for that matter, any other biblical messianic title. Our discussion has provided an answer as to why Jesus preferred such a title: taking his cue from Daniel 7 and 9 which integrated the Deuteronomic tradition, suffering servant motif, and opposed messianic king into the heavenly Son of Man but transcending them in that the latter was heavenly in nature not earthly, Jesus understood himself to be Daniel's heavenly Son of Man. In making this connection, Jesus both integrated the three earthly suffering/glory traditions into himself but transcended them. This is

---

3. Debate over the 490 years has raged among interpreters; for a summary of that debate, see C. Marvin Pate and Calvin B. Haines, *Doomsday Delusions: What's Wrong With Predictions About the End of the World* (Downers Grove, IL: InterVarsity Press, 1995), 69–75.

4. The messianic person in mind here might be Onias III, High Priest in Israel during Antiochus Epiphanes' rule of terror over ancient Jews between 171 BC and 167 BC.

why Jesus especially avoided the term "Messiah/Christ," because it connoted the idea of a political messiah who would deliver Israel from Rome. We offer two related observations regarding this perspective.

First, no doubt Jesus had learned from his Jewish heritage of the failed attempts on the part of his kindred people to establish an earthly kingdom. Zerubbabel's temple had not met the expectations of Jews in the fifth century. The Maccabean revolt was successful, but temporary, lasting only about a hundred years. Even as recently as AD 6, Judas the Galilean's failed messianic coup brought painful memories to Jesus' forebears there in Galilee. So Jesus had learned from the past failures of his people to steer clear from any connotation of an earthly messianic kingdom.

Second, Luke-Acts carefully distances Jesus from any reputation of being an insurrectionist. Luke 20:22–25 records Jesus as encouraging his fellow Jews to render respect to Caesar. Luke 22:49–53 relates that Jesus rebuked Peter for raising the sword against the authorities as they came to arrest Jesus. Furthermore, Jesus responded with disbelief to the authorities at the thought that he was leading a rebellion. At Jesus' trial, Pilate, prefect of Judea, declared three times that Jesus was innocent of the charge of rebellion. And in Acts 18:12–17, Gallio, the proconsul of Achaia, refused to accept the accusation that Christians were insurrectionists.[5]

Conclusion

This chapter has examined the message of Luke and we have concluded that the occurrence of the suffering of the Messiah leading to his glory theme spelled out in Luke 24 is the interpretive key to the third gospel. Thus, Luke's gospel is devoted to showing that the Deuteronomic tradition of the Pentateuch impacts especially Luke 19:51–19:44; that the Hebrew Prophets' predictions of the restoration of Israel through the suffering servant imprints Luke 1:1–9:50; while the opposed messianic king and the heavenly Son of Man of the Writings (the Psalms and Daniel respectively) govern Luke 9:51–23:56. Moreover, we argued that it was Daniel that integrated the preceding four suffering/glory traditions and yet viewed the heavenly Son of Man as transcending the three earthly kingdom perceptions. It is this that governed the messianic consciousness of Jesus.

---

5. From S. G. F. Brandon (*Jesus and the Zealots* [Manchester: Manchester University, 1951]) to John Dominic Crossan (*The Historical Jesus: The Life of a Mediterranean Jewish Peasant* [San Francisco: HarperSan Francisco, 1991]) to Reza Asian (*Zealot: The Life and Times of Jesus of Nazareth* [New York: Random House, 2013]) there have been notable attempts to cast Jesus as a political revolutionary against the Roman government. Yet, this always popular theory was defeated by Ernst Bammel and C. F. D. Moule in edited, *Jesus and the Politics of His Day* (Cambridge: Cambridge University Press, 1984).

REFLECTION QUESTIONS

1. What passages in Luke 24 state the author's thesis of his gospel?

2. How does that thesis explain the Deuteronomic tradition in Luke?

3. How does that thesis explain the suffering servant theme in Luke?

4. How does that thesis explain the messianic king notion in Luke?

5. How does that thesis explain the heavenly Son of Man passages in Luke?

What Is the Main Message of John About Jesus?

John 20:30–31 states the aim of the fourth gospel: to show that Jesus is the Christ, the Son of God, who offers eternal life to all who believe in him. This verse nicely summarizes the two-fold focus of John: Jesus is the Christ and those who believe in him will be blessed with eternal life. Therefore, we will use this two-fold statement to summarize the gospel of John.

Jesus Is the Christ

Here we survey five categories in John that exalt Christ: (1) Jesus Christ as the Wisdom of God; (2) Jesus' messianic titles; (3) Jesus' messianic miracles; (4) Jesus as the fulfillment of major Old Testament feasts; and (5) other indications that Jesus is the Messiah.

Jesus as the Wisdom of God

The Wisdom of God was revered in Second Temple Jewish literature as an intimate expression of God, yet without in any way compromising monotheism. The fourth gospel capitalizes on such a cherished notion by equating Jesus with the Wisdom of God. This is seen in three ways in John: in his prologue (1:1–18); in the "I am" statements; and in the descending/ascending redeemer motif applied to Jesus. First, John's prologue presents Jesus as the Wisdom of God. Note the comparisons between the two:

JOHN	WISDOM
The Word was in the beginning (John 1:1)	Wisdom was in the beginning (Prov. 8:22–23; Sirach 1:4; Wisdom of Solomon 9:9)
The Word was with God (John 1:1)	Wisdom was with God (Prov. 8:30; Sirach 1:1; Wisdom of Solomon 9:4)

JOHN	WISDOM
The Word was cocreator (John 1:1–3)	Wisdom was cocreator (Prov. 3:19; 8:25; 7:21; 9:1–2)
The Word provides light (John 1:4, 9)	Wisdom provides light (Prov. 8:22; Wisdom of Solomon 7:26; 8:13; Sirach 4:12; Baruch 4:1)
The Word as light is in contrast to darkness (John 1:5)	Wisdom as light is in contrast to darkness (Wisdom of Solomon 7:29–30)
The Word was in the world (John 1:10)	Wisdom was in the world (Wisdom of Solomon 8:1; Sirach 24:6)
The Word was rejected by its own (John 1:11)	Wisdom was rejected by its own (Sirach 15:7; Baruch 3:12; cf. 1 Enoch 42:1–2)
The Word was received by the faithful (John 1:12)	Wisdom was received by the faithful (Wisdom of Solomon 7:27; Baruch 3:37)
The Word became flesh (John 1:14)	Wisdom indwelled Israel (Sirach 24:8, 23; Baruch 3:37–42)

Second, the wisdom motif also informs the Johannine "I am" sayings, which we put here in chart form:[1]

JOHN	WISDOM
Christ is the bread of life (John 6:35)	Wisdom is the bread, the substance of life (Prov. 9:5; Sirach 15:3; Wisdom of Solomon 14:11)
Christ is the light of the world (John 8:12)	Wisdom is light (Wisdom of Solomon 7:26–30; 18:3–4)
Christ is the door of the sheep and the good shepherd (John 10:7, 11, 14)	Wisdom is the door and the good shepherd (Prov. 8:34–35; Wisdom 7257:25–27; 8:2–16; 16; Sirach 24:19–22)
Christ is life (John 11:25)	Wisdom brings life (Prov. 3:16; 8:35; 9:11; Wisdom of Solomon 8:13)
Christ is the way to truth (John 14:6)	Wisdom is the way (Prov. 3:17; 8:32–34; Sirach 6:26)

---

1. For both of the above charts and discussion, see C. Marvin Pate, *Communities of the Last Days: The Story of Israel, the Dead Sea Scrolls, and the New Testament* (Downers Grove, IL: InterVarsity Press, 2000), 227–29. The seventh "I am" statement in John—I am the vine—does not seem to correlate with Wisdom.

The point to be gleaned from these parallels is that the attributes that Jews attributed to Wisdom, the Torah of God, in reality most fully pertain to Jesus: light, the truth, provision, and so on. For John, such can be found only in Christ. The same is true of the Wisdom parallels in John 1:1–18. To state it another way, those blessings Jews thought came from Wisdom/Torah in reality only come through Christ.

Third, the descent and ascent of the revealer in John focusing on Jesus (rather than the Torah) as the revealer who descends from the Father to impart truth and then ascends back to his divine origin (John 1:47–51; 3:12–13; 6:61–62) is steeped in the wisdom tradition. Thus, like Wisdom, Jesus descends or is sent from God (thus implying his preexistence, see Sirach 24:3–17; Wisdom 9:10, 17). But like wisdom, he is removed from the unbelieving and ascends to the Father (1 Enoch 42).[2]

The preceding ideas (the prologue, the occurrences of the "I am" sayings, and the references to Jesus as the descending-ascending revealer) in John are imbued with wisdom themes, replacing the Torah with Christ and thereby highly exalting Jesus.

Jesus' Messianic Titles

John 1:19–51 attributes to Jesus a plethora of supernatural titles, including Messiah, Son of God, king of Israel, and heavenly Son of Man. We briefly define each title below

1. Rabbi (1:35–39). The two disciples of John the Baptist who followed Jesus addressed him as "Rabbi" (v. 38). "Rabbi" literally means "my great one/master," that is, "teacher." By the end of the first century, the term referred to those who were ordained teachers in Rabbinic traditions. In Jesus' day, however, the term may have been more generally used of Jewish teachers whose students followed and learned from them. It is so used of Jesus in the fourth gospel (cf. 1:38, 49; 3:2; 4:31; 6:24; 9:2; 11:8).

2. Messiah (1:40–42). We treated this title earlier. Here we observe that John is the only gospel to address Jesus as "Messiah" (Hebrew for "anointed"; cf. 4:25). All the other gospels call Jesus "Christ" (Greek for "anointed"). In the Old Testament "anointed one" variously refers to the king of Israel (1 Sam. 16:6; 2 Sam. 1:14), the high priest (Lev. 4:3), and the prophets (Ps. 105:15). The term took on messianic significance in the Psalms and in the Prophets and flourished in Second Temple Judaism (ca. 400 BC to the time of Jesus), as we documented in another chapter.

3. Moses and the Prophets (1:45). This reference probably reinforces the title "Messiah/Christ" applied to Jesus earlier. That is, Moses predicted the coming Messiah—Jesus—(Deut. 18:15, 18), as did the prophets (e.g., Isa. 9:1–7; 11:1–5, 10–12; 52:13–53:12; cf. John 5:39, 46; 6:45); Luke 24:26–27, 44–46)

---

2. See ibid., 228–29.

make a similar connection, though adding that Moses, the prophets, and "the Psalms (the writings)" anticipated the *suffering* Messiah. Nathanael found it hard to believe that Jesus was the Messiah because he thought Jesus was from Nazareth, an insignificant town compared to Bethlehem, the true birth place of the Messiah (John 1:46). Nathanael was unaware that Jesus was actually born in Bethlehem.

4. Son of God (1:49). "Son of God," Nathanael's term for Jesus, again takes us to the messianic significance of Jesus. "Son of God" in the Old Testament was applied to angels (Gen. 6:1–4; Job 1:6; 38:97), Davidic kings (2 Sam. 7:14; Pss. 2:7; 89:27), and Israel itself (Deut. 14:1; Hos. 11:1, etc.). "Son of God" was also a name for the Davidic Messiah in Jewish circles (Dead Sea Scrolls [1QSamuel 2:11–12; 4QFlorilegium 1:6–7]; *4 Ezra* 7:28–29; 13:52; *1 Enoch* 105:2). Moreover, "Son of God" was applied in pagan sources to the Pharaoh, Roman emperors, and wandering miracle workers.

5. King of Israel (1:49). Nathanael also called Jesus "the King of Israel" (cf. 12:13). Rooted in Psalm 2:6–7—which equates the Davidic King with the Son of God—"the King of Israel" no doubt refers to Jesus as the Davidic, Messianic King come to deliver Israel militarily. Jesus, however, had other ideas (John 6:15; 12:16; 18:36).

6. Son of Man (1:50–51). "Son of Man" was Jesus' favorite self-designation in the Gospels. We make here three comments about the title: its background; its classification in the Gospels; and the connection of the title to its context in John 1:50–51.

The Background of the Son of Man. "Son of Man" is a frequent phrase in Ezekiel, but there it is a synonym for mortal man. However, Daniel 7:13 attributes divinity to the heavenly Son of Man, which is probably a reference to Israel as the inheritor of the kingdom of God. In *1 Enoch*, the heavenly Son of Man is a messianic individual who delivers Israel at the end of history (46:2–4; 48:2; 62:5–17, 13–14; 69:27–29). This figure is presently hidden in heaven, but will be revealed at the end of days. Jesus' use of the title seems to presume the background of Daniel 7 and *1 Enoch*. If so, "Son of Man" was a title by which Jesus conveyed his divinity but without implying the political connotation of the term "Messiah/Christ."

The Classification of Son of Man. In the Synoptic Gospels, Jesus' application of "Son of Man" to himself falls into three categories: (a) those references to the earthly activity of the Son of Man (eating, dwelling, saving the lost, etc.); (b) those that refer to the suffering of the Son of Man; (c) those that refer to the future glory at the parousia of the Son of Man. In John's gospel, the first Son of Man classification does not occur.

Son of Man in the Context of John 1:50–51. The background of John 1:47–51 seems to be Genesis 27–28. There Jacob, called "Israel," deceived his father Isaac and became known as the "deceiver," the one filled with guile (Gen. 27:35). Because of Esau's hatred for Jacob, the latter fled for his safety from Israel to Haran. On the way he stopped at Bethel and there had a dream about angels ascending and descending to heaven. Jacob awoke and realized the place was holy ground (Gen. 28). This explains John 1:47–51. Nathanael, unlike Jacob, was an Israelite in whom there was no guile. And Nathanael, like Jacob, will witness angels ascending and descending to heaven, but not upon a ladder, but upon Jesus who is the locus of God's presence and glory. It may be that Jesus had a vision of Nathanael sitting under the fig tree reading the Jacob account. Thus, when Jesus greeted Nathanael as an Israelite without deceit, Nathanael was awestruck with Jesus' supernatural knowledge, and instantly believed in him as the Messiah.

Jesus' Messianic Miracles

We saw earlier that Isaiah envisioned that the coming Messiah would perform amazing miracles (see Isa. 26:19; 35:5–6; 61:1–3). Although Jesus performed more than the seven miracles recorded in the fourth gospel (see John 20:30–31), the seven sign/miracles emphasize that Jesus is the Messiah. Note the following chart:

JESUS' MIRACLES	MESSIANIC SIGNIFICANCE
Changing water into wine (2:1–11)	The abundance of the messianic kingdom is here
The temple cleansing (2:13–22)	Jesus is the eschatological temple that Israel expected
The healing of the nobleman's son (4:46–54)	Miracles Messiah would perform
The healing of the lame man (5:1–15)	Miracles Messiah would perform
The feeding of the multitude (6:1–15)	Messiah would once again provide miraculous food/manna that God supplied in the wilderness
The healing of the blind man (9:1–41)	Miracles Messiah would perform
The raising of Lazarus, which foreshadows Jesus' coming resurrection (11:1–44)	Only the Messiah could raise the dead

Jesus as the Fulfillment of Major Old Testament Feasts

Moreover, Jesus replaced some of Israel's key feasts (Tabernacles [John 7–8], Dedication [John 10], Passover [John 13]) as the true way to worship God. Concerning the first of these, Jews at the Feast of Tabernacles commemorated Israel's wondering in the wilderness by making shelters out of branches and then living in them for a few days. On the seventh day of the feast, the priest would pour out water in front of the temple. Jesus' calling out to those who were thirsty to drink of him indicated that he was fulfilling and replacing the Feast of Tabernacles (John 7:37–39). Regarding the Feast of

Dedication, this ceremony was conducted in memory of the Maccabean defeat of Antiochus Epiphanes in 164 BC and the rededication of the temple. An eight day feast was held to commemorate the event called Hanukkah, or the Feast of Lights. In John 8–9, Jesus draws upon that feast identifying himself as the light of the world. Finally, Passover of course annually remembered God's deliverance of Israel from bondage to Egypt. In John 13, and on the cross, John 19, Jesus is presented as the Passover lamb that was slain for the sins of the world (cf. John 1:29).

Other Indications That Jesus Is the Messiah

At least three other points indicate that Jesus is the Messiah according to the gospel of John. Jesus' triumphal entry into Jerusalem cast him as the Messianic king of Israel (though he qualified that expectation by presenting himself as the suffering Messiah, John 12). Jesus promised the coming of the Holy Spirit, the sign that the kingdom of God had arrived (John 14–19). Jesus' resurrection vindicated him as the Messiah (John 20).

Jesus Offers Eschatological Blessings to Those Who Believed in Him

We delve into the second half of John's umbrella statement in John 20:31, further dividing it into its two constituent parts: the eschatological blessings that Jesus brought and the levels of belief in John.

The Eschatological Blessings That Jesus Brought

Although the gospel of John contains both the present ("already") aspect and the future ("not yet") aspect, the focus or stress in John is clearly on the present ("already"), especially the eschatological blessings that belong now to believers. This emphasis on the "already" can be seen in John regarding the following areas: (1) Eternal life, or entrance into the kingdom of God, can be a present possession (John 6:47; 3:5–6, 36; 6:47, 51, 58; 8:51; 10:28; 11:24–26). (2) The eschatological promise of sonship is granted to the believer in Jesus now (John 1:12–13; 3:3–8; 4:14). (3) The general resurrection has already begun (John 5:25). (4) The Spirit, the gift of the end-times, currently indwells believers (John 7:37–39; 14:15–31; 15:26–27; 16:5–16; 20:22–23). (5) Last day judgment is determined by one's present response to Jesus (John 3:19; 5:22–24, 27, 30–38; 9:38; 12:31–33). (6) The spirit of anti-christ has already entered the world scene to oppose Christ (John 6:70; 13:2, 27; 14:13). (7) Jesus' death on the cross seems to absorb some elements of the messianic woes or aspects of tribulation. In other words, Jesus' passion was where the end-time holy war was raged, and his death and resurrection began the end of the forces of evil (John 15:18–16:11).

But this is not to deny that the gospel of John also includes some future ("not yet") aspects of eschatology. For example, within the gospel of John the future resurrection is still expected (John 5:26–30). Likewise the future second coming of Christ is alluded to (John 14:1–4; 21:22). Yet, the focus in the fourth gospel lies on the already aspect because Jesus is the Christ, the son of the living God who gives eternal life now to those who believe in him. But what does John mean by believe?

The Levels of Belief in John

We begin to answer this question by noting that the fourth gospel exclusively prefers the verb form of belief (*pisteuein*, "believe") to the noun form (*pistis*, "belief"), using the former ninety-eight times and the latter none. This is so because true faith for John is active and dynamic not static and fixed. As such, it is related to John's term "abiding" (occurring in the fourth gospel some forty times). Now true faith in John is often expressed by the grammatical construction *pisteuein eis* ("believe into"), which occurs thirty-six times. Only twice does that expression not portray genuine faith in Jesus (2:23–24; 12:42–43). Moreover, and here we reach the heart of the matter, faith in John is directly related to the miracles/signs that Jesus performed. And there are four such levels of faith in that regard, the first two not genuine, with the last two levels being genuine faith in Jesus. Here we put in chart form the data as identified by Raymond Brown, which is but a sampling of the verses:

Belief and Signs in John: Four Levels[3]

NEGATIVE: LEVEL 1	NEGATIVE: LEVEL 2	POSITIVE: LEVEL 3	POSITIVE: LEVEL 4
Willful unbelief in the signs of Jesus	Superficial belief in Jesus as a wonder worker	Genuine belief in Jesus because of signs	Belief in Jesus without seeing Jesus' signs (which categorizes those who did not see the historical Jesus, but believed in him anyway)
3:19–20; 11:41, 47; 15:22; etc.	2:23–25; 3:2–3; 4:45–48; 7:37	34 usages of *pisteuein eis* (including 4:43; 6:69; 9:38; 11:40) and other passages	20:29

To state the obvious, then, only those in Levels 3 and 4 are the ones who truly believe that Jesus is the Christ and therefore receive eternal life in his name.

---

3. See also Raymond Brown, *The Gospel of John I–XII*, AB 29 (Garden City, NY: Doubleday, 1966), 512–13, 530–31.

Conclusion

This chapter has delved into the message of John, which is nicely encapsulated in John 20:31: The fourth gospel was written to show that Jesus is the Messiah and that those who genuinely believe in him have the blessings of the end-time now. The first part of this thesis statement John demonstrates in a number of ways: Jesus is the Wisdom of God; Jesus bore messianic titles; he performed messianic miracles; he replaced in himself major Old Testament feasts; and other points are pressed into the service of demonstrating Jesus to be the Messiah. The second part of John 20:31 centers on the end-times blessings that presently belong to those who truly believe in Jesus: starting with eternal life, along with divine sonship, participation in the resurrection, possession of the Holy Spirit, acceptance by God now in anticipation of the final day of judgment, resistance to the spirit of antichrist, and endurance of the messianic woes. But the reception of these end-time blessings presuppose genuine belief in Jesus the Son of God.

REFLECTION QUESTIONS

1. How is Jesus the Wisdom of God according to the gospel of John?

2. What are the messianic titles John uses of Jesus?

3. How do the sign miracles in John by Jesus fulfill Old Testament claims regarding the miracles of the coming Messiah?

4. What are some of the end-time blessings predicted in the Old Testament that are already fulfilled in Jesus according to John?

5. What are the levels of belief in Jesus according to the gospel of John?

What Did the Historical Jesus Say About His Return (in the Olivet Discourse)?

Mark 13, Matthew 24, and Luke 21 contain Jesus' predictions about the future, as he taught his disciples on the Mount of Olives on the eastern side of Jerusalem. Three main interpretations of this sermon are taken among evangelicals: (1) the preterist view, (2) the futurist view, and (3) the already/ not yet view. After we summarize those views in general, we will more specifically compare the distinctive interpretations of the Synoptics. Then we will call attention to the fourth gospel's usage of the Olivet Discourse.

Three Views of the Olivet Discourse

The Preterist View

The preterist (from the Latin "gone by" or "past") view of the Olivet Discourse interprets Jesus' prophecies as being completely fulfilled at the fall of Jerusalem to the Romans in AD 70. Thus, the signs of the times forecasted by Jesus—tribulation, messianic pretenders, wars, persecution, apostasy— accompanied the failed Jewish revolt against the Romans (AD 66–73). That war brought on severe tribulation and persecution for the Jews as the Roman legions systematically conquered Palestine, culminating in the destruction of Jerusalem. Josephus documents these happenings, blaming them on the Zealots' claim that, if Jews rebelled against the Roman occupation of their land, then God would send his Messiah to deliver Israel. Indeed, numerous messianic pretenders appeared in Israel from AD 6 to AD 66 proclaiming just such a message. All of this resulted, not in the deliverance of the Jews, but their defeat and, in many cases, their subsequent loss of faith (Josephus, *Jewish Wars* 1.10.6; *Antiquities of the Jews* 10.1.3).

The preterist view, besides rooting the fulfillment of these prophecies in Josephus' first hand description of the siege of Jerusalem, appeals to two other key items in the Olivet Discourse. First, Jesus' promise in the discourse, "this generation will not pass away until all these things are fulfilled" (Mark 13:30; Matt. 24:34; Luke 21:32), is thought by this approach to fit the time period from Jesus (AD 30) to Jerusalem's demise (AD 70). Since "these things" are the signs of the times that attended the fall of Jerusalem, then the statement about this generation not passing away is to be equated with the first generation of Christians.

Second, the preterist view interprets the parousia not as Christ's second coming at the end of history, but as Christ's coming to Jerusalem in AD 70 in the form of judgment. Thus, the "second coming" of Christ and the "great tribulation" (the signs of the times in the Olivet Discourse) have already occurred.

The Futurist View

The second major view of the Olivet Discourse is the futurist school of thought, a popular view in American Christianity today. As its name suggests, this approach equates the signs of the times in Jesus' sermon with the future Great Tribulation. Accordingly, the Olivet Discourse predicts the unfolding of the end of time in three stages. Using Matthew 24, those key timeframes are as follows:

1. **Matthew 24:4–14: The First Half of the Tribulation Period.** These verses represent the beginning of God's judgment of the earth, that is, the "birth pangs." The judgments of earthquakes, famines, and wars are not referring to events of the present age; rather, they parallel the future seal judgments of Revelation 6. Also, during this time there will be a great rise in false prophets, as well as wickedness in general. But this will be countered by a worldwide preaching of the gospel of the kingdom.

2. **Matthew 24:15–28: The Second Half of the Tribulation Period (the Great Tribulation).** This period begins with the great sign of the "abomination of desolation." This terrible desecration of the rebuilt Jerusalem temple by the Antichrist and the False Prophet will be the unmistakable sign for the Jewish people to flee the land of Israel. It is at this time that terrible persecution will break forth on Jews. Also, the great outpouring of powerful and deceptive miracles will take place during this time. The Lord warned that there would be an unbelievable and massive destruction of mankind. In fact, he declared that if this period of time had not been cut short and limited to three and a half years, no flesh would survive (cf. Rev. 8–11, trumpet judgments; Rev. 15–18, bowl judgments).

It should be observed that the futurist view falls into two camps: dispensational and historic premillennialism. The former separates the return of Christ into a secret rapture of the church to heaven before the tribulation period and the second coming of Christ in glory to establish his one thousand year reign on earth. The latter equates the rapture with the second coming of Christ and has the church going through the tribulation period. The dispensational view has God dealing primarily with Israel during the tribulation period, whereas the historic premillennial position sees the church as being dealt with by God during that time.

3. **Matthew 24:29–31: The Second Coming of Christ.** This will be an event witnessed by all mankind, believers and unbelievers alike. Prior to the return of Christ, a sign will appear in the heavens indicating that Jesus Christ is now about to return. This warning will cause the unbelievers of the earth to mourn because they realize that they face immediate judgment. At this time, the nation of Israel will be re-gathered from all over the world. The judgment that determines entrance into the kingdom will occur at this time (cf. Rev. 19–20).

The Already-Not Yet View

The third major view of the prophecies of the Olivet Discourse is the already-not yet perspective. This approach understands the first half as having been fulfilled at the fall of Jerusalem in AD 70 (the already aspect) with the second half of the discourse awaiting final completion at the second coming of Christ at the end of history (the not yet aspect). According to this view Matthew 24:4–31 would be understood as follows:

THE ALREADY: THE FALL OF JERUSALEM	THE NOT YET: THE PAROUSIA
Partial fulfillment (Matt. 24:4–20; cf. Mark 13:5–23; Luke 21:8–24; Rev. 6)	Final fulfillment (Matt. 24:21–31; cf. Mark 13:24–27; Luke 21:25–36; Rev. 8–11, 15–18)
Tribulation (Matt. 24:8)	Great Tribulation (Matt. 24:21, 29)
Messianic pretenders (Matt. 24:4–5)	Messianic pretenders (Matt. 24:23–26)
Wars (Matt. 24:6–7)	Wars (Matt. 24:22)
Persecution (Matt. 24:9–10)	Persecution (Matt. 24:22)
Apostasy (Matt. 24:11–13)	Apostasy (Matt. 24:24)
Fall of Jerusalem (Matt. 24:15–20)	Parousia (Matt. 24:30–31)

According to this view, the fall of Jerusalem in AD 70 serves as the backdrop for the future return of Christ. Thus, the signs of the times began in Jesus' generation and will continue until the parousia.

The Distinctive Points of the Synoptics Regarding the Olivet Discourse

The signs of the times discussed in the Olivet Discourse as spelled out by each of the Synoptic Gospels follows in chart form:

MARK 13:1–37	MATTHEW 24:1–25:46	LUKE 21:5–36
1. Jesus has left the temple	1. Jesus has left the temple	1. No indication of Jesus leaving the temple
2. Reference to Jerusalem's destruction	2. Reference to Jerusalem's destruction	2. Reference to Jerusalem's destruction
3. Mentions Mount of Olives	3. Mentions Mount of Olives	3. No location as to where the discussion is taking place
4. Disciples ask when the destruction of Jerusalem will take place	4. Disciples ask when the destruction of Jerusalem will take place and when will be his return	4. Disciples ask when Jerusalem will fall
5. Says many will come saying, "I am He"	5. Mentions that many will come claiming to be Christ	5. Says many will come saying, "I am He"
6. Mentions they will go before rulers	6. Mentions they will be persecuted	6. Mentions that they will go before rulers
7. Mentions wars, earthquakes, famines, and pestilence	7. Mentions wars, earthquakes, famines, and pestilence	7. Mentions wars, earthquakes, famines, and pestilence
8. Instructs them to hold on to the faith	8. Says that many will turn away	8. Instructs them to hold on to the faith
9. No mention of false prophets	9. Mentions false prophets	9. No mention of false prophets
10. Alludes to Daniel with "abomination of desolation"	10. Explicitly mentions Daniel	10. No mention of Daniel
11. Mentions pregnant women	11. Mentions pregnant women	11. No mention of pregnant women
12. No reference to punishment being fulfilled	12. No reference to punishment being fulfilled	12. Reference to punishment being fulfilled
13. Says the Lord cuts the days short	13. No mention of days cutting short	13. No mention of days cutting short
14. Further warning of false Christs	14. Further warning of false Christs	14. No further warning of false Christs

MARK 13:1–37	MATTHEW 24:1–25:46	LUKE 21:5–36
15. The sun will be darkened	15. Uses the same prophets as Mark when discussing the sun	15. No use of prophets Isaiah, Ezekiel, and Joel
16. Reference to Daniel 7:13	16. Reference to Daniel 7:13	16. Reference to Daniel 7:13
17. Mentions the fig tree	17. Mentions the fig tree	17. Mentions the fig tree
18. Mentions "this generation"	18. Mentions "this generation"	18. Mentions "this generation"
19. No mention of Noah	19. Mentions the days of Noah	19. No mention of Noah
20. Ends with a command to watch	20. Ends with three parables	20. Ends with a command to watch

The key to interpreting each of the Synoptic Gospels in their own right is to catch the nuance of the disciples' question(s) to Jesus upon hearing his prediction of the coming fall of Jerusalem and the temple. Mark 13:4 presents the disciples as asking one question which, in effect, is: when will the fall of Jerusalem and its temple/the parousia happen? In Mark, which was written before AD 70 and the fall of Jerusalem to the Romans, the question presupposes that the fall of Jerusalem and the temple and the second coming of Jesus will occur simultaneously. This approximates the preterist view above in that the disciples expected their generation to witness both the fall of Jerusalem/parousia. But in Matthew 24:3, the disciples ask in effect a two-fold question: when will the fall of Jerusalem happen and when will the parousia occur? That is, the disciples seem to separate in time the fall of Jerusalem and the second coming of Christ. This creates the already/not yet construct noted above with the fall of Jerusalem in the first generation of Christians serving as the backdrop to the future parousia of Jesus. In Luke 21:7, any thought of the second coming of Jesus is omitted from the disciples' question, who in effect ask one question: when will the fall of Jerusalem and the temple happen? No mention is made of the parousia.

In terms of the parousia, we might associate the futurist view with Luke's presentation of the Olivet Discourse. Indeed, Luke is careful to highlight the present aspect of the fall of Jerusalem because it signals that Israel began to be trampled under by the Gentiles; when that period is up, then Jesus will return, presumably to restore Israel, Jerusalem, and the temple (cf. Luke 21:24 with Paul in Rom. 11:25–27).[1]

---

1. For a defense of this view see J. Bradley Chance, *Jerusalem, the Temple, and the New Age in Luke-Acts* (Mercer, GA: Mercer University Press, 1988), 115–38.

The Fourth Gospel and the Olivet Discourse

Though not often noticed, Raymond Brown insightfully observed the parallels between John 15:18–16:4a and the Olivet Discourse:[2]

PARALLELS BETWEEN JOHN 15:18–16:4A AND THE SYNOPTIC ESCHATOLOGICAL DISCOURSE		
JOHN 15:18–16:4A	**MATTHEW 10:17–25; 24:9–10**	**MARK 13:9–13; LUKE 21:12–17**
15:18: "The world hates you . . . has hated me before you"	10:22: "You will be hated by all because of my name" (also 24:9)	Mark 13:13; Luke 21:17: same as Matthew
15:20: "No servant is more important than his master"	10:24: "No servant is above his master"	
15:20: "They will persecute you"	10:23: "When they persecute you" (cf. also 23:34)	Luke 21:12: "They will persecute you"
15:21: "They will do all these things to you because of my name"	See first parallel above	See first parallel above to the disciples being persecuted
15:26: "The Paraclete . . . will bear witness on my behalf"	10:20: "The Spirit of your Father speaking through you"	Mark 13:11: "The Holy Spirit (speaking)" (cf. Luke 12:12)
15:27: "You too should bear witness"	10:18: "You will be dragged before governors and kings . . . to bear witness"	Mark 13:9; Luke 21:12–13: almost the same as Matthew
16:1: "To prevent your faith from being shaken"	24:10: "The faith of many will be shaken"	
16:2: "They are going to put you out of the synagogue"	10:17: "They will flog you in their synagogues"	Mark 13:9: "You will be beaten in synagogues"; Luke 21:12: "Delivering you up to the synagogues" (cf. also Luke 6:22)
16:2: "The man who puts you to death"	24:9: "They will put you to death"	Mark 13:12: "Children will rise against parents and will put them to death" (=Matt 10:21); Luke 21:16: "Some of you they will put to death"

---

2. Raymond Brown, *The Gospel According to John XIII–XXI*, AB 29 (Garden City, NY: Doubleday, 1966), 694.

It seems clear from this chart that the end-time tribulation described in the Olivet Discourse is applied in the gospel of John to the trials of Jesus' twelve disciples and all would-be followers. So, like Jesus, his followers also experience the messianic woes. The difference between Jesus and the disciples then and now, however, is that the former overcame the tribulation at his resurrection, whereas the latter will have to continue to battle Satan and the signs of the times until the second coming of Christ at the end of history. It would seem that this essentially matches the messages of the Synoptic Gospels as well.

Conclusion

The Olivet Discourse is presented in the Synoptics and possibly alluded to in John. How to interpret that original sermon by Jesus on the Mount of Olives forecasting the future is difficult to ascertain. Probably Mark's equation of the fall of Jerusalem and the temple and the parousia stemmed from the fact that the second gospel was written before AD 70. After that it became clear to Matthew and Luke that the fall of Jerusalem did not signal the last generation and the second coming of Christ. That generation would not occur until the complete fulfillment of the signs of the times that Jesus predicted (Mark 13:30; Matt. 24:34; Luke 21:32). The fourth gospel, while possibly drawing on the Olivet Discourse, nevertheless does not try to relate the fall of Jerusalem and its temple to the parousia. The message to be taken from this discussion is that, since our generation (like the first generation) does not know the date of the return of Christ and since the signs of the times have been in motion since the first generation of Christians, it should motivate us to be ready at a moment's notice for the glorious return of our Savior.[3]

REFLECTION QUESTIONS

1. What is the preterist view of the Olivet Discourse in terms of the return of Christ?

2. What is the dispensational premillenial view of the Olivet Discourse?

3. What is the historic premillenial view of the Olivet Discourse?

4. What is the inaugurated (already/not yet) view of the Olivet Discourse?

5. Where in the gospel of John does material with the Olivet Discourse as found in the Synoptic Gospels overlap?

---

3. For a very informative treatment of biblical prophecy in general, the reader is referred to Eckhard Schnabel's *40 Questions about the End Times* (Grand Rapids: Kregel, 2011).

PART 4

Questions About Jesus' Crucifixion and Resurrection

Questions Related
to the Crucifixion of Jesus

What Is the Significance of the Triumphal Entry?

Introduction to the Triumphal Entry

The triumphal entry of Jesus into Jerusalem both concluded his journey to the city of his destiny as well as initiated the passion narrative proper. In effect, the triumphal entry in all the gospel accounts began Jesus' Passion Week. Therefore, it seems appropriate at this junction to provide a chronological frame of reference for charting the events of the week (following Harold Hoehner's synopsis). Having done that, we will proceed to analyze the triumphal entry pericope itself, beginning with an investigation of its literary genre. Hoehner's suggested synopsis of Jesus' Passion Week runs as follows (though we rather think the triumphal entry occurred on Sunday not Monday as Hoehner suggests): A few days before the final Passover, Jesus drew near to Jerusalem (John 11:55), arriving at Bethany six days before the Passover (John 12:1), namely the Saturday before the Passion Week. That evening, Jesus was anointed at Simon the Leper's house (Matt. 26:6–13; Mark 14:3–9, John 12:1–8). On the next day (Sunday), there was a great crowd that came to Bethany to see Jesus (John 12:9–11).

Monday
    The next day (John 12:12), Monday was Jesus' triumphal entry into Jerusalem (Matt. 21:1–9; Mark 11:1–10; Luke 19:28–40; John 12:12–19), his visit to the temple (Matt. 21:10–11; Mark 11:11), and then his return to Bethany. The day of the triumphal entry would be Nisan [April] 10 when the lamb was selected for Passover. Hence, the triumphal entry was the day when Christ presented himself as Israel's paschal lamb.

Tuesday

On Tuesday on the way from Bethany to Jerusalem, Jesus cursed the fig tree (Matt. 21:18–19; Mark 11:12–14), and then he went to Jerusalem to cleanse the temple (Matt. 21:12–13; Mark 11:15–17; Luke 19:45–46). The religious leaders began to seek how they might destroy him, and that evening Jesus leaves Jerusalem, presumably returning to Bethany (Mark 11:18–19; Luke 19:47–48).

Wednesday

On the way to Jerusalem on Wednesday, the disciples saw the withered fig tree (Matt. 21:20–22; Mark 11:20–26). At the temple in Jerusalem, Jesus had a day of controversy with the religious leaders (Matt. 21:23–23:29; Mark 11:17–12:44; Luke 20:1–21:4). That afternoon Jesus went to the Mount of Olives and delivered the Olivet Discourse (Matt. 24:1–25:46; Mark 13:1–17; Luke 21:5–36). Two additional things occurred on that day: (1) Jesus predicted that in two days he would be crucified at the time of the Passover (Matt. 26:1–5; Mark 14:1–2; Luke 22:1–2); and (2) Judas planned the betrayal of Christ with the religious leaders (Matt. 26:14–16; Mark 14:10–11; Luke 22:3–6).

Thursday

On this day, he had his disciples prepare the Passover lamb (Matt. 26:17–19; Mark 14:12–16; Luke 22:7–13), and Jesus and his disciples had their Passover meal in the Upper Room (Matt. 26:20–30; Mark 14:17–26; Luke 22:14–30; John 13:1–14:31). Leaving the Upper Room, Jesus had a discourse with his disciples and offered an intercessory prayer in their behalf (Matt. 26:30–35; Mark 14:26–31; Luke 22:31–39; John 15:1–18:1). They arrived at the garden of Gethsemane, and it was here where Jesus suffered in agony (Matt. 26:36–46; Mark 14:32–42; Luke 22:39–46; John 18:1). Later that night Jesus was betrayed and arrested (Matt. 26:47–56; Mark 14:43–52; Luke 22:47–53; John 18:2–12). During the rest of that night Jesus was tried first by Annas and later by Caiaphas with the religious leaders (Matt. 26:57–75; Mark 14:53–72; Luke 22:54–65; John 18:13–27).

Friday

Early in the morning, Jesus was tried by the Sanhedrin, Pilate, Herod Antipas, and Pilate again (Matt. 27:1–30; Mark 15:1–19; Luke 22:66–23:25; John 18:28–19:16). Jesus was then led to the cross and crucified at 9:00 am and died at 3:00 p.m. and was buried later that day (Matt. 27:31–60; Mark 15:20–46; Luke 23:26–54; John 19:16–42). Christ the Paschal Lamb (1 Cor. 5:7) died at the time when the Israelites were sacrificing their Passover lambs.

Saturday

Jesus was lying in the tomb during the Sabbath, and the Pharisees secured Roman guards to keep watch of the tomb (Matt. 27:61–66; Mark 15:47; Luke 23:55–56).

Sunday
Christ was resurrected from the dead (Matt. 28:1–5; Mark 16:1–8 [9–13]; Luke 24:1–35). He is a type of the offering of the first fruits which was offered the day after the Sabbath (Lev. 23:9–14; 1 Cor. 15:23).[1]

The week of the Passion was filled with many events, beginning with the Saturday before the Passion Week and ending with the crucifixion of Christ on Friday and the resurrection on Sunday. Now we focus on the reasons Jesus entered Jerusalem on a donkey at the Triumphal Entry: to fulfill prophecy and to convey irony.

Riding to Jerusalem on a Donkey Fulfilled Old Testament Prophecy

All four of the Gospels view Jesus' riding on a donkey into Jerusalem as the messianic king as fulfillment of Zechariah 9:9. Mark and Luke allude to the Old Testament prophecy, while Matthew 21:5 and John 12:15 quote it. In its historical setting, Zechariah 9:9 no doubt referred to a Davidic king entering Jerusalem. Yet, in later rabbinic literature, Zechariah 9:9 was considered messianic (*Babylonian Berakot* 56b and *Babylonian Sanhedrin* 98a). The gospel writers certainly considered it messianic also, as they did Psalm 118:26 (cf. Matt. 23:39).

Three connotations attended a king riding on a donkey. First, obviously the donkey signified royalty. This was so in general in ancient Near Eastern enthronement ceremonies, and in particular in Israel. Thus, Solomon rode on David's donkey to Gihon to be anointed king (1 Kings 1:33, 38; cf. 2 Sam. 18:9; 19:26; cf. also mules of nobility, Judg. 5:10; 10:4; 12:13–14; 2 Sam. 13:29). Second, in rabbinic literature, the Messiah was expected to ride on a donkey (see again *Babylonian Berakot 56b* and *Babylonian Sanhedrin* 98a). Indeed, Zechariah 9:9 was the key text in such a messianic interpretation. Third, texts like *Psalms of Solomon* 17.33 and Revelation 19:11–21 present the Messiah riding on a war horse to conquer. So, on the one hand, the fact that Jesus rode into Jerusalem on a donkey did not signify that he came as "a poor common man of the people" (so Eusebius, *Demonstratio Evangelica* 8.1) nor, on the other hand, did it convey the image of a conquering king.

There is a much debated question about Matthew's version which mentions two animals (a donkey and her foal; Matt. 21:4–5) and Zechariah 9:9 which mentions only one animal. W. D. Davies and Dale C. Allison list seven theories that try to explain the so-called discrepancy:

> The Semitic parallelism of MT Zechariah 9.9 requires that the 'ass' and the 'colt, the foal of an ass', be the same animal (the LXX is ambiguous). In Matthew, however, the one

---

1. For these chronological descriptions, see Harold Hoehner, *Chronological Aspects of the Life of Christ* (Grand Rapids: Zondervan, 1977), 90–93.

animal has become two. . . . Several explanations have been forwarded. (i) The evangelist simply misread the OT (MT or LXX): he was unfamiliar with the nature of Hebrew poetry. (ii) He knew (because he was there or learned from one who was) that in fact there were two asses; or at least he had non-Markan tradition to that effect. (iii) The Matthean tradition had already made the literal misapplication of Zechariah 9.9 to the entry story . . . (iv) The newness of the colt (Mark 11.2) implied the presence of its mother. (v) 21.5 is part of a wider phenomenon, Matthew's tendency to multiply by two . . . (vi) Matthew was thinking of an oriental throne supported by two animals. (vii) . . . Matthew read Zechariah 9.9 in the light of 2 Samuel 16.1–4, where two asses are for David's household to ride upon.[2]

Many assume the first theory—Matthew misread Zechariah 9:9. But Davies and Allison disagree, offering their own intriguing solution:

One must not forget that rabbinic Judaism used Exodus 4.19 to illustrate the principle that the last redeemer (Messiah) will be as the first (Moses): 'And Moses took his wife and his sons, and set them upon an ass. Similarly will it be with the latter Redeemer, as it is stated, lowly and riding upon an ass.' Although this particular tradition is not attested early in the rabbinic corpus, the general principle it enshrines, namely, the Messiah will be like Moses, is. Further, the typological use of Exodus 4.19–20 in Matthew's infancy narrative is seemingly proof that the Old Testament text already belonged to messianic speculation by the first century. This matters because (1) throughout the First Gospel, including 21.1–11, Jesus is assimilated to Moses, (2) Moses was firmly associated with riding an ass, (3) Matthew's interest in Exodus 4.19–20 is established by its influence upon chapter 2, where the parallelism between Jesus and Moses is manifest, and (4) LXX Exodus 4.19–20 uses the plural, *hupozygia*: Moses travelled with ass*es*. We suspect that Matthew, just like the later rabbis, read Zechariah 9.9 in the light of Exodus 4.19–20, so that it was natural, given the plural in LXX Exodus 4.19–20, to find two animals in the ambiguous LXX Zechariah 9.9.[3]

---

2. W. D. Davies and Dale C. Allison, *Matthew* [XIX–XXVIII], ICC (Edinburgh: T&T Clark, 1992), 3:120.

3. Ibid., 121.

For our part, either theory 4 (newness of the colt implied the presence of its mother) or the Moses typology based on Exodus 4:19–20 just mentioned, or a combination of the two, makes sense of the quandary.

Riding on a Donkey to Jerusalem Conveyed an Irony

We mentioned that Jesus rode a donkey into Jerusalem to present himself as the messianic king, but the fact that he did not ride a war horse conveyed an irony to the Jerusalem audience that day: he was offering himself as a peaceful, even suffering Messiah, not as a political, conquering messiah.

Paul Brooks Duff has provided an insightful treatment of the triumphal entry according to Mark 11:1–14, but which also applies to Luke and Matthew.[4] Brooks finds a combination of two major ancient motifs: the Jewish Divine Warrior and the Advent of the Greco-Roman King. Duff then goes on to show that the Markan triumphal entry utilizes those motifs ironically. In effect, what Duff demonstrates is that the Divine Warrior/Greco-Roman King themes are given an ironic twist by Jesus in order to accentuate his true mission—he is a suffering Messiah, a humiliated king.

We will briefly summarize Duff's findings below, noting the four similarities emerging between the Divine Warrior motif (based on Zech. 9, 14), the advent of the Greco-Roman King (based on ancient literature ranging from Josephus to Plutarch), and the Markan triumphal entry (Mark 11:1–14). However, in the Markan narrative, it is the fourth correspondence which displays Jesus' ironic twist to the other two motifs, not to mention the expectations of the crowds: (1) The conqueror/ruler is escorted into the city by the citizens or the army of the conqueror (see Zech. 14:4–5; Josephus, *Jewish Wars* 7.132–57; Mark 11:1–7). (2) The triumphal procession into the city is accompanied by hymns and acclamations to the conqueror (see Zech. 9:9b; Plutarch, *Ameilius Paullus* 34.7; Mark 11:9–10). (3) Various elements in the procession symbolize the conqueror's enthronement over the temple (religion) and the city (state) (see Zech. 14:20–21; Josephus, *Jewish Wars* 7.153; Mark 11:11–14). It is in this last correspondence that Jesus introduced an ironic twist to the Jewish/Greco-Roman Triumphant Entry motifs for, according to Mark 11:11–14 (cf. Luke 19:45–46), Jesus cleansed the temple, disassociating himself from any connotation. Duff's conclusion concerning the Markan narrative essentially applies to Luke as well:

> But what at first glance seems to be a story of triumphal entry and temple cleansing is broken up and hence transformed by the second evangelist. By breaking up the narrative in the manner in which he does, the evangelist gives his "triumphal

---

4. Paul Brooks Duff, "The March of the Divine Warrior and the Advent of the Greco-Roman King: Mark's Account of Jesus' Entry into Jerusalem," *JBL* 111, no. 1 (1992): 55–71.

entry" an ironic twist. The echo of . . . Zechariah 14 . . . [overlaid] . . . with elements of Greco-Roman entry processions manifests this irony for the march of the divine warrior and the entry of the Greco-Roman king providing a stark contrast with the Markan account of Jesus' entry into Jerusalem. For example, in Zechariah 14, the divine warrior appears on the Mount of Olives, enters Jerusalem in procession with his holy ones, appropriates the Temple, and inaugurates a new age of blessedness centered on the Jerusalem Temple, a transformed age in which the distinction between sacred and profane has lost all meaning. Similarly, a conquering ruler from the Greco-Roman milieu would enter his city amid acclamations of his entourage, accompanied by various symbolic depictions of his authority, and immediately upon entering the city would symbolically take possession of it. On the contrary, in Mark's story, the entry parade—because of the interruption of vv. 11–14— abruptly and anticlimactically ends, and Jesus simply leaves the Temple and the city. The "appropriation" of the Temple on the following day is not really an appropriation at all but a disqualification, a fact made all the more apparent by Mark's structure, a structure that connects Jesus' entry and activity in the Temple with his cursing of the fig tree. . . . [T]he cursing of the fig tree and the subsequent "lesson" (i.e., the mountain moving logion) suggest to the reader the condemnation of the Temple. In short, the evangelist teases his readers with what seems to be triumphal allusions but never satisfies their expectations which might have been built up by those allusions. In fact, by his careful arrangement of the text and by the insertion of the fig tree episodes Mark subverts those triumphal allusions. . . . Consequently, those readers who have not really grasped the significance of Jesus' suffering messiahship and the true nature of the kingdom—that is, those readers who expect Jesus to inaugurate the kingdom in a manner resembling that of a warrior-king—will, like the characters of the disciples in Mark's Gospel, have to revise their expectations.[5]

The gospel of John is even more pronounced in demonstrating that Jesus' Triumphal Entry distinguished him from a political Messiah. Five messianic/ nationalistic responses to Jesus by the crowd can be identified in John's episode. First, the crowd greeted Jesus by waving palm branches (v. 13), a national Jewish symbol (see Josephus, *Antiquity of the Jews* 3.10.4/245; 13.13.5/372).

---

5. Ibid., 70–71.

Thus, palm branches were a prominent feature when Judas Maccabees restored the Jerusalem temple in 164 BC, after Antiochus Epiphanes desolated it three years earlier (2 Maccabees 10:7). During the two Jewish revolts against the Romans (AD 66–70 and 132–35), palms were minted on Jewish coins.

Second, the description of the crowd "going to meet him" (*eis hypantēsin*, v. 13) was the normal Greek expression used to describe the joyful escort of Hellenistic sovereigns into a city. For example, the city of Antioch came out to meet the Roman General Titus (Josephus, *Jewish Wars* 7.5.2/100); the same general, by the way, who burned Jerusalem in AD 70.

Third, the shout of "Hosanna" by the crowd meant "save now" (v. 13; see 2 Sam. 14:4; 2 Kings 6:26, esp. Pss. 113–118 [the *Hallel*]), and definitely conveyed Jewish aspirations for deliverance from the Romans.

Fourth, so also did the phrase, "Blessed is he who comes in the name of the Lord" (v. 13), a quotation of Psalm 118:26. Later Rabbinic interpretation viewed this psalm messianically (*Midrash Rabbah, Psalms* 118:22 on Ps. 118:24). Indeed, the fourth gospel associates Jesus the "coming One" with the Messiah (4:25; 7:27, 31, 41–42; 11:27; cf. 6:14).

Fifth, the next acclamation of the crowd—"Blessed is the King of Israel" (v. 13)—obviously was nationalistic. The crowd on Palm Sunday, like the crowd in John 6:15, wanted to make Jesus their king and the restorer of Israel's former glory.

In John's narrative, it is only after these acclamations that Jesus found a donkey and rode upon it into Jerusalem (v. 14). What follows, then, was Jesus' *rejection* of the crowd's nationalistic craze to make him king in order to exalt Israel. More specifically, Jesus offered himself as the suffering Messiah who came to spiritually deliver *both* Jews and Gentiles. Four pieces of data indicate that this is what Jesus was doing. First, he rode on a donkey, not the warhorse of a conquering king. That such a gesture signified humility and even death will be made clear in vv. 20–36. Second, in v. 15, right before John quotes Zechariah 9:9 ("see, your king comes to you seated on a donkey's colt") comes a quotation from Zephaniah 3:16 ("Do not be afraid, O daughter of Zion"). The last-mentioned passage envisions both the salvation of Jew and Gentile. Third, ironically in v. 19 the Pharisees confirm Jesus' mission to Gentiles, "Look, the world has gone after him." Fourth, vv. 20–36 explicitly connect the triumphal entry with Jesus' outreach to Gentiles. And it was this aspect of Jesus' Palm Sunday appearance that the disciples also failed to understand.[6]

Conclusion

We have argued that Jesus' riding on a donkey into Jerusalem at his Triumphal Entry signaled two things. First, it communicated that Jesus was

6. See C. Marvin Pate, *The Writings of John: A Survey of the Gospel, Epistles, and Apocalypse* (Grand Rapids: Zondervan, 2011), 137–38.

fulfilling messianic prophecy predicted in Zechariah 9:9 and also Psalm 118:26. Second, there was irony that day too—Jesus offered himself as the suffering, not political/conquering, Messiah. One day, however, Jesus will exchange the donkey for a white war horse at his parousia (Rev. 11:11–21), the time of his victory over the world.

REFLECTION QUESTIONS

1. How did Jesus' riding on the donkey into Jerusalem on Palm Sunday fulfill Old Testament prophecy?

2. What debate surrounds Matthew 21:4–5 and Zechariah 9:9?

3. What were the similarities between the Divine Warrior motif, the Greco-Roman King's Triumphal entry, and Jesus' entrance into Jerusalem?

4. What is the great irony about Jesus' triumphal entry into Jerusalem?

5. How does the gospel of John make it clear that Jesus rejected the connotations of a political messiah?

When and Why Did Jesus Cleanse the Temple?

Not even radical scholars deny that Jesus cleansed the temple at Jerusalem, so hostile an act it was against the Jewish authorities. The Jerusalem temple was the heart and soul of Jewish religion. Not only that, but the constant work on the temple since Herod the Great created jobs for Jews and thereby boosted the economy. The temple of Jerusalem had a storied history. It was built by Solomon in 966 BC, destroyed by the Babylonians in 587 BC, rebuilt by Zerubbabel in 516 BC, remodeled by Herod (beginning in 20/19 BC), and destroyed again by the Romans in AD 70. Josephus says in his *Antiquities of the Jews* (15.11.1/380) that the reconstruction of the temple proper (*naos*) was begun in the eighteenth year of Herod the Great (20/19 BC). Adding forty-six years to this, we arrive at AD 27 (see Luke 3:1). The restoration of the entire temple area was not completed until AD 63/64 under Herod Agrippa II and Governor Albinus (Josephus, *Antiquities of the Jews* 20.9.7/219), just a handful of years before the Romans destroyed it in AD 70. Therefore, for Jesus to attack the temple sealed his fate with the authorities.

In this chapter, we will cover a number of considerations regarding Jesus' cleansing of the Jerusalem temple: (1) a summary of the cleansing; (2) the debate as to whether the cleansing signaled the general destruction of the temple or only criticism of the abuse of certain practices; (3) the Synoptics presentation of the cleansing; (4) the cleansing of the temple according to John 2:13–25.

A Summary of Jesus' Cleansing of the Temple

We here summarize the episode of Jesus' cleansing of the temple. For convenience's sake, we will use John 2:13–25. John 2:14 and 19–21 refer to the two major areas of the temple: the outer court, the court of the Gentiles (*hieron*, v. 14), and the inner court, consisting of the court of the women, the court of the men (Jews), the Holy Place, and the Holy of Holies (*naos*, vv. 19–21).

The presence of animals and moneychangers in the Court of the Gentiles served two purposes. Because Passover pilgrims preferred not to bring their sacrificial animals with them on an arduous trip to Jerusalem, Caiaphas provided sacrificial animals for them (oxen, sheep, and, for the poor, doves). But to pay for these animals, only Tyrian coinage was permitted. Even though Tyrian shekels had an image of the pagan deities Merqarth and Heracles on one side and an eagle on the other, two factors seem to have permitted their usage in the Jerusalem temple. First, they were not Roman imperial images and second, these coins from Tyre seem to have been minted in Israel. Roman denarii and Attic drachmas were not allowed in the temple because they bore imperial and pagan imagery.[1]

The presence of the merchants in the temple with their sacrificial animals and currency exchange operation infuriated Jesus. With a whip, he drove out the animals and the merchants and overturned the tables of the moneychangers. Holy zeal consumed Jesus (cf. v. 17 with Ps. 69:9) at the thought that the merchants had commercialized God's house of worship (cf. v. 16 with Zech. 14:21; Mal. 3:1, 3). Thus, Jesus' clearing of the temple was prophetic action like that of the Old Testament prophets who condemned Jerusalem's temple for becoming spiritually barren (Isa. 56:7; Jer. 7:11; Zech. 14:21; Mal. 3:1; etc.). In addition, we learn from John 2:19–21 that Jesus' body had become the new temple. This last idea fits in with Jewish expectation that the Messiah would rebuild God's temple.[2]

What Did the Cleansing of the Temple Signify?

Here we can do no better than to draw upon Davies' and Allison's summary of the two positions based on their commentary on Matthew; we do so by way of a summary chart:[3]

DESTRUCTION OF THE TEMPLE	ONLY PROTEST CERTAIN PRACTICES
Jesus predicted the end of the temple (Matt. 24:2).	John's account singles out the business activities of the goings on in the temple.
Jesus was accused of predicting the destruction of the temple (Mark 14:53).	The Old Testament and contemporaries like the Essenes at Qumran criticized the practices of the temple without calling for its overthrow.

---

1. See Raymond E. Brown's discussion, *John I–XII*, AB 29 (Garden City, NY: Doubleday, 1966), 115. V. Eppstein discusses the possibility that Caiaphas, the High Priest of Israel at the time of Jesus, set up merchants in the outer temple precinct to rival the animal markets in the Kidron Valley or on the slopes of the Mount of Olives ("The Historicity of the Cleansing of the Temple," *ZNW* 55 [1964]: 42–58).
2. Cf. John 2:19–21; 1:14; Revelation 21:22 with Ezekiel 40–46; Tobit 13:10; 14:5; the Dead Sea Scrolls (the Temple Scroll); Mark 14:47–61.
3. W. D. Davies and Dale C. Allison, *Matthew* [XIX–XXVIII], ICC (Edinburgh: T&T Clark, 1997), 3:135–36.

DESTRUCTION OF THE TEMPLE	ONLY PROTEST CERTAIN PRACTICES
The saying about the temple's end is joined to the protest against the temple (John 2:13–22).	It was the priesthood that Jesus more opposed than the temple itself.
A prophecy of the destruction of the temple had Old Testament precedent (Jer. 26:1–11) and contemporary parallel (Jesus ben Anania).	Indeed, priests were involved in Jesus' arrest.
Moreover, in the Old Testament, prophetic object lessons signal the coming fall of the temple (Jer. 19:10–11).	Jesus did not oppose the support systems of the temple, just their abuses.
Jesus cast out both sellers and buyers, so he was not simply protesting against the latter.	One such example of abuse may have the temple authorities placing booths for selling animals were placed in the temple.

While one need not approve all of their arguments, still Davies and Allison seem to be correct in saying that both positions are correct. That is, Jesus cleansed the temple to signal its coming destruction and to criticize its abuse of certain practices. They write:

> Our own suspicion is that it is wrong to oppose the two interpretations. Rather, protestation against abuses and symbolic expression of judgment belonged together. In Jeremiah, Micah 3, Ezekiel, and 1 Enoch 83–90 criticism of priestly corruption is joined to expectation of the temple's destruction and/or hope for a new temple. It is plausible enough that Jesus, perhaps with Zechariah 14:21 in mind, indicated by both prophetic word and symbolic deed, God's eschatological judgment upon the temple, and that he opposed, not the sacrificial system itself but what he perceived to be inappropriate business proceedings, which had made the sacred secular and encouraged in the first place or confirmed in the second his thoughts of judgment. Given, however, the nearness of the tower of Antonia with its Roman cohort and the usual custom of placing additional guards around the temple during festivals (compare Josephus, *Antiquities* 20, 106) the incident must have been relatively minor. Josephus, who records many disturbances in the temple, does not notice our event.[4]

---

4. Ibid., 136–37.

The Synoptics' Presentation of the Cleansing

It seems that all four writers understood that Jesus cleansed the Jerusalem temple to both protest abuse of the above practices and to forecast its future destruction. But beyond that, each gospel author adds his own nuance to the episode. Here we consider the Synoptics' perspectives and then in the next point we consider John's viewpoint. To appreciate what the Synoptic authors are doing with this episode, we provide the following chart which is spaced to alert the reader to the differences among Mark, Luke, and Matthew (the probable chronological order of their writing):

MARK 11:12–21	LUKE 19:45–48	MATTHEW 21:12–19
Jesus Curses the Fig Tree	**Jesus Cleanses the Temple**	**Jesus Cleanses the Temple**
12 On the following day, when they came from Bethany, he was hungry. 13 And seeing in the distance a fig tree in leaf, he went to see if he could find anything on it. When he came to it, he found nothing but leaves, for it was not the season for figs. 14 And he said to it, "May no one ever eat fruit from you again." And his disciples heard it.	45 And he entered the temple and began to drive out those who sold, 46 saying to them, "It is written, 'My house shall be a house of prayer,' but you have made it a den of robbers."	12 And Jesus entered the temple and drove out all who sold and bought in the temple, and he overturned the tables of the money-changers and the seats of those who sold pigeons. 13 He said to them, "It is written, 'My house shall be called a house of prayer,' but you make it a den of robbers."
Jesus Cleanses the Temple	47 And he was teaching daily in the temple. The chief priests and the scribes and the principal men of the people were seeking to destroy him, 48 but they did not find anything they could do, for all the people were hanging on his words.	14 And the blind and the lame came to him in the temple, and he healed them. 15 But when the chief priests and the scribes saw the wonderful things that he did, and the children crying out in the temple, "Hosanna to the Son of David!" they were indignant, 16 and they said to him, "Do you hear what these are saying?" And Jesus said to them, "Yes; have you never read, "'Out of the mouth of infants and nursing babies you have prepared praise'?" 17 And leaving them, he went out of the city to Bethany and lodged there.
15 And they came to Jerusalem. And he entered the temple and began to drive out those who sold and those who bought in the temple, and he overturned the tables of the money-changers and the seats of those who sold pigeons. 16 And he would not allow anyone to carry anything through the temple. 17 And he was teaching them and saying to them, "Is it not written, 'My house shall be called a house of prayer for all the nations'? But you have made it a den of robbers." 18 And the chief priests and the scribes heard it and were seeking a way to destroy him, for they feared him, because all the crowd was astonished at his teaching. 19 And when evening came they went out of the city.		

MARK 11:12–21	LUKE 19:45–48	MATTHEW 21:12–19
THE LESSON FROM THE WITHERED FIG TREE 20 As they passed by in the morning, they saw the fig tree withered away to its roots. 21 And Peter remembered and said to him, "Rabbi, look! The fig tree that you cursed has withered."		JESUS CURSES THE FIG TREE 18 In the morning, as he was returning to the city, he became hungry. 19 And seeing a fig tree by the wayside, he went to it and found nothing on it but only leaves. And he said to it, "May no fruit ever come from you again!" And the fig tree withered at once.

It becomes clear from this chart that each author adds their respective nuance to the temple cleansing. Thus, Mark 11:12–20 breaks up Jesus' cursing of the fig tree into two parts thereby framing the cleansing of the temple. This conveys Mark's perspective on the cleansing, namely, just as the barren fig tree is cursed and dies so Jesus' cleansing of the temple is a curse on it due to its spiritual barrenness which will culminate in the temple's destruction. Luke 19:45–48, however, omits entirely the cursing of the fig tree incident. Rather, Jesus cleanses the temple to purge it so that it will be clean for his teaching sessions to be conducted there. Yet, the final destiny of the temple is not in doubt because in vv. 41–44, Jesus predicted the upcoming destruction of the temple (cf. Luke 21:20–24). Matthew 21:12–17 records Jesus' healing of the blind and the lame and accepting the praise of children in the temple. Moreover, Matthew does not separate the cursing of the fig tree into two episodes which surround the cleansing of the temple (as Mark does) but rather keeps it together, placing the incident after the cleansing of the temple. This gives the impression that the temple is not doomed so much as it is being replaced by Jesus and his followers, including the sick and children. As Davies and Allison put it, "Jesus and the church absorb the functions that were peculiar to the temple."[5]

The Cleansing of the Temple according to John 2:13–25

The fourth gospel conveys a similar basic story line and purpose(s) for the cleansing of the temple as the Synoptic Gospels. The major difference, of course, is that in John's gospel, Jesus cleanses the temple early in his ministry rather than during his passion week as the Synoptics indicate. Consequently, a debate has raged among scholars about the number of times Jesus cleansed the Jerusalem temple: One or two? And when? (1) A minority of interpreters

---

5. Ibid., 143.

think Jesus cleansed the temple twice: early on in his ministry (John 2:13–25) and at the end of his ministry (the Synoptics: Matt. 21:12–16; Mark 11:15–18; Luke 19:45–47).[6] (2) An even smaller group of scholars think Jesus cleansed the temple once and it happened early on in his ministry (John 2:13–25), not at the end of his life (the Synoptics). (3) Most scholars today, however, believe Jesus cleansed the temple only once and it was at the end of his ministry (the Synoptics). On this reading, John has taken the liberty to transpose the temple cleansing from the end to the beginning of Jesus' ministry. The main reason for the majority view is that it is inconceivable that Jesus would not have been arrested by the authorities after cleansing the temple in John 2. Jesus is not arrested as he would be during his passion week, according to the Synoptic Gospels. But in John's gospel it was the raising of Lazarus from the dead that pushed the Jerusalem leaders to the point of planning to capture and kill Jesus (John 11).

But if indeed John transposed the cleansing of the temple from its original occurrence to the beginning of Jesus' ministry, why did he do so? The most likely answer is that John attached the episode to a polemical statement by Jesus against the temple made early on in his ministry (John 2:19–22). He then saw both the anti-temple statement and the cleansing of the temple as the fulfillment of Malachi 3:1a (John the Baptist was the forerunner of the Messiah) and Malachi 3:1b (the Lord [Jesus] suddenly appears in the temple to cleanse it).

Conclusion

We have seen that Jesus most likely cleansed the Jerusalem temple both to protest its abuse of certain religious practices and to forecast its future destruction. Such an action on the part of Jesus almost certainly happened during his passion week and was the catalyst for the Roman and Jewish authorities to proceed with his arrest and subsequent execution. John, using poetic license, probably transposed that episode to the beginning of Jesus' ministry in order to reinforce Jesus' polemical remark against the temple. In other words, Jesus seems to have cleansed the temple only once, at the end of his life.[7]

---

6. Andreas J. Köstenberger provides a list of those who dissent from the majority view (view 3 above), arguing for two temple cleansings (view 1 above), *John*, BECNT (Grand Rapids: Baker, 2004), 111.

7. The Chicago Statement on Inerrancy, Article 13 states, "We further deny that inerrancy is negated by Biblical phenomena such as a lack of modern technical precision, irregularities of grammar or spelling, observational descriptions of nature, the reporting of falsehoods, the use of hyperbole and round numbers, the topical arrangement of material, variant selections of material in parallel accounts, or the use of free citations." Our position on John's account of the temple cleansing is covered by the "topical arrangement of material" and is therefore consistent with the Chicago Statement on Inerrancy.

REFLECTION QUESTIONS

1. What happened at the cleansing of the temple?

2. What were the two reasons Jesus cleansed the temple?

3. What are the respective nuances of each of the Synoptic Gospels' presentation of Jesus' cleansing of the temple?

4. When did Jesus cleanse the temple according to the gospel of John?

5. How might one explain the difference in the timing of the cleansing of the temple between the respective reports of the Synoptic Gospels on the one hand and the report of the gospel of John on the other hand?

Who Was Responsible for Jesus' Death?

One of the key criticisms raised against Mel Gibson's film, *The Passion of the Christ,* is that it is potentially anti-Semitic. More than one rabbi appeared on TV after the debut of the movie protesting its effects on Jewish/Gentile relations because of its similarities to medieval passion plays.[1] These plays are well known for contributing to the climate in Europe that culminated in the Holocaust. "Christ killers" became the motto of some of those who watched such plays, which stirred up their hatred toward the Jewish race.

In this chapter we attempt to answer the question, "Who was responsible for Jesus' death?" In responding to this query, it is crucial at this point that we maintain an awareness of history and work to interpret the events surrounding Jesus' passion as objectively as possible. There is no need to revise history in order to deny the role of some ancient Jews in their gross mistreatment of one of their own—Jesus of Nazareth. Surely modern Jews would categorically reject any attempt to revise recent history by denying the horrors of the Holocaust, and rightly so. But neither is it intellectually and morally permissible to explain away the culpability of those few Jews in the past who killed an innocent man. But after we arrive at the truth about the passion—that some Jewish leaders in AD 30 stirred up a crowd against one of their own—we will also see that such action should in no way justify anti-Semitism in any form.

---

1. Anne Catherine Emmerich's book (*The Dolorous Passion of Our Lord Jesus* [repr. Rockford, IL: TAN Books & Publishers, 1994]), exerts a strong influence on Gibson's movie. Emmerich was an Augustinian nun who was born in 1774, in Germany. She reportedly experienced the mystical phenomenon of the stigmata (the wounds of Christ). In addition, she claimed to have mystical visions. Her testimonies were written down by Clemens Brentano, her secretary, including *The Dolorous Passion of Our Lord Jesus.* Her own purported experience of the stigmata, as well as the influence of medieval passion plays, undoubtedly lies behind her graphic descriptions of Christ's passion. Emmerich died on February 9, 1824.

What, then, is the historical evidence concerning the question, "Who killed Jesus?" We begin to answer this question by observing that the source of some modern Jews' consternation about the portrayal of the death of Jesus ultimately is not Mel Gibson, but the *Gospels*—for it is they that lay the blame for Jesus' death at the feet of some ancient Jews, as well as on the shoulders of the Roman governor Pilate.

The Jews and Jesus' Death

All the Gospels indicate that the Jewish leaders initiated the plot to kill Jesus.[2] All the Gospels also indicate that Pilate's attempt to release Jesus was met with the Jewish crowd's demand for Jesus' death.[3]

The culpability of the Sanhedrin, the seventy-one Jewish leaders who governed ancient Israel, is all the more notable when one realizes how illegal the trial of Jesus was. Compared to its own laws regulating trials as recorded in the Mishnah, the ancient Jewish law code, the Sanhedrin acted improperly at Jesus' trial in at least five ways, as Bruce Corley observes:

> (1) it was improperly convened in the high priest's house (*m. Sanh.* 11:2); (2) met during the night (*m. Sanh.* 4:1); (3) on a Sabbath eve of a Feast Day (*m. Sanh.* 4:1) and (4) reached a guilty verdict on the same day (*m. Sanh. 4:1; 5:5*) (5) based on inadequate grounds for blasphemy (*m. Sanh.* 7:5).[4]

The Sanhedrin broke their own laws and convicted Jesus of blaspheming for identifying himself as the Son of God (see Mark 14:61–64 and parallel passages)—a crime punishable by death. At that time, both the Jewish leaders and the Jewish people readily accepted responsibility for their part in the death of Jesus. Matthew 27:25 is particularly powerful on this point: after demanding that Jesus be crucified, the Jewish crowd cried out to Pilate, "Let his blood be on us and our children" (NIV).

But these indictments against those Jews who rejected Jesus are not to be equated with anti-Semitism for two reasons. First, the Gospels are simply condemning Jesus' disobedient generation, just like the Old Testament prophets condemned their generation of unbelievers. Second, many Jews accepted Jesus in his day and the next generation and experienced God's grace and blessing.

In a *Time* magazine article, Richard Corliss catches this distinction in both Gibson's film and in the Gospels:

---

2. See Matthew 21:46; 26:3–4, 14–16, 47, 57–67; Mark 14:1, 43, 53–65; Luke 19:47; 20:19; 22:3–6, 47, 54, 63–65; 23:1–12; John 11:45–57; 18:2–3, 12–14.
3. See Matthew 27:20–26; Mark 15:9–14; Luke 23:13–25; John 18:39–40; 19:1–7, 15–16.
4. Bruce Corley, "Trial of Jesus," in *DJG*, ed. Joel B. Green, Scot McKnight, and I. Howard Marshall, (Downers Grove: InterVarsity Press, 1992), 851.

Is the film anti-Jewish? Well, which Jews? Start with the Sanhedrin, the Rabbinical senate that found Jesus guilty of violating temple law and handed him to the Roman authority for summary punishment. The rabbis had their reasons, they saw the upstart as dangerous, blasphemous, possibly insane for proclaiming himself the Messiah and telling his followers they would live forever if they ate his flesh and drank his blood. The film sees the rabbis as doctrinally pure but politically corrupt. Indeed, it suggests they are a rogue cell calling a midnight caucus for a frame up. But Gibson also shows many Jews (and no Romans) treating Jesus with a kindness and charity one might call Christian. We acknowledge, then, that *The Passion* is rabidly anti-Sanhedrin-opposed, as Jesus and other Jews were, to the Establishment of the time. But to charge the film with being anti-Semitic is like saying those who oppose the Bush Administration's Iraq policy are anti-American.[5]

The point is well taken. We should not confuse the Gospels' condemnation of some ancient Jews' mistreatment of Jesus with anti-Semitism. Bruce Corley expresses the matter more strongly:

A lamentable feature of Christian reaction to the trial of Jesus across the centuries has been an odious persecution of the Jews for putting Jesus to death. It has been maintained above the Evangelists did not invent the fact of Jewish involvement, but the NT never says that the Jews alone, least of all every succeeding generation, were responsible for the cross. The perennial instinct to kindle anti-Semitism by the findings of historical scholarship is deplorable in all its forms. The theological stance of the Gospels indicts us all, Jew and Gentile alike: "He was numbered with the transgressors" (Luke 22:37), yet "this man has done nothing wrong" (Luke 23:41).[6]

The Romans and Jesus' Death

But the Jews could not have pulled off the trial and execution of Jesus without the Romans' help, particularly Pilate's. John 18:31 relates how the Jewish Sanhedrin did not have the right to execute criminals; only the Roman governor did. It is interesting that at that point the Jews mixed the nature of their accusations against Jesus—he was a blasphemer (John 19:7) and an

---

5. Richard Corliss, "The Goriest Story Ever Told," *Time*, 163, no. 9, March 1, 2004, 64.

6. Corely, "The Trial of Jesus," 854.

insurrectionist (John 19:12). Introducing the latter charge necessarily involved Pilate, for now Jesus was accused of being a revolutionary. Though they could pass a death sentence, the Sanhedrin needed Pilate's approval to carry it out because the power to execute lay only in his hands as the Roman procurator (governor). This fact is corroborated by extra-canonical Jewish testimony. Corley lists the evidence from Josephus (late first century AD) and the Talmud (ancient Israel's legal writings [second to fifth centuries AD]):

> While still competent to try religious cases, the prerogatives of the Sanhedrin changed with the beginning of direct Roman rule in Judea: (1) Coponius, the first governor (AD 6), was sent out by Augustus with full powers "extending to capital punishment" (Josephus, *Jewish Wars* 2.8.1/117; cf. *Antiquities of the Jews* 18.1.1/2). (2) Tannaitic tradition confirms that "the right to try capital cases was taken from Israel forty years before the destruction of the Temple" (*Jerusalem Sanhedrin* 1.1:1.2; cf. *Babylonian Sanhedrin* 41a); (3) the Jewish death penalty was reinstated a week after the Romans lifted the siege of Jerusalem in September AD 66; "On the twenty-second of the month [Elul] the execution of malefactors began again" (*Megillat Ta'anit* 6).[7]

But there are scholars who disagree with the traditional view that only the Roman governor, not the Sanhedrin, had the power to execute criminals.[8] Those scholars typically appeal to the following cases: (1) Archeologists have discovered two of the warning inscriptions dating to the first century AD that surrounded the Jerusalem temple, forbidding Gentiles to proceed no further on pain of death at the hands of the Jewish authorities.[9] (2) Stephen was executed by the Sanhedrin (Acts 6:8–7:60). (3) Like Stephen, James, the brother of Jesus, was stoned to death at the orders of the high priest Ananus and the Sanhedrin.

But the preceding episodes are easily explained according to the traditional view. Regarding the warning inscriptions, Josephus tells his readers that Rome first gave the Sanhedrin permission to erect the barriers containing the inscriptions, and to execute trespassers.[10] In Stephen's case, while a trial procedure was initially followed by the Sanhedrin (Acts 6:11–14; 7:57–58),

---

7. Ibid., 850.

8. For example, see Paul Winter, *On the Trial of Jesus,* 2nd ed. (New York: De Gegruyter, 1974).

9. The two were discovered in 1871. They read, "No foreigner is to enter within the balustrade and enclosure around the Temple area. Whoever is caught will have himself to blame for his death which will follow," in Peter Connolly, *Living in the Time of Jesus of Nazareth* (Israel: Steimatzky, 1993), 36. Josephus quotes this inscription (see *Jewish Wars* 5.52; *Antiquities of the Jews* 15.11.5). Today the inscriptions are in the Archaeological Museum, Istanbul.

10. See Josephus, *Jewish Wars* 6.4; 124–128.

the proceedings were interrupted without proper sentencing. In other words, Stephen's death occurred as an act of lynch law at the hands of a mob, a violation of Jewish law.[11] Finally, in James' case, the brother of the Lord was killed in the interval between the rules of the Roman governors Festus and Albinus (AD 62); that is, without the approval of Rome. Consequently, the Jewish high priest, Ananus, was deposed from office by Rome. Therefore, John 18:31 stands: the Sanhedrin had to get permission from Rome to have a criminal executed. And such was the case for Jesus. Only Pilate could make it happen.

Critics of *The Passion of the Christ* accused the film of going easy on Pilate. But neither Gibson's film nor the Gospels let Pilate off the hook. All the Synoptics include Jesus' prediction that he will be handed over to the Gentiles (Matt. 20:19; Mark 10:33; Luke 18:32); and Pilate is presumably to be numbered among them. In Matthew, Pilate yields to the crowd despite the warning of his wife's dream (27:19). His washing of his hands is an empty gesture (27:24); he can no more evade his responsibility than could Judas or the high priests (27:3–7). In Luke, Pilate pronounces Jesus' innocence three times (23:4, 15, 22). However, this serves to emphasize Jesus' innocence three times (23:41, 47; Acts 13:28), not to exonerate Pilate, who in Acts is numbered among those who gather against the Anointed One (4:25–28). In Mark, Pilate's resistance to the crowd's demand is minimal. In John, he is cynical and self-serving (18:35, 38; 19:8–9). Thus, no consistent exoneration of Pilate can be traced in any of the Gospels.[12]

So if Pilate considered Jesus innocent, why he did give in to the Jewish demand to crucify Jesus? History reveals the answer. Pilate capitulated to the crowd's request to crucify Jesus because of his previous failed relationships with the Jews. Pilate, the Roman prefect of Judea from AD 26 to 36, was not well thought of by the Jews, to say the least. Josephus writes of his blundering dealings with the nation of Israel.[13] Three in particular call for comment.

First, when he became governor of Judea, Pilate sent his troops into Jerusalem with the ensigns on their standards. For the Jews, the image to Caesar was tantamount to idolatry. When the people protested Pilate's actions, he threatened them with death, but they were not intimidated. Pilate backed off from his threat.

Second, Pilate confiscated money out of the temple treasury to fund an aqueduct to bring water to Jerusalem. The Jews of Jerusalem were furious but this time the governor carried through with his threat to kill those who

---

11. See *Mishnah Sanhedrin* 6.6; Josephus *Antiquities of the Jews* 4.8.6.
12. These comments are indebted to J. A. Weatherly, "Anti-Semitism," in *DJG*, ed. Joel B. Green, Scot McKnight, and I. Howard Marshall (Downers Grove/Leicester, England: InterVarsity Press, 1992), 13–17.
13. See Josephus *Antiquities of the Jews* 18.55–62; 4.85–89.

opposed him. He did so by having his soldiers dress as civilians and then, at Pilate's signal, attack the protestors.

Third, as I have written elsewhere:

> Pilate hung votive shields engraved with Emperor Tiberius's name in the palace of Herod in Jerusalem. Before Pilate the Romans had tried to respect the Jew's abhorrence of anything that remotely resembled a graven image erected in Jerusalem. Pilate's actions crossed the line, so a Jewish delegation responded by appealing directly to the emperor, who rebuked Pilate and ordered the removal of the shields. The final straw had now come with the Jews' demand for Jesus' crucifixion. Were Pilate to refuse their request, Caesar Tiberius would surely depose the governor, especially if he tolerated a rival king (see John 19:12–15).[14]

Conclusion

So the Gospels are clear that both some ancient Jews and Romans killed Jesus of Nazareth, innocent though he was. But are they alone responsible for Jesus' death? No, for while the Gospels provide the historical reason for Jesus' death, the apostle Paul provides the theological reason for Jesus' death—Jesus died because of the whole world. The sins of humanity crucified Jesus. The key word here is "delivered up" (one word in the Greek, *paradidōmi*). This word is used in the Gospels to refer to the Jews and Romans "delivering up" Jesus to death (Matt. 17:22; 20:18–19; Mark 9:31; 10:33; Luke 9:44; 18:32; 20:20; John 18:35; 19:16). But Paul uses the word to refer to all of humanity as being responsible for Jesus' death. Note the following references:

- "He [Jesus] was delivered over to death for our sins" (Rom. 4:25).
- "by faith in the Son of God, who loved me and delivered himself up for me" (Gal. 2:20).
- "And [God] delivered him [Jesus] up for us a fragrant offering and sacrifice" (Eph. 5:2).
- "Just as Christ loved the church and delivered himself up for her" (Eph. 5:25).[15]

---

14. C. Marvin Pate, *Luke* (Chicago: Moody, 1995), 450.
15. All the preceding verses in this paragraph are the author's translation based on the Greek text (Nestle-Aland Greek-English New Testament [Stuttgart, Germany: Deustche Bibelgesellchaft, 1998]).

So to return to our question: Who killed Jesus? We all did, not just some ancient Jews and Romans. But the good news of the gospel is that we can all be saved from our sins precisely because of Jesus' death and resurrection for us.

REFLECTION QUESTIONS

1. Ultimately, who was culpable for Jesus' death?

2. What terrible danger can result from being harsh on the Jewish race regarding the death of Jesus?

3. What arguments do those who say the Jews had the legal authority to execute Jesus appeal to?

4. What past incidents in Pilate's life might have played a key role in his executing Jesus even though he was innocent?

5. In the end, who is responsible for Jesus' death?

Why Did Jesus Die?

Various reasons for Jesus' death have been discussed throughout church history (especially the imitation of Christ, ransom to Satan, Christ the Victor/messianic woes[1]), but the theory of substitutionary atonement taught in the Gospels and reiterated by the rest of the New Testament offers the best explanation in the question of why did Jesus die. We will approach this topic in six steps, substitutionary atonement in: the Old Testament, the Synoptics, John, Paul, the General Epistles, and in Revelation.

Substitutionary Atonement in the Old Testament

The Old Testament is deeply influenced by the idea of vicarious or substitutionary atonement. Three types of substitutionary atonement are described in the Hebrew Bible: The paschal lamb (Ex. 12; etc.); the sacrificial system as a whole (see esp. Lev. 1–7; etc.), the most crucial of which is the Day of Atonement (Lev. 16); and the atonement wrought by the Suffering Servant (Isa. 42:1–9; 49:1–6; 50:4–11; 52:13–53:12). All of these traditions are rooted in the conviction that a divinely designated animal or person exchanges one's righteousness, or innocence, with a devotee's sin. The Old Testament Apocrypha in the LXX adds a fourth tradition of vicarious atonement—the righteous martyr, whose suffering or death atones for Israel's sin (2 Maccabees; 4 Maccabees; Wisdom 2–5).

But the vicarious atonement traditions in the Hebrew Bible and the LXX are incomplete because they afford only temporary forgiveness. Thus, what was needed was the perfect sacrifice, one that need not be repeated. Only then could the problem of God's righteousness and human sinfulness be

---

1. For discussion of these theories of the meaning of Jesus' death along with the theory presented in this chapter, substitutionary atonement, the reader is referred to C. Marvin Pate, *From Plato to Jesus: What Does Philosophy Have to Do with Theology?* (Grand Rapids: Kregel, 2011), chapter 12.

addressed. The New Testament provides that answer—God became man in the person of Jesus Christ, whose perfect life and death atoned for the sins of the world. Finally, there was now a permanent way for humanity to satisfy the righteousness of God.

Substitutionary Atonement in the Synoptic Gospels

It might come as a surprise to learn that the Synoptic Gospels do not treat at length the meaning of the death of Jesus. But there are still statements to the effect of vicarious atonement that occur therein. We take the Synoptics in their probable chronological order.

Mark

Mark has two references to the atoning nature of Jesus' death: Mark 10:45 and 14:24. The former passage speaks of Jesus, the Son of Man, giving his life a ransom for many. It was this sort of statement that Origen (third century AD) seized on to develop his "ransom from Satan theory" of Jesus' death. In other words, Jesus' death was God's ransom paid to Satan to set humanity free from enslavement to Satan. The Cappadocian theologians (fourth century AD) tweaked Origen's idea to include the bait and hook theory. That is, Jesus' humanity was the bait that Satan took to put Jesus on the cross only to discover that the hook of Jesus' deity captured Satan at the cross and the resurrection. Thus, we have in these church fathers the combination of the ransom to Satan theory and the defeat of Satan idea. But there really is no justification for the main part of the ransom theory, not the payment to Satan nor his deception with the bait and hook dynamic. The first part of this theory would end up making Satan and God equal in power, but such dualism is not in accord with the Bible. Although Jesus did defeat Satan on the cross, it was not by tricking him. Rather, Satan tried to keep Jesus from going to the cross to accomplish his divine mission (recall the question above on the temptations of Jesus).

Mark 10:45 is best explained by Mark 14:24, which refers to Jesus' blood being poured out for many. This obviously signifies that Jesus' death was to be vicarious for sinners and thereby provide their ransom.[2] Mark labels this the "blood of the covenant," which taps into the Old Testament, especially Moses' sprinkling the blood of a sacrificed bull on the convocation of Jews to ratify the covenant (Ex. 24:1–8). In like manner, Jesus' shed blood on the cross cleanses the sinner and incorporates them into the new covenant.

---

2. For a more nuanced treatment, see C. Marvin Pate and Douglas W. Kennard, *Deliverance Now and Not Yet: The New Testament and the Great Tribulation* (New York: Peter Lang, 2004), 318–19.

Luke-Acts

Four passages in Luke-Acts associate Jesus' afflictions with the Isaianic Suffering Servant. (1) In citing Isaiah 61:1–2, Luke 4:17–21 explicitly identifies Jesus with the Servant of the Lord and, in doing so, sets forth the Isaianic background as programmatic for Luke-Acts. (2) Luke 22:37 is uttered in the context of the Lord's Supper, where Jesus announces that the scriptures are fulfilled in him and then quotes Isaiah 53:12, "And he was reckoned with the transgressors." (3) Luke 24:25–27, 44–46, at the very least, certainly include in their purview of Old Testament texts the sufferings of the Isaianic Servant and his subsequent vindication (Isa. 52:13–53:12). (4) Acts 8:32–33 is a direct quote of Isaiah 53:7–8 thereby identifying Jesus as the Servant.

These four texts seem to affirm the afflictions of Jesus the Suffering Servant to be vicarious or in the place of the sins of others. Besides the Suffering Servant passages mentioned, Acts 20:28 refers to "the church of God, which he bought with his own blood." Though there is a text critical debate here as to whether we should read "church of God" or "church of Christ," most likely the former reading is the original. Yet, surely Luke means here that it is God through the blood of Christ that purchases the church. In other words, either reading intends to present Jesus' death as vicarious.

Matthew

Here we note the influence of the Isaianic Servant upon Matthew's presentation of Jesus. In Matthew 2:13–15, Jesus' departure under the protection of his parents to Egypt anticipates his role as the servant/Israel. At his baptism, Jesus is identified as that Servant (cf. Matt. 3:17/ Mark 1:11 with Isa. 42:1) and then undergoes testing, like ancient Israel, in the wilderness; but Jesus is obedient to God whereas ancient Israel was not (4:1–11). Matthew's quotations of Isaiah 53:4 in Matthew 8:17 and Isaiah 42:1–4 in Matthew 12:18–21 further cast Jesus as the Isaianic Servant who identifies with the afflictions of Israel. This is so because, according to Matthew 11:2, which alludes to Isaiah 61:1, Jesus is the anointed one. Fittingly, Jesus is destined to embrace divine wrath in order to redeem, or establish the new covenant with Israel, according to Matthew 20:28/26:28 (cf. Isa. 35:9–10; 40:2; 41:14; 43:1, 3–4; 44:22; 51:10–11 and God's promise to redeem Israel out of exile). Therefore, Matthew, like Luke-Acts, views Jesus the suffering servant's afflictions as vicariously atoning for sin.

Substitutionary Atonement in the Gospel of John

Recent research into the provenance of the gospel of John locates that work largely in the Jewish-Christian debates in the synagogues (ca. post AD 70 and the fall of Jerusalem).[3] A key controversy generated by those

---

3. Principally based on John 9:22, 34; 12:42; 16:2, texts which speak of being expelled from the synagogue, J. L. Martyn developed the popular theory that the setting of the gospel of

discussions was the death of Jesus, particularly this question: if Jesus was truly the Messiah, why did he die, and specifically why did he die on a cross? We are not left to our imagination as to the scandal surrounding Jesus' death for Jews in antiquity. Justin Martyr's (AD 140) debating partner, Trypho the Jew, spoke for many when he said poignantly:

> Be assured that all our nation awaits the Messiah; and we admit that all the scriptures which you have quoted refer to him. Moreover, I also admit that the name of Jesus by which the son of Nun was called, has inclined me very strongly to adopt this view. But we are in doubt about whether the Messiah should be so shamefully crucified. For whoever is crucified is said in the Law to be accursed, so that I am very skeptical on this point. It is quite clear, to be sure, that the Scriptures announce that the Messiah had to suffer, but we wish to learn if you can prove it to us whether by suffering he was cursed (*Dialogue with Trypho* 89.1).

The fourth gospel's answer to that query, as Craig A. Evans has demonstrated, was that Jesus' death was in keeping with scriptural expectation. Evans identifies a twofold apologetic in John concerning the matter: Israel's rejection of Jesus the Messiah was predicted in the Old Testament (see esp. John 12:38 [Isa. 53:1] and John 12:39–40 [Isa. 6:10]); Jesus' death paradoxically was his moment of glory (John 12:23; 13:31–32; 17:5), the background of which is the exaltation of the Suffering Servant of Isaiah (cf. John 12:41 with Isa. 52:13; 53:12).[4] Evans writes:

> It is also important to understand that according to the evangelists this "glory" is the glory which the prophet Isaiah saw and of which he spoke (Jn. 12.41). The coordination of the quotations of Isa. 53.1 (Jn. 12.38) and Isa. 6.10 (Jn. 12.40) suggests that what was seen was the "glory" which the prophet beheld in his famous vision of Isaiah 6 and what was *spoken* were the words of the Suffering Servant Song. That is to say, when (or because) Isaiah saw God's *glory* he spoke about God's *servant*, who is none other than the *logos* who became flesh and tabernacle among us (Jn. 1.14).[5]

John was the aftermath of the expulsion of Jewish Christians from the synagogues (*History and Theology in the Fourth Gospel*, 2nd ed. [Nashville: Abingdon, 1979]).

4. Craig A. Evans, *Word and Glory: On the Exegetical and Theological Background of John's Prologue*, JSNTSupp 89 (Sheffield: JSOT Press, 1993), 178–80.

5. Ibid., 180–81.

That such a death was understood by John as vicariously atoning is obvious from John 1:29, 36 (Jesus is the lamb of God who takes away the sin of the world), John 19:14 (Jesus is the paschal lamb), and 1 John 2:2 (Jesus' death is a propitiation for sin).

Indeed, John's passion narrative has as its Old Testament subplot the paschal lamb, afflictions of the righteous, and the Servant of the Lord now applied to Jesus' death, as the following chart makes plain:

OT	JOHN 19
Psalm 22:18: afflictions of the righteous	John 19:24
Psalm 22:15: affliction of the righteous	John 19:28
Exodus 12:22: the paschal lamb	John 19:29–30
Isaiah 53:12: Suffering Servant of the Lord	John 19:30
Deuteronomy 21:22–23: cursed of God for humans	John 19:31
Ezekiel 36:26–27/Zechariah 12:10: Suffering Servant of the Lord	John 19:34–35
Exodus 12:46: the paschal lamb	John 19:36

Substitutionary Atonement in the Pauline Literature

Five Greek words (three of them prepositions and two of them nouns translated as "redemption") capture Paul's understanding of Jesus' death: *hyper, anti, peri,* and *apolutrōsis* and *agorazō.* These words convey the idea of vicarious atonement.[6] (1) *Hyper* ("on behalf of") as associated with Christ's vicarious death occurs in Paul in Galatians 1:4; 2:20; Romans 5:5; 1 Corinthians 11:24; Ephesians 5:2, 25; 1 Timothy 2:6; Titus 2:14. (2) *Peri* (with the genitive can mean "on behalf of") is used in Romans 8:3 of Christ's death on behalf of sin. (3) *Anti* ("in place of") occurs in Paul in combination with *lutrōsis* in 1 Timothy 2:6 to speak of Christ giving himself as a ransom for all men." (4) *Apolutrōsis* ("redemption") is used of Jesus' death in Romans 3:24; Ephesians 1:7; Colossians 1:14; Titus 2:14. A similar term, *"agorazō"* refers to Jesus' death in Galatians 3:13; 4:4–5. These five words indicate that Paul interpreted Jesus' death as a substitutionary atonement.

Paul also draws on the Suffering Servant of Isaiah 53 when reflecting on the nature of Jesus' death (i.e., Rom. 4:25; 10:16–17; 1 Cor. 15:3; and Phil. 2:6–11). These texts drawing on the Suffering Servant of Isaiah 53 reinforce the claim that Paul interpreted Jesus' death as vicarious.

And then there are those Pauline texts that unmistakably interpret Jesus' death as an atoning sacrifice (i.e., Rom. 3:25; 4:25; 5:6–10; 1 Cor. 11:23–26; 2 Cor. 5:21; Gal. 3:13–14; Eph. 2:13–18; Col. 1:19–20; and 1 Tim. 2:5–6).

---

6. See the discussion of Pate and Kennard, *Deliverance Now and Not Yet,* 136–40, 176–79.

Substitutionary Atonement in the General Epistles

Hebrews

No New Testament book emphasizes Jesus' death as atoning for sin more than Hebrews: 2:17; 5:11 (cf. 7:27; 9:12, 14–15, 25–28 [probably an allusion to LXX Isa. 53:12]; 10:18); 12:2 (cf. 1:3; 8:1; 10:12); 13:11. These passages convey the author's conviction that Jesus' death, once and for all, paid the price for sin (cf. this to the theme of the blood of Christ in Hebrews: 9:11–28; 10:10–31; 12:24; 13:12, 20).

1 and 2 Peter

The verses in 1 Peter falling under the umbrella of Jesus' death as atoning are 1:18, 19–20; 2:24; 3:18. There are two traditions informing 1:18: Isaiah 52:3 (LXX, "You were sold for nothing, and you will be atoned without silver") and Mark 10:45. The setting of the Isaianic reference (Isa. 51:17–52:12) is that of God's promise to rescue Israel from exile, who, ultimately, was not held captive by her enemies for ransom, but rather God had delivered her to the nations. The same God, therefore, would set Israel free without payment to her oppressors. According to Isaiah 52:13–53:12, however, there was a price to be paid for Israel's deliverance, and it was the suffering of God's Servant. Such a setting is reinforced in 1 Peter 1:18 by Mark 10:45, the other tradition impacting that verse.

J. Ramsey Michaels delineates four influences on 1 Peter 1:19–20 ("but with precious blood, like that of a faultless lamb—[the blood] of Christ"): (a) the Passover lamb of Exodus 12:5; (b) the blameless Suffering Servant of Isaiah 53:7; (c) Old Testament sacrificial language in general; (d) the offering up of Isaac (Gen. 22:8, 13).[7] These obviously are informed by the concept of substitutionary atonement. First Peter 1:19–20 quotes Isaiah 53:4–12. Michaels goes so far as to say that this passage is a commentary on LXX Isaiah 53:4–12.[8]

There has been much debate about 1 Peter 2:24, in particular whether it teaches the idea of imitation of Christ as the means to forgiveness of sin. But even if such a theme is present here, it is under the influence of the overall teaching of Christ's death as substitutionary atonement we have seen thus far in 1 Peter. In other words, following Jesus in no way atones for our sins; only his death did that.[9] First Peter 3:18 essentially repeats the sentiment of 2:24— Christ's death procured lasting atonement for sinners.

The only passage in 2 Peter suggesting Jesus' death was vicarious is 2 Peter 2:1, the false teachers "deny the Lord who bought [*agorasanta)* them."

---

7. J. Ramsey Michaels, *1 Peter*, WBC 49 (Waco, TX: Word, 1988), 66.
8. Ibid., 137.
9. For further discussion of this historic debate, see Pate and Kennard, *Deliverance Now and Not Yet*, 368–72.

1 John

Jesus' death as a substitutionary atonement is clearly taught in 1 John 1:7; 2:1–2; 4:10 which, in turn, shed light on 5:6.

Revelation

The following texts in Revelation speak of Jesus' death: 1:5, 18; 2:8; 5:6, 9; 17:14. The first passage sets the tone for the other texts, namely, Jesus' death was a sacrifice for sins.

Conclusion

It is obvious from the preceding data that perhaps the most significant reason Jesus died was as an atoning sacrifice for our sins. Second Corinthians 5:21 expresses this conviction well, "For He [God] has made him [Christ] sin on our behalf in order that we may might be made the righteousness of God in him [Christ]." On the cross Jesus took our sin so that through faith in him we might receive his righteousness. It is this divine exchange between Christ and sinners that satisfies a holy God.[10]

REFLECTION QUESTIONS

1. What do the Synoptic Gospels tell us about the death of Jesus?

2. What does the gospel of John tell us about the death of Jesus?

3. What does Paul teach about the death of Jesus?

4. What do the General Epistles say regarding the death of Jesus?

5. What does Revelation disclose concerning the death of Jesus?

---

10. See *The Gospel According to Isaiah 53: Encountering the Suffering Servant in Jewish and Christian Theology*, eds. Darrell L. Bock and Mitch Glaser (Grand Rapids: Kregel, 2012) for a thorough look at the influence of Isaiah 53 in the Bible.

Did Jesus Remain in the Tomb Three Days and Three Nights?

The question, "did Jesus remain in the tomb three days and three nights," has kindled heated discussion, the interpretation of which has fallen generally into two camps. There are those who vociferously argue that Jesus must have been in the grave for seventy-two hours and that those who disagree are denying Jesus' prediction in Matthew 12:40 ("For just as Jonah was three days and three nights in the belly of the sea monster, so will the Son of Man be three days and three nights in the heart of the earth"). But the other view, rightly we believe, argues that Jesus' stay in the grave Friday night, Saturday, and early Sunday morning meets the specifications of Matthew 12:40. Perhaps the best way to proceed through this debate would be to examine the key descriptions in the matter: "on the third day," "after three days," "three days and three nights," and Jesus' word to the thief on the cross with him, "Today you will be with me in Paradise" (Luke 23:43). Finally, we will touch upon Hosea 6:2.

"The Third Day"

Jewish interpreters as far back as the Midrashim (second century AD in written texts but probably earlier in oral form) have claimed that the third day motif is used in the Old Testament for God's deliverance of Israel or a righteous person.[1] The words, "the third day," are used in the New Testament especially of Jesus' death and resurrection (see Matt. 16:21; 17:23; 20:19; Luke 9:22; 24:7, 21, 46; Acts 10:40; 1 Cor. 15:4).

---

1. See, e.g., *Palestinian Sanhedrin* 97a; *Babylonian Rosh Hashanah* 31a; *Palestinian Berakoth* 5.2; *Palestinian Sanhedrin* 11.6; *Midrash Rabbah, Esther* 9.2 (on Esther 5:1); *Midrash Rabbah, Deuteronomy* 7.6 (on Deut. 28:12); *Midrash Rabbah, Genesis* 56.1 (on Gen. 22:4); *Pirke de Rabbi Eliezer* 51 (73b–74a). Note the following Old Testament examples: Genesis 22:4; 42:18; Exodus 19:11, 16; Joshua 1:11; Esther 5:1; 2 Kings 20:5; Hosea 6:2 (see our later discussion of this text).

"After Three Days"

The passion predictions in Matthew and Luke speak of Jesus being raised on "the third day," whereas the passion predictions in Mark speak of Jesus being raised "after three days." That the two phrases are synonymous is clear from Matthew 27:63–64 which speaks of Jesus' prediction that he will be raised "after three days" (cf. "the third day" earlier in Matt. 16:21; 17:23; 20:19). Moreover, Josephus uses "the third day" and "after three days" synonymously (*Antiquities of the Jews* 7.11, 6; 8.8, 1–2). So whatever these two phrases mean, they mean the same thing.

"Three Days and Three Nights"

As we mentioned above, Matthew 12:40 creates a parallel between Jonah's time in the belly of the fish and Jesus' time in the grave—"three days and three nights." It is interesting that Esther 4:16 equates "three days and nights" with "the third day" in Esther 5:1. Thus, these two phrases are also synonymous. Pulling our findings so far together, we may say that all three phrases—"the third day," "after three days," and "three days and nights"—are synonymous. It is clear that these three phrases as applied to Jesus' death and resurrection fit the ancient Jewish interpretations well in that God raised Jesus, the true Israel/the righteous Suffering Servant, from the dead. But more specifically we may say, based on the Old Testament, that the language of "three days and nights," "third day," "after three days" does not require that Jesus was in the grave for seventy-two hours, since in Jewish reckoning any part of a day could count as a day (cf. Gen. 42:17–18; 1 Sam. 30:1, 12–13; 1 Kings 20:29; 2 Chron. 10:5, 12; Esther 4:16–5:1).[2] Herein lies the answer to the question, "how long was Jesus in the grave"—for three days, namely, a part of Friday (day one), Saturday (day two), and a part of Sunday (day three).[3]

"Today You Will Be with Me in Paradise"

But does Luke 23:43 contradict Jesus' promise that he would be in the grave three (parts of) days? I write of this elsewhere:

> Traditionally, the word "today" (*sēmeron*) has been understood to be a chronological reference to a twenty-four-hour period. The difficulty with this view is its apparent conflict with biblical teaching elsewhere which suggests that Jesus first "descended" to Hades after his death (Matt. 12:40; Acts 2:31;

---

2. David L. Turner provides these references in, *Matthew* (Grand Rapids: Baker, 2008), 327.
3. See R. T. France's discussion of the relationship of the "heart of the earth" to "Hades," discounting any hint that Jesus descended to the abode of the dead between his death and resurrection (*The Gospel of Matthew* [Grand Rapids: Eerdmans, 2007], 491n. 14). We disagree with France here and will in the next chapter argue instead that Jesus did indeed descend to Hades between his death and resurrection.

Rom. 10:7) and then afterward ascended to heaven (Luke 24; Acts 1:9–11), a time span covering three days. Therefore, more contemporary scholars tend to take the time frame eschatologically, with reference to the spiritual kingdom that was present in the first coming of Christ (see Luke's use of *sēmeron* in this manner in 2:11; 4:21; 5:26). E. Earle Ellis expresses this view relative to v. 43 succinctly: "Today is sometimes a technical expression for the time of messianic salvation. Here that time is Jesus' exaltation at the resurrection. The latter view seems to be what Luke intended."[4]

Consequently, Luke 23:43 does not contradict the other Synoptics statements that Jesus predicted that he would be in the grave for three (parts of) days.

Hosea 6:2

We referred earlier to Hosea 6:2 which in the Hebrew text reads, "He will revive us after two days, on the third day he will raise us up that we may live before him." Most likely, Jesus' passion predictions regarding his resurrection on the "the third day" owe their inspiration to this text (see also 1 Cor. 15:4).[5] Indeed, already by the second century AD, the Aramaic translation of Hosea 6:2 takes this verse as predicting Israel's future resurrection:

> They will say: Come, and let us return to the service of the Lord; for he who has smitten us will heal us; and he who has brought ruin upon us will give us rest. He will revive us on the days of consolation which are about to come; on the day of the resurrection of the dead he will raise us up and we shall be revived before him.[6]

Craig Evans writes of this, "The allusion to this passage [Hos. 6:2] in all probability derives from Jesus himself and not from the evangelist or early tradents searching for a scriptural warrant [for Jesus' resurrection]."[7] With this conclusion we concur.

Conclusion

This chapter has provided an answer to the question, "did Jesus remain in the tomb three days and three nights? In light of the fact that the

---

4. C. Marvin Pate, *Luke* (Chicago: Moody, 1995), 455. The Ellis quote comes from his *The Gospel of Luke*, NCB (London: Oliphants, 1974), 368.
5. See Craig A. Evans, *Mark 8:27–16:20*, WBC 34B (Nashville: Thomas Nelson, 2001), 18.
6. Quoted in William L. Lane, *The Gospel of Mark* (Grand Rapids: Eerdmans, 1974), 302.
7. Evans, *Mark 8:27–16:20*, 17.

three phrases— "the third day," "after three days," and "three days and three nights"—are synonymous, we may say that Jesus was in the grave three (parts of) days. Luke 23:43 does not contradict this fact. And, in all likelihood, Jesus applied Hosea's prediction (Hos. 6:2) of the resurrection of true Israel/the righteous Suffering Servant to himself.

REFLECTION QUESTIONS

1. In the Old Testament and Judaism, what did the words, "the third day" mean?

2. In the Gospels and in Josephus, what did the words, "after three days" mean?

3. In the Old Testament what did the words, "three days and three nights" mean?

4. How do the words of Jesus on the cross to the thief, "today you will be with me in Paradise" factor into this discussion?

5. How does Hosea 6:2 relate to the resurrection of Jesus?

Where Did Jesus' Spirit Go While His Body Was in the Tomb?

The major passage appealed to by biblical scholars to answer the question of this chapter is 1 Peter 3:18–20, which reads:

> [He (Jesus) was] put to death in the flesh but made alive in the spirit, in which he went and proclaimed to the spirits in prison, because they formerly did not obey, when God's patience waited in the days of Noah, while the ark was being prepared, in which a few, that is, eight persons, were brought safely through water.

Three main issues regarding this text have sparked a debate for centuries among theologians: (1) What are the spirits in prison? (2) What did Christ preach to them? (3) When did Christ preach to them? In attempting to answer these questions, at least six views have emerged through the years:

- **View 1:** When Noah was building the ark, Christ "in spirit" was in Noah preaching repentance and righteousness through him to unbelievers who were on the earth then but are now "spirits in prison" (people in hell).

- **View 2:** After Christ died, he went and preached to people in hell, offering them a second chance of salvation.

- **View 3:** After Christ died, he went and preached to people in hell, proclaiming to them that he had triumphed over them and their condemnation was final.

- **View 4:** After Christ died, he proclaimed release to people who had repented just before they died in the flood, and led them out of their imprisonment (in Purgatory) into heaven.

- **View 5:** After Christ died (or: after he arose but before he ascended into heaven), he travelled to hell and proclaimed triumph over the fallen angels who had sinned by marrying human women before the flood.[1]

- **View 6:** After his resurrection, Jesus announced his victory over the spiritual principalities and powers—fallen angels—but not in a descent to hell between his death and resurrection but rather after his resurrection. In other words, 1 Peter 3:18–20 has nothing to do with Jesus descending into hell.[2]

Because it would take an entire book to examine each of these views (which Dalton has already done anyway, except for view 6), we will defend view 5, weeding out the other perspectives along the way. We proceed by answering the above three questions.

What Are the Spirits in Prison?

The choice here is one of two possibilities: the spirits are either humans or angels. In our estimation, Jobes has argued persuasively in favor of angels. She writes,

> Any theory that understands the *pneumata* (spirits) of 3:19 to refer to the souls of deceased people faces the important lexical problem of whether that noun without further qualification was used to refer to deceased souls in contemporary literature. On the basis of lexical studies, many NT commentators today claim it was not. . . . In the NT and 1 Enoch the word *pneuma*, especially in its plural form, is used overwhelmingly to refer to malevolent supernatural beings. The souls of deceased people are typically referred to with the term *psychē* in the NT. The one reference where *pneuma* in its plural form clearly refers to human beings (Heb. 12:23) is qualified by a substantive adjective, "spirits of the righteous," and it is not completely clear that this is

1. Wayne Grudem lists these five views from the pertinent literature (*1 Peter*, TNTC [Grand Rapids: Eerdmans, 1988; reprint 1999], 204). View 5 is the dominant view today thanks to the work of W. J. Dalton, *Christ's Proclamation to the Spirits* (Rome: Pontifical Biblical Institute, 1965).
2. See Karen H. Jobes, *1 Peter*, BECNT (Grand Rapids: Baker, 2005), 235–58.

a reference to the deceased. When *pneuma* is used to refer to deceased humans in 1 Enoch, it is always qualified (e.g., 20.6, "spirits of humans"; 22.3, "spirits of the souls of the dead"; 22.7, 9, 11–13). Both the lexical data and the congruence of this passage with established tradition concerning Enoch's connection to the Noah story tilt toward understanding the imprisoned spirits as the fallen angels and the spirits of their degenerate offspring.[3]

This, then, would rule out views 1 (Christ's spirit preached through Noah to those in his day who disbelieved Noah's message about the ark), 2 (Christ by his spirit descended into hell to offer salvation to the lost; that is, a post-mortem chance to be saved), 3 (Christ by his spirit descended to hell to pronounce judgment on the lost), and 4 (Christ proclaimed release to those who repented just before Noah's flood).

The reference above to *1 Enoch* provides important background to 1 Peter 3:18–20. *First Enoch* 1–36, called the Book of Watchers, is an embellishment of the mysterious story of Genesis 6:1–4, where "the sons of God went to the daughters of men and had children by them" (6:4 LXX). In Genesis, this story immediately precedes the Noah narrative and appears to give justification for the flood. Jobes writes of this:

> First Enoch tells a similar but more elaborate tale. The Watchers were the fallen angels who had abandoned heaven (12.4), slept with human women (15.3), and produced children, referred to as "giants" from whose bodies "evil spirits" have come (15.9). These evil spirits have taught people "deeds of shame, injustice, and sin" (13.2) and will continue to corrupt the earth until "the day of the great conclusion, until the great age is consummated, until everything is concluded" (16.1). The Watchers appeal to Enoch to intercede with God on behalf of themselves and the evil progeny they have produced. Enoch obliges and returns with God's proclamation to the Watchers: "[You will] not be able to ascend into heaven unto all eternity, but you shall remain inside the earth, imprisoned all the days of eternity." Moreover, the Watchers would see the destruction of their sons (referred to as "the spirits") because the petitions for themselves and for their sons (the spirits) will not be heard by God (14.5–6). These "spirits" that came from the bodies of the giants fathered by the Watchers through

---

3. Ibid., 250–51.

human women were the cause of the human evil that led to the great flood during the time of Enoch's grandson, Noah. This tradition as documented in 1 En. 12–16 appears to offer a background that fits well with 1 Pet. 3.19–20. Both involve spirits who receive a proclamation from God and who are closely associated with the story of Noah, which immediately follows in both Gen. 6:9–9:29 and 1 Pet. 3:20. If this is the assumed tradition behind 1 Pet. 3:19, then the spirits to whom Christ preached should be understood as fallen angels and/or demonic spirits. Their imprisonment represents in spatial terms God's restraining power over them, and the message Christ preached to them is the confirmation that "the day of the great conclusion," first announced by the flood, is now upon them. Christ's ascension itself may have been the proclamation of their defeat. In other words, the apostle Peter is identifying Jesus Christ as the victor over all evil in both the spirit and the human worlds forevermore.[4]

Thus, the spirits in prison, according to view 5, were the Watchers (fallen angels) who cohabitated with women resulting in a generation of giants and monstrous sin which in turn brought about divine judgment in the form of Noah's flood. God consigned those Watchers to hell and it was to them that Jesus descended between his death and resurrection to preach to them. Indeed, Jude 6 and 2 Peter 2:4 seem to allude to the same situation.

What Did Christ Preach to Them?

The key here is to look at the Greek word Peter uses for preached, namely, *kēryssō*. Jobes observes:

> The verb *kēryssō* in 1 Pet. 3:19 is often used for the preaching of the gospel in the NT (e.g., Matt. 4:23; Mark 1:14; 6:12; Acts 9:20; Rom. 10:14; 2 Cor. 1:19; Gal. 2:2; 1 Thess. 2:9). However, its semantic range is broader, and it is also used to mean "proclaim" in both the NT and the LXX (e.g., Gen. 41:43; Exod. 36:6; 2 Kings 10:20; Esth. 6:9; Jon. 1:2; Luke 4:19; 8:39; Rev. 5:2). Notably, the verb more specific to preaching the gospel, *euangelizomai* (preach the good news) is not used of Christ's proclamation in 1 Pet. 3:19.[5]

---

4. Ibid., 243–44.
5. Ibid., 250.

Therefore, it seems likely that Jesus preached judgment to the fallen angels, not the gospel. Indeed v. 22 appears to confirm this interpretation: "who [Jesus Christ] is at the right hand of God, having gone into heaven, with angels and authorities and powers subject to him."

When Did Christ Preach to Them?

The timing of Jesus' proclamation to the fallen angels centers on the parallel clauses in v. 18: "he was put to death in the flesh but made alive in the spirit." The dominant view of 1 Peter 3:18–20 is the perspective we are here defending which goes hand in hand with interpreting these clauses thusly: at Jesus' death he descended into Hell/Hades/the grave by his spirit to proclaim condemnation to the fallen angels, before acquiring his resurrection body.

Karen Jobes disagrees, arguing rather that Peter was not espousing a dualistic view of the human being—body and soul—but a monistic view such that Christ in his entirety was put to death at the crucifixion and in his entirety was made alive at the resurrection.[6] But this is not convincing because both Jesus and Paul speak of a body-soul distinction that comprises the human being (see Matt. 10:28; 2 Cor. 5:1–10).[7] It is better, therefore, to understand Peter as saying that in between his death and before his bodily resurrection Jesus was alive in spirit/soul and in that mode descended to hell to announce judgment on the fallen angels. Thus, one spirit (Jesus) announced divine judgment on other spirits (fallen angels). Having done that, Jesus assumed his resurrection body upon his return to heaven.

Conclusion

We have answered the question of this chapter in keeping with the majority view. We conclude our discussion by noting that there is a solemnity about this passage: it strongly challenges humans to accept the gospel of Christ now because there will be no opportunity to do so after death. Hebrews 9:27 puts it well, "It is appointed unto man once to die and after that the judgment." But there is also a majesty about 1 Peter 3:18–20: Jesus Christ is lord over the living and the dead; human and angelic; now and forever. To confess him now as Lord is to enjoy his majesty for all eternity.

---

6. Ibid., 241.
7. For a defense of a dualistic reading of 2 Corinthians 5:1–10 (the body dying but the believer's soul entering the presence of God), see my work, *Adam Christology as the Exegetical and Theological Substructure of 2 Corinthians 4:7–5:21* (Lanham, MD: University Press of America, 1991).

REFLECTION QUESTIONS

1. What are the spirits in prison referred to in 1 Peter 3:18–20?

2. What did Christ preach to them?

3. When did Christ preach to them?

4. Why do some have a problem with saying that Jesus' spirit was separate from his glorified body for some three days?

5. How does Karen Jobes explain this question and does your author agree with it?

Questions Related
to the Resurrection of Jesus

Did the Historical Jesus Rise from the Dead?

What do the Christian apologists Frank Morrison, Josh McDowell, and Lee Strobel have in common? All three men were once skeptics of Christianity but were converted when they studied the Gospels' accounts of the resurrection of Jesus.[1] Both believers and skeptics alike understand that the bedrock of the Christian faith is the resurrection of Jesus. There is no middle ground on this debate. Christianity rises or falls on the resurrection. If it did not happen, then Christianity is no different from any other religion. In fact, it is nothing more than an antiquated relic from the past with no meaning for today.

On the other hand, if Jesus really rose from the dead then, according to the apostle Paul in 1 Corinthians 15:12–20, the Christian faith is uniquely true, our sins are forgiven, and we will be raised one day to join our departed believing loved ones. All of this brings eternal meaning into our present existence.

So the question is clear and the stakes high: Did Jesus really rise from the dead? In this chapter we seek to answer that question in the affirmative, offering two broad categories of evidences for the bodily resurrection of Jesus Christ as culled from the four gospels and Paul. And along the way we will provide information for refuting those theories that disagree. The two broad categories of evidences are: the empty tomb and the post-resurrection appearances of Jesus.[2]

---

1. The English lawyer Frank Morrison began to write a book discrediting Jesus' resurrection, but became convinced of its historicity in the process. Ironically, his book has become a classic defense for the resurrection (*Who Moved the Stone* [repr. Grand Rapids: Zondervan, 1987]). Josh McDowell became a Christian during his skeptical college years after investigating the resurrection of Jesus (*Evidence That Demands a Verdict?*, vol. 1 [San Bernardino, CA: Here's Life Publishers, 1979]). Lee Strobel had a similar experience (*The Case for Christ: A Journalist's Personal Investigation of the Evidence for Jesus* [Grand Rapids: Zondervan, 2002]).
2. This chapter draws on C. Marvin Pate and Sheryl L. Pate, *Crucified in the Media: Finding the Real Jesus Amidst Today's Headlines* (Grand Rapids: Baker, 2005), chapter 8.

The Empty Tomb

The story of the empty tomb is found in Matthew 28:1–8; Mark 16:1–8; Luke 24:1–8; John 20:1–8; and 1 Corinthians 15:3–4. Three pieces of data combine to convince most biblical scholars, even non-conservative ones, that the tomb where Jesus was buried was found empty.

First, the testimony of the empty tomb is supported by the form criticism criterion of multiple attestation. As we learned earlier, form criticism asserts that if an event or word of Jesus in the Gospels is attested to by two or more layers of tradition, then that event or word is likely to be authentic. Such is the case with the empty tomb event, for three separate strands of testimony confirm its actuality: the Synoptics' account (Matt. 28:1–8; Mark 16:1–8; Luke 24:1–8), the Johannine account (John 20:1–8), and the Pauline account (1 Cor. 15:3–4).

Second, it is ironic that women were the first to whom the risen Jesus appeared, because in the first century AD women were not allowed to give legal testimony. Simply put, it would have been viewed as an embarrassment to the early church that the first witnesses of the empty tomb were women—Mary Magdalene, Mary the mother of James and of Jesus, and Salome (who was probably the wife of Zebedee and the mother of James and John). But this very fact serves to prove the historicity of the empty tomb because, if the church had conjured up the story, they surely would have had men, the disciples in particular, as the first witnesses of the empty tomb.

Third, if the tomb was not empty, the Jewish leadership and the Roman authorities could have easily silenced the preaching of Peter and John in the days of the early church (Acts 1–7) by taking all concerned to the place where Jesus lay. Such a move would have silenced Christianity on the spot. Later Jewish medieval legend fancied just such a scenario. But, in fact, the Jewish leadership and Roman authorities could do nothing of the kind because the tomb was indeed empty.

The Stolen Body Theory

Other than the resurrection theory, the most ancient theory explaining the empty tomb was that the disciples stole the body of Jesus and then perpetrated the fraud that Jesus had risen from the dead. This view circulated in New Testament times. Matthew records that the Jewish elders gave money to the soldiers who guarded the tomb and told the soldiers to say, "His disciples came by night and stole him away while we were asleep" (Matt. 28:13 NRSV). This explanation was also reflected in Origen's debate with Celsus in the early third century AD. Origen disposes of this fanciful explanation by arguing that men do not risk losing their lives in defense of a lie.[3]

The stolen body theory has been defended in modern times by the German scholar H. M. Reimarus. In 1778, he published a work entitled *The Goal of Jesus and His Disciples.* He argued that, after Jesus' death, the disciples were unwilling

---

3. *Against Celsus* II, LVI.

to abandon the kind of life they had led with Jesus. So they stole the body of Jesus, hid it, and proclaimed to all the world that he would soon return as the Messiah. However, they waited fifty days before making this announcement in order that the body, if it should be found, would be unrecognizable. But Origen's answer against this preposterous reasoning still stands: Men (and women) do not risk their lives and suffer martyrdom for a lie (see Acts 7:60; 12:2).

The Swoon Theory

The "swoon theory" was promoted in this century in Hugh Schonfield's *The Passover Plot* (1965), which maintained that Jesus did not really die on the cross, but rather swooned and later resuscitated in the tomb. There are records that show there were cases where individuals were crucified, taken down from the cross, and survived. He believed that the loud cry Jesus uttered on the cross was proof that Jesus was not exhausted and near death, and states that the spear thrust in the side of Jesus was only a flesh wound. Schonfield goes on to say that in response to the coolness of the tomb and the aromatic spices contained within, Jesus, who only appeared to be dead, resuscitated. An earthquake further contributed to his waking and caused the stone to roll away from the entrance of the tomb. Jesus took off his grave clothes and managed to secure a gardeners' outfit (the reason Mary mistook him for a gardener, as recorded in John 20:15).

If the swoon theory is accurate, Jesus must have lived out the rest of his life in hiding—at the very time when his disciples adamantly proclaimed his resurrection and his coming kingdom. It would appear, according to this theory, that Jesus was in solitary retreat, but that his disciples were unaware of this fact. Moreover, this theory defies credulity in underestimating the mortal impact of scourging, crucifying, and spearing as carried out by the Romans.

The Wrong Tomb Theory

The "wrong tomb" theory was popularized by the Harvard scholar Kirsopp Lake, who wrote the book *The Historical Evidence for the Resurrection of Jesus Christ*.[4] In it, he maintained that "the facts behind the tradition" of the resurrection of Jesus are as follows: Due to there being a number of tombs in the vicinity in which Jesus was buried, the women, who visited the tomb on Sunday morning, were confused as to which tomb was that of Jesus. At an empty tomb, a young man who stood at the entrance tried to tell them they had the wrong location by stating, "He is not here." Pointing to another tomb, he said, "See the place where they laid him." The women, who were frightened that someone had discovered their errand, fled. They were confused as to the meaning of the young man, mistakenly believing not only that the young man

---

4. Kirsopp Lake, *The Historical Evidence for the Resurrection of Jesus Christ* (London: Williams & Norgate; New York: Putnam's Sons, 1907), 251–53.

was more than human but also that he was announcing the resurrection of Jesus. Professor Lake concluded, "The empty tomb . . . is doctrinally indefensible and is historically insufficiently accredited."[5]

But there is a stubborn detail that single-handedly refutes the wrong tomb theory: Joseph of Arimathea owned the tomb in which Jesus was placed. And certainly, he would know which tomb was his and where he placed the body, making it easy to refute the words of the women that Jesus had risen from the dead. All he had to do was to take people to the correct tomb with the body still inside. Yet, Scripture does not indicate that he did that.

Is it possible that Joseph of Arimathea was a figment of Christian imagination designed to create the illusion of a resurrected Jesus? No. Even the most skeptical biblical scholars agree that Joseph of Arimathea was a historical person, actually a member of the Jewish Sanhedrin. As such, with the hostility which the early Christians felt toward these Jewish leaders who had put Jesus to death, it is highly unlikely that they would invent such an individual who would do the right thing regarding the burial of Jesus. Certainly Mark, who wrote that the whole Sanhedrin voted for Jesus' condemnation (Mark 14:55, 64; 15:1), would not have invented this man.

Details given in the Gospels confirm aspects of Joseph of Arimathea—he was rich (corroborated by the type and location of the tomb) and came from Arimathea (an unimportant town with no scriptural symbolism). That he was sympathetic to Jesus is attested to by Matthew and John, and also by Mark in the way he treated Jesus' body rather than those of the thieves.

William Lane Craig writes of Joseph's tomb:

> Joseph's laying the body in his own tomb is probably historical. The consistent descriptions of the tomb as an arcosolia, or bench tomb, and archaeological discoveries that such tombs were used by notables during Jesus' day makes it credible that Jesus was placed in such a tomb. The incidental details that it was new and belonged to Joseph are also probable, since Joseph could not have placed the body of a criminal in just any tomb, especially since this would defile the bodies of any family members also reposing there.[6]

The Resurrection Theory

The stolen body, swoon, and wrong tomb theories simply do not work. There really is only one explanation for the fact of the empty tomb—in

---

5. Ibid., 263.
6. "Did Jesus Rise from the Dead," in *Jesus Under Fire: Modern Scholarship Reinvents the Historical Jesus*, ed. Michael J. Wilkins and J. P. Moreland (Grand Rapids: Zondervan, 1995), 148.

accordance with the New Testament, Jesus Christ arose from the dead and, after spending time teaching his followers, ascended into heaven. But were those purported post-resurrection appearances of Jesus real?

The Post-Resurrection Appearances of Jesus Christ

The second piece of evidence is that the New Testament claims that Jesus rose from the dead three days after he was crucified and buried, after which he made his presence known to others. The following chart lists eleven such appearances:

EVENT	DATE	MATT.	MARK	LUKE	JOHN	ACTS	1 COR.
At the empty tomb outside Jerusalem	Early Sunday morning	28:1–10	16:1–8	24:1–12	20:1–9		
To Mary Magdalene at the tomb	Early Sunday morning		16:9–11?		20:11–18		
To two travelers on the road to Emmaus	Sunday at midday			24:13–32			
To Peter in Jerusalem	During the day on Sunday			24:34			15:5
To the disciples in the upper room	Sunday evening		16:14?	24:36–43	20:19–25		
To the eleven disciples in the upper room	One week later				20:26–31		15:5

EVENT	DATE	MATT.	MARK	LUKE	JOHN	ACTS	1 COR.
To seven disciples fishing on the Sea of Galilee	One day at daybreak				21:1–23		
To the eleven disciples on the mountain in Galilee	Some time later	28:16–20	16:15–18?				
To more than five hundred	Some time later						15:6
To James	Some time later						15:7
At the Ascension on the Mt. of Olives	Forty days after the resurrec-tion			24:44–49		1:3–8	

Christians in general, and many biblical scholars in particular, accept the face value of these accounts—that Jesus Christ appeared to his followers in bodily form after his death. Thus, Mary Magdalene touched him (John 20:11–18), as did Thomas (John 20:26–31). Jesus ate with his disciples (Luke 24:30, 42–43; John 21:1–15). The angels promised that Jesus' second coming would match his ascension, which was personal, visible, and corporeal (Acts 1:3–8). According to Luke 24:38–42, Jesus invited his disciples to touch him precisely to dispel the notion that he was a ghost or apparition.

Skeptics often say, however, that these reports were apologetic defenses created by the later church to combat docetism. Docetism was a late first-century to second-century AD heresy that said that Jesus was fully God but only appeared to be human. First John especially refutes that heresy (see, e.g., 1 John 1:1–4; 4:2). However, William Lane Craig correctly asserts that the Gospels were written before the rise of

doceticism. Moreover, in actuality, doceticism denied Jesus' physical incarnation but not his bodily resurrection.[7]

Beyond the anti-docetic theory, two theories are often put forth to explain away the bodily resurrection of Jesus: it was a hallucination or it was
a subjective vision (a spiritual "resurrection"). The hallucination theory asserts that the disciples were so grieved over the death of Jesus that their
longing to see him made them hallucinate and think they saw him alive,
when in fact he was not. The British New Testament professor William
Milligan, however, destroyed the hallucination theory in the early part of
the twentieth century. He pointed out some five problems with the hypothesis. First, the resurrection appearances of Jesus are varied; they do not fall
into one pattern. Second, in contrast to the hallucination theory, the disciples did not expect Jesus to rise; they were as surprised as anyone when the
news of his resurrection reached them. Third, hallucinations do not appear
to five hundred people, unless they are all strung out on drugs; there is no
evidence that such was the case. Fourth, hallucinations do not extend over
a period of forty days. Fifth, such visions do not cease with suddenness, as
the resurrection appearances of Jesus did.[8]

The second alternative theory proposed by skeptics of the resurrection
of Jesus says that he appeared in spirit, but not in body, to his followers. The
difference between this view and the hallucination hypothesis appears to
be that the former apparently allows for some type of life for Jesus beyond
the grave, but not a bodily one. For this perspective, it is the resurrection
faith of the disciples that matters, not the resurrection fact. This allows the
Jesus Seminar to say, on the one hand, that supernatural things like dead
men rising from the grave do not happen, while on the other hand, they
can affirm the faith of the disciples in the resurrected Christ. The former is
the Jesus of history (he lived and died); the latter is the Christ of faith (he
arose in Spirit or in the mind of the disciples). The introduction to *The Five
Gospels* thus asserts:

> The contemporary religious controversy . . . turns on
> whether the worldview reflected in the Bible can be carried
> forward into this scientific age and retained as an article of
> faith. . . . The Christ of creed and dogma . . . can no longer
> command the assent of those who have seen the heavens
> through Galileo's telescope.[9]

---

7. Ibid., 68.
8. William Milligan, *The Resurrection of Our Lord* (New York: Macmillan, 1927), 81–114.
9. Robert W. Funk, Roy W. Hoover, and the Jesus Seminar, *The Five Gospels: What Did
   Jesus Really Say? The Search for the Authentic Words of Jesus* (San Francisco: Harper-
   SanFrancisco, 1997), 2.

In taking this stance, the Seminar aligns itself with one of the first skeptics of the Gospels, David Friedrich Strauss:

> Strauss distinguished what he called the "mythical" (defined by him as anything legendary or supernatural) in the gospels from the historical. . . . The choice Strauss posed in his assessment of the gospels was between the super-natural Jesus— The Christ of faith—and the historical Jesus.[10]

This explains how John Dominic Crossan, one of the co-chairs of the Jesus Seminar, could say in *Time* magazine that after the crucifixion, Jesus' corpse was probably laid in a shallow grave, barely covered with dirt, and subsequently eaten by wild dogs; the story of Jesus' entombment and resurrection was the result of "wishful thinking."[11]

But here one can turn the tables on the Jesus Seminar by using their own criteria of authenticity to refute their denial of the bodily resurrection of Jesus: multiple attestation and the principle of dissimilarity. Multiple attestation works as well for the bodily resurrection of Jesus as we saw it work for the historicity of the empty tomb. Thus, three layers of New Testament tradition claim that Jesus arose from the dead in body, as the previous chart shows: the Synoptics, the gospel of John, and Paul.

The criterion of dissimilarity states that if a purported word or deed of Jesus in the Gospels is neither Jewish nor from the Hellenistic church, it is authentic. Although we still do not support the principle left unqualified, we will use it against the Jesus Seminar to support the bodily resurrection of Jesus. In the first place, Judaism at the time of the New Testament expected the Messiah to bring about the general resurrection of the dead at the *end* of history (see Dan. 12:1–3; Mark 9:9–13; John 11:24). There were, to be sure, instances in the Old Testament of the dead being brought back to life, but these dealt with a return to the earthly life and those so resuscitated eventually died again (e.g., Elijah's raising of the son of the widow at Zarephath [1 Kings 17:17–23]; Elisha's raising of the Shunammite's son [2 Kings 4:18–37]). But the Gospels' and Paul's proclamations about Jesus, an individual who was resurrected *in* history, are not paralleled in ancient Judaism.

On the other hand, Hellenism did not believe in the resurrection of the body; rather, from Plato on (ca. 350 BC) it affirmed in the immortality of the soul only. It was this very idea, for example, that Paul argued against in his

---

10. Ibid., 3.
11. Reported by Richard N. Ostling, "Jesus Christ, Plain and Simple," *Time* 10, January 1994, 32–33. That Ostling does not agree with Crossan can be seen from Ostling's endorsement of N. T. Wright's book, *The Resurrection of the Son of God*, vol. 3 of Christian Origins and the Question of God (Minneapolis: Fortress, 2003), a marvelous defense of the historicity of the bodily resurrection of Jesus Christ.

most Hellenistically inclined congregation, the church at Corinth (see 1 Cor. 15). We also see from Acts 17 that the Greek philosophers laughed Paul out of town when he started preaching the resurrection of Jesus, because they only subscribed to the belief in the immortality of the soul. So the bodily resurrection of Jesus in history proves to be distinct from both Judaism and Hellenism. Its historicity is, therefore, confirmed by the criterion of dissimilarity.

But how is it that the Jesus Seminar does not practice what it preaches about the criteria of multiple attestation and dissimilarity regarding the Gospels' accounts of Jesus' bodily resurrection? They answer, "By definition, words (and events) ascribed to Jesus after his death are not subject to historical verification."[12] The Jesus Seminar wants to have their cake and eat it too—on the one hand, they want to hold onto their criteria of authenticity, but on the other hand, they refuse to use those principles in a "non-historical" situation.

Conclusion

Jesus did indeed rise from the dead! Christianity rises or falls on the resurrection of Jesus. And the evidence is that, contrary to other religions whose founders still occupy their graves, Christianity is the only faith whose founder met with a totally different destiny. Like the angel said, "He is not here; he is risen" (Mark 16:6). This is an awesome thought, one which Christians cherish and which provides certain hope for the future.

REFLECTION QUESTION

1. What role does the empty tomb of Jesus play in demonstrating his resurrection?

2. How would you answer the stolen body theory regarding the empty tomb?

3. How would you answer the swoon theory concerning the empty tomb?

4. How would you refute the wrong tomb theory regarding the empty tomb?

5. What two theories are often offered to explain away the post-resurrection appearances of Jesus Christ?

---

12. Robert W. Funk, Roy W. Hoover, and the Jesus Seminar, *The Five Gospels,* 398.

QUESTION 40

What Is the Meaning of Jesus' Ascension?

Only Luke-Acts records the ascension of Jesus forty days after his resurrection, reporting so twice (Luke 24:50–53; Acts 1:9–11).[1] Indeed, the ascension of Jesus to heaven is recorded at the end of Luke and at the beginning of Acts. Consequently, the event must have held significant theological meaning for the author. This last chapter of our book on Jesus the Messiah attempts to address the meaning of Jesus' ascension. Two points will be made. First, the significance of the ascension was that it fulfilled the expectation dominating the messianic/royal psalms, namely, Jesus is the long-awaited Messiah who will rule the nations. Second, the already/not yet eschatological tension pertains to the ascension. We now proceed to discuss these matters.

What Was the Nature of the Ascension of Jesus?

I will argue that Jesus' ascent to heaven follows the model suggested in the royal/enthronement, or messianic, Old Testament psalms. Those Old Testament passages are as follows: Psalms 2; 18; 20; 45; 72; 89; 110. These psalms contain descriptions of David or a Davidic king being enthroned as king of Israel according to the ordinance of God. In one way or another, four components emerge in all of these psalms: (1) the Lord anoints or selects the king to be enthroned over Israel, who is a Davidic heir; (2) the nations surrounding Israel revolt at God's appointment; (3) but God defiantly enthrones his anointed as king anyway; (4) God defeats the uprising of the nations against his chosen one. One can see from these four components why the preceding labels are used of these psalms: they all deal with the *enthronement* of God's *anointed one*, who is in the *royal* lineage of David.

---

1. Luke wrote both the gospel of Luke and Acts.

These four elements nicely explain the life of Jesus according to Luke: (1) Jesus is the divine Davidic Messiah/Christ (the anointed one); (2) who was opposed by the nations (especially Rome, but also including Israel) (3) Jesus' ascension was the event when God enthroned him as Lord over his enemies; (4) from his heavenly throne Jesus will now conquer his enemies, the nations, through the conversion of the Gentiles.

Indeed, the four previous components of the royal psalms occur precisely in the contexts of the two ascension reports of Luke, as the following chart indicates:

ROYAL PSALMS	LUKE 24:50–53	ACTS 1:9–11
Divine anointed one	Jesus is the Davidic Christ/ Messiah (vv. 36/46a) and the resurrection proved him to be so (vv. 37–43/46b)	Jesus is the Lord (v. 6) and the resurrection proved him to be so (v. 3b)
Opposition of the nations	Jesus suffered at the hands of the nations (Rome and Israel, vv. 36b, 46) just as the Old Testament predicted	Jesus suffered at the hands of the nations (Rome and Israel, v. 3)
Coronation/ enthronement of the divine anointed one in the face of the nations	Jesus' ascension was his coronation/enthronement in heaven (vv. 50–51), while the disciples worshipped Jesus in the earthly temple, the counterpart of the heavenly temple (v. 53)	Jesus' ascension was his coronation/enthronement in heaven (vv. 9–11)
Divine defeat of the nations by God's Anointed king	Jesus will "conquer" the nations by converting them through the Spirit-empowered preaching of the gospel by the disciples (vv. 47–49)	Jesus will "conquer" the nations by converting them through the Spirit-empowered preaching of the gospel by the disciples (vv. 5, 8)

It seems clear that Luke presents Jesus' ascension against the backdrop of the Old Testament royal/messianic enthronement hymns because he explicitly quotes two of those hymns (i.e., Ps. 2 in Acts 4:25–27; 13:33 and Ps. 110 in Luke 20:42; Acts 2:34–35).[2]

---

2. The New Testament draws much on Psalm 2 (see, e.g., Matt. 3:17; 17:5; Acts 4:25–27; 13:33; Heb. 1:5; Rev. 1:5; 2:27; 4:2; 6:17; 12:5; 19:5) and also on Psalm 110 (Matt. 22:41–45; 26:64; Mark 12:35–37; Luke 20:41–44; Acts 2:34–35; Rom. 8:34; 1 Cor. 15:25; Eph. 1:20;

The Already/Not Yet Aspects of the Ascension

Earlier we saw that inaugurated eschatology is the key to understanding the Synoptic Gospels, including Luke. Here we focus on the eschatology of the ascension of Jesus. We may state it thusly: the ascension: Jesus' present reign in heaven and the millennium: Jesus' coming reign on earth.

The Ascension: Jesus' Present Reign in Heaven

Luke's application of Psalm 2 and Psalm 110 to Jesus' ascension (see above) indicates that Jesus is presently reigning in heaven; that is, Jesus is currently enjoying his heavenly session at the right hand of the Father. Moreover, these two Psalms also specify that Jesus is already ruling on David's throne, but in heaven not yet on earth. Furthermore, the heavenly Son of Man references in Luke's passion narrative reinforce the perspective that Jesus' kingdom now is a heavenly one, not yet a political, earthly one (Luke 21:27, 36; 22:68–70; 24:7).

The Millennium: Jesus' Future Reign on Earth

However, it is also clear that while the "already" aspect of the kingdom of God in Luke-Acts focuses on the positive Gentile response to Jesus (recall the messianic king who defeats his Gentile enemies), the "not yet" aspect of the kingdom of God anticipates the future restoration of Israel; that is the millennium (cf. Rev. 20). The first part of this statement is patently Lukan. But the other part is also Lukan, as his references to the future restoration of Israel indicate (see Luke 20:27–40; 21:24; 22:29; Acts 1:6; 28:20; cf. Rom. 11:25–27). To these passages could be added two themes in Luke-Acts. The first concerns a pattern in Luke-Acts of Jewish persons being spiritually blind to Jesus as the Messiah but who later embrace him. Elsewhere, I have argued that certain individuals in Luke dramatize the restoration of Israel in their own spiritual experiences, namely, they move from Jewish disbelief in Jesus to faith in him as the Messiah: Zechariah, John the Baptist, the twelve disciples.[3] Paul also fits the same pattern being transformed from a persecutor of Jesus and the church to the apostle to the Gentiles. Moreover, Acts 13:6–12 records the blindness that comes upon the Jewish sorcerer Bar-Jesus/Elymas for his unbelief in Jesus which results in the conversion of the Gentile proconsul Sergius Paulus; this seems to dramatize the present blindness of Israel to Jesus, but which provides the Gentile world the opportunity to believe. Indeed, Luke may have intended that this incident also portray Paul's conversion, who was spiritually blind to

Heb. 1:13; 5:6; 7:1; 8:1; 10:12–13; 1 Peter 3:22). Most interesting for our present consideration is that Psalm 110 is applied to Jesus' present rule in heaven, not just to a future reign on earth.

3. C. Marvin Pate, *Luke* (Chicago: Moody, 1995); for Zechariah, see 55–57; for John the Baptist, see 174–75, 12; for the twelve disciples, see 428–29.

the gospel as well as physically blinded by the glorious appearance of Jesus to him on the Damascus road, and who went on to preach Jesus to the Gentiles.

Second, I believe that the speeches in Acts display the Deuteronomic tradition that we saw earlier in the gospel of Luke and, as such, holding out hope for the spiritual restoration of Israel to God through their acceptance of Jesus the Christ. The following chart provides the evidence for this claim:[4]

DEUTERONOMIC TRADITION	ACTS 2:22–41	ACTS 3:12–26	ACTS 7:37–53	ACTS 10:24–48	ACTS 13:16–41	ACTS 28:17–30
Israel's sin	Israel is a wicked generation	Turn from your iniquities	Israel is stiff-necked	Implied-sickness is a picture of covenant curses	Israel's sin	Paul quotes Isaiah 6:9–19, a statement on Israel's sin
God sent prophets to Israel	Jesus the last and greatest of prophets	Jesus the prophet	Israel killed the prophets	Jesus witnessed to by the OT prophets	Read the prophets	Implied—Paul tried to convince Jews about Jesus from the OT prophets
Israel rejected the prophets	Jesus crucified by Israel	Was delivered up by Israel	Jesus the final prophet	Hung on a tree	Crucified Jesus	Jewish audience rejected Christ
God sent Israel into exile	Israel is still far off, that is, in exile	Israel will be destroyed	implied	Israel is oppressed	implied	Implied—just as Paul is imprisoned by the Romans, so is Israel

---

4. I hope to develop this notion in a forthcoming commentary on Acts to be published by Kregel.

Deuteronomic Tradition	Acts 2:22–41	Acts 3:12–26	Acts 7:37–53	Acts 10:24–48	Acts 13:16–41	Acts 28:17–30
Repentance will bring about Israel's restoration	God's promise of restoration is available to Israel based on repentance	But the times of refreshing from the Lord are here	Healing for Israel is available if she repents	The Spirit is available to Israel if she repents	Israel is waiting for the promise of the good news	The hope for Israel's restoration remains

Thus the ascension is Jesus' present reign in heaven; the already aspect of the kingdom of God. And Jesus' return will bring that kingdom to earth in his millennial rule; the not yet aspect of the kingdom of God.

Conclusion

This chapter has focused on the ascension of Jesus to heaven. Two basic points were made. First, Jesus' ascension matches the messianic/royal psalms. Second, the ascension is the already aspect of the kingdom of God: Jesus now rules in heaven;. the millennium represents the not yet aspect of the kingdom of God in Luke-Acts, the time when Jesus at his return will rule the earth for a thousand years. Since the focus of Jesus' heavenly session is on the defeat/conversion of the Gentiles it may be that Luke understood the millennium to be Jesus' rule over converted Jews. But this latter point is much debated.

REFLECTION QUESTIONS

1. What is the Old Testament background to the ascension of Jesus as recorded in Luke 24:50–53 and Acts 1:9–11?

2. What are the four components of the royal/messianic psalms that one finds in Luke's ascension narratives?

3. What is the already aspect of Jesus' reign, according to Luke?

4. What is the not yet aspect of Jesus' reign, according to Luke?

5. What two points were made to show that Israel will be restored, according to Luke-Acts?

Select Bibliography

Bauckham, Richard. *Jesus and the Eyewitnesses: The Gospels as Eyewitness Testimony*. Grand Rapids: Eerdmans, 2006.

Bird, Michael F. *Are You The One Who Is to Come? The Historical Jesus and the Messianic Question*. Grand Rapids: Baker, 2009.

Blomberg, Craig L. *The Historical Reliability of the* Gospels, 2nd ed. Downers Grove, IL: InterVarsity Press, 2007.

Bock, Darrell L. *Breaking the Da Vinci Code: Answers to the Questions Everyone's Asking*. Nashville: Nelson, 2004.

_____. "The Historical Jesus: An Evangelical View." In *The Historical Jesus: Five Views*, ed. James K. Beilby and Paul Rhodes Eddy, 249–81. Downers Grove, IL: InterVarsity Press, 2009.

_____. *Who Is Jesus? Linking the Historical Jesus with the Christ of Faith*. New York: Howard Books, 2012.

Brown, Colin. "Historical Jesus, Quest of," in *Dictionary of Jesus and the Gospels*. Edited by Joel B. Green, Scot McKnight, and I. Howard Marshall, 326–41. Downers Grove, IL: InterVarsity Press, 1992.

Charlesworth, James H, ed. *Jesus and Archaeology*. Grand Rapids: Eerdmans; Cambridge: Cambridge University Press, 2006.

Cullmann, Oscar. *Christ and Time: The Primitive Christian of Time and History*. Translation by Floyd V. Filson. Philadelphia: Westminster, 1950.

Eddy, Paul Rhodes and Gregory A. Boyd. *The Jesus Legend: A Case for the Historical Reliability of the Synoptic Jesus Tradition*. Grand Rapids: Baker, 2007.

Evans, Craig A. *Fabricating Jesus: How Modern Scholars Distort the Gospels*. Downers Grove, IL: InterVarsity Press, 2006.

_____. *Life of Jesus Research: An Annotated Bibliography.* New Testament Tools and Studies 13. Leiden: Brill, 1989.

Freyne, Sean. *Galilee from Alexander the Great to Hadrian, 323 B. C. E. to 135 C. E.: A Study of Second Temple Judaism.* Notre Dame, IN: Michael Glazier/University of Notre Dame Press, 1980.

Keener, Craig S. *The Historical Jesus of the Gospels.* Grand Rapids: Eerdmans, 2009.

_____. *Miracles: The Credibility of the New Testament Accounts,* 2 vols. Grand Rapids: Baker, 2011.

McRay, John, *Archaeology and the New Testament.* Grand Rapids: Baker, 1991.

Marshall, I. Howard. *I Believe in the Historical Jesus.* Grand Rapids: Eerdmans, 1978.

Meier, Joseph P. *A Marginal Jew.* Vol. 1 (*The Roots of the Problem and the Person*). New York: Doubleday, 1991.

Pate, C. Marvin. *Luke.* Chicago: Moody Press, 1995.

_____. "Current Challenges to the Christian Canon," in *Criswell Theological Review* 3, no.1 (Fall 2005): 3–10.

Pate, C. Marvin and Sheryl. *Crucified in the Media: Finding the Real Jesus Amidst Today's Headlines.* Grand Rapids: Baker, 2005.

Porter, Stanley. *The Criteria for Authenticity in Historical-Jesus Research: Previous Discussion and New Proposals.* Journal for the Study of the New Testament Supplement Series 191. Sheffield: Sheffield Academic Press, 2000.

Schnabel, Eckhard J. *Early Christian Mission: Jesus and the* Twelve. Downers Grove, IL: InterVarsity Press; Leicester, England: Apollos, 2004.

Shanks, Hershel and Ben Witherington III. *The Brother of Jesus: The Dramatic Story and Meaning of the First Archaeological Link to Jesus and His Family.* New York: HarperCollins, 2003.

Wilkinson, Michael F. and J. P. Moreland, ed. *Jesus Under Fire.* Grand Rapids: Zondervan, 1995.

Witherington, Ben III. *The Jesus Quest: The Third Search for the Jew of Nazareth*. Downers Grove, IL: InterVarsity Press, 1995.

_____. *The Gospel Code: Novel Claims about Jesus, Mary Magdalene and Da Vinci*. Downers Grove, IL: InterVarsity Press, 2004.

_____. "Review of *The Da Vinci Code*." *Biblical Archaeological Review* 30, no. 3 (May/June 2004): 58–61.

Wright, N. T. *Jesus and the Victory of God*. Minneapolis: Fortress, 1996.

Scripture Index

Genesis

Exodus

Leviticus

Mark

Luke

Acts

Romans

1 Corinthians

Ancient Sources Index